Japanese/Korean Linguistics

Volume 3

Japanese/Korean Linguistics

Volume 3

Edited by Soonja Choi

Published for the
STANFORD LINGUISTICS ASSOCIATION
by the
Center for the Study of Language and Information
Stanford University

Library of Congress Cataloging-in-Publication Data
(Revised for vol. 3)
Japanese/Korean linguistics.

"Papers presented at the Southern California Japanese/Korean Linguistics
Conference, held August 4-6, 1989 at the University of California, Los
Angeles"—Pref.
   Vol. 3 edited by Soonja Choi.
   Includes bibliographical references and index.
   1. Japanese language—Congresses. 2. Korean language—Congresses.
3. Japanese language—Grammar, Comparative—Korean—Congresses.
4. Korean language—Grammar, Comparative--Japanese—Congresses.
5. Linguistics—Congresses. I. Hoji, Hajime. II. Stanford Linguistics
Association. III. Center for the Study of Language and Information (U.S.) IV.
Southern California Japanese/Korean Linguistics Conference (1989 : University
of California, Los Angeles)

PL503.J36 1990 495.6   90-2550
   ISBN 0-937973-56-3 (v. 1)   ISBN 0-937073-57-1 (v. 1 : pbk.)

   ISBN 1-881526-22-4 (v. 3)
   ISBN 1-881526-21-6 (v. 3 : pbk.)

Contents

Part III
Phonology   323

Preface

This volume contains most of the papers presented at the Third Annual Southern California Japanese/Korean Linguistics Conference, held August 14–16, 1992, at San Diego State University.

This conference is intended to provide a forum for presenting research in all areas of Japanese and Korean linguistics, thereby facilitating efforts to deepen our understanding of these two typologically very similar languages. Although only a few of the papers present comparative analyses, it is clear that the phenomena discussed in one language frequently have their counterparts in the other. It is therefore hoped that the papers in this volume will help to advance future research in the emerging field of Japanese/Korean Linguistics and that the papers in subsequent conferences will bear the fruit of our collective endeavor.

The conference was organized by Soonja Choi (SDSU), Patricia Clancy (UCSB), Hajime Hoji (USC), and Noriko Akatsuka (UCLA), with the invaluable assistance of Tam Kozman, Michele Steele and Julie Brennen. Many thanks are also due to our large team of reviewers, for their help in selecting the papers for the conference.

The Department of Linguistics and Oriental Languages, the College of Arts and Letters, and the Language Acquisition Resource Center (LARC) (under a grant from the U.S. Department of Education) at San Diego State University all jointly sponsored the conference.

Part I

Discourse and Acquisition

Other-Initiated Repair Sequences in Korean Conversation as Interactional Resources

KYU-HYUN KIM

University of California at Los Angeles

1. Introduction

In talk-in-interaction, speakers frequently find themselves in a situation where they must REPAIR a variety of kinds of trouble, as problems are prone to occur in speaking, hearing, or understanding the prior talk. One type of repair is OTHER-INITIATED REPAIR, which, in most cases, takes a form in which one speaker first initiates repair, i.e. raises a problem, thus prompting the speaker of the trouble source turn to actually repair the trouble (Schegloff 1979, 1988). As Schegloff (1988) shows in English conversation, speakers use a variety of forms of OTHER-REPAIR INITIATOR's (hereafter OI's) to initiate repair, which vary in the degree of grasp of the troublesome talk.

In this paper, I mainly focus on three types of OI as they are found in spontaneous Korean conversation. The first type of OI that I will examine includes forms like *ung?* or *e?*, and their polite form *yey?* or its variant *ney?*, which all semantically correspond to English *yes*.[1] These forms pragmatically correspond to English *huh?* or *pardon?* in OI contexts. The second type of OI involves the form *mwe?*, which corresponds to English

---

I thank Prof. Emanuel Schegloff for a number of insightful comments which constitute some of the most important underlying themes of this paper. I am responsible, however, for any errors or shortcomings that remain.

[1]With falling intonation, these forms are used as an affirmative answer to a yes/no question.

3

what?. The third type of OI which this paper will address is the UNDERSTANDING CHECK by which one speaker provides a candidate understanding of what the other speaker said. In examining the interactional functions accomplished by these OI's in various interactional contexts, I will concern myself with (i) how these OI's are different in terms of the kinds of trouble being addressed, (ii) how the OI sequences are interactionally generated, and (iii) what kinds of special interactional functions are concurrently performed by them. The findings will also shed light on the cultural expectations, values, and beliefs that Korean speakers bring to bear on ordinary interactions.

The framework for this paper is conversation analysis, the major concern of which is to provide a systematic account of the recurrent practices of talking in ordinary conversational interaction by accounting for the actual ways in which language is put to use and by capturing the orientation of the participants (Sacks, Schegloff, & Jefferson 1974). The database for the present study consists of several hours of spontaneous conversation between friends. They are audio-recorded face-to-face conversations where two or more participants talk to each other. The participants are Korean graduate students studying in America and their family members. On the whole, about 70 instances of OI sequences were identified.[2]

2. Analysis
2.1. *yey?*

Among the kinds of OI's available to speakers, OI's like *e?* or *ung?*, or their polite forms *ney?* or *yey?*, are among those that signal the weakest grasp of the troublesome talk[3], and their use usually leads to the repetition of the entire trouble source turn, or a part of it. Example (1) is a case in point:[4]

```
(1) (Lunch talk)
1   H:  toyoil   -nal eti   ka-ss  -ess -eyo?                <----
        Saturday-day where go-PST-PST-POL
        Did #you# go anywhere on Saturday?
```

---

[2]The data were transcribed according to the transcription conventions of conversation analysis (Sacks, Schegloff, & Jefferson 1974, Atkinson & Heritage 1984). However, certain innovations were also used; hitches are marked by double hyphens ('- -') to distinguish them from morpheme boundaries. Also, in English glosses, a zero-marked word in original Korean utterances is enclosed by '#'.

[3]In the following discussion, where I will only address instances of *yey?*, I will use *yey?* as the representative form for these four forms, disregarding for the moment any functional differences between them.

[4]In the data, the single headed arrow marks the trouble source turn, and the double headed arrow marks the OI turn.

2   B: yey?   <<----
          yes
          Huh?

3   H: toyoil -nal
          Saturday-day
          On Saturday.

4   B: toyoil -nal, yey,=
          Saturday-day yes
          On Saturday, I see.

5   C: =uh   pati. (0.6) uhhuh
           DM party
           Party. (0.6) uhhuh

In line 1, H asks B and C, who are husband and wife, whether they went anywhere on Saturday. In line 2, B produces an OI *yey?*, and in line 3 H repairs the trouble by partially repeating the trouble source turn.

We can note here that H's trouble source turn in line 1 is a topic-initial question, which is asked after a substantial silence. Actually, the examination of the data collected strongly suggests that OI's massively occur in the turn after a topic-initial turn, which points to a close association of OI's with topic-initiating structures.

Example (2) shows another context where *yey?* is used as an OI. This segment of talk occurs in a multi-party conversation involving four participants, A, B, C, and P:

(2) (Morning talk)
    ((C is talking to P about a computer desk.))
1   C: khukey colipha -nun   -key   ani   -la:,
         much assemble-ATTR-NOML:NOM NEG:COP-CONN

2   khukey colipha -n   -key   ani   -kwu:,
         much assemble-ATTR-NOML:NOM NEG:COP-CONN

3   kunyang .h iss -nun   -ke ilehkey m//wusun yeki
         simply   exist-ATTR-thing like:this what   here

4   twu-kay iss -kwu: selhap--
        two-CL exist-CONN drawer
        It's not a big deal to assemble #it#. Not like those that are hard to assemble. It's just that there's something here like this, two drawers-

5   A: eng: kleh -telatwu yocum   -ey -n   kulehke
         I:see like:that-although these:days-LOC-TOP like:that

6   -kkaci ssa -ci   -n   anh -ulke -eyyo.   <----
         -to   cheap-CONN-TOP NEG-MOD-POL
         I see. Even so, it wouldn't be that cheap these days.

7   C: yey?   <<----
         yes
         Huh?

8   A: samsip myes   pwul (.) ku//lehkey ssa -ci   anh -ulke
         thirty how:many dollar   like:that   cheap-CONN NEG-MOD

9   -eyyo. (.) yocum   -un.
         -POL   these days-TOP
         For thirty dollars or something, no, it wouldn't be that cheap
         these days.
                                    [
10   C: kulay -yo? sasip o pwul
                                    like:that-POL forty five dollar
11   cwu -kwu   sa -ss -na?
         give-CONN buy-PST-DUB
         Really? Maybe #we# bought #it# for forty-five dollars.

In the context that precedes this segment of talk, C has been telling P that
she and her husband bought a very nice computer desk for about thirty-five
to forty dollars several months before. From line 1 through line 4, C
describes how nice the desk is. In lines 5 and 6, A challenges C by saying
that such a nice desk must cost more than thirty-five or forty dollars. As
A's utterance interrupts C's on-going talk, which is shown by the double
slashes in line 3, C produces an OI, *yey?*, in line 7. In response to the OI,
A repeats his utterance in lines 8 and 9, and C backs off in line 10.

We can note that C produces the OI at a point where she stops her on-
going interaction with P, and responds to A who just challenged her
interruptively. In this respect, there is a sense in which the speaker is using
the OI as a way of showing that she is positioning herself as an addressee
towards a new interlocutor as she disengages herself from the previously on-
going interaction with a different interlocutor. In a way, this observation
can also apply to example (1), where the person who initiates the repair
signals concurrently that she is shifting her interactional stance by
positioning herself as an addressee towards the interlocutor who just brought
up a question topic-initially.

The function of *yey?* as a marker of stance shift is further supported in
example (2), where we find that C goes ahead and responds to the trouble
source turn when just a bit of the repair response has been done. That is, in

line 10, C responds to A just at the point where A only finished a part of his utterance in line 8, which shows that C had understood the trouble source turn before A finished the repair. This observation suggests that the speaker may experience a processing delay. That is, C was presumably not yet ready to answer the trouble source turn right away and initiates repair. But, as she produces the OI, she catches up and responds to the trouble source turn while repair is underway. Such a processing delay would be associated with the marking of the speaker's stance shift in such a way that the speaker, before processing the interlocutor's topic-initial or interruptive utterance, initially positions himself/herself as an addressee of the interlocutor.

2.2. m w e ?

OI's involving *mwe?*, which corresponds to English *what?*, are used when speakers address not only generalized trouble, but also some specific trouble.[5] In the following discussion, I will only look at the latter case where various *mwe?* forms are used to target some specific trouble. Two types of *mwe?* are distinguished in terms of whether it is uttered with falling intonation or rising intonation.

Example (3) shows a context where *mwe* is used with falling intonation to deal with specific trouble. This segment of talk, which occurs in a multi-party conversation between four participants, A, B, C, and J, is situated in the following context. J and A had once visited a friend, and the friend treated them with strange food for dinner. Now the same friend just invited J for another meal, and in lines 1 and 2, J is telling A about his concern that he may be treated with the same food again:

(3) (Lunch talk)
1 J: .hh   aywu (kunyang) tto   kuttay   ku-ke   cwu-nun
        EXCL DM   again that:time that-thing give-ATTR

2   -ke   ani   -nya?   <-----
          -NOML NEG:COP-QUES
          Well, don't you think #he# will give #me# that thing again that he gave me last time?

3   (0.5)

4 A: mwe.   <<-----
        what.

---

[5]Here I am using the term *mwe?* as a representative form that subsumes a variety of OI forms involving *mwe*, such as the polite form *mwe-yo?*, or other case-marked forms like *mwe-ka?* (*mwe* + Nominative), as well as *mwe* with falling intonation, which is transcribed according to the transcription convention of conversation analysis as *mwe* followed by the period (*mwe.*).

What.

5   J: ce -p//en-ey,
          that-time-LOC
          Last time,

            [
6   A: e::: hh ku -ke, hh
          DM   that-thing
          Oh, that thing, hh.

7   J: hhh na-n   tto   taco-lul cw- ntakulay-se.....
          I -TOP again taco-ACC give-QUOT -CONN
          hhh #he# told #me# that he would treat #me# with a taco, so I
          thought..... ((J continues to tell the story to B and C.))

In lines 1 and 2, J produces a topic-initial question, which contains the demonstrative noun form *ku-ke* 'that thing'. As this question is directly addressed to A, A, in line 4, asks for specification of the reference term by producing an OI. In the next turn, J repairs the trouble in line 5 by mentioning a vague past time reference *ce-pen-ey* 'at that time' (or 'last time'). J's provision of the vague time reference point, however, turns out to be sufficient for A to figure out what J meant, and A produces a success marker *e:::* in line 6, which occurs in overlap with J's repair turn. In line 7, J begins to tell the rest of the participants what happened.

The repair sequence in example (3), then, constitutes a pre-story-telling sequence, which projects that J's story will follow. What J and A do in this repair sequence is to negotiate and confirm the shared domain of information as co-tellers of the story, which has significant import as a pre-story-telling sequence for the the projected story by heightening the other interlocutors' expectation about what they (J and A) are talking about.

Example (4) below shows another context where *mwe?* is produced as an OI, this time with rising intonation. Here the polite form *mwe-yo?* (*mwe* + politeness marker) is used:

(4) (Lunch talk)
    ((long silence))
1   H: Kim young-soon-ssi -hantey ku   pili -ess -eyo, chayk? <---
         kim Young-soon-Ms.-from   that borrow-PST-POL book
         Did #you# borrow that from Ms. Young-soon Kim? the book?

2   C: mwe-yo?   <<-----
         what-POL
         What?

3   H: Lee Sang-//jin kyoswu -nim.
         Lee Sang-jin professor-HONOR

(The book by) Professon Sang-jin Lee.

               [

4   C: ah:::, .h pillyetal -la   kulay -ss
                    DM   lend:to me-QUOT do:such-PST

5   -te   -ni,
          -RETROS-INTERR
          Ah #I# asked #her# to lend #me# #the book#, but,

6   (0.8)

7   H: an   pillyecwu-eyo?
          NEG lend   -POL
          Did #she# not lend #it# to #you#?

In line 1, H asks whether C borrowed a particular book from Ms. Young-soon Kim. Here H initially asks a question without specifying the object at hand; he simply uses a demonstrative *ku* 'that'. After he completes his utterance, he tags the generic noun *chayk* 'book' to his question for more elaboration. In response, however, C produces an OI *mwe-yo?* and shows that she did not understand which book H is talking about. H then fixes the trouble in the repair turn in line 3 by providing the name of the author of the book.

We can note that C's OI signals that the general noun *book* in line 1, which is tagged onto the utterance in the trouble source turn, does not serve as a sufficient clue,[6] thus requesting that additional clues be provided. Interestingly, this practice is reciprocated by H, who provides another clue in line 3 that further elaborates on the referent, i.e. the name of the author of the book.

Overall, if we look at examples (1) through (4) all together, we can make several observations that point to some of the similarities among them in spite of differences noticeable at a more detailed level. First, if we look at examples (1), (3), and (4), there is a sense in which the speaker of the OI turn provides a short phrasal utterance such as an adverbial of time (in (1) and (3)), or a relevant proper name (in (4)), which constitute a minimal clue for the interlocutor to grasp the trouble. Secondly, examples (2), (3) and (4) strikingly show that the initiator of the repair marks the successful repair by the interlocutor in overlap with the repair turn that is still underway. As I discussed above, example (2) is a striking instance in which the repair turn is responded to when it hardly began to be uttered. In examples (3) and (4), the repair turn is interrupted by the initiator of the

---

[6]Unlike *mwe* with falling intonation, which asks for the simple identification of a referent (cf. example (3)), *mwe* with rising intonation may raise a problem in hearing, or may ask for more clues by showing that a clue already provided in the trouble source turn is not sufficient.

repair who produces a success marker quite early (i.e. *e:::* in line 6 in (3), and *ah::* in line 4 (4)).[7]

These two observations generally point to a particular interactional mode which can be characterized in the following manner. The first observation suggests that, in response to the OI turn, the speaker of the trouble source turn increasingly provides bits of information step by step. On the other hand, the second observation suggests that the speaker of the OI turn attempts to figure out what the interlocutor meant, and displays his/her understanding quite early over the smallest clue. These tendencies, which are repeatedly observed in a number of OI sequences, point to a unique mode of interactional management through which interactants create a collusive bond and maintain intersubjectivity with one speaker over-presupposing and under-telling on the one hand, and the other speaker promptly catching up on the other.

What underlies such a practice seems to be the cultural expectations that one should figure out what the other person has in mind before it is fully conveyed in verbal terms. It is not a full ideational and verbal rendering of what one wants to communicate that counts between interactants. Rather, the Korean socio-cultural norm seems to dictate that one should attempt to guess the interlocutor's point with only the smallest clue, if possible, as interactants, through exchanges of turns, provide bits of information piece by piece on the one hand, and use them as a basis on which to infer and display understanding of what the interlocutor has in mind on the other. In this respect, what counts in a Korean interactional scene is a lot of collaborative and confirmatory effort made to be attuned to the interlocutor's utterance in such a way that the speaker, by displaying his/her understanding of the trouble source turn over the smallest clue, reduces the interlocutor's burden of fully verbalizing his/her point.

2.3. Understanding check as OI

The observation that Korean speakers tend to display their understanding of the interlocutor's trouble source utterance observably through their own collaborative effort is also supported by frequent occurrences of another form of OI, the understanding check, by which the speaker provides a candidate understanding of the interlocutor's point. In many cases, the understanding check takes the form of COLLABORATIVE COMPLETION (Schegloff 1988), by which the speaker fills in any blanks in the trouble source utterance.

In many cases, understanding checks are highly collaborative in nature in that they do not contribute very much to the interlocutor's point, at least from an informational perspective. This is illustrated in example (5):

---

[7] It is to be noted that, in (4), H's repair turn is overlapped by C, who recognizes the identity of the book in line 4 even before the name of the author is completely mentioned.

(5) (Lunch talk)
1 H: ey. k//u-- kuntey ku-- ku mal -ul   ku mal -ul (.)   <---
           yes that but   that that phrase-ACC that phrase-ACC

2   taykay--ku-- ihay   -lul mos   -ha-te   -lakwu -yo,
           usually that understanding-ACC not:able-do-RETRO-QUOT-POL
           Right. That- but that- I found #people# could not understand that
           phrase.
                   [
3 B: uhhaha
                   [
4 C: huhuhu

5 B: salam -tul-i   -yo?   <<---
           people-PL-NOM-POL
           People #couldn't understand it#?

6 H: yey.
           yes
           Yes.

7   (1.0)

8 H: ku selmyeng -ul   ha-lla   kulay -to...
           that explanation-ACC do-INTENT do:such-CONSESS
           Even though #I# tried to explain that...

In lines 1 and 2, H says that people often do not understand his explanation
of the function of a particular Korean modal marker. In this utterance, the
general noun *people* is the zero-marked subject, which is retrieved by B's
understanding check in line 5.

The highly collaborative retrieval of the already presupposed general
noun through an understanding check, which may be viewed as redundant in
terms of information distribution, has significant interactional import for
the following talk in that the initiator of the OI observably positions
himself or herself as an active recipient of the interlocutor's talk. This kind
of collaborative use of understanding checks often serves as significant
interactional resources in Korean, the grammar of which allows a high
degree of presupposition. Through an understanding check, the person
initiating repair not only attempts to confirm the correctness of his/her
candidate understanding, but also gives a go-ahead to the speaker of the
trouble source by expressing his/her interest in the topic to the effect that
further talk is built on the basis of mutual orientations to the course of the
interaction.

Another type of understanding check used as an OI takes the form in
which the speaker marks the gist of a point from the interlocutor's talk in a

question form. Example (6) is a case in point. This conversation takes place in the context where B asked H whether he has any topic in mind which might be suitable for a newly offered graduate course in sociolinguistics. Throughout the interaction, H and B talk about a variety of things, and from time to time, return to this topic. The conversation in (6) occurs in one such context where H returns to this topic after talking about something else. Therefore, H's utterance in lines 1 to 3 occurs topic-initially:[8]

(6) (Lunch talk)
```
1  H:  na-nun ce -ke    caymiiss -ul   -kes   -kat -te        <---
       I -TOP that-thing interesting-ATTR-NOML-seem-RETROS

2      -lakwu -yo, (2.2) social interaction (0.6)-ulo   ha-eya
       -QUOT-POL      social interaction     -INST do-NECESS

3      toy    -nun   -ke  -ci   -anha-yo //ku -ci   -yo?
       become-ATTR-NOML-JUDG-not -POL that-JUDG-POL
```
I found that that thing seems to be interesting, you know.
#You# are supposed to work with reference to social interaction, right?

```
4  B:  ney.
       yes
```
Yes.

```
5      (0.8)

6  H:  kuntey bilingual ha-nun    salam -tul-i,
       DM     bilingual do-ATTR person-PL-NOM
```
and bilingual people,

```
7      (1.6)

8  B:  code switching-i   -yo, ((noise in the background))<<--- (<---)
       code switching-COP-POL
```
#You mean# code switching? (= Is #it# code switching?)

```
9  H:  yey?                      (<<----)
```

---

[8]This is a case where an OI sequence is embedded in another OI sequence. B's candidate understanding in the OI turn in line 8 itself becomes the trouble source due to background noise, which triggers another OI (*yey?*) in line 9. The trouble source turn and the repair turn in the embedded OI sequence are marked by the arrows in the parentheses. In the following discussion, I focus on the first OI, i.e. H's understanding check in line 8.

yes
huh?

10 B: code s//witching-i   -yo,
     code switching -COP-POL
     #You mean# code switching?
            [
11 H: yey.
          yes
          Yes.

12 H: malha-taka, (.) konlanha   -n   -ke   yaykiha-l   -ttay
     talk-TRANS   troublesome-ATTR-NOML talk   -ATTR-time

13   -myen yenge -lo   hay. .....
     -COND English-INST do:IE
     When talking, if #they# find it difficult to say something,
     #they# use English. .....

We can note that, in line 1, H initially uses a demonstrative form *ce-ke* 'that thing' in a topic-initial turn, and this reference form cataphorically refers to what he projects as an interesting topic for the class.[9] After providing a confirmation question in lines 2 and 3 as parenthetical, H goes on in line 6 and elaborates on what kind of topic he has in mind. Then, B interrupts H in line 8 by providing a whole concept or gist of what H is attempting to explain, saying *code-switching-i-yo?* 'you mean code switching?'.

What is noteworthy in this example is that, while B's OI in line 8 marks the gist of the notion that H is explicating, it can be treated as having been directed to H's demonstrative noun form in line 1, *ce-ke*. In this respect, we find a sense in which H's explanation through lines 2, 3, and 6 is treated by B as clues for B to figure out what the demonstrative noun form refers to. Indeed, B's orientation to coming up with a candidate understanding as early as possible is very strong, to the extent that B, taking advantage of the pause in line 7 that follows H's incomplete utterance, interrupts H's on-going explanation to display his grasp and solution of the trouble.

Viewed from a broader perspective, then, example (6) shows another context where we can observe the Korean speakers' tendency to make an attempt to figure out what the interlocutor has in mind before he/she fully

---

[9]It is to be noted that *ce-ke* is differentiated from *ku-ke* from examples (3) and (4), even though they are both translated as 'that thing' in English. *Ce-ke* refers to an entity which is far from both the speaker and the hearer, while *ku-ke* refers to an entity which is far from the speaker but close to the hearer. Different types of interactional import that draw from this distinction will be discussed later (see footnote 11).

explicates it. It further illustrates a context where such a collaborative move is initiated even when it might count as a highly disjunctive and potentially face-threatening interruption. The process underlying this interactional practice, which can be formulated as 'clue-giving and catching-up', points to the Korean speakers' cultural norm that places great importance on managing intersubjectivity collaboratively and consolidating mutual understanding by successfully responding to the interlocutor who initially formulates his/her utterance in a highly indirect manner.

3. Additional remarks
3.1. *yey?* vs. *mwe-yo?* in terms of politeness-marking

Even though I did not focus on the differences between *yey?* and *mwe-yo?* in the preceding discussion, except that the former deals with generalized trouble while the latter can address both specific and generalized trouble, one interesting difference between the polite forms of these two types of OI can be found in terms of politeness-marking; the use of *mwe-yo?*, even if it clearly involves the politeness particle *yo*, is not perceived as polite, whereas *yey?* is inherently polite in contrast with its non-polite counterparts *e?* or *ung?*. That is, if a speaker is interacting with an interlocutor who is older, senior or higher in social status, and who is not close to the speaker, it is impolite to use *mwe-yo?*, even when addressing some specific trouble. In such a situation, one should use *yey?* instead.[10] Why should this be the case?

First of all, we can note that the use of *yey?* is often polite, because, as I discussed above, it serves the interactional function of marking a shift in the speaker's interactional stance by showing that the speaker is now paying full attention to the interlocutor by putting on hold or terminating the previous interaction.

Second, we can recall that *mwe-yo?* often points to some specific trouble and leads the interlocutor to fix it by asking for a clue. This stands in contrast with *yey?*, which globally targets the entire previous turn. In this respect, there is a sense in which a person of lower status is discouraged from constraining a person of higher status on what the response could be. Rather, the higher status speaker of the trouble source turn chooses what the answer will be. This may be another reason why the use of *yey?* is preferred over *mwe-yo?*.

Third, and most importantly, the preference for *yey?* over *mwe-yo?* can be explained by the fact that the latter often indexes negative affect. For instance, various forms of OI's involving *mwe* are often used in disagreement contexts where the speaker projects disagreement or downgrades the interlocutor's point. Example (7) is a case in point. From line 1 through line 3, A jokingly says that her husband helps her do the

---

[10]Another option would be to use other types of OI which inquire more specifically into the trouble source. However, presumably, this option would be dispreferred because it signals the presence of trouble in talk too overtly.

dishes at home by turning on the dishwasher. A's utterance is then interrupted by C, who challenges A's point. In response, A produces a nominative-case-marked *mwe-ka* as an OI in line 8:

(7) (Lunch talk)

1 A: selkeci-to   hay-cu -ci   -anh -ayo:, nay-k//a (0.5)
       do:dish-ADD do -give-CONN-NEG-POL I -SUB

2   dishwasher-eyta ta neh -e   -noh -umye:n (0.5)
       dishwasher-LOC all put:in-CONN-leave-COND

3   turn on the dishwasher. you know. ccak uhha.h// selkeci--
       turn on the dishwasher you know ONOM   do:dish
       *#My husband# does the dishes, you know. I put everything into
       the dishwasher, and #he# turns it on, you know, uhha,h Doing
       dish-*

4 C: (   ).hhh.hhhh

5 C: (ani) ku machankaci-ani -a, kulen -ke
       no   that same   -NEG-IE like:that-thing

6   kule -n   -ke -n.   <----
       like:that-ATTR-thing-TOP
       Well, it's the same, isn't it, that kind of thing.

7   (0.8)

8 A: >mwe-ka<.=   <<----
       what-NOM
       What's #the same#? ((= "In what respect is it the same?"))

9 C: =waip-to   machankaci-ci.
       wife-ADD same   -COMM
       *#It's# the same for the wife. ((= "It's just as easy for the wife to
       turn on the dishwasher"))*

10   (0.5)

11 A: ay kuntey elyeun -ke -n   mwe-nya   ha-myen -yo,
       DM but   difficult-thing-TOP what-QUES do-COND-POL

12   (.) ta ilehkey ssi -e   -kaciku ilehkey ilehkey
       all like:this wash-CONN-CONN like:this like:this

13   neh -e   -noh -nun -kes   iss -ci -anh-a.

put:in-CONN-leave-ATTR-NOML exist-CONN-NEG-IE
Well, but what is difficult is ((lit. "if you ask what is
difficult, it is...")) to wash the dishes all like this and put
#them# into the dishwasher, you know.

If we look more closely at C's trouble source turn in lines 5 and 6, we find that, while it clearly constitutes a challenge to A's preceding utterance, C's utterance is pragmatically formulated in such a way that it is not clear at first what it means. What A's OI *mwe-ka* does in response, then, is to prompt C to specify his point. And as indicated by the substantial pause that precedes the OI, as well as by the swiftness with which the OI is uttered,[11] there is a sense in which A is projecting disagreement. C then repairs his trouble source utterance in line 9 by specifying the subject part of the utterance which is marked by the additive particle (*wife-to* 'wife also'), implicating that what C meant is that not only the husband, but also the wife, is in the same situation as far as the ease in using the dishwasher is concerned. Not surprisingly, C's repair turn is responded to by A's extended turn where she expresses disagreement.

As I discussed above, *mwe?* often serves as a request for a clue or for some additional clue(s), which in many cases could also constitute a prospective question (Besnier 1989) by prompting the interlocutor for identification, or further specification, of the trouble source. In this respect, the use of the term *mwe* tends to index a highly inquisitive and negative attitude of the speaker towards the interlocutor by holding the interlocutor responsible for the lack of specification in the first place. Expression of such a negative stance towards someone who is older or higher in status would certainly be impolite and inappropriate in the Korean interactional world where a great deal of care and focus is given to managing hierarchical interpersonal relationships, hence the preference for the inherently polite and general form *yey?* over *mwe-yo?*.

4. Conclusions

In summary, we can say that OI's are often triggered by the tendency of Korean speakers to over-suppose and under-tell, which leads the interlocutor to initiate repair in various forms. The speaker of the trouble source turn then increasingly provides clues, and the speaker of the OI turn attempts to respond to the trouble source utterance over the smallest clue, often in overlap with the repair turn. This interactional practice was characterized as a process of 'clue-giving and catching-up', through which speakers attempt to find 'evidence of converging minds' (Schegloff, personal communication). In a way, a prompt response to an indirect saying of something often seems to serve as a measure of intimacy between the speakers.

---

[11] The symbol '> <' indicates that the enclosed part is delivered at a pace quicker than the surrounding talk (Atkinson & Heritage 1984).

What deserves our attention in this regard is why Korean speakers frequently create trouble in talk by using a highly presuppositional form topic-initially in the first place, which constitutes one of the most common trouble sources in Korean OI sequences.[12] A functional motivation for this practice may be the pressure to place a presuppositional from, rather than a full noun form, in the object position that is often utterance-initial in Korean conversational discourse. Moreover, we can point to an interactional motivation by noting that, as illustrated by examples (3) and (4), the presuppositional form produced topic-initially massively takes the demonstrative form *ku-ke* 'that thing'. This form, as one of the three deictic forms available in Korean,[13] refers to an entity that is closer to the hearer than to the speaker. Through an iconic extension, then, *ku-ke* points to something that is more in the knowledge domain of the hearer than in that of the speaker. In this sense, the topic-initial use of *ku-ke* has the significant function of inviting the interlocutor's active contribution to the identification of the referent by treating the interlocutor as a co-participant in talk. The interactional import of doing so would be to provide a mutually relevant basis on which the interlocutor is cordially led to actively and collaboratively participate as a co-teller in the course of the action being developed.[14]

As a whole, the preceding discussion suggests that what is valued in Korean OI sequences is not so much the outcome of repair *per se* as the process of repair through which interactants mutually negotiate the grounds for reaching a converging point. This practice, which could be viewed as

---

[12]I thank Prof. Patricia Clancy for bringing up this point.

[13]The other two deictic forms are *i-ke* 'this thing' and *ce-ke* 'that thing'.

[14]The use of *ku-ke*, then, stands in sharp contrast with the use of a similar demonstrative *ce-ke* in example (6), which points to something that is far from both the speaker and the hearer. As I discussed above, *ce-ke* in example (6) is used cataphorically in a context where speaker H projects an extended turn. Therefore, speaker H does not assume a higher degree of familiarity of the referent with hearer B, and does not invite the hearer's contribution to identifying the referent. It is not surprising, then, to find that B's understanding check in example (6), by which a candidate referent is provided, not only constitutes an interruption, but also is treated as such by H. That is, we can first observe in (6) that, in H's interrupted utterance in line 6, only the subject of the utterance is mentioned. After the embedded repair sequence from line 7 to line 10, H resumes his previously interrupted utterance and finishes it by starting just at the point where he stopped, i.e. by producing the predicate part which is appended to its subject part in line 6, rather than by re-starting his utterance from the beginning. By doing so, H observably shows that he is treating the intervening repair sequence as an interruption of his talk. This is an instance in which the speaker 'creates a context of interrupting' by starting up in the middle of a sentence (Fox 1985:102). This brief discussion points to an interesting relationship between grammar and interactional contexts in terms of how the former shapes and is situated in the latter in actual contexts of language use.

inefficient and not highly recipient-designed, furnishes rich interactional resources whereby speakers mutually display their orientation to the prior talk, collaboratively license further talk, and consolidate a collusive bond through intersubjectively managed 'confirming' processes.

In conclusion, it should be noted that, even though most of the observations that I presented in this paper are admittedly of a preliminary nature, they provide a handle on further examining various sequential aspects of OI sequences in terms of rich interactional uses that speakers make out of them, and explicating the relationship between language and cultural beliefs, values, and expectations that bear upon language use in general. Moreover, the interactional domain represented by OI sequences constitutes a promising area for further research by virtue of their pervasiveness and generic contingency of dealing with trouble, providing a solid basis for cross-linguistic comparisons, as well as for the explication of the basic sequence organization in spontaneous conversation (Schegloff 1988).

References

Atkinson, J. Maxwell, and John Heritage. 1984. Structures of Social Action. Cambridge: Cambridge University Press.

Besnier, Niko. 1989. Information withholding as a manipulative and collusive strategy in Nukulaelae gossip, Language in Society 18.315-41.

Fox, Barbara. 1985. On the creation of discourse by grammar. Proceedings of the First Annual Meeting of the Pacific Linguistics Conference, ed. by Scott DeLancey and Russell S. Tomlin, 97-107. University of Oregon, Eugene, Oregon.

Sacks, Harvey, Schegloff, Emanuel A., & Gail Jefferson. 1974. A simplest systematics for the organization of turn-taking for conversation. Language 50.696-735.

Schegloff, Emanuel A. 1979. The relevance of repair to syntax-for-conversation, Syntax and semantics 12: Discourse and syntax, ed. by Talmy Givon, 261-86. N.Y.: Academic Press.

_____. 1988. Other-initiated repair sequences in talk in interaction, Projected supported by NSF.

Functions of the Filler *ano* in Japanese

HARUKO MINEGISHI COOK
University of Hawaii at Manoa

1. Introduction

In the linguistic investigation of politeness in Japanese, researchers have mainly focussed on honorifics (e.g. Goldstein and Tamura 1975; Harada 1976; Ide 1989; Ide et.al. 1986; Matsumoto 1989; Niyekawa 1991; Yamanashi 1974). From a number of crosslinguistic studies of linguistic politeness such as Brown and Levinson (1987), however, it is clear that honorific expressions are not the only linguistic features that indicate politeness. These studies suggest that linguistic features that mark affect and evidentiality are major resources for indicating politeness. Recently, Maynard (1989) suggests that among other devices, fillers and final particles are resources for achieving the effect of maximum agreeableness in Japanese discourse. Studies on the final particles in recent years based on natural data have documented the way in which the particles can indicate maximum agreeableness in social interaction (e.g. Ishikawa 1988; Cook 1988; Ohta 1991; Oishi 1985) For example, Cook (1988, 1992) has shown that the particle *ne*, which indicates affective common ground, can be used to mark positive politeness (Brown and Levinson 1987), intimate social relationship between

19

the interlocutors, etc. Oishi (1985) illustrates the
way in which a nonexpert, in talking to an expert,
employs both the particles *ne* and *yo* skillfully in
order not to offend him. Further, Ohta (1991)
illustrates how the use of the final particles, among
other features, can reduce the speaker's
responsibility for his utterance. These studies show
that the final particles are an important resource for
creating and maintaining rapport in social
interaction. However, studies on fillers in Japanese
are scarce. Maynard (1989) briefly mentions that
fillers indicate the speaker's hesitant attitude or
uncertainty about the content of his message, which
gives an impression of nonimposition. Her brief
comment is about fillers in general and is rather
impressionistic. There are various fillers in Japanese
and we still do not know exactly how each of them
contributes to interpersonal rapport. Further, it
seems that certain fillers occur more frequently in
certain types of interaction than others. Studies of
fillers should include an account of such
distributional variations.

Typically, fillers occur at the utterance-initial
position in face-to-face interaction (including a
quasi face-to-face interaction such as a telephone
conversation) and generally do not occur in writing.
They are used to keep the channels of communication
open in a face-to-face interaction and are also used
to keep the current speaker's turn while he is
searching for his next word. In this way, fillers
cognitively ease the demands of production and
processing in on-going talk. Besides these cognitive
functions, I will assume that each filler is
associated with particular social functions.

This paper has two interrelated goals: i) to
identify the social functions of a particaular filler
and explain how it can index politeness and ii) to
identify ways in which this filler and a certain final
particle are used when both index politeness. The
paper discusses one of the most commonly used filler*s*
in Japanese, *ano,* and compares it with one of the most
commonly used final particles, *ne.* Since both of them
have similar social functions (they index the

interlocutors' sharedness), comparison of the two elucidates differences. The paper proposes that *ano* aligns the speaker and addressee for subsequent exchanges. Thus, it can (among other things) solicit the addressee's cooperation, function as an attention getter, highlight information, and serve as a positive politeness marker. The paper next compares the filler *ano* with the final particle *ne*. I will argue that the different positions in which they occur in an utterance can be related to differences in frequencies of occurrence.

2. Data

The data used in this study are naturally occurring: a one-hour adult family conversation and a two-hour Diet interpellation. The family conversation was audio-recorded at the dinner table in a home in Tokyo. The participants are the researcher and her parents, all of whom are middle-class speakers of Tokyo (standard) dialect. The topics of conversation are mainly family matters and gossip about the neighbors. The conversation is not argumentative. The Diet interpellation was audio-recorded from a TV broadcast in Japan. The participants of this session are two opposition party members and eleven government officials. The Diet interpellation is argumentative by nature. The opposition party members mainly question and oppose the government policies and the government officials' job is to defend their positions.

3. What does the filler *ano* mean?

Ano is used as a demonstrative adjective as well as a filler in Japanese. As a demonstrative adjective it is always immediately followed by a noun to form a noun phrase as in *ano hon* 'that book', whereas as a filler it stands alone. Also, when it is a filler, the last vowel *o* is often prolonged as in *anoo* but as a demonstrative adjective, the final vowel is not prolonged. Despite these differences, I believe that most native speakers of Japanese would agree that the filler *ano* and the demonstrative adjective *ano* are related in some way other than just being homophones. I propose that the filler is an affective extension of the deictic demonstrative adjective. In Hank's (1990, 1992) terms, I would say that as a deictic, the filler *ano* shares RELATIONAL and INDEXICAL functions with the demonstrative adjective *ano*.[1] Hanks (1990, 1992) proposes that deixis has functional components such as relational and indexical components and those of characterizing. According to him, the characterizing component describes a referent (e.g. human, regional), the relational component signals the relation between the referent and the current utterance framework (e.g. immediate, non-immediate, inclusive, non-inclusive) and the indexical component grounds the reference to the speech act participants in a speech event. For example, the English deictic word *here* denotes the region (characterizing) immediate to (relational) the speaker (indexical). When *ano* is used as a demonstrative adjective, it points to an object located at some distance from (relational) both the speaker and the addressee (indexical). In this sense, *ano* is contrasted with the other demonstrative adjectives *kono* and *sono*. *Kono* indicates that the object is in the proximity of (relational) only the speaker (indexical) and *sono* indicates that the object is in the proximity of (relational) only the addressee (indexical). This means that the use of *ano* aligns both the speaker and the addressee on the same side with respect to the object in sight. In contrast, in using *sono* and *kono*, the speaker places himself and his addressee in opposition.

I propose that the demonstrative adjective *ano* and the filler *ano* share the same relational and indexical functions. This means that the filler *ano* aligns the speaker and the addressee on the "same side." As discussed by R. Lakoff (1974) and Lyons (1977), often the meanings of locative deixis are extended to the domain of attitude and feelings, which I will call "affect". Lakoff (1974) refers to such uses of deixis as "emotional deixis" and Lyons (1977) as "empathetic deixis". Lakoff (1974: 355) claims, "there is a clear linguistic link between emotional, and spatial 'closeness' and 'distance'." She shows that in English the demonstrative pronoun *that* is used to establish emotional solidarity between the interlocutors as in

"That Henry Kissinger sure knows his way around Hollywood!." According to Lakoff (1974; 352), this use implies that the interlocutors "share the same views toward the subject of the discussion". Considering these and other examples discussed in the literature (Fillmore 1975; Hanks 1990; Levinson 1982) it is reasonable to hypothesize that the deictic functions (more specifically relational and indexical functions) of the demonstrative adjective *ano* are extended to the domain of affect when it is used as a filler. This means that the use of the filler *ano* aligns the speaker and the addressee (indexical) with respect to the subsequent utterance (relational) in face-to-face interaction.[2] Such an alignment makes the interlocutors tune into each other.

Hanks (1984; 1992), Ochs (in press) and Silverstein (1976) identify two uses of deixis, namely presupposing and creative. The former marks or points to a certain aspect of the speech context while the latter creates one in the speech context. The filler *ano* is a creative deixis in that it aligns the interlocutors and hence creates interpersonal tuning between the interlocutors. In this sense the filler *ano* differs from the demonstrative adjective *ano*, which is a case of presupposing deixis. In what follows, I will discuss the use of the filler *ano* in discourse. As we will see, the data support the proposal that the filler *ano* is a marker of alignment between the speaker and the addressee.

4. Uses of *ano* in discourse

In the data *ano* often occurs when the speaker starts a conversation or a new turn, tries to get the attention of the addressee, highlights a proposition that immediately follows *ano*, starts a new topic, or disagrees with others. This does not mean that these speech acts are always accompanied by the filler *ano* since speakers have an option of not using it, and other pragmatic features can help constitute these speech acts. Thus instances of the non-use of *ano* in these speech acts do not contradict the present analysis. Also, in some instances, *ano* conveys

simultaneously more than one of the speech acts that I
have mentioned (cf. Silverstein 1985).

Perhaps most native speakers equate the filler *ano*
with a device to start a conversation. It occurs by
itself or with the final particle *ne* as in *ano ne*.
Mizutani and Mizutani (1987) list devices for
addressing someone and state that among the devices
that they mention *ano* is the most common.

Since in the present data the interlocutors are
already engaged in conversation or speech, instances
of *ano* as a conversation starter are few. Instead, at
the beginning of a new turn, *ano* often occurs as a
tuning device.[3] Consider example (1), in which Prime
Minister Kaifu starts his turn with *ano*. Since the
prime minister is not opposing Mr. Inoki's proposal,
there is no conflict here. Thus the prime minister's
turn-initial use of *ano* is not strategic. Rather, it
is considered to be a tuning device as well as an
indicator of a new turn.

(1) [Up to this point, Mr. Inoki, an opposition party
member, has been proposing a new sport policy and
asking the Prime Minister to consider it.][4]

    Inoki: ...Arigatoo gozaimashita.
         'Thank you very much.'
   Chair: Kaifu Naikaku Soori Daijin
         'Prime Minister Kaifu.'
-->Kaifu: Anoo, sekkaku keiken ya taiken kara
         motozuita (teigen) puran o otsukurii-
         omochi to iu koto de gozaimasu kara,
         watakushi mo itadakimashite, kentoo o
         sasete itadakimasu.
         'Since you have a plan based on your
         experiences, I receive it and we will
         (humbly) consider it.'

The turn initial *ano* can simply be a tuning device as
in example (1), in which the speaker is quite
cooperative with respect to the addressee's request.
As we will later see, when the speaker disagrees with
the addressee, such a usage of *ano* simultaneously

serves as a positive politeness strategy (Brown and
Levinson 1987).

In the data, *ano* is occasionally used as an
attention getter. Consider (2) from the family
conversation data. Here H and C are talking about the
neighbors who have become rich and bought a new house
with the cash that they received as compensation from
the city due to road expansion. T wants to be part of
this conversation. In line 2, by saying *e?* 'what?', he
tries to cut into the conversation between H and C,
but he is ignored. Then in line 5 he tries to get H's
attention by saying *ano ne*. However, H ignores T again
in line 6 by talking to C.

(2)
1   H: Ja koko wa minna kyasshu de haratte (   )
        no, soshitara.
        'They paid it off all in cash, then.'
2   T: E?
        'What?'
3   H: Sugoi wa nee. (Kyasshu datta no)?
        'That's amazing. (It was cash.)'
4   C: Un. Yappa, torareta rashii, kyooseichi dooro
        ka nanka
        'Uh-huh, as expected, the land seems to
        have been taken away.
                                          [
5 -->T: Un ano nee
        dooro no kakuchoo de nee=
        'Because of the expansion of the street'
6   H:=Hu::n, sugoi.
        'Uh-hu::h, amazing.'
7   C: Sugoi okanemochi n natchatta no.
        'They have become awfully rich.'

A way to start a conversation and get the addressee's
attention is to elicit the addressee's cooperation in
paying attention to the speaker's talk. If the filler
ano is a marker of aligning the speaker with the
addressee, it can elicit the addressee's cooperation.
The fact that *ano* occurs with the final particle *ne* in
(2) does not contradict this proposal. As I have
proposed in Cook (1992), the particle *ne* as an

affective common ground marker can elicit the
addressee's involvement with the speaker. By so doing,
it can function as an attention getting device as
well. Thus, it makes sense that the sequence *ano* (a
marker of the speaker and the addressee's alignment)
ne (a marker of the speaker and the addressee's
affective common ground) is a typical attention getter
or a conversation starter.

    Ano often occurs immediately before the speaker's
point. In this way it highlights the information that
follows it. Consider example (3). Here C is talking to
H about the drought in Los Angeles. C's point is that
LA's drought stems from the fact that LA by nature is
a desert. She mentions this point twice, in lines 2
and 4, which suggests that this is a point she wants
to emphasize. In line 2, immediately before giving
this information, C uses *ano*. If the filler *ano* aligns
the speaker and the addressee and hence gets the
addressee's attention, it can give the effect of
highlighting the subsequent information since the more
attention the addressee pays to what the speaker says,
the more sailent the information becomes for the
addressee. Thus, this use of *ano* highlights the
information which immediately follows.

(3) [Up to this point C is talking about the dry spell
    in LA.]

1 C: Motomoto dakedo, Rosu to iu no wa, kiita
      n dakedomo,
     'But by nature, Los Angeles, I've heard'
2 -->ano sabaku chitai na n datte ne=
     'was a desert area, right?'
2 H:=Soo yo=
     'That's right'
4 C:=Minami Kariforunia tte sabaku chitai.
     'Southern California is a desert.'
5   Amerikajin no eichi to, sono keizairyoku de
     Kororado gawa ya nanka no, ro- Rokkii sanmyaku
     no yuki doke no mizu o
     'Because of Americans' wisdom and their economic
     power (they brought) water from the Colorado
     River and water from the snow in the Rocky

```
      Mountains'
6  H: Un.
      'Uh-huh.'
```

Example (4) comes form the Diet interpellation. Here
Mr. Konishi, an opposition party member asks the prime
minister's view on the question of transporting
plutonium from other countries to Japan. In response
to this question, Mr. Itoo, minister of
transportation, states the official point of view.
Even though Mr. Konishi's question is directly
addressed to the prime minister, the chair person
directs this question to Mr. Itoo before he does so to
the prime minister. This suggests that Mr. Itoo is
knowledgeable in this issue and knows a way to defend
the government position. Immediately before he makes
his point he uses *anoo*. This makes the addressee pay
attention to what Mr. Ito is going to say and thus has
an effect of highlighting it.

(4)
```
Konishi:  ...Soo iu men de, sono ikigomi ni tsuite ee
          soori ni okotae negaitai to omoimasu.
          '...In this respect, I'd like to ask the
          prime minister for his determination.'
  Chair:  Itoo Unyu Daijin.
          'Transportation Minister Ito'
   Itoo:  Soori tooben no mae ni hitokoto.
          'Before the prime minister's answer, I will
          say a word.'
     -->Anoo, doo goeikan o tsukuttara ii ka to iu
          koto o kentoo shite nai wake dewa arimasen.
          'It is not the case that we don't inquire
          into how to build convoys."
```

Ano often occurs before introducing a new topic. If
ano indexes the addressee's alignment with the
speaker, it makes sense that it occurs before
introducing a new topic. In order to introduce a new
topic and proceed with it, the speaker needs the
addressee's cooperation. *Ano* can elicit the
addressee's cooperation by aligning him with the
speaker. Consider examples (5) and (6). In (5) the

three family members are talking about H's schedule and in line 10, C introduces a new topic of conversation, which is preceded by *ano*.

(5)
1　H: Ashita to tabun:: tabun Doyoobi ka Nichiyoobi.
　　　'Tomorrow and pro::bably probably Saturday or Sunday.'
2　C: Doyoobi　(demo yoru　)
　　　'Saturday (but evening　)'
3　H: Yoru wa ii.
　　　'The evening will be free.'
4　C: Yoru wa ii.
　　　'The evening will be free.'
　　　　　　(1.2)
5　T: Soide
　　　'and'
　　　　[　　　]
6　C: Sore kimete.
　　　'Decide on that.'
7　T: Nijuuku sanjuu wa yoru wa kaette kun no ka
　　　'You'll be home on the evenings of the 29th and 30th.'
　　　　　　　　　　　　　　　[　　　　　　　　　　　　]
8　C:　　　　　　　　　　　　　(　　　　　　　　　)
9　H: Hiruma wa wakannai kedomo.
　　　'I don't know the schedules for the daytime though.'
10-->C: Ano ne, kondo uchi no hanashi.
　　　'We'll talk about the house now.'

Example (6) comes from the Diet interpellation. Mr. Onishi, an opposition party member is requesting that the government abolish the newly introduced sales tax bill. Then in line 3, he changes the topic to the US-Japan structural impediment initiatives. When he does so, he uses *ano*.

(6) Konishi:
1　ee Jimintoo no seijika (　　) oozei irassharu to omou n de, sono naibu de desu nee yoku kentoo shite itadaite, watashi domo ga yookyuu shite orimasu kono haishi no hookoo de mazu, sutaato

shite morau to. (4.0)
'Uh, I think that there are many Liberal Democratic
Party politicians (   ), so I request that within
the LDP you examine the problem well and begin by
taking the steps toward abolition of the bill,
which we are demanding.'
2   To iu koto o maa, shuchoo sashite itadaite, tsugi
no kadai ni utsutte ikitai to omoimasu. (2.0)
'We'd like to request this and I think we'll go to
the next item.'
3-->Ano tsugi wa desu nee, Nichibei Koozookyoogi.
'Next is the US-Japan structural impediment
initiatives.'

If the filler *ano* aligns the speaker and the
addressee, it can bring the addressee to the speaker's
side and hence make it easier to get the addressee's
cooperation.

Also, *ano* occurs often in the speech act of
disagreement. Disagreement is a speech act which
threatens the addressee's face. According to Brown and
Levinson (1987), one of the choices when the speaker
has to perform a face-threatening act is to mitigate
the act by emphasizing common ground, and by including
the addressee in the speaker's activity among others.
Brown and Levinson call this a 'positive politeness'
strategy. If the filler *ano* is a marker of a speaker-
addressee alignment, then we can explain why it occurs
often when the speaker disagrees. By aligning the
speaker and addressee, *ano* elicits the common ground
between the interlocutors, which redresses the FTA.
Consider (7) and (8) which come from the Diet
interpellation data. In (7) Mr. Konishi finds the
government policy on the illegal workers impossible.
In expressing his opposition, he uses *ano* three times:
in lines 2 and 3, where he establishes the topic of
his opposition, and in line 4 where he actually
mentions the impossibility of control.

(7)
Mr. Nomoto, Chief of Bureau of Immigration Dept.,
Ministry of Justice:
1   kore ni taisuru tekisetsu na- taioo to,

fuhooshuuroo no torishimari to koo iu koto ga
daiji daroo to omotte orimasu.
'I think it important to deal with this problem
appropriately and to control illegal working.'
((the rest of Nomoto's speech is omitted here.))
Mr. Konishi, an opposition party member:
2-->Anoo, torishimari o genjuu ni suru to iu
3-->anoo fuhooshuuroosei ne,
'Illegal student workers that you will strengthen
the control over'
(1.0)
ee, soofu ni iwareta n desu kedomo, genjitsu ni
maa,
4-->ano dekinai n ja nai desu ka.
'uh, you have said so, but in realty isn't it
impossible to control it?'

In (8), Mr. Hashimoto, minister of finance, is
defending the government position on the sales tax
bill. In line 4 Mr. Konishi, an opposition party
member disagrees with Mr. Hashimoto's view. Here he
uses *ano*.

(8)
Minister of Finance Hashimoto:
1   Mushiroo. rongi oo (2.0) ichioo, zeiseichoosakai
     toshite, omatome o itadaita mono ga, koo yuu
     katachi de ikaga deshoo ka to (1.5)
     'Rather, what is presented based on the discussion
     by the tax system commission, how about this
     format?'
2   sorotte kokumin ni oshimeshi no dekiru koto ga
     watakushi wa nozomashii sugata da to kangaete
     orimasu.
         (2.0)
     'I think it is ideal to show such a thing to the
     nation.'
Chairman: Konishi kun.
         'Mr. Konishi'
Konishi:
4-->Ee, sootoo anoo, watashi domo no kangae to zure
    ga aru yoo de arimasu ga,

'It seems that your view is quite different from ours.'

We see that in (7) and (8) *ano* functions as a positive politeness marker, redressing the face-threatening act of disagreement.[5] If *ano* is a marker of speaker-addressee alignment, it makes sense that *ano* also functions as a positive politeness marker.

As we have seen in examples (1) through (8), the function of *ano* in discourse is to obtain the addressee's cooperation by evoking the feeling that the interlocutors are on the same side with respect to the subsequent utterance. This is the way in which interpersonal rapport is created by using *ano*, which contributes to the effect of maximum agreeableness.

5. The filler *ano* and the final particle *ne*

The filler *ano* and the final particle *ne* are similar in that they mark the speaker's interpersonal involvement with the addressee. In this section, we will examine the frequencies of *ano* and *ne* in three different speech activities, namely, speeches of the government officials and the opposition party members in the Diet interpellation as well as family conversations. Our assumption is that differences in frequencies of occurrence of these features suggest different functions of these linguistic features since the uses of these features are associated with the goals of these speech activities.

If *ano* aligns the interlocutors, then we would predict that it would occur infrequently in interactions in which interpersonal involvement is minimized. As a filler, *ano* occurs only in face-to-face interaction. So we need to examine a type of face-to-face interaction, which is not oriented to interpersonal involvement, namely impersonal interaction.

Studies on the final particle *ne* (e.g. Clancy 1982, 1986; Cook 1988; Ishikawa 1988; Ohta 1991; Oishi 1985) suggest that frequent occurrence of the final particle *ne* is a good indication of interpersonal involvement. Therefore, I will use frequencies of *ne* as a measure of interpersonal involvement. Table 1 shows

frequencies of *ne* and *ano* in the three speech
activities.

TABLE 1: Frequencies of *ne* and *ano* in the data
per 2000 words[6]

	ne	*ano*
Government officials	0.52	3.36
Opposition party members	35.51	26.69
Family conversation	68.24	11.01

We see in Table 1 that *ne* occurs most frequently in
the family conversation, which we would expect, given
that *ne* occurs more frequently in intimate
interactions. Table 1 also shows that the government
officials' speeches virtually lack *ne*, which suggests
dispreference for interpersonal involvement in their
speeches. This observation concords with the native
speaker impression that government officials' speeches
are impersonal and aloof. If the government officials'
speeches are impersonal, then we would expect *ano* to
occur less frequently in their speeches because
aligning the addressee is a pragmatic act of
interpersonal involvement. In fact, Table 1 shows that
the government officials use *ano* only 3.36 times per
2000 words. This supports the present proposal.

Ne occurs almost twice as frequently in the family
conversation as in the opposition party members'
speeches. If the frequency of *ano* were in proportion
to that of *ne*, we would expect *ano* to occur more
frequently in the family conversation than in the
opposition party members' speeches. However, as we see
in Table 1, our prediction does not hold. *Ano* occurs
more frequently in the opposition party members'
speeches. The opposition party members use *ano* 26.69
per 2000 words while the family conversation
participants, only 11.01. This suggests that despite
the similarity, there are differences between the
filler *ano* and the final particle *ne*. I propose that
this distributional difference between *ano* and *ne* is
attributed to different pragmatic functions associated
with the positions in which they occur in an
utterance.[7] As a filler, *ano* occurs at the beginning

of an utterance. The utterance-initial position is an ideal position to adjust the speaker-addressee relation with respect to the subsequent utterance. *Ano* can tune the speaker and the addressee into each other before they proceed to the subsequent utterance. Thus *ano* is a good device for adjusting the relationship between interlocutors who do not share similar assumptions. It is also an effective device for tuning in with an addressee before saying something that may evoke a dispreferred response or may be difficult for the addressee to comprehend. This explanation accounts for why *ano* occurs more frequently in the opposition party members' speeches than in the family conversation, for the opposition party members' speeches are addressed to those who do not share the views of the speaker. In addition, their speeches are more face-threatening and they deal with more complex subject matters.

In contrast, because final particles typically occur in the utterance-final position except for *ne* used as an attention getter, final particles generally do not serve as a tuning device for the interlocutors prior to the subsequent utterance. Instead, they indicate how the preceeding utterance should be interpreted. For example, *ne* indicates that an utterance is to be taken with shared feelings between the speaker and the addressee. Therefore, it occurs more frequently in intimate interactions. In the present data, the frequency of *ne* is the highest in the family conversation.[8]

6. Summary

I have proposed that the filler *ano* is an affect marker which aligns the speaker and the addressee in face-to-face interaction. This function serves to obtain the addresssee's cooperation. In this way, *ano* can create interpersonal rapport. Thus it often occurs in a speech act which requires the addressee's cooperation. In this sense, the filler *ano* resembles the final particle *ne*. Both of them rarely occur in impersonal speech contexts such as government officials' speeches. However, they do differ in their

distribution in interpersonally involved interactions
due to their positions in an utterance.

As for the implications of this analysis, Ochs
(1988) suggests that a marker of affect or a
combination of affect markers can index a genre. Both
Biber (1986) and Besnier (1988) demonstrate that
genres are defined multidimensionally. The results of
my research (given in Table 1) suggest that relative
frequencies of *ano* and *ne* can index different types of
speech genre. For example, impersonal interactions are
characterized by minimal occurrences of both features.
In contrast, interpersonally involved interactions
between interlocutors who share assumptions are
characterized by high frequencies of *ne* and relatively
low frequencies of *ano.* Interactions between
interloctuors who do not share assumptions or who need
to perform a face-threatening act even when they are
interpersonally involved are characterized by
relatively higher frequencies of *ano* in relation to
those of *ne*. In order to see if we can generalize this
observation, future research covering a wide range of
genres will be required.

Notes

1. Hanks (1992) includes a broad range of contextual
features in his definition of indexical ground (e.g.
the speech act participants, the participants state of
knowledge, attention of focus, etc.). However, for the
present discussion, it is sufficient to consider only
the the speech act participants.
2. Although *ano* is used as a filler far more
frequently, *kono* and *sono* can also be used as fillers.
Unlike *ano*, they do not function as an attention
getter or a conversation starter. This is probably
because these deictic features separate the speaker
and addressee on opposite sides in relation to the
referent and do not align the interlocutors (an
alignment which is important to elicit the addressee's
attention). A further discussion of *kono* and *sono* is
beyond the scope of this paper.
3. In the Diet interpellation data, besides *ano*, the
filler *ee* often occurs at the beginning of a turn. My

observation is that while *ano* occurs in both
conversation and formal speeches, *ee* generally does
not occur in conversation by itself. When it does
occur in conversation, it is followed by the quotative
to as in *ee to*.

4. The following transcription conventions are used:

(1.0)	length of significant pause in seconds
word-	abrupt cut-off
wo::rd	vowel elongation
?	rising pitch
=	turn latching
[	turn overlapping
((text))	information for which a symbol is not available
( )	incoherent string
(word)	conjectured string
-->	position of illustrative element
'(word)'	a word that does not occur in Japanese but is necessary in English translation.

5. We observe that in the speech act of disagreement,
not only *ano* but also hedging is used as a device for
redressing face-threatening acts. Examples of hedging
are *dekinai n ja nai desu ka* 'isn't it impossible to
control it?' in (7), the filler *ee* (cf. Koide 1983),
and *yoo de arimasu ga* 'it seems that' in (8). These
expressions make the disagreement rather indirect. In
this sense these are what Brown and Levinson call
negative politeness strategies. The fact that both
negative and positive politeness strategies occur in
an utterance suggests that the assumption that
negative and positive politeness do not cooccur may
not be correct.

6. A simple frequency index is calculated by dividing
the number of times a feature occurs by the total
words uttered, then multiplying the result by 2000.
This yields an index that is interpreted as the number
of occurrences of that feature per every 2000 words.

7. Another difference between fillers and final
particles is that in personal letters, in which the
writer writes as if he is speaking to the addressee,
final particles sometimes occur whereas fillers do not

(cf. Ishikawa 1988). This seems to be attributed to the the nature of fillers as a gatekeeper of the communication channel. They have no reason to occur when the addressee is not present in the speech context.

8. In another family conversation involving 8 adults, *ne* occurs 84.6 times and *ano*, 10.9 per 2000 words.

References

Besnier, Niko. 1988. The linguistic relationships of spoken and written Nukulaelae registers. Lg 64.707-36.

Biber, Douglas. 1986. Spoken and written textual dimensions in English. Lg 62.384-414.

Brown, Penelope and Stephen Levinson. 1987. Politeness: some universals in language usage. Cambridge: Cambridge University Press.

Clancy, Patricia. 1982. Written and spoken style in Japanese narratives. Spoken and written language: exploring orality and literacy. Vol. IX Advances in discourse processes, ed. by Deborah Tannen, 55-76. Norwood: Ablex.

_____. 1986. The acquisition of communicative style in Japanese. Language socialization across cultures, ed. by Bambi. Schieffelin & Elinor Ochs, 213-50. Cambridge: Cambridge University Press.

Cook, Haruko M. 1988. Sentential particles in Japanese conversations: a study of indexicality. Doctoral dissertation, USC.

_____. 1992. Meaning of non-referential indexes: a case of the Japanese particle *ne*. *Text* 12-4.

Fillmore, Charles. 1975. Santa Crux lectures on deixis, 1971. Mimeo, Indiana University Linguistics Club.

Goldstein, B. and K. Tamura. 1975. Japan and America. Tokyo: Charles E. Tuttle.

Hanks, William F. 1984. The evidential core of deixis in Yucatec Maya. Papers from the twentieth regional meeting of the Chicago Linguistic Society, 154-72. Chicago: Chicago Linguistic Society.

_____. 1990. Referential Practice: Language and lived space among the Maya. Chicago: University of Chicago Press.

_____. 1992. The indexical ground of deictic reference. Rethinking context, ed. by Alessandro Duranti & Charles Goodwin, 46-76. Cambridge: Cambridge University Press.

Harada, S. I. 1976. Honorifics. Syntax and semantics vol. 5, ed. by Masayoshi Shibatani, 449-560. New York: Academic Press.

Ide, Sachiko. 1989. Formal forms and discernment: two neglected aspects of universals of linguistic politeness. Multilingua 8-2/3.223-48.

Ide, Sachiko, V. Hill, S. Ikuta, A. Kawasaki, and T. Ogino. 1986. Universals of linguistic politeness. Journal of Pragmatics 10.347-71.

Ishikawa, Minako. 1988. The cognitive and interactional functions of the Japanese sentence particle *ne* in written discourse. Master's thesis. The State University of New York at Buffalo.

Lakoff, Robin. 1974. Remarks on this and that. Proceedings of the Tenth Regional Meetings of the Chicago Linguistic Society. 435-56.

Levinson, Stephen. 1982. Pragmatics. Cambridge: Cambridge University Press

Lyons, John. 1977. Semantics Vol. 2. Cambridge: Cambridge University Press.

Matsumoto, Yoshiko. 1989. Politeness and conversational universal - observations from Japanese. Multilingua 8-2/3.207-21.

Maynard, Senko K. 1989. Japanese conversation. Norwood, New Jersey: Ablex.

Mizutani, Osamu and Nobuko Mizutani. 1987. How to be polite in Japanese. Tokyo: The Japan Times.

Niyekawa, Agnes. 1991. Minimum essential politeness. Tokyo: Kodansha International.

Ochs, Elinor. 1988. Culture and language development. Cambridge: Cambridge University Press.

_____. In press. Linguistic resources for socializing humanity. Rethinking Linguistic Relativity, ed. by John Gumperz and Stephen Levinson. Cambridge: Cambridge University Press.

Ohta, Amy S. 1991. Evidentiality and politeness in
    Japanese. Issues in Applied Linguistics,
    2/2.212–36.
Oishi, Toshio. 1985. A description of Japanese final
    particles in context. Unpublished doctoral
    dissertation. University of Michigan.
Silverstein, Michael. 1976. Shifters, verbal
    categories and cultural description. Meaning in
    Anthropology, ed. by K. Basso and H. Selby, 11–
    55. Albuquerque: School of American Research.
_____. 1985. The functional stratification of language
    and ontogenesis. Culture communication and
    cognition: Vygotskian perspectives, ed. by James
    Wertsch, 205–35. Cambridge: Cambridge University
    Press.
Yamanashi, Masa–aki. 1974. On minding your p's and q's
    in Japanese: a case study from honorifics.
    Papers from the tenth regional meeting of the
    Chicago Linguistic Society. Chicago, 760–71.

The Structure of the Intonation Unit in Japanese

SHOICHI IWASAKI
University of California at Los Angeles

1. Introduction

Utterances are produced in increments termed INTONATION UNITS (Chafe 1987). An intonation unit (or IU) is defined as a "stretch of speech occurring under a single unified intonation contour (Du Bois et al. 1992)." The beginning of such a unit is often, though not always, marked by a pause, hesitation noises, and/or resetting of the baseline pitch level. The ending of the intonation unit is often, again though not always, marked by a lengthening of the last syllable.[1]

Although considered, in principle, as independent of any grammatical order, it has been demonstrated that in English (at least in narratives)[2] the intonation unit often corresponds to the clause which minimally consists of the subject and predicate (Chafe 1987:38). Since the clause is a means to present a statement in which something is affirmed or denied, or a PROPOSITION as used in the predicate calculus (cf. Lyons 1977: 147ff), there exists a unity between the physical order (intonation unit), the grammatical order (clause) and the semantic order (proposition). The following is an excerpt of narrative discourse reported in Pawley and Syder (1976:39). Notice that all intonation units are a type of clause.

(1)
```
1        y'know I had four uncles-
2        (0.4) they all volunteered to go away -
3        (1.6) and ah-that was one Christmas/
4        (0.4) th't I'll always remember-
5        (0.7) because ah/ my four uncles came around/
6        they were all in uniform-
7        (1.1.) an' àh/ they are going t' have Christmas dinner with us-
```

For Japanese, though an intonation unit is identifiable with the above mentioned measures, it frequently corresponds to a smaller grammatical order, i.e. the phrase or word (Clancy 1982:73, Maynard 1989:23-27). The next segment is taken from the beginning portion of a Japanese narrative.

(2)   (from *BOMBING*)
1   *atashi   wa   nee**   I, you know.
         I   TOP   IP
2   *uchi-de   kiita   no ne?*   heard at home, you know.
         home-LOC   hear:PAST SE IP
3   *sono are   wa   ne?*   that thing, you know.
         that   that one TOP   IP
4   *hoosoo   wa   ne?*   that broadcast, you know.
         broadcast TOP IP
5   *kazoku-de.*   with my family.
         family-with

"I heard that broadcast at home with my family."

This segment of narrative consists of five intonation units which collaboratively communicate one complete proposition: "I heard the broadcast (of the Emperor's statement) at home with my family". Notice that all IUs in the segment are smaller than a clause. (Compare this with the English IU (1-7) that we examined earlier, which has a similar proposition "X do Y with Z".)

The tendency of shorter intonation units is confirmed in the five Japanese spoken discourse data sets analyzed here, which consist of two narratives, two face-to-face conversations and one telephone conversation.[3] Table 1 on the next page summarizes the types of IUs in the five data sets of 1013 IUs.[4]

The full clausal IU is defined in this paper as a non-embedded grammatical construct which has an overt predicate and at least a subject.[5] Less-than-full clauses lack overt subjects, and complex clauses are those with a complement clause with the main verb (e.g. quotation with the verb of saying), or two or more conjoined clauses. Predicate phrasal IUs are identified as those IUs that consist only of a predicate, and the associated

Clause (full)	110	10.9%	
Clause (less-than-full)	273	26.9%	
Clause (complex)	45	4.4%	
Clausal IU Total			42.2%
Predicate Phrase	88	8.7%	
Postpositional phrase	232	22.9%	
Words	265	26.2%	
Non-clausal IU Total			57.8%
Total IUs	1013	100%	

[TABLE 1]   Types of Japanese Intonation Units

noun phrases such as its subject, object and oblique information are expressed in an immediately preceding IU (and in some cases following IU). Postpositional phrases are phrases consisting of a noun and a grammatical particles such as case and topic particles. Words are lexical items such as nouns without postpositional particles, adverbs and conjunctions.

In Table 1, there are only 110 full clauses out of 1013 IUs (or 10.9% of all IUs). The number is raised only to 383 (or 37.8%) if less-than-full-clauses are included. The total number of all clause types including complex clauses is 428 (or 42.2%). On the other hand, there are 585 IUs which are shorter than a clause (or 57.8 % of all IUs). This makes a clear contrast to English IUs, of which 70 to 75% are clauses (Chafe 1980, 1987). Thus, we can conclude that there are two strategies in Japanese for producing intonation units, the clausal (or complete propositional) strategy and the phrasal/lexical (or partial propositional) strategy.

It is the hypothesis of the present paper that frequent use of the partial propositional strategy in Japanese is a consequence of the multi-faced task which the speaker must carry out in one IU. Through the analysis of the structure of predicate and postpositional phrases in Japanese, it will be shown that Japanese IUs are equipped to convey several different types of information (i.e. ideational content, cohesion marking, subjective expression and interaction management) at once. For the speaker, who attends to more than one type of information, it is easier to deal with a smaller amount of the ideational content of information. This can be achieved by producing part of the proposition, or clause. (While English speakers may attend to similar needs in conversation, they do not necessarily do it in one intonation unit.) The hypothesis is tested by analyzing actual IUs which appear in the five data sets mentioned earlier.

2. Multifunctional view of language

In linguistics, the tradition which conceives language as the means of forming and communicating propositions (statements in which something is either affirmed or denied) is strong. This encourages the method which singles out the sentence or clause as the major domain of inquiry, and disregards other factors influencing the structure of language.

Opposing this tradition, Halliday (1973, 1989) proposes a view which perceives language as a more dynamic entity comprised of three macro- (or meta-) functions; the IDEATIONAL FUNCTION, which is composed of EXPERIENTIAL and LOGICAL FUNCTIONS,   the INTERPERSONAL FUNCTION and the TEXTUAL FUNCTIOIN. In this grammar, the sentence or clause is conceived of serving these three functions simultaneously. The experiential function, one type of the ideational function, is to represent the "real world as it is apprehended in our experience" (Halliday 1989:19). Through this function, language depicts our experience by indicating things, places, actions, processes and so on. The logical function, the other type of the ideational function, represents hypotactic and paratactic relations among propositions. The interpersonal function conveys different types of speech acts such as requests and offers. The textual function creates coherent discourse.

The view proposed by Halliday finds its echo in the tradition of Japanese linguistics. In the school of linguistics represented by Tokieda (1941, 1950) (henceforth the "Tokieda school"), language is viewed not only as a vehicle to convey propositions but also as a means to reveal the speaker's internal state, or subjectivity.[6] Watanabe (1953) identifies these two elements as the acts of *jojutsu* (description) and *chinjutsu* (expression). Haga (1954) refines Watanabe's view and isolates three elements through his analysis of sentence structure. In particular, he adds the interpersonal component to the descriptive and expressive components.

Comparing the view on language by Halliday and that by the linguists of the Tokieda school, I conclude that four metafunctions must be identified in language. They are the ideational, interactional, cohesive and subjective functions.

The ideational function participates in building up a proposition and specifies the relations between propositions.

The interpersonal function is either a macro-type, which concerns complete speech acts, or a micro-type which shows sensitivity towards the addressee in the speech situation. In a conversational setting, the second type of interpersonal involvement is a very important factor which affects the structure of the utterance. In English, such phrases as "you know" or "let me tell you" serve this function. In Japanese specialized lexical items and expressions attached to utterances carry out this task. I call them INTERACTIONAL WORDS (Iwasaki to appear), which include such particles as *sa*, *ne*, and *yo* and expressions such as *deshoo* and *janai* with rising intonation.

The third function is the cohesive function, which connects one part of discourse to another in the same discourse or points to an item in the speech context. Halliday and Hasan (1976) explore many cohesion marking mechanisms in English.[7] Japanese also employs various devices which signal a cohesive tie between elements in the text including the topic marking particle *wa*, the nominalizing words *no* and *wake* (Iwasaki 1990), various conjunctives such as *kara* 'because', *noni* 'though', *kedo* 'but', and nonfinite predicate forms such as *-tara* 'if/when', and *-te* 'and/and then'.

The fourth function is the subjective function, a special concern of Japanese linguists, which does not describe, but rather expresses, the speaker's internal state such as speaker's affect, deictic relations with the outer world and epistemic (or perspective) stance. The speaker chooses, optionally or obligatorily, certain words or morphemes among several possibilities to indicate these concerns (Iwasaki 1993). These four metafunctions influence the language in various ways.

3. Analysis of the phrasal unit structure

Although Halliday and linguists of the Tokieda school share a multifunctional view of language, they differ in one important respect. Halliday (1989:23) emphasizes that the metafunctions are not isolatable in utterances and that it is wrong to assume that we can point out a word or phrase and name its function. However, the Tokieda school linguists commonly assume that functions are to a certain degree isolatable in utterances. They have found lexical items which have crystallized one of the functions, though there are also lexical items which can serve two or more functions.

Watanabe (1953) argues that morphemes are arranged in the predicate in a linear order with the morphemes representing the ideational function on the left and the morpheme representing the subjective function on the right. In particular, he shows that the verb stem and suffixes of the passive and causative which are directly attached to the stem participate in building up a proposition (ideational function) but suffixes such as the conjectural suffix *daroo* which appear away from the stem participate in expressing subjectivity. Suffixes which appear between the stem and another suffix appearing away from the stem have ambivalent status, somewhat descriptive and somewhat subjective. Subjectivity is also signified more subtly. I have argued elsewhere (Iwasaki 1993) that some verbal complexes with suffixes such as *shimau* (see also Ono and Suzuki to appear) and *miru*, which are attached to the *-te* form, express speaker's subjective attitude exclusively. The subjective component is followed by the interpersonal component which appears as the final element in an utterance (Haga 1954). At this place words such as *ne, yo, deshoo* (with rising intonation) and *janai* (rising intonation) appear.

I use the term FUNCTIONAL COMPONENT of an utterance (or simply functional component) to refer to the lexical items which represent metafunctions in a particular utterance to distinguish them from the abstract notion of metafunctions of language. The arrangement of functional components in the predicate phrasal unit of a clause proposed by Watanabe and Haga thus can be summarized as follows.

(3) [ID] [SU] [IT]
(ID = ideational component, SU = subjective component,
IT = interactional component)

Since the cohesive function is not considered by the Tokieda school linguists, its position in the predicate structure in the syntagmatic organization is not specified. I will argue, however, that it appears between the subjective and interactional components resulting in the syntagmatic structure show as (4) below.

(4) [ID] [SU] [CO] [IT] (CO = cohesive component)

This organization is supported by the following observations. First, all conjunctives such as *kara* 'so' and *kedo* 'but' attach to the subjective component (e.g. *rashii* 'seem' in (5) below). These words signal that a predicate or clause with which they appear is dependent on another clause. Second, cohesion marking morphemes such as *no* and *wake* appear exactly the same place (Iwasaki 1985, 1990). Observe the next predicate with all four component specified.

(5)
[ID]	[SU]	[CO]	[IT]
ik-ase-ta	*rashii*	*no*	*yo*
go-CAUS-PAST	seem	SE	IP

"It seems that (she) let (her) go."

I have discussed so far the syntagmatic organization of functional components in the predicate portion of a clause. Turning to the organization of postpositional phrases, we will notice that the identical organizational principle can be observed.

(6-2) is the verbal predicate phrasal unit which was just analyzed in (5). (6-1) is a postpositional noun phrasal unit with which we will be concerned here. By comparing (6-1) and (6-2), the syntagmatic organization of functional components becomes clearer across the two types of phrasal units.

(6)
1   *mami-ni   dake wa   ne.*
     (name)-to only TOP   IP
2   *ik-ase-ta   rashii no   yo.*
     go-CAUS-PAST seem   SE   IP
     "It seems that (she) let only Mami go."

A proposition of "X let Y go" is expressed across the two phrases, (6-1) and (6-2). *Mami-ni* in (6-1) is a postpositional phrase indicating the semantic role of the goal and thus functioning as an ideational component. The particle *wa* marks that the preceding phrase is identifiable through whatever means is available for the recipient of this utterance (Iwasaki 1987).[7] The final element *ne* is an interpersonal particle attempting to involve the addressee in the current speech event.

Now I propose the structural analysis of (6-1) is as follows.

(7)   [ID]   [SU]   [CO] [IT]
       mami-ni   dake   wa   ne
       (name)-to only   TOP   IP

I have not discussed the word *dake* in (7) yet. However, I contend that it is a component of the subjective function. *Dake*, along with such words as *demo* 'even', *sae* 'even', *made* 'even', *shika* 'only', *bakari* 'only', *nado*(word of approximation), *kurai* (word of approximation), and *koso* (word of emphasis), belongs to the class of HIGHLIGHTING PARTICLES. Words belonging to this class pick up a referent and compare it with other members of the same category. In the above example, *dake* singles out *Mami* among other people (e.g. friends) who are likely candidates for a recipient of the information. Numata (1989), within the tradition of the Tokieda school, shows with various supporting arguments that these words serve the subjective function involving the speaker's judgment. From this, I conclude that highlighting particles specifically convey subjectivity.

To summarize, Japanese phrasal units, both predicate and postpositional phrasal units, can be analyzed in terms of the four functional components. These four components are lined up in the same way for the both types of phrasal units.

4. The structure of intonation units

It is now possible to analyze intonation units in the data in terms of the four functional components outlined in the previous section. When we are faced with real data, however, it becomes immediately clear that two revisions are necessary. The first revision is to collapse [ID] and [SU]. This decision is based on the fact that the subjective element is very often fused with the ideational component. For example, an action/event for which the speaker has affective assessment can be communicated by the *-te* *shimau* construction. The ideational component is expressed with the verb in the *-te* form and the subjective assessment is expressed by the *shimau* component. However, more often than not, this construction is contracted as *-chau*. Thus, although it is possible to isolate the subjective functional component at an abstract level, it is not always isolatable in actual utterances, while [ID], [CO] and [IT] can be clearly separated.[8]

The second revision is to recognize the fact that there is material in IUs which are completely different in nature. An IU sometimes begins with what is usually known as pause fillers, which does not belong to any of the functional components discussed so far. I call these fillers leads. The function of a lead is to regulate the flow of conversation, signaling that more material will follow and that the speaker has the intention of keeping the floor of conversation. Thus the IU structure is identified with the following configuration.

(8)   Structure of intonation unit in Japanese
[LD] [ID] [CO] [IT] (LD = lead)

In the structure of the intonation unit [ID] and [CO] participate in the content, while the [LD] and [IT] concern the management of conversation. [LD] and [IT] differ from each other, however. The main task of the former is management of linear organization of conversation and does not have any relation to the content expressed in [ID] and [CO]. On the other hand, the task of [IT] is to show sociolinguistic sensitivity towards the addressee and/or to show speaker's understanding for the relationship between addressee's knowledge and the content expressed in the [ID].

We can summarize the structure of intonation units as follows. IUs consist of four major components, each of which attends to different needs of the language user. The lead manages the flow of conversation. The ideational and cohesive components do the propositional and textural referential work, respectively. The interactional component serves the speaker's need to show sensitivity towards the addressee.

We are now ready to analyze the actual data. The following is an example of an IU with all four components specified.

(9)   (from *LONDON*)

[LD]	[	ID	]			[CO]	[IT]
ano	*tabi-nante hitoride shita*			*koto*	*nakatta*	*no*	*ne*
uhm	trip-SOF alone	PRED:PAST NML		exist:NEG:PAST		SE	IT

"uhm I had never took a trip alone."

This intonation unit begins with a pause filler *ano*, which is the lead. After the lead, the ideational component describes "haven't ever taken a trip alone". The nominalizer *no* is a marker of cohesion. Finally the interpersonal particle *ne* solicits the involvement of the addressee in the speech situation. Although (10) contains four functional components within one intonation unit, this is far from a typical intonation unit. The next excerpt from the narrative, The Day After, contains more typical IUs.

(10)   (from *THE DAY AFTER*)

	[	ID		]	[CO]	[IT]
1	*soo-yuu*	*shito-ga*	*shiki-shi*		*-te*	*ne**
	such	person-NOM	lead-do		-TE	IP

	[	ID		]	[IT]
2	*shinin-o*	*asoko-e*	*minna*		*ne**
	corpses-ACC	there-GOAL	all		IP

	[LD]	[	ID	]	[IT]
3	*ano*	*dote-no*	*ue-e*	*sa**	
	uhm	bank-LK	top-to	IP	

	[ID]	[CO]
4	*atsume*	*-te.*
	gather	TE

	[ID]	[IT]
5	*soide*	*ne**
	and	IP

	[	ID	]	[IT]
6	*koo*	*maki-e*		*ne?*
	like this	wood-to		IP

	[LD]	[	ID	]	[CO]
7	*ano*	*maki*	*tsun*		*-de.*
	uhm	wood	pile up		TE

	[ID]	[CO]	[IT]
8	*namamaki-na*	*-n-*	*janai?*
	fresh wood-ATT-	SE	IP

	[ID]	[CO]	[IT]
9	*tsun*	*-de*	*ne:**
	pile up	TE	IP

	[	ID	]	[CO]	[IT]
10	*sekiyu*	*kake*	*-te*	*ne**
	kerosene	pour	TE	IP

```
       [           ID        ] [CO]   [IT]
11 soide  moshiten        -no    yo.
   and    burn:NONPAST-SE        IP
```

1	Those persons take the lead	[ACTION 1]
2-4	and have all the corpses gathered on the river bank	[ACTION 2]
5 -7	and pile up wood	[ACTION 3]
8	I think it was fresh wood	[METACOMMENT]
9	(they) piled (them) up	[REPEAT OF ACTION 3]
10	and poured kerosene (on the corpses)	[ACTION 4]
11	and burned (them)	[ACTION 5]

Five sequenced actions are expressed in eleven intonation units. Notice that each of the intonation units, 1, 8, 9 10 and 11, expresses complete proposition via ideational components. This is a similar pattern found in English. Unlike English, however, all but (11-1) are not full clauses. Furthermore we can notice that these intonation units have cohesive and interactional components as well. Some IUs have the non-finite -te form as the cohesive component and some have the nominalizing word no. The interactive function is exhibited by the interactional particle ne, yo and sa. This means that intonation units in Japanese are concerned not only with the transmission of propositional content but also with transmission of signals of cohesion and interaction.

Table 2 on the next page shows the distribution of the combination of functional components in IU in five different data sets. DA (The Day After) and LO (London) are first person narratives. BT (Bar Talk) and ST (Ski Trip) are face-to-face conversations. DT (Trip to Downtown) is a telephone conversation.

This table indicates that IUs with three and four functional components are not numerous: IUs with three functional components are not common (13.3 % or 158 out of 1190) and IUs with four functional components are extremely rare (only three such cases out of 1190 IUs). The preferred number of functional components is one or two: Especially those IUs with an ideational component (i.e. ID, LD-ID, ID-CO, and ID-IT,) occupy 87.4% (1040 out of 1190) of all IUs analyzed.   Among them, the most popular IU is a type which consists of an ideational component only (34.1% or 406 out of 1190). However, if we combine IUs which consist of an ideational component with a cohesive component (i.e. ID-CO) and an ideational component with the interactional component (i.e. ID-IT), this type becomes the most favored pattern (39.1%, or 465 out of 1190).

The above observation suggests the following. First, the most important task of IUs is to communicate ideational information, though this is rarely done through the form of full clause as we observed (see also Table 1). Second, though an IU might convey solely ideational information, it more often than not conveys additional information at the same time , i.e.

	DA	LO	BT	ST	DT	Total
LD	6	5	22	15	19	67
LD ID	10	5	7	0	7	29
LD CO	0	0	0	0	0	0
LD IT	2	1	13	2	4	22
LD ID CO	7	2	3	0	0	12
LD ID IT	3	0	2	1	0	6
LD ID CO IT	0	2	1	0	0	3 (0.3%)
ID	102	72	109	79	44	406 (34.1%)
ID CO	95	48	64	29	24	260 (21.8%)
ID IT	60	13	95	24	13	205 (17.2%)
ID CO IT	31	29	60	14	6	140 (11.8%)
CO	0	1	1	0	0	2
CO IT	0	0	0	0	0	0
IT	8	0	8	0	0	16
Total IU						1190 (100%)

[Table 2] Types of IUs in terms of their functional components

cohesive or interactional. Third, the speaker can incorporate up to two components in one intonation unit with ease, but not more than that. This might be due to the limitation of work that the speaker can handle within one IU. This is reminiscent of what Chafe (1987) and Pawley and Syder (1976) describe for English speakers' cognitive constraint exhibited in the IUs: English speakers are faced with the cognitive limitation which allows them to activate one concept in one intonation unit (Chafe 1987:32). Japanese speakers, on the other hand, are faced with a constraint which permits them to exercise up to two functions per intonation unit.[9] Since English speakers are not faced with the kind of limitation imposed by the structure of their language and are free from the task of indicating the cohesive marking and interactional marking as the Japanese language does, they can concentrate on producing a complete proposition with the subject and the predicate within one IU. This structural difference between Japanese and English IUs must be responsible for the length of the IU in the respective language.

5. Conclusion

The unity of physical order (intonation unit), grammatical order (clause) and the semantic order (proposition) is strong in English (at least in narratives). If judged according to this prescribed picture, Japanese intonation units appear fragmentary and very chaotic. However, if viewed in terms of the four functional components described in this paper, Japanese intonation units present themselves as having very orderly structures.

The hypothesis posited at the outset of this paper was that frequent uses of partial propositional strategy is a consequence of the multi-faced task which the speaker must carry out in one IU. It was shown that Japanese IUs have a built-in mechanism which allows the speaker to attend to different concerns of communication other than ideation itself. Since the amount of the task which the speaker can handle in one IU is limited he prefers to communicate part of proposition and also prefers to accommodate not more than two functional components.

Notes

* I offered the idea of Japanese Intonation Units presented in this paper first at a colloquium for the Linguistics Department, UC- Santa Barbara, and at the Southern California Japanese Functional Linguistics Meeting. I received many invaluable comments from the audience at both of these meetings. I would like to thank especially Wallace Chafe, Pat Clancy, Hongyin Tao and Sandra Thompson. I also acknowledge Hiroyuki Nagahara for discussion of intonation in Japanese and his assistance in examining pitch track of utterances on computer in the Phonetics Lab of the Linguistics Department at UCLA. All inadequacies remains, of course, mine. Abbreviations used in this paper are as follows. (A) *Morphemes*: ACC (accusative), ATT (attributive form), CAUS (causative), GOAL (goal), IP (interactional particle), LK (linker), LOC (locative), NEG (negative), NOM (nominative), NML (nominalizer), NONPAST (nonpast), PAST (past), PRED (predicate formative), SE (sentence extension), SOF (softening word), TE (-te form), TOP (topic marker) (B) *Intonation contours* : (.) Falling tone; (?) Rising tone; (,)Sustained tone; (*) Rise and Fall

[1] No single feature defines intonation units, but they tend to appear concurrently when one IU finishes and the next one starts. Refer to Du Bois et al (1992) for detailed discussion on identification of IU.

[2] Research on intonation units in English has been mainly on narratives. Its validity for other types of discourse such as more interactional conversation is needed for a complete statement of IUs.

[3] Two narratives (*The Day After* and *London*) and a telephone conversation (*Trip to Downtown*) were collected and transcribed by me. The two face-to-face conversations (*Bar Talk* and *Ski Trip*) were collected and transcribed by Ryoko Suzuki (UCSB) as part of the project sponsored by the University of California, Pacific Rim Studies Grant (Charles Li, Sandra Thompson and Pat Clancy as chief investigators.) I greatly appreciate their generosity for making the valuable audio-recorded data and most accurate transcription available to me.

[4]   For this study I excluded IUs which are made of non-content expressions such as backchannel expressions.

[5]   It is extremely rare for the object of a transitive verb to be overtly coded. Thus only the overt subjects are taken to be the criterion for the full clausehood.

[6]   This tradition started when Yamada (1908) recognized two types of sentences, one of which is made up of the subject and predicate and the other of which is an unanalyzable expression of the speaker's internal sensations and emotions.

[7]   Halliday and Hasan (1967:18) do not consider exophoric (situational) reference as cohesive phenomena. However, since both endophoric (textual) and exophoric (situational) involve exactly the same process of referencing (Halliday and Hasan 1976:31ff), I treat both as the same phenomenon in this paper.

[8]   Another problem is the internal structure of [ID]. There are some words in the [ID] component which have inherent cohesive function. Demonstrative words such as *kore* 'this one' or *sono* 'that' are such examples, but I did not analyze such words as [CO]. For a word to be coded as [CO], it must appear after [ID] (and [SU]) and/or before [IT]. In other words, [CO] is a language specific functional component. In a more generalized framework, [ID] and [CO] must also be collapsed.

[9]   I am distinguishing the purely cognitive limitation, with which Chafe (1987) and Pawley and Syder (1976) are concerned, and the limitation of the overall task of the speaker including the indication of sociolinguistic concern as well as   purely cognitive work of communicating the ideational information.

References

Chafe, Wallace (ed). 1980. The pear stories: Cognitive, cultural, and linguistic aspects of narrative production. Advances in discourse processes. Volume III. Norwood: Ablex Publishing Company.

Chafe, Wallace. 1987. Cognitive constraints on information flow. In R. Tomlin (ed.) Coherence and Grounding in Discourse, Typological Studies in Language, #11. Amsterdam & Philadelphia: John Benjamins.

Clancy, Patricia. 1982. Written and spoken style in Japanese narratives. In Tannen, Deborah (ed.) Spoken and written language: Exploring orality and literacy. Norwood: Ablex, pages 55-76.

Du Bois, John W, Stephan Schuetze-Coburn, Danae Paolino, and Susanna Cumming. 1992. Outline of discourse transcription. Discourse and Grammar (Santa Barbara Papers in Linguistics, vol. 2) ed. by Sandra A. Thompson, Santa Barbara: University of California, Department of Linguistics, 1988; and in Talking data: Transcription and coding methods for language research. ed. by Edwards, Jane A. and Martin D. Lampert. Hillsdale, NJ: Lawrence Erlbaum.

Haga, Yasushi. 1954. "Chinjutsu" to wa nanimono? (What is *chinjutsu*?). Kokugo-kokubun 23-4:241-255.

Halliday, M.A.K. 1973. Explorations in the functions of language. London: Edward Arnold.

Halliday, M.A.K. 1989. Language, context, and text: aspects of language in a social-semiotic perspective. London: Oxford University Press.

Halliday, M. A. K. and Ruqaya Hasan. 1976. Cohesion in English. London: Longmans.

Iwasaki, Shoichi. 1985. Cohesion, challengeability, and -n desu clauses in spoken discourse. Journal of Asian Culture (UCLA) 9:125-142.

Iwasaki, Shoichi. 1987. Identifiability, scope-setting, and the particle wa: A study of Japanese spoken expository discourse. Perspectives on topicalization: The case of Japanese wa, edited by John Hinds, Senko K. Maynard, and Shoichi Iwasaki. Amsterdam & Philadelphia: John Benjamins, pages 107-142.

Iwasaki, Shoichi. 1990. Nominalized clauses and cohesion in conversation. Paper delivered at the 1990 AAS Annual Meeting.

Iwasaki, Shoichi. 1993. Subjectivity in grammar and discourse: theoretical considerations and a case study of Japanese spoken discourse. Amsterdam & Philadelphia: John Benjamins.

Iwasaki, Shoichi. (to appear). Functional transfer in the history of Japanese language. Japanese/Korean Linguistics. (The Center for the Study of Language and Information) ed. by Clancy, Patricia.. University of Chicago Press.

Lyons, John. 1977 Semantics: 1. Cambridge: Cambridge University Press.

Maynard Senko K. 1989 Japanese conversation. Norwood: Ablex Publishing Company.

Numata, Yoshiko. 1989. Toritate-shi to muudo [Highlighting particles and mood]. Nihongo no modaritii [Modality in Japanese] ed. by Nitta, Yoshio and Takashi Masuoka. Tokyo: Kuroshio Shuppan, pages 159-192.

Ono, Tsuyoshi and Suzuki Ryoko. (to appear). The development of a marker of speaker's attitude: The pragmatic use of the Japanese grammaticized verb shimau in conversation. BLS 18.

Pawley, Andrew and Frances Syder. 1976 The one clause at a time hypothesis. Paper read at 1st congress of N.Z. Linguistics Society. Auckland.

Schuetze-Coburn, Stephan, Marian Shapley, and Elizabeth Weber. 1991. Units of intonation in discourse: Acoustic and auditory analyses in contrast. Language and Speech. 34(3): 207-234.

Tokieda, Motoki. 1941. Kokugo-gaku genron. [Basic theory of Japanese language study.] Tokyo: Iwanami.

Tokieda, Motoki. 1950. Nihon bunpoo. [Japanese grammar.] Tokyo: Iwanami.

Watanabe, Minoru. 1953. Jojutsu to chinjutsu - jutsugo-bunsetsu no koozoo [Describing and stating - the structure of predicate phrase]. Kokugogaku 13/14.

Yamada, Yoshio. 1908. Nihon bunpooron. [Theory of Japanese Grammar]. Tokyo: Hoobunkan.

Relative Clauses and Discourse Strategies

YOKO COLLIER-SANUKI

University of California at Los Angeles

0. Introduction

Analyzing the syntactic and distributional characteristics of relative clauses used in American-English conversation, Fox and Thompson 1990 claimed that the choice of relative clause constructions that English speakers use is not random but is governed by INFORMATION FLOW (Chafe 1976, 1987, Du Bois 1987, Givón 1979, 1983, 1984, and Prince 1981). On the other hand, no quantitative analyses of Japanese relative clauses have yet been done. Most studies of Japanese relative clauses, including Kuno 1973, Okutsu 1974, and Inoue 1976, have been based on the structural rules that govern English relative clauses and usually emphasize the structural differences between Japanese and English at the surface or sentence level. Furthermore, such an approach often neglects the basic but important differences between the two languages, such as word order and discourse strategies, which affect information flow, and, as Fox and Thompson have shown, in turn play an important role in determining the grammar of a language.

This paper quantitatively analyzes Japanese and English relative clauses used in written discourse to show how their differing word orders and discourse strategies affect the use of relative clauses. In so doing, I will propose, adapting Fox and Thompson's GROUNDING-mechanisms hypothesis, that the differing word orders between Japanese and English interacts with cognitive processes to determine the grammar of these languages. In addition, this paper will show that a characteristic discourse strategy of Japanese, its dependency on FRAMES which provide crucial background information, affects the use of particular types of relative clauses. Specifically, Japanese relative clauses provide frames for comprehending their head NPs. This approach provides a cognitive account for Matsumoto 1988, which claims that the understanding of Japanese relative clauses involves semantic frames evoked by linguistic clues given in noun modifier constructions. According to Hwang 1990, similar phenomena are also observed in Korean, the grammatical structure of which is similar to Japanese. On the other hand, reflecting the reversed order of head nouns and relative clauses between Japanese and English, I will point out that English relative clauses, which follow their head NPs, often provide additional information.

The remainder of this paper will be organized as follows: Section 1 will describe the type of data used in this study. Next, section 2 will present some of the results which illustrate differing usages of relative clauses between Japanese and English written discourse. Then, in section 3, we will examine some of the concepts that are important in considering information flow and discuss how and what factors affect information flow to create the differences that were presented in section 2. Lastly, section 4 will summarize the findings of this study.

1. Data

In order to assure equivalence of the amount of data being compared between the two languages, we will examine three pairs of translations into Japanese and English of novels that were originally written in languages other than these two.[1] In addition, we will compare the results with those from Fox and Thompson 1990, which analyzed 414 relative clauses found in English conversational data to consider possible differences between conversational and written discourse.

---

[1]The word count is a common unit to account for the equivalence of data quantity. However, it is not an adequate measure in Japanese, which is an agglutinative language where divisions of words are not clear. In order to help generalize the results of the analysis, novels that are examined are chosen from among those written in different original languages such as German, French and Chinese.

2. Characteristics of Japanese and English relative clauses

2.1. Frequency of use of relative clauses

Figure 1 below compares the frequency of use of relative clauses in three pairs of written text samples in English and Japanese.

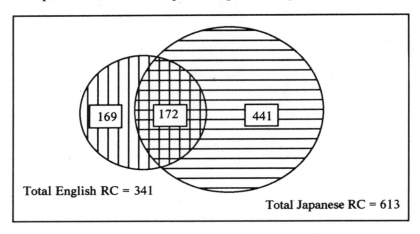

Figure 1: Number of relative clauses used in Love, Demian, and Madman.

The figure above shows that relative clauses were used twice as often in Japanese as in English. Further, the use of relative clauses in the two languages does not overlap very frequently: only about one half of the total number of English relative clauses and one fourth of the total in Japanese correspond to each other. A similar tendency was also found in an analysis by Shimura 1990. These results indicate that the use and functions of relative clauses may differ between the two languages.

2.2. Distribution of (non)humanness of relative clauses

The tables below summarize the distributions of types of head nouns. The data in table 1a are adopted from Fox and Thompson 1990. Tables 1b and 1c are the results from the English and Japanese written data examined in this study.

Head type	Frequency	
Human head	113	(30%)
Non-human head	269	(70%)
TOTAL	382	(100%)

Table 1a: Distribution of (non)humanness of head NPs in English conversations.

(= Fox and Thompson 1990)

Head type	Frequency	
Human head	82	(24%)
Non-human head	259	(76%)
TOTAL	341	(100%)

Table 1b: Distribution of (non)humanness of head NPs in English written narratives.

Head type	Frequency	
Human head	144	(23%)
Non-human head	469	(77%)
TOTAL	613	(100%)

Table 1c: Distribution of (non)humanness of head NPs in Japanese written narratives.

As seen in the tables, about 30% of the total number of relative clauses had human heads while 70 % had non-human heads. Interestingly, tables 1b and 1c exhibit slightly greater percentages of non-human heads than in table 1a. This is perhaps due to the lack of visual aids and the need to mention more about non-human objects in written stories where such items are not visible and must be described verbally. In addition, In addition, the number of human referents are limited in novels, contributing to the lesser ratios of human heads seen in the data.

2.3. Distribution of grammatical roles of head NPs

The distributions of the grammatical roles of Head NPs in main clauses show both a similarity and a difference between Japanese and English, as found in the following tables:[2]

HeadNP	Frequency	
Subject	68	(18%)
Object	125	(33%)
Predicate	75	(20%)
Existential	25	(7%)
Others	89	(23%)
TOTAL	382	(100%)

Table 2a: HeadNP types of human and Non-human referents in conversational English.
(= Summary of data in Fox and Thompson 1990)

HeadNP	Frequency	
Subject	53	(16%)
Object	83	(24%)
Predicate	25	(7%)
Existential	9	(3%)
Others	171	(50%)
TOTAL	341	(100%)

Table 2b: HeadNP types of human and Non-human referents in written English.

HeadNP	Frequency	
Subject	135	(22%)
Object	138	(23%)
Predicate	71	(12%)
Existential	30	(5%)
Others	239	(38%)
TOTAL	613	(100%)

Table 2c: HeadNP types of human and Non-human referents in written Japanese.

---

[2]Following Fox and Thompson 1990, the term Head NP refers to the Head Noun plus any determiners, but not including the relative clause. See section 3.1.

Note that Subject Heads and Object Heads together make up more than 40% of the total number of relative clauses in all three tables. Interestingly, however, the ratio of Subject Heads to Object Heads is quite different between English and Japanese: Object-Head relative clauses, a total of both direct and indirect objects, outnumber Subject-Head relative clauses by a factor of 3:2 in English while in Japanese the ratio is about 1:1. This means that subject head relative clauses are much more frequently used in Japanese than in English. Why does such a striking difference exist between the two? I hypothesize that this is due to the differences in word order between the two languages which affect the ways in which referents are introduced into discourse. We will compare below the structures of English and Japanese relative clauses and discuss how they interact with information flow.

3. Factors that affect information flow

3.1. Types of relative clauses

We will first examine the structure of relative clauses using English examples from Fox and Thompson 1990:

(1) **(a) Subject head - Object relative:**

probably **the only thing** [you'll see] is like the table

X is like the table.   (X/head noun is the subject.)
You'll see X.   (X/co-referent is the object.)

(b) Subject head - Subject relative:

the store [that sells it] is not responsible

X is not responsible.   (X/head is the subject.)
X sells it.   (X/co-referent is the subject.)

Notice that the head NPs in both (a) and (b) are in the subject position of a main clause and thus are subject heads. The difference between the two examples is that the co-referent of the head noun in each relative clause plays a different grammatical role: the co-referent is the object in (a) while it is the subject in (b). Therefore we will identify examples (a) and (b) as Subject head - Object relative and Subject head - Subject relative, respectively.

3.2.   Grounding

Before proceeding with the analysis of the structures of relative clauses, we will review one more concept: GROUNDING. As Fox and Thompson point out, for effective communication referents must be presented so as to be RELEVANT to listeners at the point where they are introduced. Grounding functions to achieve this goal. In other words, 'to ground a noun phrase is to locate its referent in conversational space by relating it to a referent whose relevance is clear, that is, to a Given referent in the immediate context' (Fox and Thompson 1990). Keeping this need for grounding in mind, let us now look at the structures of subject head and object head relative clauses in English as presented in items 2a and b:

(2) **Structure of English relative clauses.**

    (a)   Subject Head: SubNP[RC] V O.

    (b)   Object Head: S V ObjNP[RC].

Notice that a head NP in a Subject Head relative clause in English is located at the sentence initial position while that of an Object Head relative is located at the sentence final position. As we discussed, unless the head NPs in items 2a and 2b are already made clear from prior mentioning or situation, they must be made relevant in conversation by being grounded by the rest of their respective sentence elements. As schematized in 2b, in the case of Object Heads, the subject and verb of a main clause precede the head NP. Therefore, its head noun may be grounded by the main clause elements that precede it when it is heard in a conversation. On the other hand, as 2a shows, the head NP of a Subject Head relative must be grounded by its relative clause as it does not have any elements that precede it. In other words, Subject Head relative clauses are not as effective as Object Head relative clauses in English. This hypothesis predicts that Subject Head relative clauses are less likely to occur in English than Object Head relative clauses. We have already seen this tendency in tables 2a and b. Then, what about the case of Japanese? Let us next examine the cases of Japanese as illustrated in items 3a and b:

(3) **Structure of Japanese relative clauses.**

Subject Head: [RC]SubNP O V.

Object Head: (S) [RC]ObjNP   V.

Notice that in the case of Japanese, unlike in English, there are few differences between Subject and Object Head relative clauses when they are introducing head nouns. In Japanese, main-clause verbs are located at the sentence-final position and main-clause subjects are often omitted, as indicated by the parentheses. In other words, the main-clause elements do not help ground the head NP in either Subject Head or Object Head relative clauses, and Japanese Object-Head relative clauses do not have the benefit of main-clause grounding, which is available in English. This leads us to expect that there will be no particular preference for Object-Head relative clauses in Japanese. As we have already seen, this expectation is born out in table 2c. Thus we have accounted for the preference for Object Head relative clauses in English and the lack of such preference in Japanese.

Additionally, the need for a Subject Head relative clause to ground its own head also predicts a more frequent occurrence of heavily-modified and lengthy subject head relative clauses in Japanese than in English. Item 4J is such an example:

(4J) [Muttsu   no toki, otona no hito tachi ni, ekaki de   mi
     six (years) GEN when adult GEN people PL by   painter by   body

     o   tateru koto o   omoikirasareta   okagede, uwabami
     ACC establish NOMZ ACC give-up-PASS-PST   due-to   constrictor

     no   uchigawa to sotogawa no   e   o   kaku yori hoka
     GEN   inside   and outside GEN picture ACC draw than other

     wa, marukiri   e   o   kaku koto o shinakatta]   boku
     TOP not-at-all picture ACC draw NOMZ ACC do-not-PAST   I

     nandesukara.
     be-because

(Because it is **I**, [who had never drawn anything other than pictures of boas from the inside and boas from the outside due to the fact that I was made by the grown-ups to give up on pursuing my painter's career when I was six years old.][3]

While native speakers of English who are learning Japanese often become bewildered by the lengthy subjects found in Japanese, such lengthy subjects do not trouble native speakers. This is because, as we discussed above, an introduction of referents in Subject-Head relative clauses is cognitively as effective as in Object-Head relative clauses. Relative clauses like Item 4J actually occur quite frequently in Japanese.

---

[3] *Hoshi no ôjisama.*

3.3. Distribution of grammatical roles of coreferents of relative clauses

So far, we have looked at the types and grammatical roles of head NPs. Next let us examine the grammatical roles of coreferents. Tables 3a, b and c show the distributions of the grammatical roles of co-referents for each Head NP type. In these tables the category, subject relative, is further divided into its two subcategories, a-relatives and s-relatives: a-relative means that the co-referent of a head noun is the subject of a transitive verb, and s-relative means that it is the subject of an intransitive verb. For example, the subject relative in Item 1b, the store that sells it, is an example of an a-relative as a verb, to sell is a transitive verb. Now let us go on to discuss tables 3a, b and c. Table 3a is adopted from Fox and Thompson 1990:

HeadNP/NPRel	a Rel	s Rel	OBJ Rel	Others	Total
Subj Head	10(15%)	18(26%)	34(50%)	6(9%)	68 (100%)
Obj Head	21(17%)	49(39%)	48(38%)	7(6%)	125 (100%)
Pred Head	15(20%)	13(17%)	37(49%)	10(13%)	75 (100%)
Ex Head	7(28%)	13(52%)	4(16%)	1(4%)	25 (100%)
Others	8(9%)	31(35%)	41(46%)	9(10%)	89 (100%)
TOTAL	61(16%)	124(32%)	164(43%)	33(9%)	382(100%)
		<75%>			

Table 3a: Distribution of grammatical roles for human and Non-human Head NPs in oral English.
(= Summary of data in Fox and Thompson 1990)

The bottom row shows the total for each grammatical role of co-referent NPs and indicates that 32% were s-relatives and 43% were object relatives, for a total of 75% of all relative clauses. This result is in accordance with Keenan 1975. My analysis of written data also showed the same tendency both in English and Japanese. Now compare table 3a with 3b and c:

HeadNP/NPRel	a Rel	s Rel	OBJ Rel	Others	Total
Subj Head	6(11%)	20(38%)	23(43%)	4(8%)	53 (100%)
Obj Head	14(17%)	20(24%)	34(41%)	15(18%)	83 (100%)
Pred Head	2(8%)	4(16%)	12(48%)	7(28%)	25 (100%)
Ex Head	4(44%)	2(22%)	3(34%)	0(0%)	9 (100%)
Others	18(11%)	61(35%)	52(30%)	40(24%)	171 (100%)
TOTAL	44(13%)	**107(32%)**	**124(36%)**	66(19%)	341(100%)
		<68%>			

Table 3b: Distribution of grammatical roles for human and Non-human Head NPs in English translations.

HeadNP/NPRel	a Rel	s Rel	OBJ Rel	Others	Total
Subj Head	21(15%)	77(57%)	24(18%)	13(10%)	135 (100%)
Obj Head	4(3%)	96(70%)	27(19%)	11(8%)	138 (100%)
Pred Head	6(8%)	48(68%)	13(18%)	4(6%)	71 (100%)
Ex Head	4(13%)	15(50%)	4(13%)	7(24%)	30 (100%)
Others	16(7%)	155(65%)	34(14%)	34(14%)	239 (100%)
TOTAL	51(8%)	391**(64%)**	102**(17%)**	69(11%)	613(100%)
		<81%>			

Table 3c: Distribution of grammatical roles for human and Non-human Head NPs in Japanese translations.

The bottom row of table 3b, the results from the English translations, show that s-relatives and O-relatives make up 32% and 36% of the total, respectively. Their sum makes up 68% of all relative clauses. Similarly, in table 3c, results from the Japanese translations, the total of s-relatives and object-relatives makes up 81%. In sum, we find prominence of s-relatives and O-relatives in both English and Japanese. Interestingly, however, there is also an intriguing difference: while both table 5a and b from the English data indicate a slightly higher percentage of Object-relatives than s-relatives, s-relatives are far more common in Japanese, as seen in table 3c. In fact, s-relatives by themselves make up well over 60% of the total relative clauses used in Japanese. Recall that, as we discussed earlier using the examples in item 3, main clause subjects and verbs often do not help provide grounding in Japanese, and so relative clauses must ground their head nouns. While such grounding power is usually provided by object relatives in English, the low rate of object relatives in table 3c indicates that s-relatives must take up this function in Japanese. Therefore, based on these observations, I infer that s-relatives of Japanese relative clauses, as well as object relatives, have the power to help ground their head nouns. As an example of how s-relatives provide grounding power, let us reexamine example 4J, which is repeated below:

(4J)   [Muttsu no toki, otona no hito tachi ni, ekaki de mi o tateru koto o omoikirasareta okagede, uwabami no uchigawa to sotogawa no e o kaku yori hoka wa, marukiri e o kaku koto o shinakatta] **boku** nandesukara.

(Because it is I, [who had never drawn anything other than pictures of boas from the inside and boas from the outside due to the fact that I was made by the grown-ups to give up on pursuing my painter's career when I was six years old.)

Sentence 4J is an example where grounding is done by referring to the information mentioned in previous discourse. This type of grounding is called PROPOSITION LINKING by Fox and Thompson. Sentence 4J was uttered as an explanation as to why the narrator could not draw a picture well. The answer, that the narrator was made to give up a painter's career at age six, is expressed in the content of the relative clause. Actually, this information was previously discussed in the discourse. In fact, when I was six are the exact words used at the beginning of the story, and Chapter 1 is dedicated to explaining how the narrator came to be discouraged about drawing pictures. Therefore, as soon as the readers read the words, when I was six, they are able to set up a frame that relates to the head noun phrase, I. This type of usage along with others shows that Japanese relative clauses provide crucial background information, or frames for comprehending their head NPs. This hypothesis provides a cognitive account for Matsumoto 1988, who claims that the understanding of Japanese relative clauses involves semantic FRAMES evoked by linguistic clues given in noun modifier constructions. Hwang 1990 also raised similar examples of relative clauses in Korean, which she called BACK REFERENCING, as a measure to provide cohesion in discourse.

I speculate that this type of usage is possible in Japanese and Korean as relative clauses precede their head NPs in these languages, and thus are able to help create frames for up-coming discourse. On the other hand, in languages like English, where relative clauses follow their head NPs, such a task is often accomplished by a separate sentence or adverbial clause. In example 4E, which is the English translation of the same portion that was translated in 4J, two sentences are conjoined:

(4E) The grown-ups discouraged me in my painter's career when I was six years old, and I never learned to draw anything except boas from the outside and boas from the inside.[4]

Contrastingly, since relative clauses follow their head nouns in English, they can provide information on events that occur later than that described in the main clause. Observe the next example, 5E:

(5E) Dan Rather interviewed **a fifteen-year-old high school student** [who proclaimed that the Pacific War started because "Japan was isolated with no natural resources. Japan *had* to attack to get these resources."][5]

On the other hand, retention of the relative clause when translating this sentence into Japanese will result in a change of meaning, as seen in Example 5J:

(5J) Dan Rather wa [" ... " to itta] **jyûgo sai no kôkôsei** o interview shita

(Dan Rather interviewed **a fifteen-year-old high school student** [who had proclaimed that " ... ")

While the English original indicates that the quote was uttered during the interview, the Japanese translation means that the high school student had said it at some other occasion, rather than in her interview with Dan Rather. In order to avoid such alteration in meaning, the use of the relative clause must be eliminated in the Japanese translation. This example is just one indication of how differences in word order can affect the grammaticality and meaning of relative clauses. In fact, in my analysis of the three pairs of translations, the use of separate sentences or clauses was the most common strategy used when the use of relative clauses did not coincide in the two languages. In other words, 46.7% of the 169 English relative clauses which did not have relative clause counterparts in Japanese corresponded to separate sentences or clauses in Japanese.

4. Conclusion

This paper has shown that the use and functions of relative clauses differ significantly between Japanese and English. In considering

---

[4] *The Little Prince.*

[5] Daniel A. Métraux. 1991. Does Japan still shun war guilt? Annals of SEAAS. 13.50.

explanations for such differences I hypothesized, adapting Fox and Thompson 1990, that the differences in word order interact with information flow to determine the grammar of a language. Particularly, I suggested that Japanese relative clauses provide crucial background information, or frames, for comprehending their head NPs, to support Matsumoto 1988's analysis of noun modifier constructions in Japanese.

References

Chafe, Wallace L. 1976. Givenness, contrastiveness, definiteness, subjects, topic, and point of view. Subject and Topic, ed. by Charles Li, 27-55. New York: Academic Press.

_____. 1987. Cognitive constraints on information flow. Coherence and Grounding in Discourse, ed. by Russell Tomlin, 21-51. Amsterdam: John Benjamins Publishing Company.

Du Bois, John W. 1987. The discourse basis of ergativity. Language 55.59-133.

Fox, Barbara A., and Sandra Thompson. 1990. A discourse explanation of the grammar of relative clauses in English conversation. Language 66.297-316.

Givón, Talmy. 1979. On Understanding Grammar. New York: Academic Press.

_____(ed.). 1983. Topic continuity in discourse. Amsterdam: Benjamins.

_____. 1984. Syntax, Vol. I. Amsterdam: Benjamins.

Hwang, Shin Ja Joo. 1990. The relative clause in narrative discourse. Language Research (Seoul: Korea) 22.45-72.

Inoue Kazuko. 1976. Henkeibunpô to nihongo (Jô) (Transformational Grammar and Japanese 1). Tokyo: Taishûkan.

Keenan, Edward L. 1975. Variation in universal grammar. Analyzing Variation in Language, ed. by Roger W. Shuy and Ralph W. Fasold, 136-148. Washington, D.C.: Georgetown University Press.

Kuno, Susumu. 1973. The Structure of the Japanese Language. Cambridge, Massachusetts: The MIT Press.

Matsumoto, Yoshiko. 1988. Grammar and Semantics of Adnominal Clauses in Japanese. Ph.D. dissertation. University of California, Berkeley.

Okutsu Keiichiro. 1974. Seisei nihongo bunpô ron: Meishi-ku no kôzô (On Generative Japanese Grammar: The structure of noun phrases). Tokyo: Taishûkan.

Prince, Ellen F. 1981. Toward a taxonomy of given/new information. Radical Pragmatics, ed. by P. Cole, 223-255. New York: Academic Press.

Shimura, Akihiko. 1990. Why do the Japanese learners produce fewer relative clauses in English? University of Hawai'i at Manoa. Photocopy.

Some Observations in Humble Expressions in Japanese: Distribution of *o-* V(stem) *suru* and 'V(causative) *itadaku*

JUNKO MORI
University of Wisconsin at Madison

1. Introduction

Honorifics is one of the characteristics of Japanese language, and has been studied by many linguists. There are three planes of honorific markers for predicates: *sonkei-go* (subject honorific), *kenjoo-go* (non-subject honorific), and *teinei-go* (hearer honorific). A speaker has to choose the appropriate form from the three, depending on who is the referent of the subject and to whom he/she has to show respect.

(1). *Yamada-sensei   ga   tegami o   <u>o-kaki-ni naru.</u>*
Yamada-teacher NOM letter ACC write(subject-honorific)
' Teacher Yamada writes letters.'

(2). *Watakushi   ga   Yamada-sensei   ni tegami o*
 I   NOM Yamada-teacher to letter ACC
<u>*o-kaki suru.*</u>
 wite(non-subject honorific)
  ' I write letters to Teacher Yamada.'

(3). *Watakushi ga   tegami o   <u>kaki-masu.</u>*
 I   NOM letter ACC write(hearer-honorific)
 ' I write letters.'   (Kuno, 1987: 99)

According to Kuno(1987:100), 'Subject honorific elevates the referent of the subject in the speaker's deference, while nonsubject honorific elevates the referent of a non-subject element and downgrades that of the subject.' On the other hand, hearer honorific does not express the speaker's deference to the exalted person, but 'the speaker's politeness to, or distance from, the hearer(p. 125).' The purspose of the present study is to discuss the syntactic and pragmatic constraints in the use of the regular construction of this non-subject honorific, _o-V(stem) suru_, by comparing it with another humble expression _V(causative) itadaku_.[1]

2. Benefactivity of nonsubject honorific

Among the three different honorific markers, in fact, nonsubject honorific is the most complicated one in its use, in terms of the kind of verbs that it can undergo, the syntactic position of the exalted person, and the pragmatic, contextual constraints. While the regular subject honorific construction _o-V(stem) ni naru_ can be applied to either action or stative verbs, nonsubject honorific construction _o-V(stem) suru_ is possible 'only when the predicate denotes a voluntary action(Harada, 1976: 527). So, for instance a verb like _wakaru_ (to understand) can be _o-wakari ni naru_ with the subject honorific, but cannot be _o-wakari suru_ with the nonsubject honorific. Further, while subject honorifics always mark the subject as the exalted person, 'the exalted person in non-subject honorifics can be NPs of various functions except of the subject(Kuno, 1983:25, translated by J.M.).'

(4). *Sensei   o   o-mimai shita.*   (theme)
    teacher ACC inquired
    'I inquired of my teacher.'

(5). *Sensei   ni o-hanashi shita.*   (goal)
    teacher to talked
    'I talked to my teacher.'

---

[1] Although nonsubject honorifics can be used to elevate a third person who is not in the context, the primarily focus of this study is the situations where the exalted person is the same person as the addressee.

(6). *Sensei   kara o-kiki shita.*   (source)
teacher from heard
'I heard it from my teacher.'

(7). *Sensei no   otaku no   mae o o-toori shita.* (possessor)
teacher GEN house GEN front ACC passed
'I passed my teacher's house.'

(8). *Kopii-dai wa   watashi ga   kaikei ni chokusetsu o-harai*
copy-bill TOP   I   NOM cashier to directly   pay
shimasu.   (beneficiary)
'As for the bill for the copies, I will pay at the cashier (for
you.)'   (Kuno, 1983:25)

As we see in (8), even if the exalted person is not explicit in the
surface form, it has to be an element of the verb (Kuno, 1983).
According to Harada(1976: 527), these features of nonsubject
honorifics 'inherently relate to the fact that nonsuppletive object
honorifics ('regular nonsubject honorifics' in this article[2]) often
have a benefactive interpretation.'
This pragmatic notion of 'benefactivity' has been widely
accepted as a feature of this construction, <u>o-Vstem *suru*</u>. This
notion is especially efficient in explaining cases like (8) where
there is no specific exalted referent in the sentence. Because of
the frequency of its use and because of the fewer exceptions in
the situation, this construction is usually introduced to the
language leaners, along with the speech act of 'offering sevices to
someone superior to the speaker.' In other words, as long as the
utterance is made in order to offer service, the use of nonsubject
honorifics is grammatical as in (9).

(9). *O-cha o   o-ire shimashoo.*
tea   ACC make
'I will make some tea (for you).'

However, this pragmatic constraint of 'benefactivity,' is
questioned in the light of the following examples where the

---

[2] There are several different translations of *kenjoo-go* , such as 'object
honorifics(Harada, 1976)', 'non-actor type honorifics(Wenger, 1983)',
'nonsubject honorifics(Kuno,1987)'.

speaker is asking the hearer for his/her permission:

(10). a. *Denwa   o   tsukatte mo   ii   desu ka.*
       telephone ACC use   even good
    b. **O-denwa o o-tsukai shite mo yoroshii deshoo ka.*
       'May I use the phone?'

(11). a. *Denwa   o   karite mo   ii   desu ka.*
       telephone ACC borrow even good
    b. *O-denwa o o-kari shite mo yoroshii deshoo ka.*
       'May I borrow(=use) the phone?

Both (10) and (11) describe the same event. Although (10a) and (10b) without honorific are grammatical, the application of non-subject honorific grammatically fails in (10b) but is fine in (11b). The ungrammaticality of (10b) can be explained by the fact of the action is not benefactive to the exalted person. However, the notion of 'benefactivity' cannot account for the grammaticality of (11b), since the beneficiary is not the exalted person but the speaker. Moreover, when the construction is used for the report of a past event, there are some cases where the action can hardly be interpreted as benefactive.

(12). *Sensei   no   otaku   no   mae   o   o-toori-shita.*   (=7)
      teacher GEN house GEN front ACC passed
      'I passed the teacher's house.'

(13). *Chuusha-joo de sensei   no o-kuruma o   o-mikake-shita.*[3]
      parking-lot at teacher GEN car   ACC   saw

---

[3] For some native speaker of Japanese, these sentences seem not to be acceptable. But the utterances like the followings may sound better.

Yuube osoku made o-shigoto shite rasshatta n desu nee, sensei. Ichiji goro otaku no mae o o-toori shitara, mada denki ga tsuite itande bikkuri shita n desu yo.
'You seem to have worked till late last night. When I passed your   house around one a.m., the light was still on so that I was surprised.'

Kochira ni irassharu to omotte ta n desu yo. Chuusha joo de o-kuruma o-mikake shita mono desu kara.
'I tought you were here, because I saw your car at the parking lot.'

'I saw the teacher's car at the parking lot.'

These examples suggest that the pragmatic constraints on this construction o-Vstem *suru* need to be reexamined or specified in more detail. In this study, I will attempt the specification of the pragmatic constraints through the comparison between this construction o-V(stem) *suru* with the other possible substitute, V(causative) *itadaku.* That is, given the situations where the speaker has to show respect to the addressee, if o-Vstem *suru* is not available, he/she can use V(causative) *itadaku.*

(14). a. *O-denwa o o-tsukai shite mo yoroshii deshoo ka.* (=10b)
     b. *O-denwa   o   tsukawasete   itadake masen ka.*
       telephone ACC use(causative) receive
       'May I use the phone?'

The structure of V(causative) *itadaku* construction is shown in (15).

(15). a. *Watashi ga shimasu.*   'I will do (it.)'
     b. *Watashi ga X ni [X ga watashi ni [watashi ga su-]-asete]*
       itadakimasu.
     c. *Watashi ga X ni sasete itadakimasu*
     ' I will receive the (exalted) favor of X's letting me do (it).'

(A) is the sentence which is embedded in the causative sentence, that is embedded again in the matrix sentence of receiving as shown in (b). And (c) is the final sentence of Vcausative *itadaku* construction. Ohta(1987) claims that **'permission'** and **'favor-receipt'** are two important semantic features of this construction because of the fact that causative construction and the receiving verb are involved in this construction.

    There have been studies for each construction by Harada, Wenger, Hamano, Ohta, and so on, but none of them have dealt with the comparison between the two constructions, in spite of the fact that both of them may be used for the same purpose of being humble. In the following sections, I will introduce the distribution of these two constructions and discuss the regularities in their use.

3. Request for permission
    In this section, I will discuss the cases where the speaker asks the exalted person for the permission, as in (10b) and (11b) introduced here again as (16) and (17).

(16).*O-denwa   o   o-tsukai shite mo yoroshii deshoo ka?   (=10b)
　　　telephone ACC use　　　even good
　　　'Is it all right if I use the phone?'

(17). O-denwa   o   o-kari shite mo yoroshii deshoo ka. (=11b)
　　　telephone ACC borrow　　even good
　　　'Is it all right if I borrow(=use) the phone?'

Argument versus non-argument status of the exalted person
　　　The only difference between (16) and (17) is the verbs,
kariru which is transactional and *tsukau* which is non-transactional. In other words, while *kariru* is a three place predicate which takes **agent, theme,** and **source** as its argument, *tsukau* is a two place predicate which takes only **agent** and **theme.** Thus, the ellipted parts of the sentences can be recovered as:

(16)'.*Watashi ga o-denwa o o-tsukai shitemo yoroshii desu ka.
(17)'. Watashi ga sensei kara o-denwa o o-kari shitemo yoroshii
　　　desu ka.

The difference between (16) and (17) suggests that the applicability of o-V(stem) suru is dependent on whether the exalted person is an argument of the verb or not.[4] Here are more cases for '+argument' to support this claim.

(18). Kono hon, ashita   o-kaeshi shite mo yoroshii deshoo ka.
　　　this book tomorrow return　・even good
　　　'Is it all right if I return this book to **you** tomorrow?'

(19). Ima chotto konde irunde, hachi-ji goro o-todoke shite mo
　　　now little crowded　　eight-o'clock deliver　　　even
　　　yoroshii deshoo ka.
　　　good
　　　'As we are busy now, is it all right if we deliver it to **you**
　　　around eight?'

---

[4] Hamano(1988) reports various status of the exalted person in the construction of nonsubject honorifics, which can be characterized as arguments.

(20). *Konban o-denwa shite mo yoroshii deshoo ka.*
    tonight call   even good
    'Is it all right if I call **you** tonight?'

(21). *Kaigi-chuu ni   denwa   ga hairi mashi tara,*
    meeting-during telephone NOM enter   if
    o-tsunagi shite mo yoroshii deshoo ka.
    transfer   even good
    'If there is a phone call during the meeting, is it all right if
    I connect it to **you**?'

(22). *Chotto o-kiki shite mo yoroshii deshoo ka.*
    little   ask   even good
    'Is it all right if I ask **you** a few questions?'

(23). *Kono hon o-kari shite mo yoroshii deshoo ka.*
    this   book borrow   even good
    'Is it all right if I borrow this book from **you**?'

On the other hand, if the exalted person is not an argument, o-
V(stem) *suru* cannot undergo non-subject honorification.

(24).**Kono ronbun o-yomi shite mo yoroshii deshoo ka.*
    this article read   even good
    'Is it all right if I read this article?'

(25).**Kono hon kopii o   o-tori shite mo yoroshii deshoo ka.*
    this book copy ACC take   even good
    'Is it all right if I make a copy of this book?'

(26).**Piano o   o-hiki shite mo yoroshii deshoo ka.*
    piano ACC play   even good
    'Is it all right if I play this piano?'

(27).**Kono jisho   o-tsukai shite mo yoroshii deshoo ka.*
    this dictionary use   even good
    'Is it all right if I use this dictionary.'

The relationship between argument status of the exalted person and benefactivity

    However, even if the exalted person is not an argument, if

the sentence has the 'benefactive' interpretation, o-V(stem) *suru* is applicable.

(28). *Ima o-heya o   o-sooji shite mo yoroshii deshoo ka.*
     now room ACC clean   even good
     'Is it all right if I clean your room now?'

(29). *Kono kami de o-tsutsumi shite mo yoroshii deshoo ka.*
     this paper with wrap   even good
     'Is it all right if I wrap it with this paper?'

That is, 'benefactivity' becomes crucial only when the exalted person is not an argument. In other words, nonsubject honorification is always applicable if the exalted person is an argument of the verb, whether or not the sentence has benefactive interpretation.

The use of V(causative) *itadaku*

How can the speaker humbly ask for permission when o-V(stem) *suru*   is not available as in (24)~(27), or in the cases of '- argument, -benefactivity'? In these cases, the other construction V(causative) *itadaku*   tends to be used.

(30). *Kono ronbun yomasete   itadakemasen   ka.*
     this article read(causative) receive(potential-neg.)
     'Could you give me the favor of letting me read this article?'
     = 'May I read this article?'

(31). *Kono hon kopii o   torasete itadakemasen ka.*
     this book copy ACC take(causative)
     'May I make a copy of this book?'

(32). *Piano o   hikasete itadakemasen ka.*
     piano ACC play(causative)
     'May I play the piano?'

(33). *Kono jisho   tsukawasete itadakemasen ka.*
     this dictionary use(causative)
     'May I use this dictionary?'

One of the important semantic features of V(causative) *itadaku* is 'permission'. However, it is not always the best choice for the purpose of asking permission. Consider these pairs of sentences.

(34). a.*Kono hon, ashita   o-kaeshi shite mo yoroshii deshoo ka.*
      this book tomorrow return   even good
      b.*Kono hon, ashita kaesasete itadakemasen ka.*
                         return(causative)
      'May I return this book to **you** tomorrow?'

(35). a.*Ima chotto konde runde, hachi-ji goro o-todoke shite mo*
         yoroshii deshoo ka. (=19)
      b.*Ima chotto konde runde, hachi-ji goro todokesasete*
         itadakemasen ka.
      'As we are busy now, may we deliver it to **you** around
       eight?'

(36). a.*Konban o-denwa shite mo yoroshii deshoo ka.* (=20)
      b.*Konban denwa sasete itadakemasen ka.*
      'May I call **you** tonight?'

(37). a.*Kaigi-chuu ni denwa ga hairi mashitara, o-tsunagi shite mo*
         yoroshii deshoo ka. (=21)
      b.*Kaigi-chuu ni denwa ga hairi mashitara, tsunagasete*
         itadakemasen ka.
      'If there is a phone call during the meeting, may I connect it
       to **you**?'

(38). a.*Chotto o-kiki shite mo yoroshii deshoo ka.* (=22)
      b.*Chotto kikasete itadakemasen ka.*
      'May I ask **you** a few questions?'

(39). a. *Shucchoo de sochira ni mairi masu node, zehi o-ai shitai n*
         business-trip there   go   because   meet want
         desu ga.

      b.**Shucchoo de sochira ni mairi masu no de, zehi awasete*
                                               meet(causative)
         itadaki tai n desu ga.
         receive want
         'As I am going there for my business, I would like to meet
         you, but...'

Vcausative *itadaku* seems available for most of these cases, yet what is crucial here is that (b) with <u>Vcausative *itadaku*</u> sounds more imposing than (a) with <u>*o*-Vstem *suru*.</u> Thus (b) sounds as if the speaker is pushing the speaker's own convenience too far. That is, when the speaker has to or wants to insist on his/her need, he/she may use 'Vcausative *itadaku*', but if this is not the case, the preferred choice seems to be (a). The same kind of imposition is observed when the predicate has benefactive interpretation as follows:

(40). a. *Ima o-heya o o-sooji shite mo yoroshii deshoo ka.* (=28)
    b. *Ima o-heya o sooji sasete itadakemasen ka.*
    'May I clean your room now?'

(41). a. *Kono kami de o-tsutsumi shite mo yoroshii deshoo ka.* (=29)
    b. *Kono kami de tsutsumasete itadakemasen ka.*
    'May I wrap it with this paper?'

In both cases, (b) is more imposing than (a). Remember that <u>V(causative) *itadaku*</u> has two important semantic features, namely 'permission' and 'favor-receipt'. In (b), the aspect of 'favor-receipt' seems to affect the imposing connotation. That is, when the speaker actually asks for the favor, it is considered to be more polite to ask the exalted person indirectly about his/her psychological state by using '~ *te mo yoroshii desuka* (Is it all right with you if ~)' than to refer to the possibility of 'favor-receipt' directly. So, as long as the nonsubject honorifics is available to give deference to the addressee, the speaker should choose this construction followed by ' ~*te mo yoroshii desu ka?*' to avoid imposition.

Summary

What I have discussed so far is summarized in Chart 1.

	o-V(stem) *suru*	V(causative) *itadaku*
+argument	+	+/- (imposing/ungramm.)
-argument, +argument	+	+ (imposing)
-argument, -argument	-	+

Chart 1. The distribution of the two constructions (request)

When the exalted person is an argument of the verb, nonsubject honorifics is always applicable. When the exalted person is not an argument, if the utterance has benefactive interpretation, nonsubject honorifics can be used. V(causative) *itadaku* can be used in the wide range of situations.[5] Yet, to avoid imposition, the speaker should use *o-V(stem) itadaku* , as long as it is available.

4. Report of past events

I will consider next the cases where the speaker reports past events to someone superior to him/her. The findings from the previous section may predict the grammaticality of the following cases (42)~(45).

(42). *Senshuu   o-kari shita hon wa, kinoo   o-keshi shita to*
last-week borrowed   book TOP yesterday returned   COP
omoimasu ga.
think
'As for the book I borrowed last week, I think I returned it to you yesterday. '

(43). *Yuube   o-hanashi shita ken desu ga..*
last-night talked   case
'About the issue I talked to you last night...'

(44). *O-nimotsu o   o-mochi shimashita.*
luggage   ACC brought
'I brought your luggage.'

(45). *Ima   kuuraa   o   o-tsuke shimashita kara*
now air-conditioner ACC turn-on   because
sugu suzushiku naru   to   omoimasu.
soon cool   become COP think
' I turned on the air conditioner now, so I think it will be cooler soon.'

---

[5] There are some cases where the use of V(causative) *itadaku* is rather awkward.

Chotto hanasasete itadaki tai koto ga aru n desu ga....
'I have things that I would like to talk to you, but ...'

Misesasete itadaki tai mono ga aru n desu ga.....
'I have a thing that I would like to show you, but ...'

(42) and (43) are the cases where the exalted person is an argument of the verb, while (44) and (45) are the cases where there is benefactive interpretation. Therefore, in these cases, o-Vstem *suru* is available.

What is different from the previous findings is that there are cases where o-Vstem *suru* is available even in the cases of the third category of '-argument, -benefactive', in the 'report of past events'. For instance, Hamano(1988) claims that the following examples are acceptable 'if the exalted parties (members of the exalted party) are present at the time of the speech act (p.2).'

(46). *Sensei   no go-hon o   musuko kara o-kari shimashita.*
      teacher GEN book ACC son   from borrowed
      'I borrowed Teacher's (=your) book from my son.'

(47). *O-kaeri ni naru to   musume kara o-kiki shimashita ga.*
      go-home   COP daughter from heard
      'I heard from my daughter that you are leaving.'

Although the verbs are transactional in these examples, the arguments (source) are the in-group members of the speaker who should not be exalted. The exalted person is the possessor of the object in (46) and the referent of the subject of the embedded clause in (47), and there is no benefactive interpretation in both cases. Here are some more examples with non-transactional verbs.

(48). *Sensei no otaku no mae o o-toori shimashita.*(=7, 12)
      'I passed your house last night.'

(49). *Sensei no o-kuruma o chuusha- joo de o-mikake shimashita node... (=13)*
      'As I saw your car at the parking lot...'

One may point out the unity between the exalted person and the object or information which belongs to him/her. That is, the object has equal quality to the possessor him/herself, so that the object or information can be exalted as if it is a human object. Nevertheless, this is not always the case. Although the exalted person is a possessor of the object in (50) and (51), the object cannot be treated as a representation of the person.

(50).*Rusu-chuu ni   denwa   o   o-tsukai shimashita.
　　absent-during telephone ACC used
　　'I used your telephone while you were gone.'

(51).*Sensei   no ronbun, kopii o   o-tori shimashita.
　　teacher GEN article   copy ACC took
　　'I made a copy of your paper (for my convenience).'

In these cases, Vcausative *itadaku* is the appropriate
construction to use as we have seen in the other situations.

(52). *Rusu-chuu ni denwa o tsukawasete   itadakimashita.*
　　　　　　　　　　　use(causative) received
　　'I used your phone while you were gone.'

(53). *Sensei no ronbun, kopii o torasete   itadakimashita.*
　　　　　　　　　　　take(causative) received
　　'I made a copy of your paper.'

As for (46)~(49), on the other hand, it seems rather awkward to
use V(causative) *itadaku.*

(54).?*Sensei no go-hon o musuko kara karisasete itadakimashita.*
　　　　　　　　　　　　borrow(causative) received
　　'I borrowed your book from my son.'

(55).*O-kaeri ni naru to musume kara kikasete itadakimashita ga.*
　　　　　　　　　　　hear(causative) received
　　'I heard from my daughter that you are leaving.'

(56).?*Sensei no otaku no mae o torasete itadakimashita.*
　　　　　　　　　　　pass(causative) received
　　'I passed your house.'

(57).*Sensei no o-kuruma o mikake sasete itadakimashita.*
　　　　　　　　　　　see(causative) received
　　'I saw your car.'

The use of V(causative) *itadaku* and 'face threatening acts'
What is crucial here seems whether or not the speaker's

action is socially believed as one which requires the exalted person's permission. For the purpose of further explanation, let me introduce the model of politeness suggested by Brown and Levinson(1987).

Brown and Levinson claim that every langiage has its own way to achieve 'politeness'. They equate the universal features of politeness with the expression of the speaker's intention to mitigate face threats. They define 'face' as:

'the public self image that every member wants to claim for himself, consisting in two related aspects:
  (a) negative face: the basic claim to territories personal preserves, rights to non-distraction -- i.e. to freedom of action and freedom from imposition
  (b) positive face: the positive consistent self-image or "personality"(crucially including the desire that this self-image be appreciated and approved of) claimed by interactants (p.66)'

Based on this idea of 'face', especially 'negative face', the actions in (50) and (51) are the ones which conceptually require the exalted person's permission, because they interfere with the addressee's territory. Thus, even if the action actually took place without the permission, it should be reported with V(causative)_itadaku_ to mark the authority of the addressee. Otherwise, the speaker's utterance would result in threatening the addressee's face by ignoring the authority. However, the actions in (46) ~ (49) are not ones which are considered to require the exalted person's permission, or these utterances simply report the speaker's experience which is somehow related to the addressee. Consider the following examples.

(58).*_Setsumee_   _o   o-hajime shita._
          explanation ACC started
          'I started the explanation.'

(59). _Setsumee_   _o   o-tuzuke shita._
          explanation ACC resumed
          'I resumed the explanation.'

(60).*_Setsumee_   _o   o-oe shita._
          explanation ACC complete

'I completed the explanation.'

These examples are quoted from Hamano(1988). Here she attempts to explain this difference in the acceptability of nonsubject honorifics as one where '"maintenance" is considered a service activity, while "initiation/completion" is not(p.8)' What she calls 'service activity' is the similar concept that Harada calls 'benefactive'. But I would like to suggest the factor of 'permission' for a better explanation of the difference between (59) and (58) or (61). That is, 'initiation' and 'completion' are the actions which interfere with the exalted person's territory, and thus require his/her permission, while 'maintenance' is a natural consequence which does not require the permission.

The summary of this section is shown in Chart 2.

	o-V(stem) *suru*	V(causative) *itadaku*
+arg.	+	-
-arg., +benef.	+	-/+? (favor-receipt)
-arg., -benef., -perm.	+	-/+ (favor-receipt)
-arg., -benef., +perm.	-	+

Chart 2. The distribution of the two constructions (past events)

With my definition, the factor of 'benefactivity' can be eliminated from this chart, as the actions of '+benefactive' fall into the category of '-permission'. That is, what I define as '+permission' is not the actual permission but is related to the idea of face-threatening acts. Thus the actions of '+benefactive' would not be face-threatening acts even if it is done without permission.

The obligatory versus optional use of V(causative) *itadaku*

Finally I would like to add some comment on V(causative) *itadaku* used for the actions of '-permission' in chart 2.

(61). a. *O-kuruma o-yobi shimashita.*
      car   called
   b. *O-kuruma o yobasete itadakimashita.*
      car   call(causative) received

'I called a taxi (for you).'[6]

(62). a. *Sensei   no   kooen   o-kiki shimashita.*
   teacher GEN lecture listened
  b. *Sensei   no   kooen   kikasete   itadaki mashita.*
   teacher GEN lecture listen(causative) received
   'I listened to your lecture.'

The actions in (61) and (62) are not necessarily 'permission required' acts, as both of them are rather benefactive to the addressee or the exalted person. In fact *o-V(stem) suru* can be also used. In these cases, the aspect of favor-receipt is emphasized rather than permission, to show the speaker's appreciation of the benefit he/she received from the experience. That is, these are optional use of V(causative) *itadaku*, whereas in the cases of '+permission' such as (52) or (53), the use of this construction is obligatory.

5. Summary and concluding remarks

In this paper, I have discussed the constraints on the use of nonsubject honorifics, comparing it to that of V(causative) *itadaku*. While the factor of 'benefactivity' suggested by Harada(1976) is efficient for some speech acts such as 'offering services', the examination of the other speech acts reveals that we need to consider other factors than 'benefactivity'.

Through the observation of the cases of 'requests for permission', we now know that the 'benefactivity' is crutial only when the exalted person is not an argument. When the exalted person is an argument, *o-V(stem) suru* is always applicable even without the benefactive interpretation. Further, the cases of 'reports of past events' demonstrate that we need the factor of 'permission required act' to explain the distribution of the two constructions. For, even if the action is not benefative to the addressee, nonsubject honorifics may be used if the action is not a 'permission required' one. Given the two possible ways of humble expressions, in some cases, the unavailability of V(causative)

---

6 Kawanishi(in personal communication) suggested that there is a difference in (61a) and (61b). That is, while (61a) simply reports the fact that the speaker called a taxi, (61b) has a connotation of the speaker's feeling sorry for not providing a ride by him/herself. I think it is this feeling that motivates the use of V(causative) *itadaku* or the emphasis of favor-receipt, i.e. want for forgiveness.

itadaku seems to force the speaker to use *o-V(stem) suru* with a risk of producing unacceptable utterances(see note 3).

The shortcoming of this study is the lack of discussion on the relationship between the syntactic constraint and the pragmatic constraints. In other words, what is not answered is why nonsubject honorific is always available if the exalted person is an argument, or why we need the pragmatic constraints if the exalted person is not an argument. Further, this study is solely based on native speakers' judgements of the sentences made up artificially, and the unacceptable sentences produced by the second language leaners. In that sense, this is a preliminary study of the pragmatic aspects of these humble expressions. For further discussion, it is necessary to have some natual data and analyze the speaker's actual use of these expressions, including the 'mis-use' or 'over-use' of them, in order to refine what we consider as 'permission required' acts.

* I would like to thank Naomi H. McGloin for her comments on the earlier version of this paper and her encouragement for presenting this paper at the preceding conference. I also acknowledge Nanako Machida for introducing me the problem I discussed in this paper. My special appreciation goes to George R. Johnson who has supported my study.

References

Brown, Penelope. and Levinson, Stephen. C. 1987. Politeness: Some universals in language usage. Cambridge: Cambridge University Press.

Hamano, Shoko. 1988. 'Service activities' and 'non-service' activities in Japanese Grammar. Presented at the Honorific Conference at Portland State University.

Harada, S. I. 1976. Honorifics. In Syntax and semantics 5: Japanese generative grammar. San Diego: Academic Press.

Kuno, Susumu. 1983. Shin nihon bunpoo no kenkyuu. Tokyo: Taishuukan shoten.

Kuno, Susumu. 1987. Honorific marking in Japanese and the word formatio hypothesis of causatives and passives. Studies in language. 11-1. 99-128.

Ohta, Kaoru. 1987. Japanese humble expression sasete itadaku : linguistic, social, and psychological perspectives. Selecta. 8. 17-26.

Wenger, James. 1983. Variation and change in Japanese honorific forms. Papers in Japanese linguistics. 16. 267-301.

Referential Structure in Japanese Children's Narratives: The Acquisition of *wa* and *ga*

KEI NAKAMURA
University of California at Berkeley

The study of discourse functions has recently become a popular area of research in child language development. Functionalist approaches have focused on how children acquire relations among linguistic devices on one hand, and communicative functions and context on the other hand. They claim that the 'development of forms cannot take place only at the intra-utterance level, since discourse and pragmatic functions constitute necessary developmental mechanisms, regardless of what other factors might be involved during the acquisition of formal machinery within utterances (Hickman, Liang and van Crevel 1989:2-3). Some functionalist proponents would even say that children's acquisition of forms is primarily determined by the communicative functions they serve, where the term 'function' includes semantic as well as discourse/pragmatic functions. Discourse cohesion is one of the universal discourse principles that determines how forms are used, and that must be acquired by all children in order to communicate smoothly.

Successful discourse depends on the speaker's ability to utilize different formal devices to manage information flow, by packaging information in a manner that is organized and easily accessible to the hearer. Language permits the transfer of information from the mind of the speaker to the hearer. The listener must be able to comprehend what is being referred to, and what is being said about the referent. In order for effective communication to take place, the speaker must be sensitive to the informational status of the of the listener and figure out what knowledge s/he shares with the listener and how to communicate what is unshared. In genres as different as informal conversation and formal lectures, the speaker must present information across clauses in a manner which can be easily followed by the listener, establishing participants and topics, and maintaining their continuity through various events, states, and locations. In order to do so, the speaker must use cohesive devices which assist the listener in identifying the topic and maintaining topic continuity.

One of the tasks of the child is to learn the forms, functions and rules which govern the relationship between accessible and inaccessible information, both at the level of the sentence and at the level of discourse. In English, speakers rely on grammatical tactics such as zero anaphora, pronouns, definite noun phrases, left dislocation, right dislocation, and demonstrative pronouns to mark topic continuity (Givón 1983). There is a growing body of literature which examines children's use of referring expressions beyond the sentence-level. Some of these studies conclude that children acquire the major features of the referential system of their languages around the age of 3 (e.g., Maratsos 1976, MacWhinney & Bates 1978), while others have argued that young children use referential expressions mainly in a deictic manner, and that only older children are able to use them appropriately (e.g., Warden 1976, Karmiloff-Smith 1979, 1980, Bamberg 1987). Such views support Piaget's (1955) observations that young children seem to be egocentric, and lack the ability to place themselves according to the listener's point of view. Piaget claimed that 5- and 6-year-olds are unable to adopt the perspectives of their listeners, and therefore, their utterances are often independent of the listener's level of comprehension and whatever feedback they may receive.

In general, it seems that most of the current studies on the acquisition of referential structure seem to support the view that although children start to master referential devices at a relatively early age, their understanding of the discourse pragmatics of topic continuity emerges gradually. Peterson (1990: 444) states that 'competent and fully explicit orientation to narrative participants is something which is seldom seen in children under 3-1/2 and which will undergo considerable improvement with age.' Children often ellipt the referent, use ambiguous pronominal forms, and rely heavily on deictic and non-verbal cues. Most of this research has focused on English and other Indo-European languages (e.g., French, Italian, German).

This paper addresses how Japanese children become increasingly capable of using language-specific referential strategies in narrative construction. In order to facilitate the listener's comprehension, children must acquire ways of distinguishing referent introduction from referent maintenance and marking referents based on the degree to which the identity of the entities can be more or less presupposed from the context, based on factors such as the number of characters that are involved and distance from last mention (e.g., Clancy 1980, Givón 1983). In Japanese, referent continuity is achieved through the use of a number of devices, such as the postpositional particles *wa* and *ga*, zero anaphora and word stress.

There is a substantial amount of literature on the topic of participant identification in Japanese, focusing on the means by which a speaker introduces a character and makes subsequent reference to that character. Hinds and Hinds (1979) describe a classical three-step progression in the identification of participants in a narrative:

First Mention:	NP + *ga (ni, o)*
Second Mention:	NP + *wa*
Subsequent Mention:	ellipsis

On first mention, a participant is introduced into a narrative with a non-topicalizing particle. If this particle is an agent, the particle is *ga*. If the participant is introduced as a non-agent, such as a direct object, or indirect object, the appropriate particle indicating the grammatical role of the noun phrase will be used (e.g., *o, ni*).

On second mention, the participant is referred to with a topicalized noun phrase marked by *wa*. This assures the audience that additional information about the character is coming and gives the addressee a chance to anchor the new referent in mind before the speaker continues the story line using ellipsis.

On subsequent mention, the participant is usually referred to by ellipsis (except in cases such as when there are episode shifts in terms of participant orientation, temporal or physical setting changes or the speaker chooses not to use ellipsis for emphasis).

In their analysis of oral narratives based on cartoons and videotapes, Clancy and Downing (1987) found that the classical model described by Hinds and Hinds (1979) did not always hold up. They found that the use of NP+*ga* for first mention was often followed by ellipsis on second mention (an average of 68% of all instances) and that NP+ *wa* was relatively rare. Research has shown that grammatical subjects are ellipted as much as 74% of the time in normal conversational interaction (Martin 1975:185). Often in Japanese conversation, the tendency is to leave as much unsaid as possible and to trust the partner to infer the intended meaning. It is grammatically acceptable to omit overt reference to any element is a sentence that the speaker assumes is understood. The classic model, in which NP+ *ga* is used for first mention, followed by NP+ *wa* for second mention and ellipsis for subsequent mention, does not seem to hold up well in actual discourse contexts.

As for the development of these two postpositional particles, Japanese sources report that *wa* and *ga* emerge as early as 2;2 (Okubo 1967, Miyahara & Miyahara 1973, Maeda 1979, Hayashi 1982), but in the early stages, the rate of deletion is extremely high. Although omission of *ga* in 2-year-olds quickly decreases to an adult rate, *wa* deletion in children as old as age 5 still remains high. Studies on the acquisition of discourse functions reveal relatively late acquisition. In a study examining the development of discourse functions in *wa* and *ga*, Ito and Tahara (1985) report that 4- and 5-year-old children tend to use *ga* regardless of context, while 6- to 12-year-olds begin to use *wa* for previously mentioned referents, but not consistently. Only the 14-year-old and adult narrators were able to systematically differentiate *wa* and *ga* according to discourse function. They claim that although *wa* and *ga* emerge as early as the two-word stage, complete acquisition of these particles occurs very late.

Method

This study examines oral narratives which were elicited from over 100 Japanese monolingual children and adults. Subjects were asked to narrate a picture storybook that presents a clear plot with no verbal text. This research is part of a larger study that was designed by Dan I. Slobin in collaboration with Ruth A. Berman to collect comparable speech samples from children and adults from across a wide range of languages, using a method developed by Michael Bamberg (1987). This method allows us to compare the ways in which speakers of different ages, speaking different languages talk about the same events. Data has been collected in the United States, Spain, Germany, Israel, Turkey, Chile, Argentina, China and Japan. Data for this study has been gathered from six age groups: 3-, 4-, 5-, 7-, 9-year-olds and adults.

The picture book, *Frog where are you?* by Mercer Mayer (1969) consists of set of 24 pictures. The story depicts a boy and a dog in search of their pet frog, which has escaped from its jar. During their search for the frog, the boy and the dog wander outside, encountering various animals (bees, a mole, a deer, an owl) and obstacles before they find their frog. The plot involves two main characters and a variety of peripheral characters, and moves from place to place, requiring causal and temporal description and careful tracking of referents across scenes. The simultaneous activities of the boy and the dog, in addition to the various other characters, are ideal for eliciting referential devices in narrative. By using an elicited narrative task, uniformity of the content is ensured across narrators.

Each narrator was presented with the picture book and told: 'This is a story about a boy, a dog, and a frog.' As this was said, the experimenter pointed to each character on the first page of the book. The child or adult was then asked to look through the book silently, page-by-page, to acquire familiarity with the plot. The investigator then opened the book to the first page, asking the subject to tell the story. The texts were tape-recorded and then transcribed. The length of the child stories ranged from a minimum of 15 clauses in a story by a 3-year-old to 107 clauses in a story by a 7-year-old. The data were analyzed in terms of the development of grammatical means for marking referential structure: namely referent introduction, referent maintenance and referent re-introduction.

Results and Discussion

The first analysis conducted was a tabulation of the percentage of subjects using *-wa* and *-ga* in their construction of the Frog narrative. As seen in Table 1, usage of *ga* is established relatively quickly, while *wa* seems to emerge gradually. 75% of the 3-year-olds were already using *ga* productively, and 100% of the subjects older than 4 years of age used *ga*. However, only one-fourth of the 3-year-olds used *wa* . Usage of this particle increased gradually with age. Although 100% of the 4-year-olds were able to use *ga* in their narratives, 100% usage of *wa* was only demonstrated by the adults.

	3 years	4 years	5 years	7 years	9 years	Adults
WA	25	35	50	84	88	100
GA	75	100	100	100	100	100

Table 1: Percentage of Subjects Using wa/ga by Age

In the literature, *wa* and *ga* have been described as emerging in spontaneous speech as early as 2;3. As reported by Goto (1988) and others, although *ga* emerges at an early age, *wa* seems to be omitted until much later. Here we see that this indeed seems to be the case.

The average number of *wa* and *ga* used by each subject by age was calculated to estimate frequency of usage. Table 2 illustrates that *ga* usage always exceed *wa* usage, except in the adults, who use a larger number of *wa* than *ga*. This would be expected, if the narrator is able to establish referent continuity with one of the main characters in the story.

	3 years	4 years	5 years	7 years	9 years	Adults
WA	0.1	0.4	4.1	8.5	7.5	18.2
GA	3.4	11.2	14.4	14.6	10.3	13.3
Ratio	1:30	1:28	1:4	1:1.7	1:1.4	1:0.7

Table 2: Average Number of wa/ga Used Per Subject by Age

The 3-year-olds hardly use any particles at all. This is because they tend to omit them completely. Between the ages of four and five there is a dramatic increase in *wa* usage resulting from clearer marking of noun phrases with *wa* and less deletion of particles. One issue to keep in mind is that of input. Much of the input the child received differs from standard adult speech, having the characteristics of child-directed speech (usually shorter and simpler, with clear articulation and exaggerated rise in pitch). In Japanese child-directed speech, particles are often omitted. Miyazaki (as cited in Cook, 1985) found that *ga* was omitted in 10.2% and *wa* in 25.5% of potential contexts in adult-adult conversation, whereas the corresponding figures in mother's speech to a 2-year-old were 30% and 70% omission for *ga* and *wa* respectively. How is the child expected to learn particles correctly if they appear so sporadically in the input?

Another explanation for the high degree of particle omission in young children is cognitive. Young children have a very restricted short-term memory capacity, which in turn constrains sentence production. 'Unimportant' words such as auxiliaries, prepositions, conjunctions and particles such as *wa* and *ga* may simply be left out, even though the child is aware of their presence in adult speech and understands some aspects of their meaning.

The overall increase in particles is also related to the increasing length of the narratives, since the older the narrators, the longer are the narratives. Another jump in *wa* usage occurs between 5 and 7 years of age. This seems to be caused by the children's increasing efforts to mark referent continuity. However, this increase is followed by a slight decrease in usage by the 9-year-olds. The 9-year-olds, on the average, also produced narratives about the same length as the 5-year-olds. Poor performance in 9-year-olds has also been documented by researchers such as Ito and Tahara (1985). They propose that children experience a developmental retreat around this age as they attempt to grapple with the multifunctional nature of these particles. However, the fact that the narratives are also shorter points to the possibility that this task is less exciting for children this age, and therefore, they may lack the motivation to perform well.

Adults follow the expected pattern of using more *wa* than *ga*. In the case that a narrator is attempting to create narrative coherence by maintaining topic-referent continuity, one would expect more *wa* to be used than *ga*. *Ga* should be reserved for situations in which one is introducing new information, such as a new character (e.g. the mole, owl, deer) or when an old character gets reintroduced (e.g. the frog).

In some of the children around the age of 5, there is a strong tendency to overmark with *ga*. Early *ga* usage is relatively indiscriminate. Children use *ga* to mark most of the referents. The overuse of this particle supports Slobin's (1973) claim that once learned, children apparently prefer to use grammatical functors whenever possible. The less frequent usage of *wa* is probably caused by the fact that it is less clearly marked acoustically and is used for many different functions.

Looking at the *wa* /*ga* ratios, one finds a clear age-related trend: with increasing age, the proportion of *wa* increases until it is used more frequently than *ga*.

Participant Introduction : According to Hinds and Hinds (1979), the classic model for referent introduction and maintenance in Japanese is that referents are introduced into the discourse with NP+ *ga*, then referred to with NP+ *wa*, and on subsequent mention, are referred to by ellipsis. Strategies used for referent introduction are presented by age in Table 3.

As discussed above, a participant is almost always introduced into a narrative with a nontopicalizing particle. If this participant is an agent, the particle is *ga* , as in the following examples:

(1) *Inu to otoko no ko ga kaeru wo miteru.* (4;00)
   A dog and a boy are watching a frog.

(2) *Hachi ga bunbun tonde kita.* (4;11)
   Bees came flying (making a) buzzing (noise).

	3 yrs	4 yrs	5 yrs	7 yrs	9 yrs	Adults
NP+ga	17.5	46.4	54.7	61.7	62.1	57.8
NP only	54.2	26.5	23.0	1.6		
Ellipsis	10.0	10.4	5.2	3.1	4.5	3.3
Copula	15.5	1.4	5.6	3.4	1.8	5.9
NP+other prt.	2.9	11.9	11.7	24.9	25.0	29.4
NP+ wa		0.8		4.6	6.8	5.3
NP + mo		2.4		0.8		

Table 3: Strategies Used for Referent Introduction (Percentages by Age)

In most of the referent introductions, the referent was introduced with a full noun phrase + *ga* as would be predicted by the classical model. However, more than half of the 3-year-old referent introductions were made with a full noun phrase alone. Even 4-

and 5-year-olds frequently omitted particles. However, this tendency disappears by age 7. Particle deletion in young children has been well-documented in the literature (e.g. Noji 1976).

Another striking finding is the frequency with which children introduce referents with ellipsis. Perhaps the children (and even some adults) use ellipsis to introduce the main characters because the three main characters are clearly referred to by the experimenter prior to the telling of the narrative. It is possible that they assume the referent information is 'given'. Another possibility is that they are relying on the presence of the picture book and consider the referent to be given information because the characters are visible in the book to both the child and the experimenter. With increasing age, ellipsis, too, seems to decrease as a referent-introducing device. Clancy (1982) also reports that children often use ellipsis to introduce referents. Clearly, one task the child faces is to learn when one must be explicit.

It is important to note that not all participants are introduced into narratives as agents. Copulas can also be used to introduce referents:

(3) *Sono yama wa shika-san datta no desu!* (5;05)
That mountain was (actually) Mr. Deer!

The introduction of referents with particles other than *wa* and *ga* (e.g. *ni, to, mo*) also increases with age, such as in the following examples:

(4) *Shika ni otoko no ko ga hikkakatta no.* (5;04)
The boy got caught on a deer.

(5) *Inu mo miteru.* (4;11)
A dog is also looking.

There are also cases in which children marked the first reference to a character with the topicalizing . It is possible that they are doing this because they consider the referent to be 'given' (as discussed above) or perhaps they do not have a clear understanding of the function of *wa* . As Hinds and Hinds (1979: 203) discovered, even adults occasionally introduce referents with the topicalizing particle *wa* when the names of the referents appear in the title of the story.

Referent   Re-introduction: This analysis was based on the reappearance of the frog towards the end of the story. Here, even the youngest children seem to be strongly motivated to mark full noun phrases with *ga* as in (6) and (7).

(6) *Kaeru ga iru.* (3;2). The frog is there.

(7) *Ushiro wo mitara, kaeru ga ita.* (5;2)
    When they looked behind, there was the frog!

	3 yrs	4 yrs	5 yrs	7 yrs	9 yrs	Adults
NP+ga	62.5	76.5	68.6	73.7	87.5	100.0
NP only	37.5	17.6		5.3		
Ellipsis		5.9		10.5	6.3	
Copula			12.5	5.3		
NP+other prt.			12.5	5.3	6.3	
NP +wa			6.3			

Table 4 Strategies Used for Referent Reintroduction (Percentages by Age)

In Table **4**, we find that once again, the youngest children are using noun phrases without particles to introduce the frog. However, as compared with the figures on referent introduction, we find that fewer narrators across ages use ellipsis and full noun phrases with *wa*. It is clear that the discovery of the lost frog is a highly salient event and the clearest way to mark this is with an NP + *ga*.

Second Mention: Due to the large number of characters, continuous reference was relatively rare. In fact, in each scene of the picture book, there are two or more characters. None of the characters is ever alone. However, second mentions were relatively common.

(8) First mention: *koko kodomo ga miteru.* (3;00)
                 The child's looking here.
    Second mention: *nohara Ø detetta.*
                 (He) went out to the meadow.

(9) First mention: *Maikeru to Jon ga petto no kerochan wo*
     nozokikonde imasu. (adult)
     Michael and John are looking at their pet, Kerochan.
     Second mention: *soshite kakera wa oyasuminasai wo iimashita.*
     And then (they) said goodnight (to the frog).

	3 yrs	4 yrs	5 yrs	7 yrs	9 yrs	Adults
Ellipsis	94	83	74	83	88	83
NP + wa			9	8	6	13
NP + ga	6	17	12	9	5	4
NP only			4			

Table 5: Strategies Used for Second Mention (Percentages By Age)

As illustrated in Table 5, all age groups showed a strong tendency to go straight from full noun phrase + *ga* marking to ellipsis. (8) is an example of this tendency. Some of the older children and adults use the 'classical' noun phrase + *wa* marking, but not as many as might be expected. An example of this is presented in (9). This supports Clancy and Downing's (1987) view that different genres and elicitation tasks depend on different referential strategies (e.g. written narratives vs. oral narratives).

Some of the younger children used the NP + *ga* marking for second mention. This was especially true of some of the 3- and 4-year-olds who seemed to be using *ga* somewhat excessively. Most of the noun phrase + *ga* uses in the older children and the adults, however, seemed to be involved in subordinate clauses. Finally, unlike English-speaking children who use anaphoric third person pronouns to maintain reference, use of third person pronouns was rare: only two of the adults used them.

Subsequent Mention: For subsequent mentions, marking with ellipsis was more common than in the case of second mentions, as the characters were clearly more well-established. Here, marking with full noun phrase + *wa*, at all ages, was less common than in the case of second mentions. In general, usage of NP + *ga* also decreased in subsequent mention as compared to second mention.

	3 yrs	4 yrs	5 yrs	7 yrs	9 yrs	Adults
Ellipsis	100	83	91	84	92	88
NP + wa			5	8	2	10
NP + ga		15	3	8	7	2
NP only		2	2			

Table 6: Strategies Used for Subsequent Mention (Percentages By Age)

(10) (After third mention) (3;00)

Okotteru no.	(He's) angry.
Noboreta no.	(He) was able to climb up.
Doronko no naka ni iru.	(He) was in the mud.

As seen in the examples under (10), with a clearly established referent, narrators usually choose ellipsis to illustrate referent continuity.

Overall, the more complicated the scene (in terms of the numbers of characters), the stronger the tendency to mark referents clearly with NP + *ga* or *wa*. There also seemed to be some strong individual differences. Some people will rely on ellipsis right away, demanding more of the listener. One adult referred to the boy over 13 clauses with ellipsis, regardless of the fact that he also referred to other characters during that time. Others will meticulously mark every clause throughout the story with a noun phrase and *wa/ga*.

One interesting aspect of the data presented thus far is the fact that subjects are not using very many NP+*wa* 's for marking second and subsequent reference, as might be expected. This is probably due to the large number of referents involved in the story plot. Clancy and Downing (1987) ranked the characters in their stories according to the number of pages on which they appeared in order to examine the relationship between the saliency of each character and *wa*-marking. In the Frog story, there are eight characters with varying degrees of prominence. Here they are listed in order of their initial appearance, with percentages indicating the number of pages on which they appear out of the 24 pages in the book:

1. the boy (100%)
2. the dog (96%)
3. the frog (21%)
4. the bees (21%)
5. the mole (4%)
6. the owl (17%)
7. the deer (13%)
8. the frog's family (13%)

In order to check that the subjects were using *wa* -marking in a logical fashion, percentages of *wa*- marking on the various referents were calculated.

	Boy	Dog	Frog	Bees	Mole	Owl	Deer	Misc
3 yrs	100							
4 yrs	17	17	17				17	33
5 yrs	38	43	4	3	1	3	1	7
7 yrs	50	36	4	2		2	5	1
9 yrs	45	36	9	2		2	4	2
Adults	42	36	14	1		1	2	4

Table 7: Percentage of Wa-Marking on Referents

In general, the usage of *wa*-marking follows the hierarchy of referents- except for the prominence of the frog. Although it only appears in 21% of the scenes, the frog is a key character (it is the main motivation behind the boy and the dog's long search). The deer also is slightly emphasized, perhaps due to the fact that it plays a active role in pushing the boy and dog off the cliff into the scene where they find their long-lost frog. In the Frog story, there are eight main characters. Therefore, although the subjects are not always using NP +*wa* to mark second and subsequent reference, they seem to be frequently using it to mark switch reference. This topic merits further investigation.

Conclusion

The focus of this study is to examine the development of referential structure in oral narratives elicited from Japanese adults and children by analyzing their usage of the postpositional particles, *wa* and *ga,* as well as other devices such as zero anaphora. As children grow older, they become more capable of marking referent introduction, reintroduction and maintenance with the appropriate linguistic devices. By the age of 5, a majority of the children are able to introduce referents with a full noun phrase . Children also become increasingly capable of introducing the referent with non-agentive particles. In the case of referent re-introduction, even the youngest children showed a strong tendency to mark the referent with a full noun phrase + *ga.* Very few narrators used ellipsis to re-introduce the referent. Contrary to Piaget's expectations, children as young as 3 and 4 were able to take the listener's needs into consideration, making adult-like referential choices in contexts calling for explicit nominal reference.

Regarding second mention, narrators perform somewhat differently from the classical model- they tend to jump right into ellipsis, without marking the referent with *wa* , as one might predict. Children who were not using ellipsis for second mention relied on full noun phrases + *ga*. This can be explained in two ways: (1) children are overusing *ga* and overmarking referents, or (2) children are using *ga* repetitively to ensure the salience of the referent. Finally, both children and adults showed an even stronger tendency to use ellipsis for the referent in the case of subsequent mention, as would be expected from the classical model. In general, the data support the view that children begin to master referential devices at a relatively early age, but that their understanding of the discourse pragmatics of referential structure emerges gradually.

The difference between these results and what would be predicted can also be explained in terms of genre. Adults performed more closely to the predicted pattern. Perhaps this is because of their familiarity with oral narrative as a genre. The children's less predictable performance may be related to their unfamiliarity with the task, as well as with the genre. In addition, they may have a different understanding of the listener's perspective (e.g. a different sense of what is 'understood'). Clancy (1982, in press) found that child and adult referential choice vary across discourse contexts, types of referent and narrative situations. Clearly these factors need to be examined more closely. More studies need to be conducted across a wider spectrum of contexts and languages in order to gain a better understanding of children's use of referential structures.

References

Bamberg, Michael. 1987. The acquisition of narratives: learning to use language. Berlin: Mouton de Grutyer.

Clancy, Patricia. 1980. Referential choice in English and Japanese narrative discourse. The pear stories: cognitive, cultural and linguistic aspects of narrative production, ed. by Wallace Chafe, 127-202. Norwood, NJ: Ablex.

Clancy, Patricia.1982. Referential strategies in the narratives of Japanese children. Paper presented at the 7th Annual Boston

University Conference on Language Development, Oct. 8-10, 1982.

Clancy, Patricia. In press. Referential strategies in the narratives of Japanese children. Discourse Processes.

Clancy, Patricia & Downing, Pamela. 1987. Theuse of *wa* as a cohesion marker in Japanese oral narratives. Perspectives on topicalization: the case of Japanese*wa*, ed. by John Hinds, Senko Maynard & Shoichi Iwasaki, 3-56. Amsterdam: John Benjamins.

Cook, Haruko. 1985. Frequency of nominal markers in the speech of a Japanese child and his caretakers: a case study. Descriptive and Applied Linguistics 18. 13-24.

Givón, T. 1983.Topic continuity in discourse: an introduction. Topic continuity in discourse: a quantitative cross-linguistic study, ed. by T. Givon, 5-41. Amsterdam:John Benjamins.

Goto, Keiko. 1988. Pre-school children's production of the case particles *ga* and *wo* and their judgment in simple transitive sentences. Mita Working Papers in Psycholinguistics 1. 39-49.

Hayashi, D. 1982. Zusetsu nihongo.Tokyo: Kadokawa Shoten.

Hickman, Maya, Liang, J. & van Crevel, M. 1989. The given/ new distinction in children's narratives: a cross-linguistic analysis. Paper presented at the Tenth Biennial Meeting of the International Society for the Study of Behavioral Development, July 9-13, 1989, Finland.

Hinds, John & Hinds, Wako. 1979. Participant identification in Japanese narrative discourse. Explorations in linguistics, ed. by G. Bedell, E. Kobayashi & M. Muraki, 201-212. Tokyo: Kenkyusha.

Ito, Takehiko & Tahara, Shunji. 1985. A psycholinguistic approach to the acquisition of multifunctionality in Japanese particles *wa* and *ga*. Descriptive and applied linguistics 18. 97-108.

Karmiloff-Smith, Annette. 1979. A functional approach to child language: a study of determiners and reference. Cambridge: Cambridge University Press.

Karmiloff-Smith, Annette.1981.The grammatical marking of thematic structure in the development of language production. The child's construction of language, ed. by W. Deutsch, 121-147. London: Academic Press.

MacWhinney, Brian & Bates, Elizabeth. 1978. Sentential devices for conveying givenness and newness: a cross-cultural developmental study. Journal of Verbal Learning and Verbal Behavior 17. 539-558.

Maeda, K. 1979. Nyuyoji no gengo hattatsu ni kansuru chosa kenkyuu VI. Nihon Kyooiku-shinrigakkai 19. 172-173.

Maratsos, Michael. 1976. The use of definite and indefinite reference in young children: an experimental study in semantic acquisition. Cambridge: Cambridge University Press.

Martin, Samuel. 1975. A reference grammar of Japanese. New Haven: Yale University Press

Mayer, Mercer. 1969. Frog, where are you? New York: Dial Press.

Miyahara, K. & Miyahara, H. 1973. Yooji- ni okeru bunpoo hattatsu no shoosoo. Nihon shinrigakkai 37. 698-699.

Noji, J. 1976. Yoojiki no gengo seikatsu no jittai. Hiroshima: Bunka Hyooron.

Okubo, Ai. 1967. Yooji gengo no hattatsu. Tokyo: Tokyo-do.

Peterson, C. 1990. The who, when and where of early narratives. Journal of Child Language 17. 433-455.

Piaget, Jean. 1955. The language and thought of the child. New York: Harcourt Brace

Slobin, Dan.1973.Cognitive prerequisites for the development of grammar. Studies of child language development, ed. by Charles Ferguson and Dan Slobin. New York:Holt, Rinehart & Winston.

Warden, D. 1976. The influence of context on children's use of identifying expressions and references. British Journal of Psychology 67: 101-112.

Grammatical Factors in the Acquisition of Complex Structures in Japanese

WENDY SNYDER

California State University at Northridge

1. Introduction
1.1 Acquisition Background

Much of the first language acquisition literature in English, Japanese, and other languages has focused on the use of processing strategies by young children. Many of these strategies are largely dependent on children's sensitivity to linguistic forms that are evident on the surface (the acoustic stream), such as the order in which words appear. For example, Bever 1970 proposed that young English-speaking children follow what is often called an NVN strategy, whereby they interpret any Noun-Verb-Noun sequence, even that of a passive sentence, as an agent-action-patient description. Various strategies have also been discussed in the literature surrounding children's acquisition of complex structures, particularly that of relative clauses. Smith 1974, de Villiers, Tager Flusberg, Hakuta, and Cohen 1979, and others have argued that observed differences in the imitation or comprehension of different types of relative clauses can be at least partially attributed to a reliance on an NVN strategy. In testing 3-6 year old children's comprehension of sentences such as those in 1, de Villiers et al. found that children more often correctly acted out the first part of sentences like 1a and 1d, which conform to a basic English NVN canonical sentence, than they did the first part of sentences like 1b and 1c, which begin with an NNV sequence.[1]

---

[1] Note here that in the abbreviations used to refer to relative clause types (e.g. SS, SO), the first letter designates the role of the NP head in the matrix clause and the second letter the role of the gap inside the relative clause.

1a. SS: The gorilla that bumped the elephant kissed the sheep. ($= N_1\text{-}V\text{-}N_2\text{-}V\text{-}N_3$)

 b. SO: The turkey that the gorilla patted pushed the pig. ($= N_1\text{-}N_2\text{-}V\text{-}V\text{-}N_3$)

 c. SI: The giraffe that the turkey yelled to pushed the zebra. ($= N_1\text{-}N_2\text{-}V\text{-}V\text{-}N_3$)

 d. OS: The kangaroo kissed the camel that shoved the elephant. ($= N_1\text{-}V\text{-}N_2\text{-}V\text{-}N_3$)

Another widely discussed strategy that relies on the surface order of linguistic units is what is often called the anti-interruption strategy. For example, Slobin 1973 argued that such a strategy, whereby the interruption of linguistic units is avoided, underlies findings that sentence-final relatives in English, as in 2a, are acquired before center-embedded ones, as in 2b.

2a. I met a man who was sick.
 b. The man who was sick went home.

Much of the Japanese first language acquisition literature has also focused on strategies, especially that involving relative clause acquisition. For example, researchers such as Harada, Uyeno, Hayashibe, and Yamada 1976, Hakuta 1981, and several others have argued for the equivalent of the English NVN strategy, i.e. an NNV strategy for Japanese. A common result in these studies was for children to mistakenly interpret the initial NNV sequence of center-embedding relative clause structures such as those shown in 3c and 3d as one sentential unit; thus, for example, in 3c children would act out a bear jumping over a dog instead of a rabbit.[2]

3a. SS/SOV: [ø Usagi-san o taosita]   inu-san ga kuma-san o tobikoeta.
 (LB)   rabbit   knocked-down   dog   bear   jumped over
        'The dog that knocked down the rabbit jumped over the bear.'

 b. SO/SOV: [Kirin-san ga ø tataita] zoo-san ga uma-san o taosita.
 (LB)   giraffe   hit   elephant   horse   knocked down
        'The elephant that the giraffe hit knocked down the horse.'

---

[2]In abbreviations denoting Japanese relative clause types as well, the first letter designates the role of the NP head in the matrix clause and the second letter the role of the gap inside the relative clause.

Please note that the particles *wa*, *ga*, and *o* are left unglossed in this paper. They are topic, nominative, and accusative particles respectively.

c. OS/SOV: **Kuma-san ga [ø inu-san o tobikoeta]   usagi-san o taosita.**
    (CE)   bear   dog   jumped over   rabbit   knocked-down
                'The bear knocked down the rabbit that jumped over the deer.'

d. OO/SOV: **Kirin-san ga [zoo-san ga ø tataita] inu-san o tobikoeta.**
    (CE)   giraffe   elephant   hit   dog   jumped over
                'The giraffe jumped over the dog that the elephant hit.'

Thus, while the NVN strategy in English was argued to help children give correct semantic interpretations to at least the initial portions of certain types of relative clauses, the NNV strategy in Japanese has been argued to account for children's "garden-path" misinterpretations of center-embedded relatives.

Poor performance on center-embedded relative clauses has also been attributed at least partially to an anti-interruption strategy by several researchers (e.g. K. Harada 1976 and Asano 1979). And Clancy, Lee, and Zoh 1986 have provided evidence that a variety of processing strategies may work additively in children's treatment of relative clause structures not only in Japanese but in English and Korean as well.

A common result in many of the Japanese relative clause studies is the overall low success rate found. For example, Harada et al. and Asano found 3 and 4 year old children performing with a success rate of nearly 0% for most relative clause types, and Hakuta found the success rate of even 5 and 6 year olds to be less than 50% for most types.

1.2 Linguistic Background for Current Study

The apparent dependence of young Japanese children on surface phenomena like word order, their propensity to garden-path misinterpretations of many relative clause structures, and their overall low performance in previous experiments leaves open the question of whether children have the competence to access the underlying bracketing and configuration required for such structures. At the same time, the adult Japanese grammar itself has often been characterized as having a possibly "flatter" syntactic structure than languages like English. Properties in Japanese such as relatively free word order, frequent null pronouns, and a rich case system have provided support for setting this language on the so-called "non-configurational" side of a possible configurationality parameter posited, for example, by Hale 1980. If Japanese is less configurational than some other languages, it could mean that Japanese children need less of a sensitivity to abstract configuration. On the other hand, more recent literature (e.g. works by Saito 1985, Hoji 1985, and Whitman 1982) has provided evidence for characterizing Japanese with more configurational properties, for example the presence of a VP, and NP movement.

The current study set out to explore whether the use of surface strategies previously found in Japanese relative clause acquisition studies was indicative of a lack of grammatical competence. Specifically, this study questioned whether young children have any knowledge of the grammatical structure of relative clauses, and whether they can distinguish these from other grammatical structures such as *kara* 'because' and *-te* '...ing' or '...and'. As the examples in 4 show, sentences that contain these structures can look very similar on the surface in terms of the concatenation of nouns, verbs, and particles.

4a.[ø$_i$ E   o kakiowatta   kodomo$_i$] wa kureyon o simatta.
    picture   draw-finished   child   crayon   put away
    'The child$_i$ who ø$_i$ finished drawing the picture put away the crayons.'

b.[ø$_i$ E   o kakiowatta] kara   kodomo$_i$ wa kureyon o simatta.
    picture   draw-finished because   child   crayon   put away
    'Because ø finished drawing the picture, the child$_i$ put away the crayons.'

c.[ø$_i$ E   o kakiowatte]   kodomo$_i$ wa kureyon o simatta.
    picture   draw-finishing child   crayon   put away
    'ø Finishing drawing the picture, the child$_i$ put away the crayons.'

Furthermore, all these structures involve sentential embedding, all can contain null backward anaphora, and, as shown in 5, all allow gaps to have non-subject roles.

5a.[Otoosan ga ø$_i$ otosita] tokee$_i$ wa dame ni natta.
    father   dropped watch   bad   became
    'The watch that (the) father dropped became bad/broke.'

b.[Otoosan ga ø$_i$ otosita   kara]   tokee$_i$ wa dame ni natta.
    father   dropped because watch   bad   became
    'Because (the) father dropped (it), the watch broke.'

c.[Otoosan ga ø$_i$ otosite] tokee$_i$ wa dame ni natta.
    father   dropping watch   bad   became
    '(The) father dropping it, the watch broke.'

However, besides semantic differences, there are of course several basic grammatical differences among these structures. Only the relative clause forms a constituent with the NP it precedes, and generally requires that there be an anaphoric relation, whereby a null is bound to an NP head, forming backward anaphora. *Kara* clause structures need not contain any anaphoric relation, and when a *kara* clause does contain a null it is not bound but free; as 6 shows, given the proper context, a null in an embedded *kara* clause may refer to an NP completely outside the sentence, whether the *kara* clause is left-branching as in 6b or center-embedded as in 6c.

6a. SPEAKER 1: **Taroo$_i$ wa yakyuu ga zyoozu de   ii desu nee.**
       baseball   skillful being good
   'It's nice that Taro is good at baseball, isn't it.'

 b. SPEAKER 2's Response (LB): **Ee,[ø$_i$ kinoo   siai   ni katta kara]**
              yes yesterday game   at won because
              ryoosin ga totemo yorokonda no.
              parents   very delighted
   'Yes, because ø$_i$ won the game, his parents were completely delighted.'

 c. SPEAKER 2's Response (CE): **Ee, ryoosin wa [ø$_i$ kinoo siai ni katta**
              kara] totemo yorokonda.
   'Yes, (his) parents, because ø$_i$ won the game, were completely delighted.'

When *-te* clauses are left-branching they often pattern like *kara* clauses, but when they are center-embedded they show several differences. For example, center-embedded *-te* clauses that contain an overt subject are clearly more marked then their left-branching counterparts and often unacceptable, as shown in 7. And when center-embedded *-te* clauses do contain subject nulls, they appear to necessarily co-refer to the matrix subject; compare the unacceptability of 8a for *-te* with the acceptability of 8b for *kara*.

7a.(?) **Sensee wa [Taroo ga e   o kakiowatte]   kureyon o simatta.**
   teacher   picture draw-finishing crayon   put away
      'The teacher, Taro finishing drawing the picture, put away the crayons.'

 b. ***Kodomo wa [okaasan ga ø$_i$ atatamete] miruku$_i$ o nonda.**
    child   mother   heating   milk   drank
    'The child, the mother heating (it) drank the milk.'

8a. ***Hanako wa [ø$_i$ hon o   yabutte] syoonen$_i$ o sikatta.**
          book   tearing boy   scolded
      'Hanako, ø$_i$ tearing the book, scolded the boy$_i$.'

 b. **Hanako wa [ø$_i$ hon o yabutta kara] syoonen$_i$ o sikatta.**
          book   tore because boy   scolded
      'Hanako, because he tore the book, scolded the boy.'

To account for these and other sorts of differences, it was suggested in Snyder 1987 that while both left-branching and center-embedded *kara* clauses may be Chomsky-adjoined outside the matrix sentence (the center-embedding structure is shown in 9), the most basic structure for center-embedded *-te* clauses may involve embedding under the matrix S, possibly under the VP, as shown in 10.[3] Subject gaps may then be in a control domain as defined by Huang 1986.[4]

9.

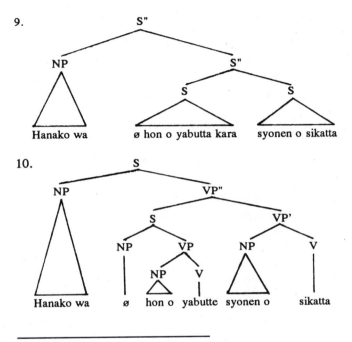

10.

---

[3] See Snyder 1987 for a more detailed analysis.

[4] Huang's definition is as follows:
   α is the control domain of ß iff
a. α is the lowest cyclic node (S or NP) that contains ß
   or the minimal maximal category containing ß, and
b. α contains a SUBJECT accessible to ß.

SUBJECT: The SUBJECT of a clause is $[AGR_i,S]$ if there is one,
   otherwise $[NP_i,S]$ or $[NP_i,NP]$ (where [X,Y] means "the X immediately
   dominated by Y" (modulo such nodes as INFL and AUX)). (van
   Riemsdijk and Williams 1986)

Accessibility: α is accessible to ß if and only if α c-commands ß and the
   assignment of the index of α to ß does not lead to a violation of the i-
   within-i Condition. (van Riemsdijk and Williams 1986)

i-within-i Condition: $*[_r \ldots \delta \ldots]_r$ where r and δ have the same
   index (van Riemsdijk and Williams 1986)

2. Current Acquisition Experiment
2.1 Methods

The current study used an elicited imitation task to test 40 monolingual Japanese children aged 3 1/2 to 4 1/2 on sentences containing *relative clause*, *kara*, or *-te* embedding.[5] The test sentences were designed to contain just two nouns and two verbs each, so that they all comprised NVNV surface concatenations. It was hypothesized that if young children are not sensitive to grammatical factors that go beyond the surface level, and if they generally depend only on surface strategies to map linguistic data to meaning, then they should treat *relative clause*, *kara*, and *-te* structures similarly, both in terms of the amount of correct responses and the types of errors made.

Three analyses were performed in this study. In Analysis I, eight *relative clause* and *kara* sentence types were considered according to the factors of *Subordination Type* (i.e. *relative clause* or *kara*), *Embedding Position/ Matrix Role of the Antecedent* (*left-branching* with *subject antecedent* or *center-embedding* with *object antecedent*), and *Gap Role* (*subject* or *object*). Examples of the test sentences are shown in Table 1.[6] So that *kara* and

---

[5]See Lust, Chien, and Flynn 1987 for extensive evidence that the elicited imitation method does not involve rote repetition of the stimulus sentence but rather a reconstruction of the stimulus according to the child's own grammar.

[6]Table 1 shows Battery A sentences only. Battery B sentences were as follows (numbers correspond to sentence types in Table 1):

1b. [φ Okasi o mituketa] oniisan wa yorokonda.
    candy   found   brother   became glad
    'The older brother who found the candy became glad'

2b. [Otoosan ga φ tukutta] kikai wa kowareta.
    father   made machine   broke (Vi)
    'The machine which the father made broke'

3b. [φ Saihu o otosita kara] tomodati wa komatta.
    wallet   dropped because friend   got-troubled
    'Because (he) dropped the wallet, the friend became troubled'

4b. [Syasyoo ga φ osita kara]   basu wa ugoita.
    driver   pushed because bus   moved
    'Because the driver pushed (it), the bus moved'

5b. Obaasan wa [φ yabuketa] zookin o suteta.
    grandmother   tore (Vi)   rag   threw-away
    'The grandmother threw away the rag which tore'

6b. Sensee wa [φ φ aratta] osara o simatta.
    teacher   washed dish   put-away
    'The teacher put away the dishes (she) washed'

7b. Obasan wa [φ nureta kara] yoohuku o hosita.
    aunt   got wet because clothes   hung-up
    'The aunt, because (they) got wet, hung the clothes (out to dry)'

8b. Kodomo wa [φ φ nageta kara] omotya o kowasita.
    child   threw because toy   broke (Vi)
    'The child, because (he) threw (it), broke the toy'

relative clause sentence types would maximally resemble one another on the surface, in all cases the subordinate clause immediately preceded the matrix NP that served as an antecedent for the embedded gap, producing backward anaphora. Since the design maintained SOV word order, there was necessarily a confounding of *Embedding Position* and *Matrix Role of the Antecedent*. Also, in order to maintain the NVNV pattern, the OO sentence types actually contained two nulls, one referring to the matrix topic, and one to the object, as shown in sentences 6 and 8 in Table 1.[7]

		SS	1.[φ **Tokee o nusunda**] <u>**tomodati**</u> **wa kakureta.** watch stole friend hid 'The friend who stole the watch hid (Intrans)'
	RC		
		SO	2.[**Okaasan ga** φ **yaita**] <u>**sakana**</u> **wa kogeta.** mother grilled fish got burned 'The fish which the mother grilled got burned'
LB			
		SS	3.[φ **Isi o hakonda kara**] <u>**oneesan**</u> **wa tukareta.** stone carried because sister tired 'Because (she) carried a stone, the older sister got tired'
	KARA		
		SO	4.[**Oniisan ga** φ **tataita kara**] <u>**garasu**</u> **wa wareta.** brother hit because glass broke 'Because the older-brother hit (it), the glass broke'
		OS	5. **Obasan wa** [φ **nokotta**] <u>**sinbun**</u> **o moyasita.** aunt remained(Vt) newspaper burned 'The aunt burned the newspapers which were left over'
	RC		
		OO	6. **Syasyoo wa** [φ φ **atumeta**] <u>**okane o**</u> **kazoeta.** conductor gathered money counted 'The conductor counted the money which (he) collected'
CE			
		OS	7. **Ozisan wa** [φ **yogoreta kara**] <u>**kutu**</u> **o migaita.** uncle dirty(Vi) because shoes polished 'The uncle, because (they) got dirty, polished the shoes'
	KARA		
		OO	8. **Sensee wa** [φ φ **yogosita kara**] <u>**tukue**</u> **o huita.** teacher dirty(Vt) because desk wiped 'The teacher, because (he) made (it) dirty, wiped the desk'

Table 1: Analyses I Test Sentences (Battery A)

The second analysis added four more sentence types, this time with embedded *-te* clauses, as shown in Table 2. As with the first analysis, these

---

[7]Please note that for *kara* and *-te* clauses also, abbreviations such as SS, SO, etc. designate first the role of the NP antecedent and second the role of the gap in the embedded clause.

sentences varied according to the factors of *Embedding Position* (*left-branching* or *center-embedding*) and *Gap Role* (*subject* or *object*). However, the *-te* sentences differed from the sentences of Analysis I in that the *center-embedding subject-gap* sentence type (sentence 11 in Table 2) had a *subject* antecedent rather than an *object* antecedent, and consequently entailed forward anaphora. This was done because a *-te* sentence parallel to the center-embedding OS *relative clause* and *kara* structures was considered ungrammatical by Japanese adults.

		9a. [φ **Kaban o motte**] <u>**otoosan**</u> **wa dekaketa.** case holding father went out 'Holding the briefcase, the father went out'
	SS	
		b. [φ **Ningyoo o nakusite**] <u>**oneesan**</u> **wa naita.** doll losing sister cried 'Having lost the doll, the older sister cried.'
LB		
		10a. [**Kodomo ga** φ **sodatete**] <u>**tyuurippu**</u> **wa saita.** child raising(Vt) tulip bloomed 'The child raising (them), the tulips bloomed'
	SO	
		b. [**Akatyan ga** φ **kette**] <u>**booru**</u> **wa korogatta.** baby kicking ball rolled 'The baby having kicked (it), the ball rolled'

		11a. <u>**Oziisan**</u> **wa** [φ **suwatte**] **manga o yonda.** grandfather sitting comics read 'The grandfather, having sat down, read the comics'
	SS (FWD. ANPH.)	b. <u>**Okaasan**</u> **wa** [φ **tatte**] **kaaten o simeta.** mother standing curtains closed 'The mother, having stood up, closed the curtains'
CE		
		12a. **Obaasan** **wa** [φ φ **atatamete**] <u>**miruku**</u> **o nonda.** grandmother warming(Vt) milk drank 'The grandmother, having heated (it), drank the milk'
	OO	
		b. **Ozisan wa** [φ φ **yudete**] <u>**oudon**</u> **o tabeta.** uncle boiling(Vt) noodles ate 'The uncle, having boiled (them), ate the noodles'

Table 2: Analyses II Test Sentences (Batteries A and B)

A third analysis which added one more sentence type for *kara* was also included in this study. This will be briefly mentioned below in discussing the results.

There were two tokens for each sentence type, making a total of 26 sentences, presented to each child in random order in two batteries by a native speaker of Japanese.[8]

2.2 Results
2.2.1 Analysis I

A first major result of this study was that *relative clause* structures did not elicit particularly poor performance. As Table 3 shows, more than 50% of the sentences with *relative clauses* were correctly imitated, in contrast to previous studies. Furthermore *relative clause* sentences elicited significantly better performance than *kara* clause sentences (T(87,432)=2.83, p=.0048).

Emb. Pos.	Ant.Role/ Gap Role	Relative Clause	Kara	Totals
LB	SS	1.075	1.100	ALL LB: 1.031
	SO	0.975	0.975	
CE	OS	1.175	0.500	ALL CE: 0.850
	OO	0.950	0.775	
Totals		1.044	0.838	0.941

Table 3: Mean Number of Correct Responses for Analyses 1[9]

Results of Analysis I did find *Embedding Position* to be significant, with *center-embedding* sentences eliciting significantly more errors than *left-branching* ones (T(87,432=2.49, p=.0131). Furthermore, error analysis showed that children changed center-embedding to left-branching, as exemplified in 11 below, more than four times as often as they made the opposite type of error.[10]

---

[8]The sentence types were tested by a 3-way ANOVA which took *Group*, *Subject nested within Group*, and *Sentence Type* as main effects. Various interactions were also tested. (See Snyder 1987 for more detailed explanation of methods and hypotheses, and more detailed analysis of results). For all tests the level of significance was p < .01.

[9]As there were 2 tokens for each sentence type, the maximum possible score was 2.

[10]Note that letters E and C indicate what the experimenter and child said respectively.

11.E: <u>Sensee_i wa</u> [ø_i ø_j yogosita   kara]   tukue_j o huita.
teacher   made dirty because desk   wiped
'The teacher, because (she) got (it) dirty, wiped the desk.'

C: [ø ø yogosita kara] <u>sensee wa</u> tukue o huita.

An important result of Analysis I was a significant interaction between *Subordination Type* and *Embedding Position* $(T(87,432)=3.01, p=.0028)$. As Figure 1 suggests, *Embedding Position* was significant for *kara* $(T(87,432)=3.89, p=.0001)$, where it greatly depressed sentences with *center-embedding*, but it did not significantly affect *relative clause* sentences; in fact, *center-embedding relative clause* structures elicited a slightly higher number of correct responses.

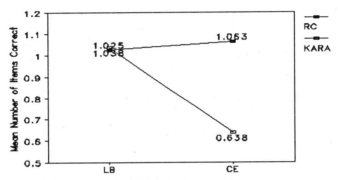

Figure 1: Interaction of *Subordination Type* and *Embedding Position*

Analysis I did not find *Gap Role* to be significant overall or within either *left-branching* or *center-embedding* sentences, or *relative clause* or *kara* sentences. Furthermore, *Gap Role* did not interact with *Subordination Type*.

A major result of Analysis I was that children distinguished *relative clause* and *kara* sentences in terms of anaphora errors. Anaphora errors consisted of cases where children elaborated gaps, as in 12, changed the direction of anaphora, as in 13, omitted the NP antecedent, as in 14, or made substitutions such that there was no longer any anaphoric relation, as in 15. As Table 4 shows, anaphora errors characterized nearly half the incorrect two-clause responses in Analysis I, but the great majority of these errors were in response to *kara* structures. Note that while such responses for *kara* were scored as incorrect since they deviated from the stimulus sentences, they are acceptable sentences in Japanese grammar. Furthermore, in at least one-third of the cases where children made anaphora errors in response to *relative clause* sentences, they replaced the *relative clause* structure with some other type of subordination.

Emb. Pos.	Ant.Role/ Gap Role	Relative Clause	Kara	Totals
LB	SS	12 {15.0} (57.1)	13 {16.3} (54.2)	ALL LB: 49 {15.3} (45.8)
	SO	6 { 7.5} (20.0)	18 {22.5} (56.3)	
CE	OS	2 { 2.5} (10.5)	31 {38.8} (86.1)	ALL CE: 55 {17.2} (50.9)
	OO	2 { 2.5} (14.3)	20 {25.0} (51.3)	
Totals		22 { 6.9} (26.2)	82 {25.6} (62.6)	104 {16.3} (48.4)

Table 4: Total Anaphora Errors for Analysis I[11]

12.E: **Oniisan ga ø tataita kara   garasu wa wareta.**
    brother   hit   because   glass   broke
    'Because the older brother hit it, the glass broke.'

   C: **Oniityan ga garasu o watta kara   garasu wa wareta.**
      brother   glass   hit because   glass   broke
      'Because the older brother hit the glass the glass broke.'

13.E: **Ozisan wa ø yogoreta kara   kutu o migaita.**
    uncle   got dirty because shoes   polished
    'The uncle, because they got dirty, polished the shoes.'

   C: **O-Oniisan wa kutu ga yogoreta kara ø migaita.**
      older brother   shoes got dirty because   polished
      'The older brother, because the shoes got dirty, polished them.'

14.E: **[ø₁ Saihu o otosita kara]   tomodati₁ wa komatta.**
       wallet   dropped because friend   got troubled
       'Because (he) dropped the wallet, the friend became troubled.'

   C: **[ø Saihu o otosita kara] ø komatta.**

---

[11]In this table and Table 6 below, unenclosed numbers represent the actual number of responses with such errors, numbers enclosed in curly brackets { } represent the percent of total responses, and numbers enclosed in brackets ( ) represent the percent of incorrect 2-clause responses per item.

15.E: **Sensee$_i$ wa [ø$_i$ ø$_j$ yogosita   kara]   tukue$_j$ o huita.**
   teacher   made dirty because desk   wiped
   'The teacher, because (he) made it dirty, wiped the desk.'

C: **...Ozisan wa [tukue nureta kara]   kutu o huita.**
   uncle   desk got wet because shoes   wiped
   'Uncle, because the desk got wet, wiped the shoes.'

In analyzing the source of the center-embedding problem, there was little evidence for "garden-path" type errors where the initial NV sequence of center-embedding sentences would be misanalyzed as one clausal unit. The sentence that would be most susceptible to such a false interpretation is the *center-embedding* OS. In examining responses to the OS *kara* sentences, there were only two cases that might suggest a garden-path interpretation, one shown in 16 and one where the child repeated just the first noun and verb. On the other hand, many errors provided evidence against garden-path interpretations. For example, about 75% of the incorrect 2-clause responses to OS *kara* sentences maintained center-embedding but contained anaphora direction change or elaboration as described earlier, providing evidence that children understood the embedding and intended grammatical relations. Furthermore, 85% of the incorrect 2-clause responses to the *center-embedding* OO *kara* sentence type also maintained center-embedding. For this sentence type as well, anaphora was a major source of difficulty. Nearly 30% of the 2-clause incorrect responses to these structures involved a change in anaphora, and over half the 2-clause errors involved a change in transitivity of the embedded verb or the matrix verb, suggesting a possible change in the grammatical role of either the gap or the NP antecedent, as shown in 17.

16.E: **Obasan wa ø$_i$ nureta   kara   yoohuku$_i$ o   hosita.**
   aunt   got wet because clothes   hung to dry
   'The aunt, because (they) got wet, hung the clothes out to dry.'

C: **Obasan wa nureta   kara   oyoohuku nureta.**
   aunt   got wet because clothes got wet
   'Because the aunt got wet the clothes got wet.'

17.E: **Sensee$_i$ wa [ø$_i$ ø$_j$ yogosita   kara]   tukue$_j$ o huita.**
   teacher   made dirty because desk   wiped
   'The teacher, because (she) got (it) dirty, wiped them desk.'

C: **Sensee wa yogoreta kara tukue o huita.**
   teacher   got dirty because desk   wiped
   'The teacher, because (it) got dirty, wiped the desk.'

2.2.2 Analysis II

Results of Analysis II found -*te* sentence types not to differ significantly from *relative clause* sentence types in terms of overall correct responses, but, like the *relative clause* structures, to elicit significantly better performance than *kara* structures (T(87,432)=4.98, p=.0001), as shown in Figure 2 below. Also like *relative clause* and unlike *kara*, *Embedding Position* was not found to be significant for -*te*. As shown in Table 5, *center-embedding* structures were not found to be particularly difficult and in fact elicited slightly better performance than *left-branching* structures. Furthermore, error analysis showed that nearly 70% of the 2-clause incorrect responses to *center-embedding* -*te* structures maintained center-embedding.

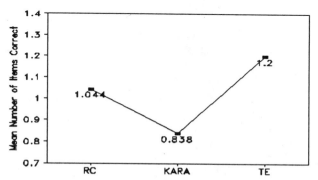

Figure 2: Mean Number of Correct Responses to Overall *RC* and *Kara* Sentence Types in Analyses I and -*Te* Sentence Types in Analyses II

Emb. Pos.	Ant.Role	Subject Gap	Object Gap	Totals
LB	S	1.375	0.850	1.113
CE	S/O	1.500	1.075	1.288
Totals		1.438	0.963	1.201

Table 5: Mean Number of Correct Responses for Analyses II

Unlike Analysis I for *relative clause* and *kara*, Analysis II did find *Gap Role* to be significant for -*te* (T(87,432)=4.62, p=.0001). There was no interaction between *Gap Role* and *Embedding Position*; as Figure 3 shows, *subject-gap* sentences elicited significantly better performance than *object-gap* sentences, both within *left-branching* and *center-embedding* conditions.

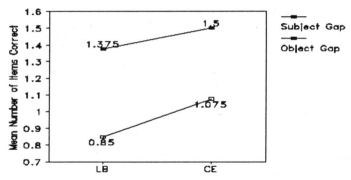

Figure 3: Mean Number of Correct Responses to *LB* and CE -Te
Sentences by *Gap Role* in Analyses II

Error analysis for -*te* structure responses also provided evidence that
children were distinguishing this structure from *relative clause* or *kara*
structures. For example, a comparison of Table 6 below with Table 4 above
shows that while anaphora errors for -*te* (e.g. elaborating gaps or dropping
NP antecedents) occurred with less frequency than they did for *kara*, they
occurred nearly twice as often as they did for *relative clauses*, suggesting
a sensitivity to the fact that anaphora in *relative clauses* is always bound and
backward while it is free for -*te* in certain positions.

Emb. Pos.	Ant.Role	Subject Gap	Object Gap	Totals
LB	S	10 {12.5} (45.5)	9 {11.3} (29.0)	19 {11.9}: (35.8)
CE	S/0	4 { 5.0} (33.3)	12 {15.0} (63.2)	16 {10.0}: (51.6)
Totals		14 { 8.8} (41.2)	21 {13.1} (42.0)	35 {10.9} (41.7)

Table 6: Total Anaphora Errors for Analysis II

Other errors provided evidence for a sensitivity to the possible control
structure of the center-embedding -*te* sentence type. For example, while
embedding change errors from both left-branching to center-embedding
structures and vice versa were found for three of the -*te* sentence types,
there was an interesting lack of such an error for *left-branching* SO
sentences, where such an error would entail producing an overt embedded
subject in a center-embedded -*te* clause (e.g., *Booru wa [akatyan ga ø kette]
korogatta*), something problematic in the adult grammar. Furthermore,

while object gaps were occasionally elaborated in both left-branching and center-embedding cases, and subject gaps occasionally elaborated in left-branching sentences, no such elaboration errors ever characterized the subject gaps in center-embedding -te sentences, again consistent with a possible control structure.

3. Summary and Discussion

The results of this study suggest first that children by age 3 do have at least a basic competence for S under NP embedding, and that the poor results found in many prior studies may have been due to other factors.[12] *Relative clause* embedding was not found to be more difficult than *kara* or -te embedding, and did not elicit particularly poor performance. Secondly, this study did not find center-embeddedness to replicate as a source of difficulty for *relative clause* structures, nor was it found to be problematic for -te structures. On the other hand, center-embedding was found to be a source of difficulty for *kara* structures. Error analysis suggested that a major factor in the difficulty of the center-embedding *kara* sentence type was the anaphora structure. This is further supported by a third analysis done in this study that considered an additional *kara* sentence type that was *center-embedding* but had a *subject* NP antecedent and *subject* gap, as shown in 18, and parallel to the -te sentence type 11 in Table 2. Remember that in Analysis I, the factors of *Embedding Position* and *Antecedent Role* were confounded for *relative clause* and *kara* structures. Analysis III results showed the additional *kara* sentence to elicit significantly superior performance to the *center-embedding* OS *kara* sentence of Analysis I ($T(87,432)=2.75$, $p=.0062$), but similar performance to the *left-branching* SS *kara* sentence type, as shown in Figure 4. This suggests that the center-embedding difficulty for *kara* in Analysis I was not independent of the grammatical role of the NP antecedent.

18. Analysis III *CE SS Kara* Sentence Type Sentences (Batteries A and B):

    a. **Akatyan wa [ø koronda kara]   hiza o surimuita.**
       baby   fell   because knee   scraped
       'The baby, because (he) fell, scraped his knees'

    b. **Ojiisan   wa [ø isoida kara]   kasa   o wasureta.**
       grandfather   hurried because umbrella   forgot
       'The grandfather, because (he) hurried, forgot the umbrella'

---

[12]Note that sentences in many previous studies contained three animate nouns and reversible actions and may have presented special memory load demands.

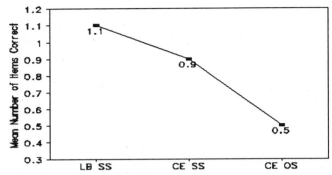

Figure 4: Mean Number of Correct Responses to *LB SS*, *CE SS*, and *CE OS Kara* Sentence Types in Analyses I and III

Further research is necessary to examine more precisely the nature of the center-embedding effect for *kara* found in this study, but the fact that such an effect was not found for the other structures tested suggests it is modulated by grammatical configuration.

Additional evidence that children distinguished the differing types of grammatical structures comes from the fact that *Gap Role* was significant only for *-te*, whereby sentences with *subject* gaps were found to be easier than those with *object* gaps. This may suggest that children distinguish a subject antecedent/subject gap anaphoric relation in *-te* as unmarked in comparison to other types of anaphora, and is consistent with the suggestion that the most basic configuration for *-te* clauses may be under the VP in a control structure.

It is important to note that while the results of the current study do not provide evidence for the use of strategies, this does not deny that children may have indeed used strategies in other experiments or that they may sometimes use them in non-test situations. However, the present study suggests that even if strategies are sometimes used, they do not exhaust the child's linguistic competence. It does not appear that Japanese children analyze all sentences as flat structures, in spite of the fact that Japanese can be argued to have many non-configurational properties. It suggests that while 3 and 4 year old children may not have the adult control for the structures tested, the nature of their competence already includes a sensitivity to abstract configurational hierarchy and various types of anaphoric relations which may be the consequence of configurational structure.

References

Asano, A. 1979. On strategies for processing Japanese relative clauses. Attempts in linguistics and literature: papers in honor of Kazuko Inoue, vol. 6. 15-26. Society of Linguistics and Literature, International Christian University,

Bever, T.G. 1970. The cognitive basis for linguistic structures. Cognition and the development of language, ed. by J.R. Hayes. New York: Wiley.

Clancy, P.M., H. Lee, and M.-H. Zoh. 1986. Processing strategies in the acquisition of relative clauses: universal principles and language-specific realizations. Unpublished manuscript. University of Southern California and Seoul National University.

de Villiers, J. G., H. B. Tager Flusberg, K. Hakuta, and M. Cohen. 1979. Children's comprehension of relative clauses. Journal of Psycholinguistic Research 8:5. 499-518.

Hakuta,K. 1981. Grammatical description versus configurational arrangement in language acquisition: the case of relative clauses in Japanese. Cognition 9. 197-236.

Hale, K. 1980. Remarks on Japanese phrase structure: comments on the papers on Japanese syntax. Theoretical issues in Japanese linguistics, MIT Working Papers in Linguistics, vol. 2, ed. by Y. Otsu and K. Farmer.

Harada, K. 1976. Acquisition of relative clauses: a case study on a two-year-old. Annual Reports 1. Division of Languages, International Christian University.

Harada, S.I., T. Uyeno, H. Hayashibe, and H. Yamada. 1976. On the development of perceptual strategies in children: a case study on the Japanese child's comprehension of the relative clause constructions. Annual Bulletin No. 10. 199-224. Research Institute of Logopedics and Phoniatrics, University of Tokyo.

Hoji, H. 1985. Logical form constraints and configurational structures in Japanese. Doctoral dissertation. University of Washington.

Huang, C.-T. J. 1986. Pro-Drop in Chinese: a generalized control approach. Unpublished manuscript. Cornell University.

Lust, B., Y-C Chien, and S. Flynn. 1987. What children know: a comparison of methods in the study of the acquisition of anaphora. Studies in the acquisition of anaphora, vol. 2, Applying the constraints, ed. by B. Lust. Dordrecht: Reidel Press.

Reimsdijk, H. van, and E. Williams. 1986. Introduction to the theory of grammar. Cambridge: MIT Press.

Saito, M. 1985. Some asymmetries in Japanese and their theoretical implications. Doctoral dissertation. MIT.

Slobin, D.I. 1973. Cognitive prerequisites for the development of grammar. Studies of child language development, ed. by C.A. Ferguson and D.I. Slobin. 175-208. New York: Holt, Rinehart and Winston, Inc.

Smith, M.D. 1974. Relative clause formation between 29-36 months: a preliminary report. Papers and reports on child language development 8. 104-110. Committee on Linguistics, Stanford University.

Snyder, W. 1987. Grammatical and processing factors in the first language acquisition of complex structures in Japanese. Doctoral Dissertation. Cornell University.

Whitman, J. 1982. Configurationality parameters. Unpublished manuscript. Harvard University.

Part II

Syntax and Semantics

Adjuncts and Event Argument in Restructuring

NATSUKO TSUJIMURA

Indiana University

0. Introduction

Restructuring phenomena have been viewed as resulting from a rule that changes a bi-clausal structure to a mono-clausal structure. The rule is often triggered by a particular group of verbs such as motion verbs. Restructuring has been claimed to exist in various languages including Japanese. In Japanese, for instance, Miyagawa (1986) and Matsumoto (1991) show that purpose clauses and gerundive clauses as in (1-2) can create Restructuring environments.[1]

---

[1]Although both Miyagawa (1986) and Matsumoto (1991) discuss Restructuring phenomena in Japanese, Miyagawa adopts a transformational approach while Matsumoto supports a lexical analysis.

(1)   Taroo-ga hon-o   kai-NI   itta.
         -Nom book-Acc buy-purpose went
      'Taro went to buy books.'
(2)   Taroo-ga hon-o   kat-TE   kita.
         -Nom book-Acc buy-gerund came
      'Taro (came back, having) bought books.'

In both constructions the matrix verbs are typically
motion verbs.[2] In (1) -NI is a purpose morpheme
suffixed to a verbal stem, and -TE in (2) is the
gerundive suffix that takes a verbal root.

   Restructuring phenomena in purpose clauses and
gerundive clauses are observed with negative polarity
binding and the Nominative Case assignment on the
object associated with the potential morpheme (rar)e.
Negative polarity items like sika must be bound by
negation within the same clause in order to be
interpreted as 'only'. This is shown in (3-4).

(3)   Taroo-ga   sakana-sika tabe-nai.
         -Nom fish-SIKA   eat-NEG
      'Taro eats only fish.'
(4) *Hanako-ga [Taroo-ga   sakana-sika tabe-ru]-
         -Nom   -Nom fish-SIKA   eat-nonpast-
      to iw-ana-katta.
      COMP say-NEG-past
      'Hanako said that Taro eats only fish.'

When sika is not bound clause-internally as in (4),
the sentence is ungrammatical. Given the condition
that negative polarity items must be bound clause-
internally, we would expect that the purpose clause
and gerundive clause in (5-6) would be ill-formed if
we analyze them as bi-clausal.

---

[2]Matrix verbs in gerundive clauses also include
giving/receiving verbs such as ageru 'give' and morau
'receive', but in this paper I will restrict the
discussion to the gerundive clauses with motion verbs
as their matrix verbs.

(5) Taroo-ga   Kanda-ni   [hon-_sika_ kai-NI]   ik-
         -Nom   -to   book-SIKA buy-purpose   go-
     ana-katta.
     NEG-past
     'Taro went to Kanda to buy only books.'

(6) Taroo-ga [nihon-no   eiga-_sika_ mi-TE]   ko-
         -Nom   Japan-Gen movie-SIKA see-gerund come-
     _na_-katta.
     NEG-past
     'Taro (came back, having) seen only a Japanese
     movie.'

Consequently, it can be concluded that the grammaticality of these sentences suggests the mono-clausal status of the constructions.

Miyagawa and Matsumoto demonstrate the same point in regard to the Nominative Case assignment involved in the potential morpheme _(rar)e_. When the potential morpheme _(rar)e_ is suffixed to a verb, the direct object of the verb can either be marked with Nominative Case -_ga_ or Accusative Case -_o_. However, the Nominative Case is assigned to the direct object only when the complex of the verb and the potential morpheme is clausemate with the direct object. This is shown in (7-10).

(7) Taroo-ga tyuukaryoori-o   umaku tukuru.
         -Nom Chinese food-Acc well make
     'Taro cooks Chinese food well.'

(8) Taroo-ga tyuukaryoori-o/_ga_   umaku tukur-
         -Nom Chinese food-Acc/Nom well make-
     _e_-ru.
     potential-nonpast
     'Taro can cook Chinese food well.'

(9) Tanakasan-ni   [PRO tyuukaryoori-o   asita
     Mr. Tanaka-Dat   Chinese food-Acc tomorrow
     tukuru ka] kik-_e_-masu   ka?
     make   Q   ask-potential-nonpast   Q
     'Can you ask Mr. Tanaka if he will cook Chinese
     food tomorrow?'

(10) *Tanakasan-ni   [PRO tyuukaryoori-_ga_ asita
      Mr. Tanaka-Dat   Chinese food-Nom tomorrow

> tukuru ka] kik-<u>e</u>-masu   ka?
> make   Q   ask-potential-nonpast Q
> 'Can you ask Mr. Tanaka if he will cook Chinese
> food tomorrow?'

In (10) the Nominative Case and the potential morpheme are not within the same clause, which leads to the ungrammaticality. Given the clausemate condition on the Nominative Case assignment, it would be predicted that the purpose clause and gerundive clause in (11-12) are ill-formed since the condition is violated.

(11)   Tanakasan-no   musuko-wa hitoride [eiga-
       Mr. Tanaka-Gen son-Top   alone   movie
       o/<u>ga</u>   mi-NI]   ik-<u>e</u>-masu.
       Acc/Nom see-purpose go-potential-nonpast
       'Mr. Tanaka's son can go see a movie alone.'
(12)   Tanakasan-no   musuko-wa   hitoride [eiga-
       Mr. Tanaka-Gen son-top   alone   movie-
       o/<u>ga</u> mi-TE]   ko-<u>re</u>-ru   no?
       Acc/Nom see-gerund come-potential-nonpast Q
       'Can Mr. Tanaka's son go see a movie alone (and
       come back)?'

Contrary to the prediction, the sentences in (11) and (12) are grammatical. This suggests that they are mono-clausal.

     In this paper I shall show that despite the similarities we have observed above in Restructuring environments between purpose clauses and gerundive clauses, they demonstrate quite different behavior in selection of adjuncts. I will claim that the difference results from the distribution of event argument. I will further show that the they are different in their syntactic behavior, and claim that the difference can be attributed to argument/non-argument status of the two clause types.

1. Adjunct Selection

While we have observed that purpose clauses and gerundive clauses exhibit similar behavior with respect to Restructuring phenomena, there is a striking difference between these two clause types in their ways of selecting adjuncts. The generalization to be captured is that sentences with purpose clauses can select only the adjuncts that modify the matrix verb, while those with gerundive clauses allow only the adjuncts modifying the embedded verb. We shall look at the validity of this generalization with respect to (i) locative/directional adjuncts, (ii) comitative adjuncts, (iii) instrumental adjuncts, and (iv) depictive predicates.

First, in a sentence with a purpose clause, a locative/directional phrase can modify the matrix verb, but it cannot modify the embedded verb. Consider (13).

(13) a. Taroo-ga tosyokan-e manga-sika   kari-
                 -Nom library-to comic book-SIKA borrow-
         ni   ik-ana-katta.
         purpose go-NEG-past

         'Taro went to the library to borrow only comic books.'

     b. *Taroo-ga tosyokan-de manga-sika
                 -Nom library-at comic book-SIKA
         kari-ni   ik-ana-katta.
         borrow-purpose go-NEG-past
         'Taro went to borrow only comic books at the library.'

Both sentences in (13) are Restructured sentences, as indicated by the sika...nai construction, which was considered as triggering a Restructuring environment. The directional phrase in (13a) tosyokan-e 'to the library' modifies the matrix verb, while the locative phrase in (13b) tosyokan-de 'at the library' is intended to modify the embedded verb. As the ungrammatical status of (13b) suggests, locative/directional adjuncts are licensed only by the matrix verb in a sentence with a purpose clause.

The situation is opposite in sentences with gerundive clauses. With gerundive clauses, locative/directional phrases can modify the embedded verb but not the matrix verb. This is illustrated by (14).

(14) a. Taroo-ga <u>tosyokan-de</u> manga-sika
           -Nom library-at comic book-SIKA
         kari-te   ko-na-katta.
         borrow-gerund come-NEG-past
         'Taro came back, having borrowed only comic
         books at the library.'
     b. *Taroo-ga <u>tosyokan-kara</u> manga-sika
           -Nom library-from comic book-SIKA
         kari-te   ko-na-katta.
         borrow-gerund come-NEG-past
         'Taro came back from the library, having
         borrowed only comic books.'

The polarity binding construction with <u>sika...nai</u> suggests that the sentences in (14) are in the Restructuring environment. In (14a) the locative phrase <u>tosyokan-de</u> 'at the library' modifies the embedded verb, and the sentence is grammatical. By contrast, the directional phrase in (14b), <u>tosyokan-kara</u> 'from the library' is intended to modify the matrix verb, rather than the embedded verb, but the sentence is ill-formed. Hence, with gerundive clauses, locative/directional adjuncts are licensed only by the embedded verb.

Second, the selection of comitative phrases points toward the same generalization. (15) and (16) contain a purpose clause and a gerundive clause, respectively, and each has a comitative phrase.

(15) Taroo-ga (Tookyoo-e) hon-sika <u>Hanako-to</u>
          -Nom (Tokyo-to) book-SIKA   -with
       kai-ni   ik-ana-katta.
       buy-purpose go-NEG-past
       'Taro went (to Tokyo) to buy only books with
       Hanako.'

(16) Taroo-ga susi-sika Hanako-to   tabe-te
       -Nom sushi-SIKA   -with eat-gerund
      ko-na-katta.
      come-NEG-past
      'Taro (came back, having) eaten only sushi with
      Hanako.'

The comitative phrase in (15), Hanako-to 'with Hanako', is interpreted as "go and buy books with Hanako", but is never construed as "Taro went to Tokyo alone and bought books with Hanako (after meeting with her somewhere, for example)." The comitative phrase, then, must have its scope over the event of going. The comitative phrase in (16), on the other hand, is interpreted such that Taro ate sushi with Hanako, but crucially it cannot be construed as Taro came back with Hanako. That is, in (16) the comitative phrase modifies only the embedded VP. Hence, comitative adjuncts are licensed by the matrix verb in a sentence with a purpose clause while they are licensed by the embedded verb in a sentence with a gerundive clause.

Third, the same generalization holds for the interpretation of instrumental adjuncts as well. Consider the sentence with a purpose clause in (17) and the sentence with a gerundive clause in (18).

(17) Taroo-ga Hanako-no megana-sika zitensya-de
          -Nom   -Gen glasses-SIKA bicycle-with
      kowasi-ni   ik-ana-katta.
      break-purpose go-NEG-past
      'Taro went to break only Hanako's glasses
      (??)with a bicycle/by bicycle.'
(18) Taroo-ga Hanako-no megane-sika zitensya-de
          -Nom   -Gen glasses-SIKA bicycle-with
      kowasi-te   ko-na-katta.
      break-gerund come-NEG-past
      'Taro (came back, having) broken Hanako's
      glasses with a bicycle.'
      '*Taro (came back by bicycle, having) broken
      Hanako's glasses.'

The instrumental phrase <u>zitensya-de</u> 'by bicycle' in (17) is interpreted as modifying the matrix verb, whereby a bicycle is used as a transportational device. In (18), by contrast, the instrumental adjunct can only modify the embedded verb, so that the bicycle is interpreted as being an instrument used to break Hanako's glasses rather than as a transportational device. Again, we can observe that with a purpose clause, an instrumental adjunct is licensed by the matrix verb, while with a gerundive clause, it is licensed by the embedded verb.

Finally, the selection of secondary depictive predicates in Restructuring environments is consistent with the generalization under discussion. Contrast (19) and (20).

(19)   Taroo-ga   Ziroo-sika <u>hadakade</u> naguri-ni   ik-
          -Nom   -SIKA naked   hit-purpose go-
       ana-katta.
       NEG-past
       'Taro went naked to hit only Ziro.'
(20)   Taro-ga   Ziroo-sika <u>hadakade</u> nagut-te   ko-
          -Nom   -SIKA naked   hit-gerund come-
       na-katta.
       NEG-past
       'Taro (came back, having) hit Ziro naked.'

In the sentences with a purpose clause in (19), the secondary depictive predicate <u>hadakade</u> 'naked' can relate only to the matrix verb: that is, the person who is naked in (19) is Taro, rather than Ziro. In the sentence with a gerundive clause in (20), on the other hand, the depictive phrase can only modify the embedded object, namely, Ziro. So, the person who was naked is Ziro rather than Taro in (20). This suggests that object-oriented depictives can cooccur with gerundive clauses but not with purpose clauses.

To summarize so far, we have observed an interesting contrast between the two Restructuring environments, purpose clauses and gerundive clauses. The data from locative/directional, comitative, and instrumental adjuncts all demonstrate that these adjuncts can relate only to the matrix verb with purpose clauses while they can relate only to the embedded verb with gerundive clauses. Furthermore, purpose clauses and gerundive clauses are different in that purpose clauses disallow object-oriented depictive predicates while gerundive clauses allow them.

2. Event Argument

Given these observations about adjunct selection, I will claim that the different behavior manifested between purpose clauses and gerundive clauses has to do with the temporal properties associated with the two clauses, which ultimately lead to the difference in the distribution of event argument.

Recall, first, that object-oriented depictive predicates can appear in gerundive clauses but not in purpose clauses. This was shown in (19-20). The secondary depictive predicate <u>hadakade</u> 'naked' can only take the subject, Taro, as its antecedent in (19), while the object is the antecedent of the depictive in (20). Upon closer examination, furthermore, this contrast shows up even when the sentences do not contain anything that forces Restructuring, such as the presence of the negative polarity item like the <u>sika...nai</u> sequence. This is shown in (21-22).

(21) Taroo-ga Ziroo-o <u>hadakade</u> naguri-ni itta.
       -Nom   -Acc naked   hit-purpose went
     'Taro went to hit Ziro naked.'
(22) Taroo-ga Ziroo-o <u>hadakade</u> nagut-te   kita.
       -Nom   -Acc naked   hit-gerund came
     'Taro (came back, after having) hit Ziro
     naked.'

In (21) the depictive <u>hadakade</u> 'naked' is predicated of the subject, Taro, and can never be interpreted with the object, Ziro. The interpretation in which the object Ziro is the antecedent of the depictive is available in (22). Hence, even in the absence of any factors that generate Restructuring as in (21-22), an object-oriented depictive is still not possible in purpose clauses while it is allowed in gerundive clauses. This indicates that a potential difference between the two structures to which this contrast can be attributed is an inherent difference between the purpose morpheme -ni and the gerundive suffix -te. A possible inherent property that separates the two appears to be the temporal properties that accompany them. The gerundive morpheme -te is presumably specified as [-Tense] for its infinitival property. By contrast, -ni is not specified for the feature [Tense]: it only bears aspectual property of irrealis, as Iida (1987) points out. Whatever the exact nature of the temporal/aspectual feature specification is, it seems reasonable to posit that such a feature specification is playing a crucial role in distinguishing the behavior of depictives in (21) and (22). That is, assuming that object-oriented depictives must be governed by the feature [Tense], the interpretation of the depictives in (21) and (22) has a straightforward explanation. In (21) the purpose morpheme does not bear the feature [Tense], and thus, it cannot govern the object-oriented depictive. In (22), by contrast, the gerundive suffix is specified for [-Tense], which governs the depictive phrase, and therefore, the depictive can be predicated of the object.

Turning to the different selectional properties for adjuncts observed in purpose clauses and gerundive clauses, I contend that feature specification of [tense] is again relevant. Let us suppose that the feature [Tense] sanctions an event argument, and that the event argument in turn licenses adjuncts. Given this assumption, the distribution of adjuncts in purpose sentences and gerundive sentences is explained as follows. In the case of sentences with purpose clauses, the purpose morpheme is not specified for [Tense], and thus, it cannot sanction an event argument. This, in turn, means that adjuncts are not licensed internal to the purpose clause, which is consistent with the data given above. The matrix verb, on the other hand, does bear the [+Tense] feature, as evidenced by the inflection on it. In the presence of this feature, the matrix clause can have an event argument, which enables adjuncts to be licensed. This is why in purpose constructions adjuncts are allowed only when they modify the matrix predicate.

In the case of sentences with gerundive clauses, the situation is opposite. The gerundive suffix bears the feature of [-Tense], which sanctions an event argument internal to the gerundive clause. The event argument within the gerundive clause, then, licenses adjuncts that modify the embedded verb. This property departs from the construction with purpose clauses, as we have just explained. Hence, gerundive clauses can have their own adjuncts internal to them. Notice, however, that the matrix clause is also specified as [+Tense], just as in the sentences with purpose clauses. Nevertheless, we have observed that the matrix clause that cooccurs with a gerundive clause cannot license adjuncts.

This situation with gerundive clauses is reminiscent of Italian Restructuring sentences, as analyzed by Napoli (1982). Napoli claims that after Restructuring, the matrix verbs, most of which are modals, aspectuals, and motion verbs, are "semantic auxiliaries", acting to modify the infinitival verb. She further demonstrates that if the matrix verb becomes too strong semantically by way of adding modifiers to it, for example, then, Restructuring is impossible. Interestingly enough, the adjunct selection in Italian Restructuring sentences patterns with sentences with gerundive clauses in Japanese. The contrast in (23) illustrates that a directional adjunct which is intended to modify the matrix verb disallows clitic climbing. In other words, in a Restructured sentence, a directional adjunct cannot modify a matrix verb.

(23) a. Piero verra   in biblioteca   a
                will come to the library to
          parla<u>ti</u>   di   parapsicologia.
          speak to you about parapsychology
          'Piero will come to the library to speak to
          you about parapsychology.'
      b. *Piero <u>ti</u> verra a parlare di parapsicologia
          in biblioteca.

The analysis of main verbs as "semantic auxiliaries" in Italian Restructuring sentences can be extended to the Restructuring sentences with gerundive clauses in Japanese. Since the main verb becomes a semantic auxiliary after Restructuring, it loses the function of denoting an event, which the same verb would otherwise have expressed. Therefore, as a semantic auxiliary, the matrix verb involved in a sentence with a gerundive clause fails to bear an event argument, and as a consequence, it cannot license adjuncts internal to that clause.

3. Syntactic Differences

We have so far looked at the different behavior in adjunct selection in purpose clauses and gerundive clauses, and have attributed the difference to the distribution of event argument. For the remainder of the paper I would like to point out that there are other syntactic differences between the two clause types. I will limit the discussion only to two instances of such syntactic behavior.[3]

First, purpose clauses can be scrambled whereas gerundive clauses cannot. This is shown in (24-25).

(24) [Hon-o   kai-ni]$_i$ Taroo-ga Kanda-e   t$_i$
       book-Acc buy-purpose   -Nom   -to
       itta.
       went

---

[3]For fuller discussion, see Tsujimura (in preparation).

'Taro went to Kanda to buy books.'
(25) *[Kanda-de   hon-o   kat-te]$_i$ Taroo-ga   t$_i$
        -at   book-Acc   buy-gerund   -Nom
     kita.
     came
     'Taro (came back after having) bought books at
     Kanda.'

Second, the two types of clauses demonstrate
different behavior with respect to iterativity, as
(26-27) show.

(26) *Taroo-ga   Sinzyuku-e   hon-o   kai-ni,
         -Nom   -to book-Acc   buy-purpose
      susi-o   tabe-ni,   eiga-o   mi-ni
      sushi-Acc eat-purpose movie-Acc see-purpose
      itta.
      went
      'Taro went to Shinjuku to buy books, eat sushi,
      and see a movie.'
(27) Taroo-ga   Sinzyuku-de hon-o   kat-te,
          -Nom   -at book-Acc   buy-gerund
       susi-o   tabe-te,   eiga-o   mi-te
       sushi-Acc eat-gerund   movie-Acc see-gerund

       kita.
       came
       'Taro (came back after having) bought books,
       eaten sushi, and seen a movie in Shinjuku.'

I propose that these two differences are
consequences of their syntactic status: more
specifically I contend that a purpose clause is an
argument of a limited set of motion verbs while a
gerundive clause is a mono-clausal structure with a
motion verb as a syntactic as well as semantic
auxiliary element. Under such a claim the difference
in scramblability and iterativity as we have observed
in (24-27) can be straightforwardly accounted for.
The purpose clause in (24) is an argument of the
motion verb _itta_ 'went', and, hence, can be scrambled
since the trace left behind is properly governed by

the verb. As for the impossibility of scrambling with a gerundive clause in (25), it should be attributed to a more general constraint that, unlike in English, no auxiliary element can be stranded in Japanese. Consider (28-30).

(28) a. Taroo-ga Hanako-ni hon-o   kat-te
          -Nom   -Dat book-Acc buy-gerund
         ageta.
         give
         'Taro bought Hanako a book.'
     b. *[Hanako-ni hon-o kat-te]$_i$ Taroo-ga t$_i$ ageta.
(29) a. Watasi-wa asita   byooin-e   iku
         I-Top   tomorrow hospital-to go
         tumori-desu.
         intention-be
         'I intend to go to hospital tomorrow.'
     b. *[Asita byooin-e iku]$_i$ watasi-wa t$_i$ tumori-desu.
(30) a. Taroo-wa moo   uti-e   kaetta hazu-da.
          -Top already home-to return expected-be
         'Taro is expected to have already gone home.'
     b. *[Moo uti-e kaetta]$_i$ Taroo-wa t$_i$ hazu-da.

Ageta 'gave' in (28), tumori-desu 'intend' in (29), and hazu-da 'is expected to' in (30) are arguably considered as auxiliary elements. Whether the verbal form that precedes them is gerundive, as in (28), or morphologically inflected for tense, as in (29-30), to scramble a VP, leaving the auxiliary elements behind, leads to ungrammaticality.

The iterativity facts follow from the argument status of purpose clauses. Recall that gerundive clauses can be iterative while purpose clauses cannot. This was observed in (26-27). Larson (1988) discusses the difference in iterativity between arguments and adjuncts: that is, adjuncts are iterative while arguments are not. (31-32), which are taken from Larson (p.171), illustrate such a difference.

(31)   Fred <u>deftly</u> [MANNER] handed the toy to the
baby <u>by reaching behind his back</u> [MANNER] <u>over</u>
<u>lunch</u> [TEMP] <u>at noon</u> [TEMP] <u>in a restaurant</u>
[LOC] <u>last Sunday</u> [TEMP] <u>in Back Bay</u> [LOC]
without interrupting the discussion.

(32)   a. *John ate that meat that beef.
        b. *The job paid steadily well.

Adjuncts can be repeated an indefinite number of
times while arguments that exceed the number (and
type) that a predicate subcategorizes for are
rejected. The ungrammaticality of (26), then,
follows from the argument status of purpose clauses
while the same restriction does not apply to
gerundive clauses in (27).

4.   Summary

In this paper I have examined two Restructuring
environments in Japanese, purpose clauses and
gerundive clauses. These two sentence types behave
differently with respect to adjunct selection. That
is, in the sentence with a purpose clause, adjuncts
are only associated with the matrix clause. In the
sentence with a gerundive clause, adjuncts are
licensed only internal to the gerundive clause. I
have argued that the difference should be attributed
to the presence of the feature specification for
[Tense]. A purpose clause lacks such feature, and as
a result, it also lacks an event argument which would
otherwise license an adjunct internal to it. The
matrix clause that accompanies a purpose clause, on
the other hand, bears the feature [Tense], and thus,
can license an adjunct. As for the sentences with
gerundive clauses, the gerundive clause bears the
feature [-Tense], which allows for an adjunct
internal to the gerundive clause. The matrix verb in
this construction, however, functions as a "semantic
auxiliary" in the sense of Napoli (1982). As a
semantic auxiliary, the matrix verb lacks an event
argument, and hence cannot license any adjunct
internal to that clause.

It has also been shown that purpose clauses and gerundive clauses are different in their scramblability and iterativity. An account has been posited in which a purpose clause is an argument of a motion verb, and thus it can scramble though it cannot iterate.

References

Iida, Masayo. 1987. Case Assignment by Nominals in Japanese. Working Papers in Grammatical Theory and Discourse Structure: Interactions of Morphology, Syntax, and Discourse, ed. by M. Iida, S. Wechsler, & D. Zec, 93-138. Stanford: CSLI.

Larson, Richard. 1988. Implicit Arguments in Situation Semantics. Linguistics and Philosophy 11.169-201.

Matsumoto, Yo. 1991. On the Nature of Purposive and Participial Complex Motion Predicates in Japanese. BLS.

Miyagawa, Shigeru. 1986. Restructuring in Japanese. Issues in Japanese Linguistics, ed. by T. Imai & M. Saito, 273-300. Dordrecht:Foris.

Napoli, Danna Jo. 1982. Semantic Interpretation vs. Lexical Governance: Clitic Climbing in Italian. Language 57.841-887.

Tsujimura, Natsuko. (in preparation) Adjunct Licensing and Restructuring. Ms. Indiana University.

On the Syntactic Properties of the Passive Morpheme in Japanese

HIROTO HOSHI
University of Connecticut

1. Introduction

The purpose of this paper is to clarify the syntactic nature of the passive morpheme in Japanese and to explore its implications.

Consider first the following pair:

(1) a. Mary-ga John-o   nagut-ta
         -Nom   -Acc hit-Pst
      'Mary hit John'
    b. John-ga Mary-ni nagur-are-ta
         -Nom   -by hit-Pass-Pst
      'John$_i$ was affected by Mary's hitting him$_i$'

(1a) is an active sentence; (1b) is a *ni* direct passive. The logical object in (1a), *John*, is in the subject position in (1b). Although (1b) seems like a regular passive involving NP movement, Kuroda (1965) argues that the passive morpheme *(r)are* of the *ni* direct passive assigns an external θ-role to the subject and that NP movement does not take place in this type of construction.[1] The structure he proposes for (1b) is (2).

(2) $[_S$ John$_i$-ga $[_S$ Mary-ni John$_i$ nagur] are ta]

       ↓

      ø (Kuroda 1965, 1979)

Under Kuroda's analysis, the embedded object is deleted, if it is identical with the matrix subject.[2]

Kuno (1973) proposes an alternative analysis of the *ni* direct passive, which differs from Kuroda's in two respects. He argues that the passive morpheme of the *ni* direct passive triggers NP movement but does not have an external θ-role to assign.[3] The structure proposed by Kuno is (3).

(3) $[_S$ John$_i$-ga $[_{VP}$ Mary-ni t_i nagur-are-ta]]

                                    (Kuno 1973)

In Hoshi (1991), I argued that Kuroda's and Kuno's proposals are both basically correct, in that the passive morpheme of this type not only assigns an external θ-role but also triggers NP movement. Further, I sketched a way to reconcile those two syntactic operations. Consider (4a-b).

(4) a. John $[_{VP}$ Mary   PRO nagur] are ta

                                          (D-S)

    b. John$_i$-ga $[_{VP}$ PRO$_i$ Mary-ni t_i nagur] are ta

                                      (after D-S)

Under this analysis, the subject *John* is base-generated in the matrix subject position where it receives an external θ-role from *(r)are*. The subject within VP, *Mary*, is demoted and the objective Case of the verb *nagur* 'hit' is absorbed by the passive morpheme. An empty category, PRO, which is base-generated in the complement position of the verb, is forced to move to the SPEC of VP to be controlled by *John*.[4] This analysis, thus, reconciles the two conflicting proposals sketched above. In this paper, I pursue this proposal and develop it, taking Larson's (1988) theory of θ-role assignment and Pesetsky's (1985) proposal for affix raising.

In section 2, I briefly show Kuroda's analysis and Saito's (1982) argument for Kuno's NP movement analysis. After discussing those two conflicting proposals, I show how Hoshi (1991) tried to reconcile those proposals but with a problem left, concerning the dual syntactic nature of the passive morpheme of the *ni* direct passive. In section 3, I develop my earlier proposal. Specifically, I argue that: At D-structure, the passive morpheme of the *ni* direct passive forms a complex unit with a verb and triggers passivization VP-internally, i.e. dative shift in Larsonian terms[5]; then, it excorporates from the verb and moves up, to assign an external θ-role to the subject in a higher clause. Section 4 explores two consequences of the proposed analysis. In section 5, I summarize the conclusion.

2. Theta-subject and NP Movement
2.1. Theta-subject Analysis

Consider the *ni* direct passive (5a) and the *ni yotte* passive (5b).[6]

(5) a. John-ga Mary-ni nagur-are-ta   (= 1b)
         -Nom   -by hit-Pass-Pst
      'John$_i$ was affected by Mary's hitting him$_i$'
    b. John-ga   Mary-ni yotte nagur-are-ta
         -Nom   -to due hit-Pass-Pst
      'John was hit by Mary'

In (5a-b), the logical object *John* surfaces in the subject position. At first glance, the only difference between them seems to be *ni* vs. *ni yotte*, both of which are considered to correspond to *by* in English.

However, Kuroda (1979), led by Inoue's (1976) observation concerning the difference between the *ni* direct passive and the *ni yotte* passive, proposes (6a-b) for (5a-b), respectively.

(6)a. [$_S$ John$_i$-ga [$_S$ Mary-ni John$_i$ nagur] are ta]
                         ↓   (= 2)
                         ø (Kuroda 1965, 1979)
   b. [$_S$ John$_i$-ga [$_{VP}$ Mary-ni yotte t_i nagur-are-ta]]
                              (Kuroda 1979)

Under this analysis, two types of Japanese passives are assigned completely different structures. Kuroda proposes that the passive morpheme of the *ni* direct passive assigns an external θ-role (and requires that the subject be an affectee), while that of the *ni yotte* passive does not have an external θ-role to assign. This analysis correctly explains the paradigm in (7).

(7) a.   John-ga   chuui-o   harat-ta
          -Nom   heed-Acc   pay-Pst
       'John paid heed'
   b. *chuui-ga John-ni haraw-are-ta
        heed-Nom   -by pay-Pass-Pst
       'Heed$_i$ was affected by John's paying it$_i$'
   c.   chuui-ga John-ni yotte haraw-are-ta
        heed-Nom   -to due   pay-Pass-Pst
       'Heed was paid by John'

(7a) is an active sentence which contains the verb phrase idiom *chuui-o haraw* 'pay heed'. There is a grammatical difference between (7b), the *ni* direct passive, and (7c), the *ni yotte* passive. (7c) is grammatical, whereas (7b) is not. Since NPs such as *chuui* cannot be an affectee, (7b) is ruled out due to the violation of the selectional restriction imposed by *(r)are*, under Kuroda's proposal. On the other hand, *(r)are* of the *ni yotte* passive imposes no such requirement on the subject in his analysis. Hence, (7c) is correctly ruled in.

2.2. NP Movement Analysis

In contrast with Kuroda's proposal, Kuno proposes an NP movement analysis for both the *ni* direct passive and the *ni yotte* passive. His structures for (5a-b) are (8a-b), respectively. As is seen, Kuno does not assume any syntactic difference between (5a) and (5b), except from *ni* vs. *ni yotte*.

(8) a. [$_S$ John$_i$-ga [$_{VP}$ Mary-ni t_i nagur-are-ta]]
                                              (= 3)
    b. [$_S$ John$_i$-ga [$_{VP}$ Mary-ni yotte t_i nagur-are-ta]]
                                         (Kuno 1973)

Observe that Kuroda and Kuno assign exactly the same structure to the *ni yotte* passive (5b) (cf. 6b and 8b). Notice, however, that under Kuno's analysis, the subject position is a non-θ position and NP movement is involved in (5a) as well as in (5b). Thus, if we take Kuno's proposal, a problem arises as to how to explain the contrast in (7a-b), which

Kuroda's proposal explains straightforwardly. On the other hand, there is strong evidence for Kuno's analysis provided by Saito (1982).

Saito's original argument relies on Harada's (1973) double-*o* constraint. Just for ease of discussion, in place of Harada's constraint, here I make use of a constraint on abstract Case assignment in (9), which Saito (1985) assumed on the basis of Kuroda's (1978) and Poser's (1981) development of Harada's double-*o* constraint.

(9) A verb can assign objective Case to at most one NP. (Saito 1985)

Given the constraint (9), examine the example (10).

(10) Mary-ga   John-o/ni   [PRO Tom-ni *e* sikar-
     -Nom   -Acc/Dat   -by   scold-
     are]-sase-ta
     Pass-Cause-Pst
     'Mary made John be scolded by Tom' (Saito 1982)

In (10), a *ni* direct passive is embedded in a causative sentence. Notice that the existence of an empty category in the embedded clause does not prevent the causee *John* from being marked with objective Case by the complex predicate *sik-are-sase*. If the empty category in (10) receives abstract objective Case, the condition (9) should prevent *John* from receiving objective Case. But that is not the case in (10). Thus, Saito argues that the empty category in (10) is an NP trace, which does not require Case, and concludes that the *ni* direct passive involves NP movement.

Given this argument, we are left in a paradoxical situation, regarding the analysis of (5a). Recall that the previous discussion concerning the ungrammaticality of (7b) supported Kuroda's θ-subject analysis of the *ni* direct passive. Conversely, Saito's argument provides substantial support for Kuno's NP movement analysis of the same type of passive.

2.3. Reconciling the Two Conflicting Proposals

Given the arguments above, I argued in Hoshi

(1991) that we have to maintain Kuroda's θ/θ'-subject dichotomy between the *ni* direct passive and the *ni yotte* passive but that the correct analysis of the *ni* direct passive must subsume Kuno's NP movement analysis under Kuroda's θ-subject analysis. The representations that I suggested for (5a) are in (11).

(11)a. John   [$_{VP}$ Mary   PRO nagur] are ta
                                                      (D-S)

   b. John$_i$-ga [$_{VP}$ PRO$_i$ Mary-ni t_i nagur] are ta
                                     (after D-S)(= 4)

Under this proposal, Kuno's analysis is incorporated into Kuroda's in a desirable way:
   a) The subject of the *ni* direct passive, *John*, is base-generated in the matrix subject position as shown in (11a). In that position, it receives an external θ-role from the passive morpheme.
   b) A PRO is base-generated in the complement position of the embedded verb. At a later point of the derivation, it moves to the VP SPEC position to be controlled by the matrix subject as in (11b). Notice that under this analysis, it is not the subject *John* itself but the PRO that undergoes NP movement.
   While this reconciliation brings us a desirable consequence, it raises an interesting question concerning the dual syntactic nature of the passive morpheme of the *ni* direct passive. Notice that in this proposal, the passive morpheme of the *ni* direct passive is assumed to perform two different operations. More specifically, it is assumed that this type of passive morpheme, on the one hand, assigns an external θ-role in the higher clause; it, on the other hand, triggers passivization in the embedded clause, i.e. VP. Thus, a question arises as to how the passive morpheme of this type of passive fulfills those two operations in different structural positions.

3. Toward a Cross-linguistic Analysis of Passive
3.1. Domain of Passivization and θ-role Assignment

Keeping in mind the problem concerning the dual syntactic nature of the passive morpheme of the *ni* direct passive, consider (12) and (13a-b).

(12)   [$_{IP}$ John$_i$ was beaten t_i by Mary]

(13) a.　　John gave　a book to Mary
　　　b.　　John gave　Mary　　a book

Observing some similarity between the dative shift construction (13b) and the IP passive (12), Larson (1988) proposes that (13b) derives from (13a) via NP movement as in (12). Then, he argues that the difference between those two lies in the domain of NP movement. Dative shift sentences involve NP movement within VP, while IP passives involve it within IP.

Examine Larson's structures (14a–b) for (13b).

(14) a. $[_{VP1}$ John $[_{V'}$ e $[_{VP2}$ e $[[\text{give}_i$ Mary$_j]$ a book $]]]]$
　　　　　　　　　　　　　　　　　　　　　　　　　　　　(D-S)

　　　b. $[_{VP1}$ John $[_{V'}$ give$_i$ $[_{VP2}$ Mary$_j$ $[[t_i$ $t_j]$ a book$]]]]$
　　　　　　　　　　　　　　　　　　　　　　　　　　　　(S-S)

Larson proposes that the dative shift triggering verb *give* in (14a) triggers passivization within VP$_2$ and, then, moves up to the higher empty V position in order to assign its external θ-role. The subject in VP$_2$, *a book*, in Larsonian terms, is demoted and the inherent Case of *give*, i.e. *to*, is withdrawn in (14a). For Case reasons, *Mary* undergoes NP movement to the VP$_2$ SPEC position. Then, as shown in (14b), *give* moves up to the empty V position where it assigns its external θ-role to *John* and assigns abstract Case to *Mary* in the VP$_2$ SPEC position. In this analysis, thus, it is proposed that θ-role assignment can be done at any point of the derivation. Consequently, this allows the dative shift verb *give* to perform two syntactic operations, namely triggering passivization in the lower clause and assigning an external θ-role in the higher clause.

Notice that there is an interesting similarity between Larson's proposal for the verb *give* of (13b) and Hoshi's (1991) proposal for *(r)are* of (5a).[8] *Give* and *(r)are* both trigger passivization in a lower clause and assign their external θ-roles in a higher clause. Given this significant similarity and taking Larson's theory of θ-role assignment and Pesetsky's proposal that a part of a word is capable of splitting off, I will next set forth an analysis of the *ni* direct passive in Japanese. Kitagawa (1986) first adopts Pesetsky's affix raising analysis for constructions such as Japanese causatives and passives and argues that all types of causative and passive morphemes in Japanese are detached in LF. First incorporating Pesetsky's and Kitagawa's affix raising analysis into Larson's theory, Washio (1989–1990), on the other hand, argues that the passive morpheme of the *ni* indirect passive excorporates in syntax, while that of the *ni* direct passive does not. I, however, argue that the excorporation is involved in all the types of the *ni* passive in LF, although it is involved neither in the *ni yotte* passive nor in Japanese causatives.

3.2. A Proposal

The structures I propose for the *ni* direct passive (5a) are (15a–b).[9]

(15) a. $[_{VP1}$ John $[_{V'} [_{VP2}$ e $[_{V'}$ Mary [PRO nagur-are]]] e]] (D–S)

b. $[_{VP1}$ John$_i$-ga $[_{V'} [_{VP2}$ PRO$_i$ $[_{V'}$ Mary-ni [t_i nagur-t_j]]] are$_j$]] (after D–S)

Under this proposal, the *ni* direct passive (5a) is generated in the following way:

a) The passive morpheme *(r)are*, first, forms a complex unit with the verb *nagur* 'hit' as in (15a); it demotes the subject of the verb, *Mary*, and absorbs Case from it.

b) The empty VP shell, i.e. VP$_1$, is licensed over the VP$_2$, which is headed by the complex verb *nagur-are*, because *(r)are* has an external θ-role to assign. Within the higher clause, i.e. the empty VP shell, the higher subject *John* is generated, as in (15a).

c) The PRO, which is base-generated in the complement position of the complex verb, is allowed to move into the VP$_2$ SPEC position to be controlled by the matrix subject, since the passivization by *(r)are* makes the SPEC of VP$_2$ vacant. I argue that this VP-internal movement done by PRO is the NP movement, involved in the *ni* direct passive. I further propose that this VP internal passivization is one of the operations which the English dative shift sentence and the *ni* direct passive have in common.

d) In LF, *(r)are* excorporates from the verb *nagur* and moves up to the empty V position, to assign its external θ-role to *John* in the SPEC of VP$_1$.

Summarizing the discussion so far, I have presented an analysis of (5a) which proposes that there is a striking similarity between the *ni* direct passive and the English dative shift construction, i.e., that both of those constructions involve VP-internal passivization. Moreover, I have shown that the analysis not only subsumes Kuroda's θ-subject analysis and Kuno's NP movement analysis, but also accounts for the puzzling dual syntactic behavior of the passive morpheme of the *ni* direct passive (5a).

3.3. Three Types of Japanese Passive

So far the discussion in this paper has concentrated only on the examination of syntactic properties of the *ni* direct passive. In this subsection, it will be shown how the other types of passive are related to the *ni* direct passive.

Regarding the syntactic nature of *(r)are* of the *ni* direct passive, a question arises why that type of passive morpheme has the dual function. Combining Saito's (1982) and Marantz's (1984) proposal that the passive morpheme in Japanese optionally triggers passivization with Kuroda's (1979) proposal that the passive morpheme optionally assigns an external θ-role, I suggest the following lexical specifications:

(16) *Rare*:
a) +/−Experiencer [+Affected]
b) +/−Passivization = External θ-role suppression & Case absorption

Given (16), we predict that there should be four types of *(r)are* with the following features in Japanese: 1) [+Experiencer/+Passivization]; 2) [−Experiencer/+Passivization]; 3) [+Experiencer/−Passivization]; 4) [−Experiencer/−Passivization]. This is in fact the case.

3.3.1. The first type of the passive morpheme has the features [+Experiencer/+Passivization]. Hence, it not only triggers passivization, but also assigns an external θ-role. These are, in fact, the syntactic properties of the passive morpheme of the *ni* direct passive. See the proposed structures in (15), assigned for this type of passive.

3.3.2. The second type has the passive morpheme which triggers passivization but does not assign an external θ-role. This is the syntactic property of the passive morpheme of the *ni yotte* passive. Consider the examples in (17).

(17) a. John-ga   Mary-ni yotte nagur-are-ta
        -Nom   -to due   hit-Pass-Pst
   'John was hit by Mary'   (= 5b)
   b. *John-ga   kodomo-ni yotte sin-are-ta
        -Nom   child-to   due   die-Pass-Pst

(17a) is grammatical but (17b) is not. Sentences with intransitive verbs such as *sin* 'die', as in (17b), cannot be *ni yotte* passivized, as noticed by Kuno (1973). This is so, because the passive morpheme of *ni yotte* passives cannot trigger passivization to the intransitive verb *sin*. Notice that the translation of (17a) indicates that the subject *John* does not bear an experiencer role. I propose (18a-b) for (17a).

(18)a. [$_{IP}$ e [$_{VP}$ e Mary-ni yotte John nagur-are]]   (D-S)
   b. [$_{IP}$ John$_i$-ga [$_{VP}$ (t_i) Mary-ni yotte t_i nagur-are]]
                                 (after D-S)

In (18a), *(r)are* of the *ni yotte* passive triggers passivization. However, *(r)are* in (18a) cannot license an empty VP shell, since it does not have an external θ-role to assign. Due to the passivization by *(r)are*, the internal argument *John* moves up to the IP SPEC position for Case reasons, as seen in (18b).

3.3.3. The third type of the passive morpheme does not trigger passivization but assigns its external θ-role. This is the syntactic property of the passive morpheme of the *ni* indirect passive. Consider (19).

(19)   John-ga   kodomo-ni sin-are-ta
        -Nom child-by   die-Pass-Pst
   'John was affected by his child's dying'

Notice that the this type of *ni* passive is grammatical with the intransitive verb *sin*. Observe further that the subject *John* receives an experiencer role from *(r)are*, as indicated in the translation. I propose the structures in (20) for (19).

(20) a. $[_{VP1}$ John $[_{V'}$ $[_{VP2}$ kodomo sin-are]] e]]   (D-S)

b. $[_{VP1}$ John-ga $[_{V'}$ $[_{VP2}$ kodomo-ni sin-t_j]] are$_j$]]

(after D-S)

The passive morpheme of the *ni* indirect passive does not trigger passivization within VP$_2$ as in (20a). However, it licenses an empty VP shell over the VP$_2$, since it has an external θ-role to assign. Thus, the subject *John* is base-generated in the SPEC of VP$_1$. At a later point of the derivation (19b), i.e. LF, *(r)are* excorporates and moves up to the empty V position and assigns an external θ-role to *John*.

3.3.4. Last, (16) leads us to expect that there should exist a passive morpheme with the features [-Experiencer/-Passivization]. Contrary to this expectation, such a passive morpheme is not found. I suggest that this type of passive morpheme exists but cannot surface, because of the Principle of Morphological Nonredundancy proposed by Zubizarreta (1985), which prohibits a passive morpheme with no positive feature from surfacing.

In this subsection, I have suggested that the lexical properties of the passive morpheme vary along the features [+/-Experiencer], [+/-Passivization], as shown in (16). I have extended my analysis of the *ni* direct passive to the analyses of the *ni yotte* passive and the *ni* indirect passive. Given the proposal in this section, I will explore two consequences in section 4. The proposed analysis correctly predicts some difference between *ni* direct passives and *ni* indirect passives and between causatives and *ni* passives.

4. Consequences
4.1. VP-internal Passivization

Kuno (1973) and N. A. McCawley (1972) independently observe the following difference between the *ni* direct and the *ni* indirect passives.

(21) a. John$_i$-ga   Mary$_j$-ni   zibun$_{i/*j}$-no uti-de

-Nom   '-by self-Gen   house-in

koros-are-ta
kill-Pass-Pst
'John$_i$ was affected by Mary$_j$'s killing him$_j$ in
self$_{i/*j}$'s house' (ni direct passive)

b. John$_i$-ga Mary$_j$-ni zibun$_{i/j}$-no koto-o
-Nom   -by self-Gen, matter-Acc

zimans-are-ta
boast-Pass-Pst
'John$_i$ was affected by Mary$_j$'s bragging about
self$_{i/j}$'s matter' (ni indirect passive)

In (21a), only *John* can be the antecedent of the
long distance subject-oriented anaphor *zibun*. In
(21b), either *John* or *Mary* can be the antecedent of
zibun. I argue that this difference between (21a-b)
arises from whether or not VP-internal passivization
is involved. Consider the LF representation (22) for
the *ni* direct passive (21a).

(22)$[_{VP1}$ John$_i$-ga $[_{VP2}$ PRO$_i$ $[_{V'}$ Mary$_j$-ni zibun-no uti-de t_i
koros-t_k]] are$_k$] (LF)

In (21a), *(r)are* triggers passivization within VP$_2$.
Because of the demotion of the VP$_2$ subject *Mary*, the
SPEC of VP$_2$ is empty at D-S. Thus, at a later point
of the derivation, PRO moves into the VP$_2$ SPEC to be
controlled by *John$_i$*, as in (22). Notice that PRO
occupies the VP$_2$ SPEC position, because of the VP-
internal passivization. If we assume that NPs in the
VP SPEC position count as subjects for *zibun* and, if
we further assume that LF is relevant for the
Binding Theory, then we can explain the fact that
only *John* is a possible antecedent of *zibun* in (21a).
This is so, because, in (22), John$_i$ and PRO$_i$ are in
the VP SPEC position but Mary$_j$ is not.

Consider now the LF representation (23) for (21b).

(23)$[_{VP1}$ John$_i$-ga $[_{VP2}$ Mary$_j$-ni zibun-no koto-o
zimans-t_k] are$_k$] (LF)

The passive morpheme of the *ni* indirect passive
(21b) does not trigger VP-internal passivization.
Thus, not only *John* but also *Mary* is in the VP SPEC
position in (23). Therefore, either *John* or *Mary* can
be an antecedent of *zibun* in (21b).

4.2. Excorporation and Binding Domain

Consider the causative (24a) and the *ni* passive (24b).

(24)a. John-ga Mary-ni hon-o   kaw-ase-ta
       -Nom   -Dat book-Acc buy-Cause-Pst
       'John made/let Mary buy a book'
   b. John-ga Mary-ni hon-o   kaw-are-ta
       -Nom   -by book-Acc buy-Pass-Pst
       'John was affected by Mary's buying a book'

The representations proposed by Kuroda for the (24a-b) are in (25) and (26), respectively.[10]

(25)a. [$_S$ John   [$_S$ Mary   hon   kaw] ase ta] (D-S)
    b. [$_S$ John-ga [$_S$ Mary-ni hon-o t_i] kaw$_i$-ase-ta]
                                                  (after D-S)
(26)a. [$_S$ John   [$_S$ Mary   hon   kaw] are ta] (D-S)
    b. [$_S$ John-ga [$_S$ Mary-ni hon-o t_i] kaw$_i$-are-ta]
                                         (after D-S)(Kuroda 1965)

In (25a) and (26a), the causative morpheme *(s)ase* and the passive morpheme *(r)are* function as matrix verbs. In (25b) and (26b), the verb *kaw* 'buy' in the embedded clause moves up and forms a complex predicate with those morphemes. Notice that under this analysis, the *ni* passive (24b) as well as the causative (24a) is generated exactly in the same way by verb raising. In this section, I argue that Kuroda's verb raising analysis is correct for the causative, whereas the excorporation analysis is correct for the *ni* passive.

Examine the contrast between the causative (27a) and the *ni* passive (27b).

(27) a. John$_i$-ga   Bill-ni kare$_i$-o sinyoos-ase-ta
          -Nom   -Dat he-Acc trust-Cause-Pst
       'John$_i$ made Bill trust him$_i$'   (Oshima 1979)
     b. *John$_i$-ga Bill-ni kare$_i$-o sinyoos-are-ta
          -Nom   -by he-Acc trust-Pass-Pst
       'John$_i$ was affected by Bill's trusting him$_i$'
       (Saito (p.c.), Kitagawa and Kuroda (1992))

There is a sharp difference in grammaticality between (27a) and (27b). As Oshima (1979) observes, pronouns such as *kare* 'he' in the embedded object position of a causative sentence can be coindexed with the matrix subject as in (27a). In contrast, Mamoru Saito, in personal communication, and Kitagawa and Kuroda (1992) point out that embedded pronominal objects cannot be coindexed with matrix subjects in *ni* passives, as in (27b).

Recall that under Kuroda's theory, the causative sentence and the *ni* passive are generated exactly in the same way by verb raising. Hence, in his proposal, it is expected that the causative sentence and the *ni* passive behave similarly with respect to the pronominal coreference in (27). However, it turns out that their syntactic behavior is different. Hence, a question arises as to what differentiates them in (27). In this subsection, I propose that this difference emerges, because Japanese causatives involve verb raising as Kuroda argues, while Japanese *ni* passives involve excorporation of the passive morpheme *(r)are* as I have argued. Let us now see how this proposal correctly explains the facts observed in (27).

Examine (28a-b) for the causative (27a) and the *ni* passive (29a-b) for (27b). (28b) involves verb raising, whereas (29b) involves excorporation.

(28) a. [$_{VP1}$ John [$_{VP2}$ Bill kare sinyoos] ase]   (D-S)
    b. [$_{VP1}$ John$_i$-ga [$_{VP2}$ Bill-ni kare$_i$-o t_j] sinyoos$_j$-ase]
                                             (after D-S)
(29) a. [$_{VP1}$ John [$_{VP2}$ Bill kare [sinyoos-are]] e] (D-S)
    b. *[$_{VP1}$ John$_i$-ga [$_{VP2}$ Bill-ni kare$_i$-o [$_{V0}$ sinyoos-t_k]]are$_k$]
                                             (after D-S)

Given these distinct representations for the causative sentence (27a) and the *ni* passive (27b), and the notion "Complete Functional Complex (henceforth CFC)" proposed by Chomsky (1986), we can correctly account for the contrast in (27).

Chomsky proposes that a pronominal must be free in its CFC, i.e. the minimal domain containing α in which all grammatical relations compatible with its head are realized. If so, the CFC for the pronoun *kare* in (28b) is VP$_2$, because the governor of *kare* in (28b) is the trace of *sinyoos* 'trust' and all the grammatical relations compatible with that verb are realized within VP$_2$. Observe that thus, the pronoun *kare* is not bound by its antecedent *John* in its governing category in (28b). Therefore, Kuroda's verb raising analysis correctly predicts that in (27a), *kare* can be coreferential with the matrix subject. Recall, however, that in Kuroda's theory, the causative (27a) and the *ni* passive (27b) are generated in the same way, and, thus, his theory incorrectly predicts that in (27b), *kare* is allowed to be coreferential with the matrix subject as in (27a).

If, however, we take the excorporation analysis of Japanese *ni* passives, the CFC for *kare* is VP_1 in (29b). Notice that in contrast with (28b), in the *ni* passive (29b), all the grammatical relations of the governor, i.e. $[_{V0} \; sinyoos\text{-}t_i \;]$, for *kare* are not expressed within VP_2, but are realized within VP_1. This is because the passive morpheme, i.e. the part of complex predicate $[_{V0} \; sinyoos\text{-}are_j \;]$, moves up to the empty V position to assign its external θ-role under the excorporation analysis. Given this, we can correctly account for the impossibility of the pronominal coreference in (27b), because the pronoun *kare_i* is bound by *John* in its governing category, i.e. VP_1, and violates Binding Condition B in (29b).

5. Conclusion

In this paper, I argued that at D-S, the passive morpheme of the *ni* direct passive forms a complex unit with an embedded verb, triggering passivization VP-internally; then, it excorporates from the verb, assigning an external θ-role to the matrix subject. I have explained the contrast between the *ni* direct passive and the *ni* indirect passive, concerning the possible antecedent of *zibun*, by appealing to one important distinction between those two types of passive, i.e. the presence or absence of the VP-internal passivization. Finally, I have demonstrated that the excorporation analysis of the *ni* passive brings us a desirable way to explain the contrast between the causative and the *ni* passive. There, I have argued that Japanese causatives involve verb raising, but *ni* passives involve excorporation.

Notes

* I am grateful to Jun Abe, Mona Anderson, Hajime Hoji, Yasuo Ishii, Yoshihisa Kitagawa, S.-Y. Kuroda, Howard Lasnik, Diane Lillo-Martin, Shigeru Miyagawa, Naoko Nemoto, Noriko Yoshimura, Shûichi Yatabe, and especially to Javier Ormazabal, Mamoru Saito, and Myriam Uribe-Etxebarria for their valuable comments, suggestions, and criticisms. Needless to say, all the shortcomings are mine.

1. See Kitagawa (1986), and Kitagawa and Kuroda (1992), among others, for arguments for this type of analysis.

2. In Kuroda's analysis, if the object in the embedded clause is not coreferential with the matrix subject, then the deletion operation does not take place and the *ni* indirect passive is generated.

3. The reader is referred to Saito (1982), Miyagawa (1989), among others, for arguments for the NP movement analysis.

4. PRO must not be governed to satisfy Binding Conditions A and B (cf. Chomsky 1981, 1982). In (4b), PRO is not governed by the verb *nagur* 'hit'. It, however, is governed by the passive morpheme *(r)are*. I leave this problem for future research.

5. In this paper, I mean by passivization a combination of the following operations: suppression of an external argument and absorption of Case.

6. I adopt Howard and Niyekawa-Howard's (1976) terms, the direct passive, and the indirect passive. Adopting Kuroda's (1979) terms, I call the passive construction with *ni*, the *ni* passive, and the passive construction with *ni yotte*, the *ni yotte* passive.

7. Notice that Larson's theory of θ-role assignment denies the Projection Principle (henceforth PP), which informally states that all the argument relations are represented at all levels in syntax (Chomsky 1981). Thus, if his theory is correct, it also invalidates the Generalized Projection Principle (henceforth GPP), which I suggested in Hoshi (1991) by incorporating adjunct θ-requirements into the PP. Later in this paper, I follow Larson, rejecting both the GPP and the PP.

8. I am very grateful to Mamoru Saito (personal communication) who pointed out this similarity to me.

9. In this paper, I assume Saito's (1982) mechanism of Case assignment in Japanese: nominative case *ga* is structurally assigned to an NP which is immediately dominated by IP; accusative Case *o* is assigned to an object; as for dative *ni*, it is assigned to an argument of a verb which cannot surface with either nominative case *ga* or accusative Case *o*. However, just for ease of exposition, I show the structures where nominative case is assigned in the VP SPEC position, not in the SPEC of IP position.

10. Kuroda argues that there exist two distinct representations for the causative sentences such as (24a), i.e. the *ni* causative version and the *o* causative version. The representations in (25) are the ones for the *ni* causative. Just for ease of exposition, I make use of his representation for the *ni* causative here.

References

Bedell, George, Eichi Kobayashi and Masatake Muraki, eds. 1979. *Exploration in Linguistics: Papers in Honor of Kazuko Inoue*, Kenkyusha, Tokyo.

Chomsky, Noam. 1981. *Lectures on Government and Binding*, Foris Publications, Dordrecht.

Chomsky, Noam. 1982. *Some Concepts and Consequences of the Theory of Government and Binding*, MIT Press, Cambridge, Massachusetts.

Chomsky, Noam. 1986. *Knowledge of Language: Its Nature, Origins and Use*, Praeger, New York.

Harada, Shin-Ichi. 1973. Counter Equi NP Deletion, *Annual Bulletin*, 7, Research Institute of Logopedics and Phoniatrics, University of Tokyo, 113-147.

Hoshi, Hiroto. 1991. The Generalized Projection Principle and Its Implications for Passive Constructions, *Journal of Japanese linguistics* 13, 53-89.

Howard, Irwin and Agnes M. Niyekawa-Howard. 1976. Passivization, in M. Shibatani, (ed.), *Japanese Generative Grammar: Syntax and Semantics* 5, Academic Press, New York, 201-237.

Inoue, Kazuko. 1976. *Henkeibunpoo to Nihongo* [Generative Grammar and Japanese], Taisyukan, Tokyo.

Kitagawa, Yoshihisa. 1986. *Subjects in Japanese and English*, PhD dissertation, University of Massachusetts, Amherst.

Kitagawa, Yoshihisa and Kuroda S.-Y. 1992. Passive in Japanese, ms., University of Rochester and University of California at San Diego.

Kuno, Susumu. 1973. *The Structure of the Japanese Language*, MIT Press, Cambridge, Massachusetts.

Kuroda, S.-Y. 1965. *Generative Grammatical Studies in the Japanese Language*, PhD dissertation, MIT.

Kuroda, S.-Y. 1978. Case Marking, Canonical Sentence Patterns, and Counter Equi in Japanese, in J. Hinds and I. Howards (eds.), *Problems in Japanese Syntax and Semantics*, Kaitakusya, Tokyo.

Kuroda, S.-Y. 1979. On Japanese Passives, in G. Bedell, E. Kobayashi and M. Muraki, eds., 305-347.

Larson, Richard. 1988. On the Double Object Construction, *LI* 19, 335-391.

Marantz, Alec. 1984. *On the Nature of Grammatical Relations*, MIT Press, Cambridge, Massachusetts.

McCawley, Noriko Akatuska. 1972. On the Treatment of Japanese Passives, *CLS* 8, 256-270.

Miyagawa, Shigeru. 1989. *Structure and Case Marking in Japanese: Syntax and Semantics* 22, Academic Press, New York.

Oshima, Shin. 1979. Conditions on Rules: anaphora in Japanese, in G. Bedell, E. Kobayashi and M. Muraki, eds., 423-448.

Pesetsky, David. 1985. Morphology and Logical Form, *LI* 16, 193-246.

Poser, William. 1981. The 'Double-*o* Constraint': Evidence for a Direct Object Relation in Japanese, ms., MIT.

Saito, Mamoru. 1982. Case Marking in Japanese: A Preliminary Study, ms., MIT.

Saito, Mamoru. 1985. *Some Asymmetries in Japanese and Their Theoretical Implications*, PhD dissertation, MIT.

Washio, Ryuichi. 1989-1990. The Japanese Passive, *Linguistic Review* 6, 227-263.

Zubizarreta, Maria Luisa. 1985. The Relation between Morphophonology and Morphosyntax: The Case of Romance Causatives, *LI* 16, 247-289.

The Affected Construction in Korean and Japanese

TAEGOO CHUNG

The University of Texas at Austin

0. Introduction

Korean and Japanese have indirect/adversity passives, which I call the affected constructions (hereafter, AC's), as shown below:

(1) a. Korean:
  John-un   phi-lul   hulu-li-ess-ta.
  John-Top blood-Acc run-Passive-Past-Dec
  'John had bleeding.'
b. Japanese:
  Taroo-wa   kodomo-ni   sin-are-ta.
  Taro-Top   child-Dat   die-Passive-Past
  'Taro's child died on him.'   (Oehrle and Nishio 1981:163)

---

* This is an extended and revised version of Chung (1992), in which only Korean is dealt with. I thank Professor C. L. Baker, Professor S. Wechsler, and Professor J. Maling for their comments and suggestions on earlier versions of this paper. I also appreciate the valuable comments of Professor C. -M. Lee, Professor Y.-J. Kim, and Kathy Hoyt. I am grateful to K. Yabushita and M. Kawamura for their discussions and judgments of the Japanese data. All errors are mine.

Two related questions about this construction are so far unanswered in the literature[1]: First, is this construction a passive or not, and second, if so, how can we account for accusative case and argument addition?

In this study, I claim that an AC is a psychological causative construction. It is not a passive, because it involves argument addition and no case absorption. The causative approach to AC's enables us to account for argument addition and no case absorption because a causative construction has these two characteristics. The present study is based on the data of Korean and Japanese.

This paper is organized as follows. Section 1 discusses the form and meaning of AC's and some of their basic properties. Section 2 presents a causative approach to AC's. Section 3 discusses Case in this construction, and Section 4 looks into its argument structure. Section 5 compares AC's with causatives and passives, and Korean AC's with Japanese AC's. Section 6 concludes the study.

1. What is an AC?
1.1. Form of AC

An AC is formed morphologically in Korean and Japanese. Korean employs the morpheme /hi/, which is an archimorpheme for -i-, -hi-, -li-, and -ki-, and Japanese employs the morpheme /rare/, as shown in (1). Both morphemes are homophonous with passive morphemes in these languages, which is one of the reasons that this construction has often been treated as a passive construction.[2]

Both languages have AC forms which are not formed with /hi/ or /rare/. In Korean, some simple lexical verbs may be AC's as in (2a). In Japanese, the causative morpheme /sase/ may form an AC, as in (2b):[3]

(2) a. Korean:
Mary-ka   John-eykey kiss-lul   tangha-ess-ta.
Mary-Nom John-Dat   kiss-Acc   adversely receive-Past-Dec
'Mary got (adversely) kissed by John.'   (Yang 1972:121)

---

[1] For Korean, see C.-M. Lee (1975), Im (1978), Kang (1986), K.-H. Lee (1988), Kim (1990), Hong (1991), and Maling and Kim (1992), among others. For Japanese, McCawley (1972), Kuno (1973), Howard and Niyekawa-Howard (1976), Miyagawa (1989), Washio (1990), and Washio (1991), among others.

[2] The Korean morpheme /hi/ is ambiguous between a causative and a passive. The Japanese morpheme /rare/is a passive.

[3] Interestingly, even in English, the same verb may be interpreted ambiguously between a causative and an AC. The verb *have* below has the ambiguity:

(i) John had his house burned down.

Sentence (i) may be interpreted in two ways: (a) John burned his house down intentionally; or (b) he did not cause his house to be burned down, but he was affected adversely by his house being burned down. See Washio (1992) for the alternation between a causative and an AC in other languages.

b. Japanese:
Titioya-wa kodomo-o sin-ase-ta.
father-Top child-Acc die-Causative-Past
'The father had his child die on him.'[4]   (Oehrle and Nishio 1981:166)

One interesting observation here is that both languages use the same morphemes for AC's; i.e., the passive or causative morphemes. I will leave open the question of the relation of AC's, passives, and causatives in the two languages.[5]

1.2. Affected Meaning of AC's

An AC has an affected meaning; that is, the surface subject is adversely affected by some event. Here, affectedness means that a psychological change to the subject is involved.[6] This is why the subjects are required to be sentient, as shown below:[7,8]

(3) Korean:
a. John-i   koyangi-hantey elkwul-lul halkwuy-i-ess-ta.
   John-Nom   cat - Dat   face-Acc   scratch-HI-past-Dec
   'John had (his) face scratched by the cat.'
b. *ku chayk- i   koyangi-hantey pyoci-lul   halkwuy-i-ess-ta.
   the-book-Nom   cat - Dat   cover-Acc   scratch-HI-past-Dec
   'The book had its cover scratched by the cat.'

---

4 According to Oehrle and Nishio (1981:166), sentence (2b) may be interpreted in four ways: (i) The father intentionally brought on his child's death; (ii) the father let his child die; (iii) the father caused his child's death, inadvertently; or (iv) the father did not cause his child's death, intentionally or otherwise, but he was adversely affected by this child's death. The fourth interpretation is called the 'adversity causative' by Oehrle and Nishio (1981).

5 For the relation between passives and causatives, see S.-O. Lee (1972), Yang (1979), K. Park (1988), and H. Lee (1991), for Korean; and Washio (1992), among others, for Japanese.

6 Following Anderson (1978) and Tenny (1987), we can define the affectedness in an AC as requiring that the mental state of the subject undergo change gradually. It is worthwhile to note that McCawley (1972) states that Japanese adversity passives are always associated with the implication that the subject is affected, which is missing in plain passives. Thus, she posits the underlying verb AFFECT for the adversative passive.

7 For Korean, this is pointed out by C-M. Lee (1973:150), Y.-J. Kim (1990:287), and Maling and Kim (1992:50-51), among others, as an animacy constraint on the subject of an AC. For Japanese, it is pointed out by McCawley (1972), Kuno (1973), Dubinsky (1985), Miyagawa (1989), Rosen (1989), and Shibatani (1990), among others.

8 Hereafter, I will use the gloss HI for the Korean morpheme /hi/ and RARE for the Japanese morpheme /rare/, which is ambiguous between a passive and an AC.

(4) Japanese:[9]
a. Hirosi-wa kodomo-ni terebi-o   itazura s-rare-ta.
   Hirosi-Top child-Dat   television-Acc put out of commission-RARE-Past
   'Hirosi was subject to a child putting his television out of commission.'
b. *Telebi-wa kodomo-ni antena-o   itazura s-rare-ta.
   Hirosi-Top child-Dat   antena -Acc put out of commission-RARE-Past
   'The TV set was subject to a child putting its antena out of commission.'
                                                        (McCawley 1972:261-2)

The psychological affectedness of the subject is caused by some event where
the subject is involved. The subject may be involved in the causing event
either directly or indirectly, as shown below:

(5) Korean:
a. John-un   nolum-eyse caysan-ul   motwu nal-li-ess-ta.
   John-Top gambling-at property-Acc   all   fly -HI-Past-Dec
   'John experienced (his) property all being blown away in the gambling.'
b. Swunca-nun tongsayng-eykey ilki-lul   ilk-hi-ess-ta.
   Swunca-Top   brother-BY   diary-Acc   read-HI-Past-Dec
   'Swunca was affected by her diary being read by her brother.'
                                                          (Washio 1992:21)

(6) Japanese:
a. Tanaka-san-wa dareka-ni   saihu-o   nusum-rare-ta.
   Tanaka-Mr-Top somebody-Dat purse-Acc steal-RARE-past
   'Tanaka was subjected to somebody stealing his purse.'
b. John-ga   ame-ni hur-are-ta
   John Nom rain by   fall-RARE-Past
   'It rained and as a result John was affected adversely.' (Kuno 1973:23-24)

Examples (5a) and (6a) show that the subject is implicated directly in the
causing event. In (5b), however, it is not clear whether the subject's
involvement is direct or not. In (6b), however, the subject must not be
involved directly in the causing event. Thus, sentence (6b) may be interpreted
as 'It rained, to John's dismay'. (See Kuno 1973:24.)[10]
   It is important to note that the affected meaning is related to the speaker's
belief. That is, the speaker believes that the surface subject of an AC is

---

9 One of the Japanese informants disagrees with the judgment of sentence (4b). I
think that speaker's belief or empathy is involved in the animacy constraint in
Japanese as well as in Korean. This will be discussed in this section.
10 Interestingly, Washio (1991) develops his claim based on the 'exclusion' and
'inclusion' relations; if the subject is not directly involved in the causing event,
then it is 'excluded'. Although his observation is very insightful, Washio's claim
that the lack of 'intransitive passives' in Korean reduces to the lack of 'adversity by
exclusion' is not correct. Korean has 'intransitive passives,' such as sentences (1a)
and (5a).

psychologically affected by some event denoted by the predicate. The speaker's belief is related to the grammaticality of sentences as shown in the following Korean examples:

(7) a. ku salam-i   kom-hantey   tali-lul   mwuli-i-ess-ta.
       the man-Nom bear-Dat   leg-Acc bit-HI-Past-Dec
       'The man had his leg bitten by the bear.'
    b. ?ku cwukun salam-i   kom-hantey   tali-lul mwuli-i-ess-ta.
       the dead   man-Nom bear-Dat   leg-Acc bit-HI-Past-Dec
       'The dead man had his leg bitten by the bear.'

The contrast shown above is related to the animacy constraint on the subject. If the speaker believes that an inanimate being is sentient, then the sentence will be good; otherwise, it will be bad:

(8) ku cip-i   nwunintul-hantey pyek-ul   hel-li-ess-ta.
    the house-Nom soldiers-Dat   wall-Acc demolish-HI-Past-Dec
    'The house had its wall demolished by the soldiers.'

Some linguists (Im 1978:111 and K.-H. Lee 1988:215) judge sentence (8) to be grammatical, whereas other linguists (C.-M. Lee 1973:150) judge it ungrammatical. The different grammaticality judgments are due to the speaker's belief.

I call the construction under consideration the affected construction (AC) because of the affected meaning. The affectedness does not always need to be adversative, which is the reason that AC's should not be called 'adversity passives'.[11] I rather assume that the affectedness can be either positive, negative, or neutral, depending on the relation of the subject to the event denoted by the predicate, although most of the cases are negative.

2. A Causative Approach to AC's

Here, I argue that AC's are causative constructions. The causative approach will provide an account of two AC characteristics: argument addition and no case absorption.

Causation involves two events, a causing event and a caused event. It is known that there are two conditions on causation (cf. Shibatani 1976 and Dowty 1979):

(9) a. the speaker believes that the caused event would not take place
       without the causing event.

---

[11] McCawley (1972), Oehrle and Nishio (1981), Dubinsky (1985), and Shibatani (1990) point out that in Japanese, the AC's do not always have to be adversative:
   (i) Kirei na ozyoosan ni nak-rare-ru to   tyotto uresii mono da.
       pretty girl   by cry-Passive when little   glad
   'It's kind of nice when a beautiful girl cries over you.' (McCawley 1972:262, (18))

b. the speaker believes that the caused event takes place after the causing event.

When these two conditions hold, the two events constitute a causative relation. Now let's look at the causative relation in AC's. Consider the following repeated examples and their rough semantic relations:

(10) Korean:
a. ku salam-i   kom-hantey tali-lul   mwuli-i-ess-ta.
   the man-Nom bear-Dat   leg-Acc bit-HI-Past-Dec
   'The man had his leg bitten by the bear.'   (=7a)
b. bite (the bear, the man) CAUSE affected (the man)

(11) Japanese:
a. Tanaka-san-wa   dareka-ni   saihu-o   nusum-are-ta.
   Tanaka-Mr-Top somebody-Dat purse-Acc steal-RARE-past   (=6a)
   'Tanaka was subjected to somebody stealing his purse.'
b. steal (somebody, Tanaka's purse) CAUSE affected (Tanaka)

We can see that there are two events in an AC and that the two conditions on causation in (9) are satisfied in the semantic representations of AC's in (10b) and (11b). Thus, AC's can be argued to be causatives.

One special property of AC's is that the causation is reversed, compared with that of plain causatives. That is, in a plain causative, the subject is the causer, whereas in an AC it is a causee. Thus, we may assume that there are two types of causatives: [-reversed] and [+reversed]. An AC is then a [+reversed] causative.

The claim that an AC is a causative accounts for the two problems, argument addition and no case absorption, because a causative involves argument addition and does not absorb case. These two problems cannot be accounted for by a passive approach to AC's because passives involve argument suppression and case absorption, but never argument addition.

3. Case and AC's

This section will show that Case in AC's is assigned as in plain causatives. If AC's are causatives, then it is predicted that the case pattern of the AC is the same as that of the plain causative. This prediction is born out. The following Korean data show that the case patterns in AC's and plain causatives are exactly in parallel:

(12) when a verb stem is intransitive:
a. Causative: John-i   so-lul   cwuk-i-ess-ta.
             John-Nom cow-**Acc**   die-HI(causative)-Dec
             'John killed the cow.'
b. AC: John-i   ku saep-eyse caysan-ul   motwu nal-li-ess-ta.
      John-Nom the business-in property-**Acc**   all   fly-HI-Past-Dec

'John had (his) property all blown away in the business.'

(13) when a verb stem is transitive :
a.Causative: John-i   Mary-eykey chayk-ul   ilk-hi-ess-ta.
           John-Nom Mary-**Dat** book-**Acc** read-HI-Past -Dec
           'John made Mary read a book.'
b. AC: John-un   koyangi-hantey elkwul-lul halkwu-i-ess-ta.
      John-Top   cat - **Dat**   face-**Acc** scratch-HI-past-Dec
      'John had (his) face scratched by the cat.'

It does not seem to be accidental that the case patterns of the two constructions are in parallel. The feature [+causative] in causatives and AC's is responsible for the accusative case and the dative case. Thus, an AC verb is a causative-transitive verb.[12]
    Now let's look at the case patterns in AC's and causatives in Japanese. The following Japanese data also show that the case patterns of the two constructions are in parallel:

(14) when a verb stem is intransitive:
a. Causative: Taroo-wa   kodomo-ni/o   ko-sase-ta.
           Taro-Top   child - **Dat/Acc** come-Causative-Past
           'Taro let/made the child come.'
b. AC: Taroo-wa kodomo-ni   ko-rare-ta.
      Taro-Top child - **Dat** come-RARE-Past
      'Taroo had the child come on him.'

(15) When a stem verb is transitive,
a. Causative: Taroo-wa John-ni   watasi-no kao-o   kizutuke-sase-ta.
           Taro -Top John-**Dat** I - Gen face-**Acc** hurt -Causative-Past
           'Taroo made John hurt my face.'
b. AC: watasi-wa John-ni   kao-o   kizutuke-rare-ta.
      I - Top   John-**Dat** face-**Acc** hurt-RARE-Past
      'I had my face hurt by John on me.'

One thing we need to explain is why the AC of the intransitive verb in (14b) has dative case only, whereas the causative counterpart in (14a) shows case alternation between dative and accusative. As shown in the English translation in (14a), the causative is interpreted ambiguously, depending on the case markers. When there is dative case, it is interpreted as a 'permissive'(or noncoercive) causative which is translated by English *let* , and when there is accusative case it is interpreted as a coercive causative which is translated by *make*.[13] The semantic interpretation of Japanese causatives according to case

---

12 Maling (p.c.) has pointed out that the present position is in accord with the assumption taken by Maling (1989) and Maling and Kim (1992).
13 See Shibatani (1973) for the semantics of Japanese causatives.

markers predicts that an AC will be interpreted as a noncoercive causative.[14] The causing event in the AC does not coercively cause the subject to be affected. Therefore, an AC should be treated as a noncoercive causative and thus it has dative case only, but not accusative case.

4. Argument Structure of AC's
4.1 Argument Addition

As a causative, an AC shows the property of argument addition. The following examples show how the AC adds an argument from its corresponding simple verb:

(16) Korean:
a. John-uy   elkwul-eyse phi-ka   hulu - ess - ta.
   John-Gen face-from   blood-Nom run-Past-Dec
   'Blood ran from John's face.'
b. John-i   phi-lul   hulu-li-ess-ta.
   John-Nom blood-Acc run-HI-Past -Dec
   'John experienced bleeding.'
c. *John-i   phi-lul   hulu-ess-ta.
   John-Nom blood-Acc run-Past-Dec
   'John ran blood.'

(17) a. (Theme): simple verb 'run' in (16a)
      b. (Experiencer (Theme)): AC verb 'run-HI' in (16b) [15]

Examples (16a) and (16b) show a simple verb *hulu-* 'run' and its corresponding AC. Example (16c) shows that the simple verb *hulu-* 'run' is not a transitive verb. (17) shows that the AC has got an additional argument, experiencer, compared with its simple verb. Japanese shows exactly the same thing:

(18) Japanese:
a. Ame-ga   hut-ta.
   rain-Nom fall-Past
   'It rained'
b. John-ga   ame-ni   hur-are-ta.
   John-Nom rain-Dat   fall-RARE-Past
   'John was fallen by rain and he was affected adversely by it.'
c. *John-ga   ame-ni/o   hut-ta.
   John-Nom rain-Dat/Acc   fall-Past
   'John fell rain.'

---

[14] Because, in an AC, the causing event is an event, it cannot be interpreted as a permissive causative.
[15] A parenthesis indicates an argument structure of one predicate. Thus, in (17b), the argument structure of 'run' is embedded in that of /hi/.

(19) a. (Theme): simple verb 'fall' in (18a)
    b. (Experiencer (Theme)): AC verb 'fall-RARE' in (18b)

It is predicted that this experiencer argument is added in an AC because the AC is a psychological causative, and the affectedness of the surface subject is psychological.[16]

4.2 Argument Suppression in AC's?

The question of whether an AC involves argument suppression is related to that of whether an AC is a passive, because passivization is known as an operation where the highest argument is suppressed and case is absorbed. Thus, if an AC involves argument suppression, it may be argued that it is a passive, ignoring case absorption.[17] In this section, however, I suggest that AC's do not suppress an argument.

First, let's look at Japanese. The present question is whether or not dative-marked NP's are suppressed in the following AC examples:

(20) Japanese:
a. Taroo-wa   kodomo-ni   sin-are-ta.
    Taro-Top   child-Dat   die-RARE-Past
    'Taro's child died on him.'   (=1b)
b. John-wa kodomo-ni saihu-o   nusum-rare-ta.
    John-Top child-Dat purse-Acc steal-RARE-Past
    'John had his purse stolen by the children on him.'

Japanese has two pieces of evidence that the dative-marked arguments in AC's are not suppressed. The first one is the behavior of the anaphor *zibun* 'self'. It is known in Japanese that only a subject may antecede the anaphor. The following sentences are not ambiguous because only subjects can antecede the anaphor:

(21) Japanese:
    John$_i$-ga   Bill$_k$-ni zibun$_i$/*$_k$-no koto-o   hanasi-ta.
    John-Nom Bill-Dat self-gen   matter-Acc talk-Past
    'John talked to Bill self's matter.'   (Kuno 1973:292)

---

16 The property of argument addition holds in an AC where the simple verb is transitive as in (13b) and (15b). That is, the subject is an added argument, and has its independent argument status because it cannot be omitted.

17 See Sobin (1985) for a language where passivization involves only argument suppression, but does not absorb case. However, note that causativization may also involve argument suppression in other languages like Chichewa (See Baker 1988 and Alsina 1992). Argument suppression does not necessarily imply that an AC is not a causative because argument addition seems to be a more important characteristic of causativization than argument suppression.

The example above shows that nonsubjects may not antecede the anaphor. The examples in (22) show that a dative-marked argument in an AC antecedes the anaphor:

(22) a. Taroo$_i$-wa kodomo$_k$-ni zibun$_{i/k}$-no heya-de sin-are-ta.
    Taro-Top son-Dat self - Gen room-in die-RARE-Past
    'Taro's son died in self's room on him.'
b. John$_i$-wa Mary$_k$-ni zibun$_{i/k}$-no koto-o zimans-are-ta.
    John-Top Mary-Dat self-Gen matter-Acc boast-RARE-Past
    'John suffered from Mary's bragging about self's matter.' (Farmer 1984:94)

The sentences in (22) are ambiguous because the subject and the dative-marked NP can both be antecedents.[18] This indicates that the dative-marked NP's are not suppressed.

The second piece of evidence comes from quantifier floating. It is known in Japanese that only an argument may antecede a numeral quantifier, as shown below:

(23) a. Kodomo-ga 3-min kita.
    children-Nom 3-CL came
    Three children came.'
b. *Taroo-wa sensei-ni 2-ri hon-o moratta.
    Taro-Top teachers-from 2-CL book-Acc got
    'Taro got books from two teachers.' (Miyagawa 1989:24-25)

The following AC shows that the dative-marked argument in an AC can antecede a numeral quantifier:[19]

(24) a. Hahaoya-ga kodomo-ni 2-ri sin-are-ta.
    mother-Nom child-Dat 2-CL die-RARE-Past
    'Two children died on their mother.' (Miyagawa 1989:169)

---

[18] A dative-marked argument in a Japanese causative shows the same antecedenthood of the anaphor *zibun*:
  (i) John$_i$-ga Mary$_k$-ni zibun$_{i/k}$-no uti-de hon-o yom-ase-ta.
    John-Nom Mary-Dat self-Gen house in book-Acc read-Causative-Past
    'John made Mary read books in (lit) self's house.' (Kuno 1973:294)
Sentence (i) shows the same ambiguity as that in (22). This also indicates the parallelism between a plain causative and an AC.
[19] I owe sentence (24b) to M. Kawamura. But note that when a simple verb is transitive, the dative-marked NP in an AC does not always antecede a quantifier:
  (i) *John-wa kodomo-ni 2-ri saihu-o nusum-are-ta.
    John-Top child-Dat 2-CL purse-Acc steal-RARE-Past
    'John had his purse stolen by two children on him.'
This requires further study on quantifier floating in Japanese.

b. Tanaka-san-wa   jyosei-ni 2-ri   ai-o   kokuhaku-sare-ta
Tanaka-Mr.-Top lady-Dat 2-CL love-Acc confess-RARE-Past
'Mr. Tanaka was affected by the love of two ladies being confessed.'

Japanese clearly shows that the dative-marked argument in an AC is not suppressed, and thus the AC does not involve argument suppression.[20]
    Now let's look at Korean AC's. First, it is clear that when the simple verb is intransitive, the corresponding AC does not involve argument suppression, because the presence of the single argument of the simple verb is obligatory:

(25) a. John-i   phi-lul   hul-li-ess-ta.
        John-Nom blood-Acc run-HI-Past -Dec
        'John experienced bleeding.'   (=16b)
b. *John-i   hul-li-ess-ta.
    John-Nom run-HI-Past -Dec
    '?'

    Now let's look at an AC whose corresponding simple verb is transitive:

(26) John-un   koyangi-hantey elkwul-lul halkwu-i-ess-ta.
     John-Top   cat - Dat   face-Acc   scratch-HI-Past-Dec
     'John had (his) face scratched by the cat.'

Now the question is whether or not the dative-marked NP in (26) is suppressed, which is the highest argument of the simple verb.
    It is not clear what may antecede the anaphor *caki* 'self' and a floated numeral quantifier in Korean, because there are some cases where some adjuncts as well as subjects may antecede them (See Hong 1991 for the examples.). Furthermore, there is no clear test for argumenthood in Korean. Here, I will not discuss what may antecede the anaphor *caki* and numeral quantifiers. Instead, I will show that the status of the dative-marked argument in an AC is the same as that in a plain causative, and thus the dative-marked NP in an AC is an argument. This is so because, in a plain causative, the argument must not be suppressed, since it cannot be omitted.
    First, the dative-marked argument in both an AC and a plain causative do not antecede the anaphor *caki* 'self', as shown below:

(27) a. AC:
Mary$_i$-ka John$_k$-eykey caki$_{i/*k}$ pang-eyse ton-ul   ppayas-ki-ess-ta.
Mary-Nom John-Dat   self   room-in   money-Acc take away-HI-Dec

---

[20] Marantz (1984) assumes that the dative-marked argument in Japanese is suppressed, without giving evidence. Washio (1990:230-235) gives three pieces of evidence for the suppression of the dative-marked argument in Japanese. But they are not convincing to me.

'Mary had (her) money taken away by John in her/*his room.'
b. Causative:

John$_i$-i   Mary$_k$-eykey caki$_{i/*k}$ chayk-ul   ilk-hi-ess-ta.
John-Nom Mary-Dat   self   book-Acc read-HI-Past-Dec
'John made Mary read his/*her book.'

Secondly, quantifier floating tells us the same thing; i.e., that the dative-marked argument behaves like that in a plain causative. It is known that in Korean, as in other languages, subjects or objects may only antecede floated numeral quantifiers in general (See Hong (1991) for examples.). However, dative-marked arguments in both an AC and a plain causative do not seem to antecede numeral quantifiers:[21]

(28) a. AC:
*John-un   koyangi-hantey sey-mali-hantey elkwul-ul halkwu-i-ess-ta.
John-Top   cat-dat   three-CL-Dat   face-Acc   scratch-HI-Past-Dec
'John had his face scratched by three cats.'
b. Plain Causative:
*John-i   haksayng-hantey seys-hantey chayk-ul   ilk-hi-ess-ta.
John-Nom student-Dat   three-Dat   book-Acc read-HI-Past-Dec
'John made three students read books.'

To conclude the discussion regarding the argumenthood of the dative-marked argument in Korean AC's, we do not have any direct evidence that it is either suppressed or not suppressed. What we can say is that its status is the same as that of a plain causative which is assumed to be an argument.[22,23] Although Korean does not show the desired contrast clearly, as does Japanese, we may argue that a dative-marked argument in an AC is not suppressed and thus the AC does not involve argument suppression in either of the two languages.

---

21 Hong (1991) shows that if dative-marked NP's occur with delimiters (*man* 'only' and *to* 'also'), or with the contrastive marker *nun*, then they can antecede numeral quantifiers.

22 One possible test for the argumenthood of an NP is whether or not its presence is obligatory. The dative-marked argument does not seem to be:

  (i) Mary-ka   (John-eykey)   ton-ul   ppayas-ki-ess-ta.
    Mary-Nom (John-Dat)   money-Acc take away-HI-Dec
    'Mary had (her) money taken away (by John).'

Here we need to check whether the omitted NP is a discourse-related element, i.e. a topic. If it is a topic, we may assume an empty element such as small pro for the omitted NP. Otherwise, we might assume that AC's involve argument suppression. But this assumption still requires us to explain why an argument of a simple verb should occur obligatorily in its corresponding AC.

23 The present issue is related to what constitutes a test for argumenthood in Korean, which is still unknown. Note that Kim (1990) and Hong (1991) both assume that the dative-marked argument in an AC is not suppressed.

5. Discussion
5.1 AC's, Causatives, and Passives

The present approach to AC's is that an AC is a causative. There are, however, some differences between AC's and plain causatives. First, as mentioned in section 2, an AC is a reversed causative, where the causee is mapped to the surface subject, in contrast to a plain causative, where the causer is mapped to the surface subject.[24]

The second difference between AC's and plain causatives is that AC's do not allow double accusative marking,[25] whereas plain causatives do, which is pointed out by Y.-J. Kim (p.c), as shown below:

(29) Plain Causative:
a. sensayngnim-i haksangtul-eykey chayk-ul   ilk-hi-ess-ta.
   teacher-Nom   students-Dat   book-Acc read-HI-Past-Dec
   'The teacher made/caused students (to) read books.'
b. sensayngnim-i haksangtul-ul chayk-ul   ilk-hi-ess-ta.
   teacher-Nom   students-Acc book-Acc read-HI-Past-Dec
   'The teacher made students read books.'

(30) AC:
a. John-i   koyangi-hantey elkwul-lul halkwuy-i-ess-ta.
   John-Nom cat - Dat   face-Acc   scratch-HI-past-Dec
   'John had (his) face scratched by the cat.'   (=3a)
b. *John-i   koyangi-lul elkwul-lul halkwuy-i-ess-ta.
   John-Nom   cat - Dat face-Acc   scratch-HI-past-Dec
   'John had (his) face scratched by the cat.'

This contrast can be accounted for by a semantic condition on accusative-marked arguments in Korean causatives: when a causative shows the case alternation (Dat-Acc, or Nom-Acc[26]), the accusative-marked argument is

---

[24] Grimshaw (1990) explains the matching of the experiencer argument to the surface subject in an English psychological causative by assuming that the aspectual dimension overrides the thematic dimension and thus the causer, not Experiencer, is mapped to the surface subject. In Korean AC's such as in (30), we can see that this is not the case: that is, an experiencer causee is mapped to the subject position. The reversed direction of causation in AC's requires further study.
[25] Japanese does not allow double accusatives. This is known as the 'Double O Constraint'.
[26] The Nom-Acc alternation occurs in the periphrastic causative construction:
      (i) John-i   Mary-ka   chayk-ul ilk-key   ha-ess-ta.
          John-Nom Mary-Nom book-Acc read-KEY cause-Past-Dec
          'John caused Mary to read books.'
      (ii) John-i   Mary-lul   chayk-ul ilk-key   ha-ess-ta.
          John-Nom Mary-Acc book-Acc read-KEY cause-Past-Dec
          'John made Mary read books.'

interpreted as an affected entity.[27] The dative-marked agent argument in an AC cannot be interpreted as an affected entity. This is why an AC does not allow double accusative.

Now let's compare AC's and passives. If AC's are causatives, not passives, it should be possible to passivize them. Theoretically, passivization of AC's is possible. However, in fact, it is not possible in either Korean or Japanese. Let's look at a Korean AC first:[28]

(31) a. AC: John-i   caysan-lul   nal-li-ess-ta.
       John-Nom property-Acc fly-HI-Past -Dec
       'John experienced losing his property.'
  b. HI-passive: *caysan-i   John-ey uyhay nal-li-li-ess-ta.
       property-Nom John-by   fly-HI-HI-Past-Dec
       (Lit) '(John's) property was flown by John.'
  c. CI-passive: caysan-i   John-ey uyhay nal-lie ci-ess-ta.
       property-Nom John-by   fly-HI CI-Past-Dec
       (Lit) '(John's) property was flown by John.'

Of the two passives, HI and CI passives, the HI passive in (31b) is ungrammatical, whereas the CI passive in (31c) is grammatical. But note that the CI passive in (31c) is a passivization of the causative of (31a), not of the AC. Note that all AC's in Korean are ambiguous between an AC and a causative. The ungrammaticality of (31b) and of the AC (31c) can be explained by the double /hi/ constraint, which does not allow two /hi/'s to appear in the same verb. Theoretically, it is possible to have two /hi/s; one of which is a passive and the other of which is a causative. But this double /hi/ construction is always ungrammatical in Korean.

Now let's look at a Japanese AC and its passivized counterpart:

(32) a. AC: John-wa dareka-ni   saihu-o   nusum-rare-ta.
       John-Top somebody-Dat purse-Acc steal-RARE-past
       'John was subjected to somebody stealing his purse.'   (=6a)
  b. Passivized AC:
    *John-wa dareka-ni   saihu-ga   nusum-are-rare-ta.
    John-Top somebody-Dat purse-Nom steal-RARE-RARE-past
    'As for John, his purse was stolen by somebody.'

---

[27] Hong (1991) develops a theory of case in Korean, where accusative case is associated with an affected entity. Although this is correct in general, it is not always the case. First, the affected argument in an AC is associated with nominative case. Secondly, accusative-marked NP's in Korean light verb constructions and in some perception verb constructions are not affected entities.
28 Note that Korean has two types of passives: the HI passives where the morpheme /hi/ is employed, and the CI passive where the auxiliary verb -ci 'become' is employed. It is assumed that HI passivization is lexical and CI passivization is syntactic. See Kim (1990) and Hong (1991). For the meaning difference between the two passives, see K. Lee (1987).

The ungrammaticality of the passivized AC in (32b) can also be explained by the double /rare/ constraint in Japanese. Alternatively, we may suggest that an AC cannot be passivized semantically. An AC has a passive meaning in that the surface subject is affected and thus passivization of a semantic passive will be awkward semantically.

5.2. Differences between Korean AC's and Japanese AC's

There are some differences between AC's in Korean and Japanese. First, in Korean the AC morpheme is /hi/, which is the same in form as the passive morpheme and the causative as well. Note that the other passive morpheme CI is never used in an AC. In Japanese, the morpheme /rare/ which is the passive morpheme, is employed. And note that the causative morpheme /sase/ is also used in Japanese. I will leave open the question of why the morpheme which is the same in form as the passive or the causative is employed in the languages.

Secondly, Korean AC's are restricted, whereas Japanese AC's are considerably unrestricted. Ditransitive verbs in Korean do not have AC counterparts, and the number of intransitive verbs with AC counterparts is very small. The reason that ditransitive verbs in Korean do not form AC's is because they do not have any /hi/ causatives and passives. One possible account for the difference between the two languages is that Korean AC's are lexical and Japanese AC's are syntactic.

6. Concluding Remarks

In this study, I have claimed that AC's are psychological causatives. This claim based on the semantics of such constructions can account both for argument addition and for the case pattern found in AC's, which have been problematic in the literature.

Many linguists[29] have treated AC's as passives. As long as they assume that AC's are passives, however, they encounter problems with argument addition and nonabsorbed accusative case. They need to make some stipulations or devise special mechanisms to solve the problems.[30]

The present causative approach to AC's does not require any stipulations or special mechanisms. Because it is a causative, an AC involves argument addition and does not absorb case. Even in the nonuniform approach to Japanese AC's, they just assume that there are two types of passives but do not explain why one passive (an adversity passive) involves argument addition and does not absorb case. However, the causative approach to AC's explains

---

[29] For Korean, they are Im (1977), Kang (1986), Kim (1990), and Hong (1991), among others. For Japanese, they include the uniform advocates like Howard and Nyekawa-Howard (1976), Miyagawa (1989), and Washio (1990), among others.
[30] This is the case in Kang (1986), Kim (1990), and Han (1991) for Korean, and Marantz (1984), Miyagawa (1989), and Washio (1990) for Japanese.

such properties of AC's without cost, which is a big advantage over the other approaches.

References

Alsina, Alex. 1992. On the Argument Structure of Causatives, LI 23:4. 517-555.

Anderson, Mona. 1978. NP Pre-posing in Noun Phrases, In NELS 8. 12-21.

Baker, Mark. 1988. Incorporation, Chicago: The University of Chicago Press.

Chung, Taegoo. 1992. The Affected Construction and Case in Korean, SICOL 92 Proceedings, 1992 Seoul International Conference on Linguistics, The Linguistics Society of Korea.

Dowty, David. 1979. Word Meaning and Montague Grammar, Dordrecht: D. Reidel Publishing Company.

Dubinsky, Stanley. 1985. A Union Analysis for Japanese 'Adversity Passives', In Wayne Harbert and Sarah Fagan (eds.), Cornell Working Papers 7, Cornell University.

Farmer, Ann K. 1984. Modularity in Syntax: A Study of Japanese and English, Cambridge: The MIT Press.

Grimshaw, Jane. 1990. Argument Structure, Linguistic Inquiry Monograph 18, Cambridge, Massachusetts: The MIT Press.

Han, Hak-Sung. (1991) The Case of Korean Adjectives and Passive Verbs, Studies in Generative Grammar, The Generative Grammar Circle, Kul Press, Seoul.

Hong, Ki-Sun. 1991. Argument Selection and Case Marking in Korean, Ph.D. Dissertation, Stanford University.

Howard, Irwin and Agnes Niyekawa-Howard. 1976. Passivization, in M. Shibatani, (ed.) Syntax and Semantics 5: Japanese Generative Grammar, New York: Academic Press.

Im, Hong-Pin. 1978. Kwuke Phidonghwauy Uymi, [The Meaning of Passivity in Korean], Cindanhakpo 45.

Kang, Young-Se. 1986. Korean Syntax and Universal Grammar, Ph.D. Dissertation, Harvard University.

Kim, Young-Joo. 1990. The Syntax and Semantics of Korean Case: The interaction between Lexical and Syntactic Levels of Representation, Ph.D. Dissertation, Harvard University.

Kuno, Susumu. 1973. The Structure of the Japanese Language, The MIT Press, Cambridge.

Lee, Chung-Min. 1973. Abstract Syntax and Korean with Reference to English, Ph.D. Dissertation, Indiana University.

Lee, Hyangcheon. 1991. The Meaning of Passive and Its Origin, Ph. D. Dissertation, Seoul National University, Seoul, Korea.

Lee, Keedong. 1987. 'The Meanings of the Two Passives in Korean,' Language Research 23. 185-201.

Lee, Kwang-Ho. 1988. A Study of the Case Marker 'ul/lul' in Korean, Kwukehakchongse 12, Kwukehakhoy.

Lee, Sang-Oak. 1972. Kwukeuy Sadong-phidong Kwumun Yenkwu, [A Study of Korean Causative-passive Constructions], Kwuke Yenkwu 26.

Marantz, Alec. 1984. On the Nature of Grammatical Relations, The MIT Press, Cambridge, Massachusetts.

McCawley, Noriko A. 1972. On the Treatment of Japanese Passive, CLS 8: 259-270.

Maling, Joan. 1989. Adverbials and Structural Case in Korean, In Kuno et. al (eds.) Harvard Studies in Korean Linguistics III.

Maling, Joan. and Soowon Kim 1992. 'Case Assignment in the Inalienable Possession Construction in Korean,' Journal of East Asian Linguistics 1, No 1, 37-68.

Miyagawa, Shigeru 1989. Syntax and Semantics 22: Structure and Case Marking in Japanese, Academic Press, New York.

Oehrle, Richard T. and Hiroko Nishio. 1981. Adversity, Coyote Papers 2, University of Arizona.

Rosen, Sara T. 1989. Argument Structure and Complex Predicates, Ph.D. Dissertation, Brandeis University.

Shibatani, Masayoshi. 1973. Semantics of Japanese Causativization, Foundations of Language 9. 327-373.

Shibatani, Masayoshi. 1976. The Grammar of Causative Constructions: A Conspectus, In M. Shibatani (ed.) Syntax and Semantics 6, New York: Academic Press.

Shibatani, Masayoshi. 1990. The Languages of Japan, New York: Cambridge University Press.

Sobin, Nicholas J. 1985. Case Assignment in Ukrainian Morphological Passive Constructions, LI 16. 649-662.

Tenny, Carol L. 1987. 'Grammaticalizing Aspect and Affectedness,' Ph.D. Dissertation, MIT.

Washio, Ryuichi 1990. The Japanese Passive, In Linguistic Review 6, 227-263.

Washio, Ryuichi 1991. When Causatives mean Passives: A Cross-linguistic Perspective. Ms.University of Tsukuba, Japan.

Yang, In-Seok. 1972. Korean Syntax: Case Markers, Delimiters, Complementation, and Relativization, Ph.D. Dissertation, Working Papers in Linguistics 4, No 6, University of Hawaii.

Yang, Dong-Whee. 1979. The Passive-Causative in Korean, In Hankul 166:33-49.

Numeral Classifier Phrases Inside DP and the Specificity Effect

HISATSUGU KITAHARA
Harvard University

This paper examines three types of Japanese nominal phrases each containing a numeral classifier:

(1)   a.   Type I

Taro-ga	hon-o	san-satu	katta
T-Nom	book-Acc	3-Class	bought

'Taro bought three books.'

        b.   Type II

Taro-ga	hon	san-satu-o	katta
T-Nom	book	3-Class-Acc	bought

        c.   Type III

Taro-ga	san-satu	hon-o	katta
T-Nom	3-Class	book-Acc	bought

---

*   I would like to thank Noam Chomsky, Ruriko Kawashima, Susumu Kuno, and especially Samuel D. Epstein for valuable comments and helpful discussion. In addition, I am grateful to Jun Abe, Masatoshi Koizumi, Shigeru Miyagawa, Yoichi Miyamoto, Masayuki Oishi, Shigeo Tonoike, Akira Watanabe, and participants at the 3rd Japanese/Korean Linguistics Conference for clarifying remarks and helpful suggestions. All errors are my own.

In type I, the NP with an overt case particle precedes its numeral classifier. In type II, the bare NP precedes its numeral classifier with an overt case particle. And in type III, its numeral classifier precedes the NP with an overt case particle.

The paper consists of three sections. In section 1, I review the single-constituent analyses provided in Kamio (1983) and Terada (1990). In section 2, I propose an alternative analysis within Checking Theory (Chomsky (1992)). In section 3, I discuss a constraint on the scrambling of numeral classifiers (Miyagawa (1989)).

1. The Single-Constituent Analyses

Kamio (1983) observes the following contrasts in Coordination and Pseudo-Cleft constructions.[1]

(2)	a.	Type I		
		Taro-ga	hon-o	san-satu-to
		T-Nom	book-Acc	3-Class-and
		pen-o	san-bon	katta
		pen-Acc	3-Class	bought

'Taro bought three books and three pens.'

	b.	Type II		
		Taro-ga	hon	san-satu-to
		T-Nom	book	3-Class-and
		pen	san-bon-o	katta
		pen	3-Class-Acc	bought

	c.	Type III		
		*Taro-ga	san-satu	hon-to
		T-Nom	3-Class	book-and
		san-bon	pen-o	katta
		3-Class	pen-Acc	bought

---

[1] The case particle must drop in a position immediately preceding the conjunction -to. This remains unexplained.

(3)   a. Type I

```
Taro-ga      katta-no-wa
T-Nom        bought-Comp-Top
hon-o        san-satu   da
book-Acc     3-Class    Copula
'It is three books that Tom bought.'
```

        b. Type II

```
Taro-ga      katta-no-wa
T-Nom        bought-Comp-Top
hon      san-satu-o      da
book     3-Class-Acc     Copula
```

        c. Type III

```
*Taro-ga     katta-no-wa
T-Nom        bought-Comp-Top
san-satu     hon-o      da
3-Class      book-Acc   Copula
```

These two well-known constituency tests suggest that the NP and its numeral classifier (henceforth, NC) form a constituent in type I and type II, but not in type III.

Terada (1990), following Kamio (1983), argues that a constituent formed in type I is a QP whose head Q is an NC, as shown in (4):

(4) $[_{QP}$ $[_{NP}$ hon-o] $[_{Q'}$ san-satu]]

Her QP analysis is consistent with the assumption that Japanese is a strict head-final language. Further, agreement between the NP and its NC can be construed as Spec-Head agreement (Chomsky (1986b)). She also argues (following Sportiche (1988)) that when the NP is separated from its NC, the NP is indeed scrambled out of the QP and adjoined to the IP (Saito (1985)), as shown in (5):

(5)   a.

```
hon-o      Taro-ga     san-satu    katta
book-Acc   T-Nom       3-Class     bought
'Taro bought three books.'
```

        b. $[_{IP}$ hon$_i$-o $[_{IP}$ Taro-ga $[_{QP}$ t_i $[_{Q'}$ san-satu]] katta]]

Assuming the *Barriers* framework (Chomsky (1986a)), the QP occupying the complement position of the verb *katta* is L-marked; hence, the movement does not cross a barrier.

While Terada's QP analysis provides an elegant account of type I; her extension of it to type II and type III, confronts both empirical and conceptual problems.

Regarding type II (in which an NC is realized with an overt case particle), she stipulates that an NC is categorially ambiguous between a head Q and a head N. Given this, she argues that a constituent formed by the NP and its NC in type II is an NP whose head N is an NC, as shown in (6):

(6)   [NP [NP hon] [N' san-satu-o]]

Although she does not provide the internal structure of the NP (headed by the NC *san-satu-o*) in (6); the NP *hon* must occupy the Spec of the NP to enter into Spec-Head agreement with its NC. This analysis of type II is empirically inadequate in that it incorrectly allows the scrambling of the NP *hon* out of the NP whose head N is the NC *san-satu-o.* Consider (7):

(7)   a. *hon   Taro-ga   san-satu-o   katta
           book   T-Nom   3-Class-Acc   bought
           'Taro bought three books.'

        b. [IP [NP hon]i [IP Taro-ga
           [NP ti [N' san-satu-o]] katta]]

The direct object NP is L-marked by the verb -*katta;* hence, the movement does not cross a barrier.

Turning to type III, Terada argues that type III is derived from type I. The NC is scrambled out of the QP and adjoined to the VP. Consider (8):

(8)   a. Taro-ga   san-satu   hon-o   katta
           T-Nom   3-Class   book-Acc bought
           'Taro bought three books.'

        b. Taro-ga [VP san-satui [VP [QP hon-o ti]
           katta]]

This adjunction of the head Q *san-satu* (see (4)) to the maximal projection VP violates Structure Preservation. To avoid this, she stipulates that the NC itself may constitute a maximal projection QP. Given this; type I is structurally ambiguous between (9a) and (9b), and only the latter yields type III.

(9)   a.   [$_{QP}$ hon-o [$_{Q'}$ san-satu]]

        b.   [$_{QP}$ hon-o [$_{QP}$ san-satu]]

Now, her analysis (including the two stipulations) satisfies Structure Preservation, but it makes unclear how the NP *hon-o* can enter into Spec-Head agreement with the NC *san-satu* (= QP) in (9b).

    To summarize, Terada's QP analysis provides an elegant account of type I; however, regarding type II, it stipulates that an NC is categorially ambiguous between Q and N. Even with this stipulation, the ungrammaticality of (7) remains unexplained. Regarding type III, it stipulates that an NC is structurally ambiguous between Q and QP. This stipulation makes unclear how the NP in the adjoined position of the QP can enter into Spec-Head agreement with its NC.

    In the following section, I propose an alternative analysis within Checking Theory (Chomsky (1992)), which solves Terada's (empirical and conceptual) problems.

2. An Alternative Analysis

2.1. Agreement Inside DP

Chomsky (1992) argues that categories bearing certain morphological features (e.g. Case-features) must move to a position where these features can be checked off. Given that the features are checked off when they are matched in a Spec-Head configuration; I assume that nominal categories (e.g. N, D) may bear a Case-feature. When overt nominal categories bear a Case-feature in Japanese, they are morphologically realized with an overt case particle. Further, they must move to a position where their Case-features may be checked off. Following insights in Fukui (1986), I argue that the Spec of the DP whose covert head D bears a Case-feature is a position where the checking of Case-features takes place.[2] Consider (10):

(10)   a. [$_{DP}$ [$_{D'}$ [$_{NP}$ hon-o] D$_{<+Acc>}$]]
                     book-Acc

       b. [$_{DP}$ [$_{NP}$ hon-o]$_i$ [$_{D'}$ t$_i$ D$_{<+Acc>}$]]
                  book-Acc

In (10a), the NP whose head N *hon-o* bears accusative case (henceforth, [+Acc]) is base-generated in the complement position of the covert D which also bears [+Acc]. In (10b), the NP moves to the Spec of the DP where [+Acc] is checked off. The movement is driven by a general principle: Morphological features must be checked off in the course of the derivation (Chomsky (1992)).

Assuming Checking Theory, consider agreement between an NP and its NC, as shown in (11):

(11)   a. gakusei-o   san-nin
           student-Acc   3-Class

       b. *hon-o   san-nin
            book-Acc   3-Class

       c. *gakusei-o   san-satu
            student-Acc   3-Class

       d. hon-o   san-satu
           book-Acc   3-Class

The classifier *-nin* is used for counting humans whereas the classifier *-satu* is used for counting books. The ungrammatical (11b, c) suggest that some features borne by the NP and its NC in each example fail to be matched (in other words, some features fail to be checked off) whereas in (11a, d), the relevant features are correctly matched and checked off.

Within Checking Theory, the feature checking operations occur in Spec-Head configurations.[3] Given that Japanese is a strict

---

[2]   This paper does not discuss a checking relation between a verb and its complement DP in Japanese. See Miyagawa (1991) for relevant discussion of this point.

[3]   See Chomsky (1992) for the precise definition of checking domain.

head-final language; I propose the following structure of the nominal phrase with its NC:

(12)   [$_{DP}$ [$_{D'}$ [$_{NCP}$ [$_{NC'}$ NP NC]] D]]

In (12), the NC heads its own maximal projection, Numeral Classifier Phrase (henceforth, NCP) (dominated by DP and dominating NP). The NP realized with a case particle first moves to the Spec of the NCP to enter into a checking relation with the head NC, then it moves to the Spec of the DP where its Case-feature is checked off.

2.2.   A   Unified   Analysis

Recall types I, II, and III:

(1)   a. Type I
            Taro-ga   hon-o   san-satu   katta
            T-Nom   book-Acc   3-Class   bought
            'Taro bought three books.'

        b. Type II
            Taro-ga   hon   san-satu-o   katta
            T-Nom   book   3-Class-Acc   bought

        c. Type III
            Taro-ga   san-satu   hon-o   katta
            T-Nom   3-Class   book-Acc   bought

For ease of exposition; let us use the following schematic structures:

(13)   a.   NP-Acc   NC   (type I)

        b.   NP   NC-Acc   (type II)

        c.   NC   NP-Acc   (type III)

Given (12); the relevant aspects of the derivation of type I are as follows:

(14) a. $[_{DP} [_{D'} [_{NCP} [_{NC'} \text{ NP-Acc NC}]] \text{ D}_{<+Acc>}]]$

b. $[_{DP} [_{D'} [_{NCP} \text{NP}_i\text{-Acc } [_{NC'} \text{ t}_i \text{ NC}]] \text{ D}_{<+Acc>}]]$

c. $[_{DP} \text{NP}_i\text{-Acc} [_{D'} [_{NCP} \text{ t}'_i [_{NC'} \text{ t}_i \text{ NC}]] \text{ D}_{<+Acc>}]]$

The NP-Acc base-generated in the complement position of the NC ((14a)) moves to the Spec of the NCP to enter into a checking relation with the NC ((14b)), and then the NP-Acc moves to the Spec of the DP where [+Acc] is checked off ((14c)). Consider type II:

(15) a. $[_{DP} [_{D'} [_{NCP} [_{NC'} \text{ NP NC-Acc}]] \text{ D}_{<+Acc>}]]$

b. $[_{DP} [_{D'} [_{NCP} \text{NP}_i [_{NC'} \text{ t}_i \text{ NC-Acc}]] \text{ D}_{<+Acc>}]]$

c. $[_{DP} [_{NCP} \text{NP}_i [_{NC'} \text{ t}_i \text{ NC-Acc}]]_j$
$[_{D'} \text{ t}_j \text{ D}_{<+Acc>}]]$

The bare NP base-generated in the complement position of the NC-Acc ((15a)) moves to the Spec of the NCP to enter into a checking relation with the NC-Acc ((15b)), and then the NCP whose head bears [+Acc] moves to the Spec of the DP where [+Acc] is checked off ((15c)).[4] Now, consider type III:

(16) a. $[_{DP} [_{D'} [_{NCP} [_{NC'} \text{ NP-Acc NC}]] \text{ D}_{<+Acc>}]]$

b. $[_{DP} [_{D'} [_{NCP} \text{NP}_i\text{-Acc } [_{NC'} \text{ t}_i \text{ NC}]] \text{ D}_{<+Acc>}]]$

c. $[_{DP} \text{NP}_i\text{-Acc} [_{D'} [_{NCP} \text{ t}'_i [_{NC'} \text{ t}_i \text{ NC}]] \text{ D}_{<+Acc>}]]$

d. $[_{NCP} \text{ t}'_i [_{NC'} \text{ t}_i \text{ NC}]]_j \ldots$
$[_{DP} \text{NP}_i\text{-Acc} [_{D'} \text{ t}_j \text{ D}_{<+Acc>}]]$

---

[4] I assume (with Murasugi (1991)) that an NC is a nominal category which may bear a Case-feature.

(16a-c) are identical to (14a-c). In (16d), however, the NCP is scrambled out of the DP. Thus, the scrambled NCP and the DP do not form a constituent.[5]

Recall that the result of the constituency tests suggests that the NP and its NC forms a constituent in type I and type II, but not in type III (Kamio (1983), Terada (1990)). The proposed analysis explains this result by assigning (14c), (15c), and (16d) to types I, II, and III, respectively. Now consider the following sentences (which led Terada to stipulate that an NC is both categorially (Q vs. N) and structurally (Q vs. QP) ambiguous):

(17) a. hon-o   Taro-ga   san-satu   katta
         book-Acc   T-Nom   3-Class   bought
         'Taro bought three books.'

   b. $[_{IP}$ $[_{NP}$ hon-o$]_i$ $[_{IP}$ Taro-ga $[_{DP}$ t"$_i$ $[_{D'}$
         $[_{NCP}$ t'$_i$ $[_{NC'}$ t$_i$ san-satu$]]$ D$_{<+Acc>}$ $]]$
         katta $]]$

(18) a. Taro-ga   san-satu   hon-o   katta
         T-Nom   3-Class   book-Acc   bought
         'Taro bought three books.'

   b. Taro-ga $[_{VP}$ $[_{NCP}$ t'$_i$ $[_{NC'}$ t$_i$ san-satu $]]_j$
         $[_{VP}$ $[_{DP}$ $[_{NP}$ hon-o$]_i$ $[_{D'}$ t$_j$ D$_{<+Acc>}$ $]]$
         katta $]]$

Given that the transitive verb *katta* L-marks the DP in its complement position; the extraction of either the NP or the NCP out of the DP crosses no barrier. Let us finally consider the ungrammatical (7), repeated in (19), which was a problem for the QP analysis.

(19) a. *hon   Taro-ga   san-satu-o   katta
         book   T-Nom   3-Class-Acc   bought
         'Taro bought three books.'

   b. $[_{IP}$ $[_{NP}$ hon$]_i$ $[_{IP}$ Taro-ga
         $[_{DP}$ $[_{NCP}$ t'$_i$ $[_{NC'}$ t$_i$ san-satu-o $]]_j$
         $[_{D'}$ t$_j$ D$_{<+Acc>}$ $]]$ katta $]]$

---

[5] I assume (with Barss (1986)) that the unbound trace occupying the Spec of the NCP is an anaphor which is chain-bound by its antecedent NP occupying the Spec of the DP.

The extraction of the NP *hon* from both the NCP and the DP crosses a barrier (= the NCP) and the maximal projection immediately dominating the barrier (= the DP); thus, the trace t'_i occupying the Spec of the NCP violates the Empty Category Principle (ECP).[6]

As shown above, the proposed analysis of types I, II, and III renders unnecessary the stipulations (that an NC is both categorially and structurally ambiguous) while at the same time, it correctly excludes the ungrammatical (19) (= (7)).

3. On the Scrambling of NCPs

In this section, the proposed analysis of an NP and its NC will be extended to the constraint on the scrambling of NCs, observed by Miyagawa (1989). The constraint will be shown to be a Specificity Effect (Chomsky (1973), Fiengo and Higginbotham (1981)).

3.1. Theme vs. Non-Theme

Miyagawa (1989) observes that an NC linked to a theme argument can be scrambled ((20a)) whereas an NC linked to a non-theme argument cannot ((20b)).[7]

```
(20)    a.  san-satu    Taro-ga
            3-Class     T-Nom
            gengogaku-no        hon-o       yonda
            linguistics-Gen     book-Acc    read
            'Taro read three linguistics books.'

        b.?*san-nin    Taro-ga
            3-Class     T-Nom
            Harvard-no      gakusei-o       matta
            H-Gen           student-Acc     waited
            'Taro waited for three Harvard
            students.'
```

---

6 Assuming the framework of Lasnik and Saito (1992); in (19b), the DP immediately dominating the NCP fails to dominate the antecedent-governor of the trace t'_i; hence, the trace t'_i violates the ECP. The definition of 'antecedent-government' is 'A antecedent-governs B iff A is X^0, A binds B, and B is subjacent to A.'

7 Ueda (1986) also observes and discusses a constraint on the scrambling of NCs.

To account for this contrast, Miyagawa stipulates that an NC (being a predicate) can leave a trace only in a position governed by a verb which assigns the role Theme. Given this; his Mutual C-Command Requirement (MCR), which requires an NP (or its trace) and an NC (or its trace) to c-command one another, explains the contrast, assigning the following structures:

(21)   a.   san-satu$_i$ Taro-ga
              3-Class   T-Nom
              [$_{VP}$ gengogaku-no   hon-o t_i yonda]
                  linguistics-Gen book-Acc   read

       b.?*san-nin$_i$ Taro-ga
              3-Class   T-Nom
              [$_{VP}$ Harvard-no   gakusei-o ø matta]
                  H-Gen   student-Acc waited

In (21b), the NC fails to leave its trace within the VP; consequently, the MCR is violated.[8] Under the standard assumption that an argument NP may leave a trace; however, the following contrast shows that the trace-leaving stipulation is not empirically sufficient.

(22)   a. [$_{NP}$ gengogaku-no   hon-o]$_i$ Taro-ga
                  linguistics-Gen book-Acc T-Nom
             [$_{VP}$ t_i san-satu yonda]
                   3-Class   read

       b.?*[$_{NP}$ Harvard-no   gakusei-o]$_i$ Taro-ga
                 H-Gen   student-Acc T-Nom
              [$_{VP}$ t_i san-nin matta]
                   3-Class waited

In (22), argument NPs are scrambled (while in (21), NCs are scrambled). Both (22a) and (22b) satisfy the MCR; hence, Miyagawa's analysis incorporating the trace-leaving stipulation still fails to explain the contrast in (22).

---

[8]   Miyagawa (1989) assumes that the NP and its NC are in a sister relation to the verb at D-structure.

3.2. Specific vs. Non-Specific

The analysis proposed here assigns the following structures to the object DPs in (20) and (22), before scrambling takes place.

(23) a. [$_{DP}$ [$_{NP}$ gengogaku-no   hon-o]$_i$ [$_{D'}$
                  linguistics-Gen   book-Acc
          [$_{NCP}$ t'$_i$ [$_{NC'}$ t$_i$ san-satu]] D$_{<+Acc>}$]]
                              3-Class

      b. [$_{DP}$ [$_{NP}$ Harvard-no   gakusei-o]$_i$ [$_{D'}$
                  H-Gen   student-Acc
          [$_{NCP}$ t'$_i$ [$_{NC'}$ t$_i$ san-nin]] D$_{<+Acc>}$]]
                              3-Class

In our analysis, the constraint on the scrambling of NCPs ((20)) and NPs ((22)) is stated as: Extraction out of a non-theme DP is prohibited (while extraction out of a theme DP is allowed). To account for this constraint; let us examine the difference in interpretation between the two relevant object DPs. First, consider the following.[9]

(24) (watashi-wa) **keiji-ga**   Taro-no
          I-Top   detective-Nom T-Gen
      ie-ni   kita-to   kiiteita-kedo
      house-Dat   came-Comp   heard-while
         ø   Hanako-no ie-ni-mo
                     H-Gen   house-Dat-too
      kita-rashiiyo
      came-seem
      'While I have heard that a detective came to
      Taro's house, it seems that (a detective)
      came to Hanako's house, too.'

In (24), the detective who came to Hanako's house may be different from the one who came to Taro's house. Now consider the following:

---

[9]   A nominal phrase in bold face is an antecedent of a deleted phrase.

(25)   (watashi-wa) **Jiro-no office-ni**
           I-Top   J-Gen   office-Dat
    denwa-o shita keiji-ga   Taro-no
    call-Acc made   detective-Nom T-Gen
    ie-ni   kita-to   kiiteita-kedo
    house-Dat came-Comp heard-while
         ø   Hanako-no ie-ni-mo
                 H-Gen   house-Dat-too
    kita-rashiiyo
    came-seem
    'While I have heard that a detective who
    made a call to Jiro's office came to Taro's
    house, it seems that (a detective who made a
    call to Jiro's office) came to Hanako's
    house, too.'

In (25), on the other hand, the detective who came to Hanako's house is the same one who came to Taro's house. Given that the relative clause renders the indefinite DP specific (cf. Heim (1982), Enç (1991), Ludlow and Neale (1991)); let us assume that when an antecedent DP is specific, its deleted counterpart refers to the same referent of the antecedent DP.[10] Given this; let us consider the following contrast.

(26)   (watashi-wa) Taro-ga   **gengogaku-no**
           I-Top   T-Nom   linguistics-Gen
    hon-o   san-satu   yonda-to
    book-Acc 3-Class   read-Comp
    kiiteita-kedo Hanako-mo   ø
    heard-while   H-too
    yonda-rashiiyo
    read-seem
    'While I have heard that Taro read three
    linguistics books, it seems that Hanako read
    (three linguistics books), too.'

---

[10] See Ludlow and Neale (1991) for recent discussion of interpretation of the indefinite nominal phrases.

```
(27)    (watashi-wa)   Taro-ga    Harvard-no
         I-Top         T-Nom      Harvard-Gen
        gakusei-o      san-nin    matta-to
        student-Acc    3-Class    waited-Comp
        kiiteita-kedo  Hanako-mo    ø
        heard-while    H-too
        matta-rashiiyo
        waited-seem
        'While I heard that Taro waited for three
        Harvard students, it seems that Hanako
        waited for (three Harvard students), too.'
```

In (26), the three linguistics books that Hanako read may be different from the three that Taro read. But in (27), the three Harvard students that Hanako waited for are the same three that Taro waited for. Given this contrast; the constraint on the scrambling of NCPs ((20)) and NPs ((22)) is now restated as follows: Extraction out of a specific DP is prohibited (while extraction out of a non-specific DP is allowed).[11] This constraint is readily construed as a Specificity Effect, which prohibits variables from appearing within a specific nominal phrase (Chomsky (1973), Fiengo and Higginbotham (1981)).[12]

   The proposed analysis, as we argued, eliminates the trace-leaving stipulation and reduces the constraint on the scrambling of NCPs and NPs to the Specificity Effect.[13]

---

[11]   Kawashima (1992), following Diesing (1992), examines a certain class of verbs which induce specific interpretation of nominal phrases in their complement position. She extends her analysis to the constraint observed by Miyagawa (1989) and shows that the constraint is construed as a Specificity Effect.

[12]   Kitahara (1992) examines the wide range of data discussed in Miyagawa (1989). The result of extending the current analysis to subject of transitive, ergative, and unergative verbs, in addition to theme and non-theme objects is summarized in (i):

				extraction
(i)	a.	theme object	specific/non-specific	ok
	b.	non-theme object	specific	*
	c.	transitive subject	specific	*
	d.	ergative subject	specific/non-specific	ok
	e.	unergative subject	specific	*

The facts in (i) are readily construed as the Specificity Effect.

[13]   See Diesing (1992) and Mahajan (1992) for recent discussion explaining the Specificity Effect.

4. Concluding Remarks

In section 1, we discussed the single-constituent analyses of an NP and its NC (Kamio (1983), Terada (1990)). In section 2, we articulated the structure of an NP and its NC, in which the NC heads its own maximal projection NCP (dominated by DP and dominating NP). The proposed analysis solves the problems confronting the previous analyses. In section 3, the constraint on the scrambling of NCPs and NPs (Miyagawa (1989)) was shown to be a Specificity Effect (Chomsky (1973), Fiengo and Higginbotham (1981)).

References

Barss, Andy. 1986. Chains and Anaphoric Dependencies. Doctoral dissertation, MIT.

Chomsky, Noam. 1973. Conditions on Transformation. Essays on Form and Interpretation. North-Holland.

Chomsky, Noam. 1986a. Barriers. The MIT Press.

Chomsky, Noam. 1986b. Knowledge of Language: Its Nature, Origin, and Use. Praeger.

Chomsky, Noam. 1992. A Minimalist Program for Linguistic Theory. MIT Occasional Papers in Linguistics. No. 1. MITWPL.

Diesing, Molly. 1992. Indefinites. The MIT Press.

Enç, Mürvet. 1991. The Semantics of Specificity. LI 22.1. 1-25.

Fiengo, Robert and James Higginbotham. 1981. Opacity in NP. Linguistic Analysis 7.4. 395-421.

Fukui, Naoki. 1986. A Theory of Category Projection and its Application. Doctoral dissertation, MIT.

Heim, Irene. 1982. The Semantics of Definite and Indefinite Noun Phrases. Doctoral dissertation, UMASS, Amherst.

Kamio, Akio. 1983. Meishi-ku-no Kozo. Nihongo-no Kihon Kozo. ed. by Kazuko Inoue. Sanseido.

Kawashima, Ruriko. 1992. ACC Case and Specificity. ms. Cornell University.

Kitahara, Hisatsugu. 1992. Floating Numeral Classifiers in Japanese and the Specificity Effect. ms. Harvard University.

Lasnik, Howard and Mamoru Saito. 1992. Move α: Conditions on Its Application and Output. The MIT Press.

Ludlow, Peter and Stephen Neale. 1991. Indefinite Descriptions: In Defense of Russell. L&P 14. 171-202.

Mahajan, Anoop. 1992. The Specificity Condition and the CED. LI 23.3. 510-516

Miyagawa, Shigeru. 1989. Syntax and Semantics 22: Structure and Case Marking in Japanese. Academic Press.

Miyagawa, Shigeru. 1991. Case Realization and Scrambling. ms. MIT.

Murasugi, Keiko. 1991. Noun Phrase in Japanese and English: A Study in Syntax, Learnability and Acquisition. Doctoral dissertation, The University of Connecticut.

Saito, Mamoru. 1985. Some Asymmetries in Japanese and their Theoretical Consequences. Doctoral dissertation, MIT.

Sportiche, Dominique. 1988. A Theory of Floating Quantifiers and Its Corollaries for Constituent Structure. LI 19.3. 425-449.

Terada, Michiko. 1990. Incorporation and Argument Structure in Japanese. Doctoral dissertation, UMASS, Amherst.

Ueda, Masanobu. 1986. On Quantifier Float in Japanese. Oriental Linguistics. ed. by N. Hasegawa and Y. Kitagawa. UMASS, Amherst.

Floating Quantifiers, Scrambling and the ECP

Myung-Kwan Park and Keun-Won Sohn
University of Connecticut

1. Introduction

This paper explores the behavior of floating quantifiers (FQs) in Korean and Japanese.[1] Starting from Miyagawa's (1986, 89) ECP-related problem, we propose that an FQ adjoins to its modified NP at LF to have an appropriate interpretation and thereby can get out of an island without violating the ECP. We show that this adjunction procedure can account for the distribution of FQs, which has been previously accounted for by Miyagawa's (1986, 89) Mutual C-command Condition (MCC). Additionally, it is shown that the data presented in this paper corroborate the hypothesis that traces can be licensed in the course of a derivation (Chomsky (1989); Saito (1992)).

The paper is organized as follows. Section 2 discusses Miyagawa's (1986) observation that a wh-FQ within an island can move out of the island at LF without inducing an ECP violation. We show that existing analyses (especially, Miyagawa (1986, 89) and Terada (1990)) do not offer an adequate account for the island insensitivity of FQs at LF. In section 3, we propose an alternative analysis,

---

[1] The constructions to be discussed are of the following form; [NP-Case FQ]. Although it has been argued in the literature that these quantifiers are not floated, but base generated, we will use this term *FQ* for convenience in our paper.

where we argue that an FQ adjoins to and forms one unit with its modified NP at LF to have a proper interpretation. This adjunction procedure resolves the ECP problem, because an FQ moves out of the island together with its modified NP as a unit. In section 4, we deduce Miyagawa's MCC from this adjunction operation as there is much redundancy between these two approaches. We show that most cases accounted for by MCC are also accounted for by our LF adjunction approach. Finally, possible explanations are suggested for some problematic cases.

2. Extraction of a Wh-FQ out of an Island

2.1. Miyagawa's (1986, 89) MCC

Miyagawa (1986, 89) argued that FQs are secondary predicates subject to the Mutual C-command Condition (cf. Williams (1980)).

```
(1) Miyagawa's Mutual C-command Condition (MCC)
For a predicate to predicate of an NP, the NP or its trace
and the predicate or its trace must c-command each other.
```

Miyagawa gives the following structures for subject modifying FQs and object modifying FQs, respectively:

```
(2)  a.    IP                    b.    VP
       / | \                       / | \
     NP  FQ  I'                   NP  FQ  V
```

His proposal accommodates cases where an FQ[2] cannot appear together with an NP followed by a postposition:[3]

```
(3)a.  haksayng-i   tases-myeng  wassta
       student-Nom  5-Cl         came
       '5 students came'

   b.  John-i   chayk-ul   sey-kwen  ilkessta
       -Nom     book-Acc   3-Cl      read
       'John read 3 books'

   c. *John-i  chinkwu-eke  sey-myeng  sacin-ul      poyecwuessta
       -Nom    friend-Dat   3-Cl       picture-Acc   showed
       'John showed a picture to three friends'
```

---

[2] To facilitate understanding, we give some characteristics of FQs. First, an FQ is composed of two parts; a numeral followed by a classifier. Second, there is a coocurrence restriction between an FQ and its modified NP. The classifier of an FQ should agree with its related NP with respect to some features such as [+/- human], [+/- animate], [+/- countable] and etc.. See Chae (1983) and Ahn (1992) for some relevant discussion. We will return to this property of FQs in section 3.

[3] We underline both an FQ and its modified NP.

Miyagawa claims that postpositions including the Dative Case marker, being theta role assigners, project their own projections (PP) and thus the MCC is not satisfied. This is why (3c) is ungrammatical. On the other hand, the Nominative or Accusative Case markers, not being theta assigners, do not have their own projections. These Case markers will not block the modified NP from c-commanding the FQ in (3a,b).

Miyagawa's analysis accounts for cases where an FQ cannot appear as the head of a relative clause:

```
(4) *[NP[IPJohn-i haksayng-ul ttaylin] sey-myeng]
        -Nom   student-Acc   hit      3-Cl
    'the three students who John hit'
```

In (4), the FQ that heads a relative clause is not in a mutual c-command relationship with its modified NP, and this explains the ungrammaticality of (4).

But the grammaticality of examples like (5) has posed a nontrivial problem for Miyagawa's analysis:

```
(5) [[haksayng-i myech-myeng chamkaha-n] tayhoy]-eyse
     student-Nom how many- Cl  participate contest-Loc
     ku-ka  sang-ul  tha-ess-ni
     he-Nom prize-Acc win-past-Q
     'Q he won the prize in [the contest in which
     how many students have participated]'
```

(5) contains a wh-FQ *myech myeng* within the relative clause, which is linked to the matrix Q-morpheme. This FQ should move, crossing an island, into the matrix spec of a [+wh] Comp at LF. The grammaticality of (5) poses a problem for Miyagawa's analysis of FQs as secondary predicates, since it is not possible to extract typical secondary predicates out of an island.

Let us look at the following examples containing secondary predicates in Korean:

```
(6)a. John-i   cichyese tolawassta
        -Nom    tired    returned
      'John returned tired'

   b. John-i elmana  cichyese tolawass-ni
        Nom   how     tired    returned-Q
      'How tired did John return?'

   c. *Ne-nun [ elmana cichyese tolaon   salam]-lul  mannass-ni
       you-Top  how     tired    returned person-Acc  met-Q
      'Q you met [a person that returned how tired]'

(7)a. John-i   koki-lul  cal ikhiese  mekessta
        -Nom meat-Acc well done      ate
      'John ate the meat well done'

   b. John-i   koki-lul  elmana ikhiese   mekess-ni
        -Nom meat-Acc how     well-done ate-Q
      'How well-done did John eat the meat'
```

```
c. *Mary-nun [ koki-lul elmana ikhiese    mekun salam]-ul
      Top        meat-Acc how   well-done eat    person-Acc
   silheha-ni
   hated-Q
   'Q Mary hates [a person that ate the meat how well done]'
```

In the above examples, a secondary predicate for a subject (= 6) and one for an object (= 7) are tested. Both of them can be interrogated as shown in (6b) and (7b). But (6c) and (7c) show that extraction of them out of an island results in ungrammaticality. The ungrammaticality of these examples is attributed to the violation of the ECP, because the trace of the secondary predicates within a complex NP can neither be lexically nor antecedent governed.

The discussion above poses a problem for Miyagawa's claim that FQs are secondary predicates, because, unlike other secondary predicates, they seem to be able to move out of an island as shown in (5). Acknowledging this problem, Miyagawa suggests that an FQ moves together with its modified NP at LF, satisfying the ECP. It is clear, however, that his suggestion cannot be supported by the structure he has proposed for FQs, since an FQ and its modified NP are not a constituent as we can see in (2). Thus we conclude that (5) poses a real difficulty for Miyagawa's secondary predicate analysis. In the next section, we turn to Terada's (1990) view that an NP and its modifying FQ are a constituent.

2.2 Terada's (1990) Constituent (QP) Analysis

Terada (1990) has proposed that an NP and an FQ in the [NP-Case FQ] constructions form a constituent, QP. The following is the structure of the [NP-Case FQ] proposed by Terada (1990):

(8) [$_{QP}$ [$_{Q'}$ NP-Case [$_Q$ Num + Cl]]]

Terada claims that Case goes to NP, not to QP in (8), since NP but not QP requires Case to satisfy the Case filter (Chomsky (1981)).

If Terada's analysis holds, Miyagawa's ECP-related problem might not arise, because the unit [NP-Case FQ], being in argument position, can move out of an island without violating the ECP. Two questions, however, come to mind. One concerns the constituency of an NP and an FQ. Terada uses the conjunction test as evidence for this. Look at the example (9) taken from Terada (1990):

```
(9) Taroo-wa [ringo-o    niko] to [mikan-o    yonko] tabeta
      Top  apple-Acc two   and orange-Acc four      ate
   'Taro ate two apples and four oranges'
```

Under the assumption that only constituents can be conjoined, Terada's position seems to be well supported by (9), where two [NP-Case FQ]s are conjoined.

However, despite various similarities between Korean and Japanese FQ constructions, they exhibit different behavior with respect to the conjunction test. (10), unlike the corresponding example in Japanese (9), is ungrammatical in Korean:

(10) *John-i [sakwa-lul twu kay]-wa [kywul-lul ney kay] makessta
      -Nom apple-Acc two Cl and orange-Acc four Cl   ate
   'John ate two apples and four oranges'

Given the impossibility of the conjunction in (10), it is clear that the modified NP and the FQ are not a constituent in Korean. This might lead to a conjecture that [NP-Case FQ] is a constituent in Japanese but not in Korean. But the grammaticality of (11) in Japanese makes us doubt the validity of the conjunction test as a measure for constituency:

(11)
   Taroo-wa [ringo-o kinoo niko] to [mikan-o kyoo yonko] tabeta
      Top apple-Acc yesterday two and orange-Acc today four ate
   'Taro ate two apples yesterday and four oranges today'

In each bracketed conjunct of (11), there is an adverb intervening between the NP and the FQ, indicating that the sequence [NP-adverb-FQ] is not a constituent. Still,, the conjunction of these non-constituent items is allowed in (11). In short, we cannot rely on the conjunction test as a diagnosis for constituency.[4]

Another argument against Terada's analysis comes from the scramblability of FQs. Let us consider (12):

(12)
   [[John-i   myech-kay   ipeney   kummeytal-ul ttasesstanun]
      -Nom how many-Cl this time gold medal-Acc won
   kisa]-lul   ne-nun   ilk-ess-ni
   report-Acc you-Topic read-past-Q
   'Q You read a report that John won how many medal this time'

In (12), the FQ has been scrambled over its modified NP. Further, FQs can be long distance scrambled across the clause boundary, as in (13):

(13) 3-pyeng$_i$ Tom-i [Sue-ka maykcwu-lul t$_i$ masiesstako] hayssta
      Cl   -Nom   -Nom beer-Acc   drank   said
   'Tom said that Sue drank 3 bottles of beer'

If the structure in (8) is the D-structure of the NP and the FQ in examples like (12), there is no way to account for their grammaticality. As the FQ is a head of the QP, it cannot undergo long distance scrambling as Terada herself admits. The only option left is that the entire QP moves to the sentence initial position after the complement

---

4 Probably, the impossibility of a conjunction as in (10) reflects a non-constituency of the conjoined items while the reverse is not true. This, however, is subject to empirical testing. See Fujita (1991) for some arguments against the constituent analysis.

NP *maykcwu-lul (beer)* in (13) has scrambled out of this QP and adjoins to some maximal projection (probably VP). But as in (15), the trace of the moved NP is not bound by its antecedent, violating the Proper Binding Condition (Fiengo (1977)).

(14) **Proper Binding Condition (PBC)**
     Traces must be bound.

(15) $[_{IP}[_{QP}[t_i \ Q]]_j[_{IP}\text{---}[_{CP}[_{IP}\text{---}[_{VP}\underline{NP}_i[_{VP} \ t_j \ V]]]]]]$

Noticing this problem, Terada claims that an NP and an FQ in (12) and (13) where an FQ is scrambled have the structure (16), not (8):

(16) $[_{QP} \ NP \ [_{QP}...]]$

This structure closely resembles that of a relative clause. With (16) assumed, Terada suggests that what is moved in (12) and (13) is the lower QP in (16). Therefore, according to her, [NP-Case FQ] has two sources; (8) and (16). But the problem is that there seems to be no rationale for the structure (16). The only reason she posits (16) is to generate sentences like (12) and (13). This makes us doubt the validity of the dual structures for the [NP-Case FQ]. Due to these considerations, we will not adopt Terada's QP analysis. In section 3, we propose an alternative analysis for (5), which leads us to a different view on the nature of FQs.[5]

3. LF Adjunction of an FQ to Its Antecedent NP

In section 2, it has been shown that neither of the previous analyses accounts for the grammaticality of examples like (5). To address this issue, we propose the following condition:

(17) **An FQ adjoins to its modified NP at LF.**

This condition requires an FQ to form a unit with its modified NP at LF. A wh-FQ within an island as in (5) does not induce an ECP violation since it can move out of the island together with its modified NP as a unit.

---

[5] Still another possibility is that an FQ in (5), in fact, does not move out of an island, but a complex NP containing it moves to the matrix spec of Comp. This type of approach has been advocated by Nishigauchi (1986) and Choe (1987) under the name of 'Pied Piping' approach (PPA). But, as Lasnik & Saito (1992) have argued, there are both conceptual and empirical issues which require further elaboration of the PPA, although it definitely has some attractive aspects. Readers are referred to Lasnik & Saito (1992), and Fiengo, Huang, Lasnik, and Reinhart (1988).

If this is the case, we should ask what is the purpose of this adjunction. A plausible answer would be that an FQ adjoins to its antecedent NP to have an appropriate interpretation. As is well documented, there is a cooccurrence restriction between an FQ and its modified NP (Chae (1983) among others). More precisely, a classifier within an FQ should agree with its linked NP with respect to features like [+/-animate], [+/-countable], [+/-human] and so on. Furthermore, a classifier is indeterminate in the sense that its meaning requires further specification. As one classifier can be used for a set of NPs, we cannot fully interpret its meaning until we see an NP it is related to. For example, the classifier 'myeng' can be used for human beings, but a further specification is needed to determine which subgroup of human beings it modifies; viz., whether it is a unit of students or teachers, and what not. We propose that LF adjunction allows for the proper interpretation of FQs.

The proposed analysis not only accounts for the ECP dilemma of Miyagawa (1986), but is also in line with a recent proposal related to anaphor binding in Korean and Japanese (Abe (1991)). *Caki* in Korean and *zibun* in Japanese always take an atomic individual as their semantic value. Further, it has been observed that they can be used not only with an NP denoting a single individual, but also with a bare plural NP (Kawasaki (1989) among others).[6] Consider the following contrast:[7]

(18)a. Haksayng-tul-i   caki-lul saranghanta
       students-pl-Nom self-Acc   love
       'Students love themselves'

   b. Gakusei-tati-ga zibun-o   aisiteiru
      student-pl-Nom   self-Acc   love

(18a-b) only have a distributive reading such as *Each of the students loves himself or herself*. Noting this, Abe (1991) proposes that the Japanese reflexive *zibun* moves at LF as a distributor. Let us assume that his approach can be extended to the Korean anaphor *caki*. Then we have the indexing shown in (19b) rather than (19a).

(19)a. Haksayng-tul$_i$-i   caki$_i$-lul saranghanta
    b. Haksayng-tul$_j$-i   caki$_i$-lul saranghanta

---

[6] The English reflexive anaphor cannot be used with a bare plural subject:

(i) *Students love himself/herself

The reason (i) is bad would be due to the mismatch of the number feature between the antecedent NP and the anaphor.

[7] Note that, in (18), the English translation differs in reading from the Korean or Japanese example. It can have the collective reading as well as the distributive reading.

Now at LF, the anaphor *caki* adjoins to its antecedent as in (20a), and Quantifier Raising (QR) applies to the whole NP to get (20b).

(20)a. [[Haksayng-tul$_j$]caki$_i$]$_i$ t$_i$-lul   saranghanta
     b. [$_{IP}$[[Haksayng-tul$_j$]caki$_i$]$_i$[$_{IP}$ t'$_i$ t$_i$-lul saranghanta]]

This LF representation gives us the interpretation *[NP$_j$caki$_i$]* α → *all x, x is a member of the NP$_j$, then x has the property represented by* α.

Under these considerations, let us see what will happen when there is an FQ modifying the antecedent of an anaphor:

(21)a. <u>Haksayng-tul-i</u> caki-uy cip-uro <u>sey myeng</u>   kaessta
       students-pl-Nom self-Gen house-to 3-Cl   went
       'Three students went to self's house'

   b. [$_{IP}$[[<u>Haksayng-tul</u>$_j$] caki$_i$]$_i$ [$_{IP}$ t'$_i$ t$_i$-uy cip-uro
      <u>sey myeng</u> ka-ess-ta]]

Without assuming the adjunction operation, (21b) will be the LF representation of (21a). In (21b), the anaphor *caki* has been adjoined to the antecedent NP and the whole NP has undergone QR. It is doubtful that this structure can represent the intended meaning *Each of the three students went to self's house*.

But if we adopt the hypothesis that an FQ is adjoined to its antecedent NP at LF, the resulting representation in (22) does not seem to pose any problem:

(22) [$_{IP}$[[<u>Haksayng-tul</u>$_j$] <u>sey myeng</u>$_k$]$_j$ caki$_i$]$_i$[$_{IP}$ t'$_i$---

In the LF representation (22), *caki* is correctly distributed over the 3 members of the set of students. Thus our adjunction analysis gets support from the anaphor binding interpretation as in examples like (21a).

Let us now focus on the exact mechanism needed to apply our adjunction analysis. One immediate question concerns the nature of the chain created by this adjunction operation. This adjunction occurs from an A′-position to an A-position, which is not a usual type of movement. However, Saito (1992) proposes the same type of movement to explain the grammatical status of the examples like the following:

(23)
  a. *John-wa [sono hon-o NAZE katta hito]-o sagasiteru no
        Top that book-Acc why buy   person-Acc looking for Q
     'Q John is looking for [a person that bought that book why]'

  b. ??John-wa [NANI-o NAZE katta hito]-o   sagasiteru no
        -Top what-Acc why bought person-Acc looking for Q
     'Q John is looking for [a person that bought what why]'

Extraction of an adjunct wh phrase *naze* out of an island is not allowed due to an ECP violation as shown in (23a). In (23b), *naze* is also located within an island and coocurs with an argument wh phrase in the higher position of the same clause. This sentence is predicted to be ungrammatical due to a violation of the ECP. But this example does not have the status of an ECP violation. Observing this, Saito (1992) proposes that an adjunct wh-phrase can adjoin to an argument wh-phrase in the higher position of the same clause as in (24) and use this as a *free ride* strategy.[8]

(24) the structure of an embedded VP at LF after adjunction

After this adjunction as in (24), *naze* can move out of an island together with the argument wh phrase *nani-o* as a unit satisfying the ECP. How about the original trace of *naze*? Let us look at the following LF representation:

(25) $[_{CP} [NAZE_j [NANI_i\text{-}o]]_i [_{TP} John\text{-}wa [_{NP} [_{CP}\text{---} [_{VP} t_i [_{VP} t_j [_{VP} t_i katta]]]] hito]\text{-}o sagasiteru] no]^{VP} t_i$

It is clear from the above representation that the antecedent *naze* is too far from its trace (t_j) to antecedent govern it. Thus, Saito (1992) adopts the hypothesis that a trace can be licensed in the course of a derivation.[9] Given this hypothesis, the trace of *naze* in (23a) is licensed at the time when it is created.

---

[8]   Saito (1992) argues that antecedent government is allowed from head- or A-adjoined positions but not from A′-adjoined positions. We will assume this without discussion. Note that, in (24), the VP adjoined position created by *shortest* scrambling is assumed to be an A-position (cf. Tada (1990)).

[9]   Given that, an immediate question arises, then, how to rule out (ia) while allowing (ib):

(i) a. *Who fixed the car how
    b. Who bought what

Suppose *how* first adjoin to VP and licenses its original trace. Next, it adjoins to *who* in spec of Comp. Although the intermediate trace cannot be antecedent governed from an A′-adjoined position, the intermediate trace can delete. Thus no offending trace. But Chomsky's (1989) proposal on the legitimate chains gives a plausible way to distinguish between these two

The proposed adjunction analysis for FQs is in the same vein as Saito's (1992) adjunction analysis. Just as the adjunct wh phrase within an island can avoid violating the ECP by adjoining to the argument wh phrase, so can an FQ move out of an island by adjoining to its modified NP. Let us consider (5) which is repeated as (26a):[10]

```
(26)a. [[haksayng-i  myech - myeng  chamkaha-n] tayhoi]-eyse
          student-Nom  how many -  Cl  participate contest-Loc
          ku-ka    sang-ul    tha-ess-ni
          he-Nom prize-Acc win-past-Q
          'Q he won the prize in [the contest in which how many
          students have participated]'

    b. [IP[NP myech myengj[NP haksayng]][I' tj [I' ...
```

(26b) is the post adjunction structure of the embedded IP of (26a). As in (26b), the FQ adjoins to the subject NP to which it is related.[11] It licenses govern its trace at the time when it is created; if not, it will be too far to antecedent govern its trace. Then, the whole adjoined phrase having a [+wh] feature can move directly to the matrix spec of [+wh] Comp, avoiding the ECP effect. This explains the grammaticality of examples like (5).

To sum up, in this section, we have argued that a wh-FQ located within an island can avoid violating the ECP by adjoining to its antecedent NP and moving out of that island together with the NP.

---

cases:

```
(ii)  a.  [ A,...,A,...A ] (uniform A-chain)
      b.  [ A',..,A',..A'] (uniform A'-chain)
      c.  [ A'.........A ] (operator-variable chain)
```

The crucial assumption here is that deletion is a last resort, that is, allowed only when it creates a legitimate chain. Now let us look at the chain created in (ia) and (ib). The chain created by movement of *how* in (ia) is already a legitimate one since it is of the form (iib), a uniform A'-chain. Then the intermediate trace cannot delete, eventually violating the ECP. Thus this example is ruled out correctly. On the other hand, the chain created by the movement of *what* is not a legitimate chain as it has the following members [A',A',A]. Now the intermediate trace can delete since deletion of this trace will create a legitimate chain of the type (iic). Thus there is still a plausible way to distinguish (ia) and (ib) even if we adopt the assumption that traces can be licensed in the course of a derivation.

[10] We assume strict binary branching as in Hoji (1985). Thus, the subject modifying FQ is assumed to appear in I'-adjoined or VP-adjoined position. The object modifying FQ is assumed to appear in the V'-adjoined position.

[11] The adjunction of an FQ to its host NP is always an instance of A'-to-A movement since the host NP is either a subject or an object in Korean and Japanese.

If our analysis in this section is correct, we have found further evidence for the claim that traces can be licensed in the course of a derivation.

4. Deriving the MCC from LF Adjunction

In section 3, we proposed that an FQ adjoins to its modified NP at LF and by doing so can avoid violating the ECP. We suggested that the purpose of the LF adjunction is to have a proper interpretation. In this section, we derive the effect of the MCC from our LF adjunction approach. As both LF adjunction and the MCC are licensing mechanisms to allow for a proper interpretation of FQs, there seems to be redundancy between them. But, in the former section, we showed that the LF adjunction of an FQ is independently required whether we adopt Miyagawa's approach or not. Given that, it would be desirable to deduce the MCC from LF adjunction. Assuming that FQs are nominal adjuncts which can freely appear at any place in a sentence, we show below that the distribution of FQs can be subsumed under the LF adjunction approach without resorting to any other specific conditions.

Let us look at the examples in (3) which are repeated as (27):

(27)a. <u>Haksayng-i</u> <u>tases myeng</u> wassta
     student-Nom   5-Cl   came
     '5 students came'

   b. John-i   <u>chayk-ul</u> <u>sey kwen</u>   ilkessta
       Nom   book-Acc   3-Cl   read
      'John   read   3 books'

   c. *John-i <u>chinkwu-eykey</u> <u>sey myeng</u> kurim-ul poyecwuessta
       Nom friend-Dat   3-Cl   picture-Acc showed
      'John showed pictures to three friends'

As pointed out, Miyagawa (1986, 89) attributed the ungrammaticality of (27c) to the assumption that the maximal projection (PP) of the postposition or Dative Case marker blocks the NP from c-commanding its modifying FQ. But Nominative or Accusative Case markers do not have their own projections, which accounts for the grammaticality of (27a-b).

Our LF adjunction approach provides an equally plausible analysis for the same data. Suppose that at LF, an FQ must adjoin to its antecedent NP. Below, we give the LF representations of (27b) and (27c).

(28)a. [VP [V' [NP sey kwen$_j$ [NP chayk-ul]][t_j ilk]]]
   b. [VP [V' [PP [NP sey myeng$_j$ [NP chinkwu]]-eykey]]
     [V' t_j kurim-ul]...

In (28a), the FQ can antecedent govern its trace, t_i, from the adjoined position as there is no intervening maximal projection between them.[12] In (28b), on the other hand, there is an intervening maximal projection (PP) blocking the FQ from c-commanding its trace. This results in an ECP violation or an PBC violation, thus correctly ruling out the ungrammatical example (27c).

The nonoccurrence of an FQ as the head of a relative clause also can be accounted for by the same considerations:

```
(29)(=4)  *  [NP[IPJohn-i  haksayng-ul  ttalin]  sey myeng]
              Nom   student-Acc   hit      3 - Cl
```

Suppose that the relative head FQ in (29) adjoins to its antecedent NP at LF. As the antecedent NP is located in the hierarchically lower position than the FQ, the trace of this FQ induces a PBC violation. Therefore, the data which provided empirical support for Miyagawa's analysis are also well accounted for within our analysis.

Now, we discuss other types of examples, where an NP and its modifying FQ are not clausemates at S-structure. Consider the following example where the FQ appears in a clause lower than the one containing its antecedent NP:

```
(30)
  a. [IPUysa-ka [CPhwanca-ka sey myeng oessta-ko] malhaessta]
      doctor-Nom  patient-Nom  3 - Cl   came-Comp said
      'A doctor said that three patients came'

  b. *[IPUysa-ka [CPhwanca-ka sey myeng oessta-ko] malhaessta]
      'intended reading: Three doctors said that a patient came'
```

If, as in (30a), the FQ is construed with the subject NP in the same clause, i.e., with *hwanca-ka*, the example is grammatical. But if, as in (30b), the FQ in the embedded clause is construed with the subject NP in the matrix clause, i.e., with *uysa-ka*, the example is ungrammatical. This contrast is also accounted for by the LF adjunction approach. In (30a), the FQ can adjoin to the embedded subject NP and license its trace from the adjoined position. On the other hand, (30b) is ruled out as there is no legitimate derivation. Two derivations need to be examined for (30b). In one derivation, the FQ moves successive cyclically and adjoins to the matrix subject NP. The resulting chain of this movement would be of the following form; $[A,...A',...A',...,A']$. We assume, following Saito (1992) and Takahashi (1992), that this chain formation does not count as a single operation in that it contains two different chains: an A-chain $[A...A']$ and an A'-chain $[A',...A',...A']$. Besides this derivation, there is another derivation, where the FQ adjoins to the matrix subject NP in one step. This movement is one operation in that it creates only one chain; an

---

[12] We assume, following May (1985), Chomsky (1986a) and Saito (1992), that one segment of a category does not count as a full maximal projection.

A-chain [A...A']. Between the two derivations considered, under economy considerations (Chomsky (1989)), the latter derivation is chosen over the former. This economical derivation, however, is not legitimate since the FQ is too far from its trace to antecedent govern it. Thus there is no legitimate derivation for the example (30b), where the FQ is construed with the matrix subject.

Next, let us consider an example where an FQ is in a higher clause than one containing its antecedent NP.

(31) <u>Sey pyeng,</u> Tom-i [Sue-ka <u>maykcwu-lul</u> masiessta-ko] mitnunta
    3 Cl   Nom   Nom beer-Acc   drank-Comp   believe
    'Tom believes that Sue drank three bottles of beer'

In (31), the FQ can be considered to be base generated in or scrambled to its S-structure position. If the FQ has been base generated, (31) will be ruled out since the trace of the FQ left after downward adjunction will not satisfy the PBC. If it has been scrambled, two structures need to be examined; one where the FQ is generated in the sentence medial position higher than the modified NP, and one where it is generated in the position lower than the modified NP as a clausemate. Both structures are given below schematically:

(32)a. [FQ$_i$ --- (t$_i$)---[$_{CP}$ (t$_i$)--- antecedent NP---]]
    b. [FQ$_i$ --- [$_{CP}$ --- antecedent NP --- t$_i$]]

In (32a), the FQ is higher than its antecedent NP at D-structure. (32a) will be ruled out due to a PBC violation, whether undoing of the scrambled FQ occurs or not. This is because there will be an unbound trace after the LF adjunction of the FQ. In (32b), on the other hand, at D-structure the FQ is lower than its antecedent NP within the same clause. If the scrambled FQ is undone at LF in (32b), it creates a context where an FQ adjoins to its modified NP without violating any principle. Thus we have a legitimate derivation for the grammatical sentence (31).

Another configuration that is to be examined is the case where the antecedent NP of an FQ has scrambled to a higher position. The issue is whether the FQ can adjoin to its antecedent NP which has undergone long distance scrambling. Given LF undoing of scrambling, long distance scrambling does not seem to pose any problem for the LF adjunction analysis. Consider the following example:

(33) <u>Maykcwu-lul</u>$_i$ Tom-i [Sue-ka t$_i$ <u>sey pyeng</u> saesstako] mitnunta
    beer-Acc   Nom   Nom   3- Cl   bought   believe
    'Tom believes that Sue bought 3 bottles of beer'

First, let us see what happens if the scrambled NP in (33) stays in its S-structure position. One fell swoop adjunction of the FQ to the preposed antecedent NP will not be allowed since the trace left after that movement will not satisfy the ECP. Second, what if the FQ moves successive cyclically to the antecedent NP? To discuss this derivation, we assume that long distance scrambling is uniformly an A'-movement while short distance scrambling can be either an A' or A-movement (Mahajan (1989), Tada (1990), Saito (1991)). Given this assumption, the landing site of the long distance scrambled phrase in (33) will be an A'-position. Then, the successive movement of the FQ to the long distance scrambled phrase in A'-position will not be allowed, because the last intermediate trace is not antecedent governed by the A'-adjoined FQ (See footnote (8).). The FQ, being in A'-adjoined position, cannot license (or γ-mark in the sense of Lasnik & Saito (1984)) that last intermediate trace. The only way the trace can avoid an ECP violation is to delete at LF. In the former section, however, we have adopted Chomsky's (1989) notion of legitimate chains and the related claim about the deletion procedure. According to Chomsky, a trace can delete only as a last resort, that is, to create a legitimate chain (See footnote (9).). Now, consider the chain formed by the successive cyclic movement of the FQ. It is already a legitimate chain being composed of [A',...A',...A']. Thus the offending trace cannot be deleted in this chain and this forces the derivation we are considering to be ruled out due to an ECP violation. In short, regardless of whether the FQ adjoins to its modified NP in one step or successive cyclically, the derivations where the NP stays in its S-structure position as in (33) are all ruled out under the LF adjunction analysis.

Again, the undoing operation accounts for the grammaticality of (33). Suppose that undoing happens at LF and returns the scrambled NP to its D-structure position (canonical object position). Then the FQ can adjoin to its antecedent NP in one step, and this derivation will satisfy the requirement for antecedent government. In short, long distance scrambling of either an FQ or an NP can be accounted for by our LF adjunction analysis without postulating any other mechanisms.

Now let us consider cases where an FQ or an antecedent NP has undergone short distance scrambling.

(34)a. Maykcwu-lul$_i$ John-i t$_i$ sey pyeng masiessta
       beer-Acc   Nom   Cl   drank
       'John drank 3 bottles of beer'

   b. Sey pyeng$_i$ John-i maykcwu-lul t$_i$ masiessta
       3-Cl   Nom   beer-Acc   drank

As short distance scrambling can be an A-movement, the FQ in (34a) can directly adjoin to the scrambled NP which is reanalyzed as an A-position at LF (Saito (1991)). Or it can adjoin to the antecedent NP after the latter has undergone undoing. On the other hand, in (34b) where the FQ has scrambled over its antecedent NP, we have the option of undoing at LF, which will create a legitimate adjunction context.

We have shown that our adjunction approach can handle various cases where an FQ and its antecedent NP have been separated from each other. Now let us discuss a potential problem for our analysis.[13] Let us look at the following example:

(35)a. Haksayng-i sey myeng maykcwu-lul masiessta
        Student-Nom 3-Cl   beer-Acc   drank
        'Three students drank beer'

   b. ?*Haksayng-i maykcwu-lul sey myeng masiessta
        student-Nom beer-Acc   3-Cl   drank
        'Three students drank beer'

(35b) shows that the intervention of an object between a subject and its modifying FQ results in ungrammaticality. The ungrammaticality of this example is accounted for by the MCC coupled with the assumption that a subject cannot be scrambled (Saito (1985)). Suppose that an FQ is base generated under the VP node. This structure will be ruled out due to a violation of the MCC. Suppose that the string in (35b) is derived by scrambling of the object followed by scrambling of the subject. We can rule out this derivation with recourse to the ban on scrambling of a subject (Saito (1985)). Saito (1985) attributes the impossibility of subject scrambling to the following condition:

(36) Variables must have Case (Chomsky (1981))

Saito claims that Nominative Case in Japanese is default and is given to an NP which is a daughter of an IP. Saito further argues that, when the subject NP is scrambled, the trace left after this A′-movement violates (36).[14]

---

[13] Besides the problem dealt with in the text, one potential problem would be the case where the long distance moved NP cannot undergo undoing procedure. The relevant example is of the following sort:

(i) Enu pan haksayng-ul$_i$ Tom-un [Sue-ka t$_i$ myech myeng
    students in which class-Acc Top Nom   how many Cl
    poessnun-ci] alko sip-ni
    see -   Q   want to know-Q
    'Q Tom wants to know [Q Sue saw how many students
    of which class]'

Some people get only the wide scope reading for the wh phrase which has been scrambled to the sentence initial position in (i), though others get the narrow scope reading, as well. If this scrambled wh phrase has only the wide scope reading, this means that it cannot be undone at LF. This might serve as counterevidence to our analysis, since the FQ cannot adjoin to the antecedent NP within the scrambled wh phrase, being too far from this antecedent NP. See Sohn (1992) for relevant discussion.

[14] For details, readers are referred to Saito (1985).

It is difficult to rule out the example (35b) within our analysis, because, after adjunction to its modified NP, the FQ is close enough to antecedent govern its trace. Thus, our analysis incorrectly rules in (35b). We have no definite answer for the ungrammaticality of this example at this point. But the existence of the following examples in Korean seems to provide some implications for this issue:

(37)a. **Haksayng-i** **sey myeng-i** maykcwu-lul masiessta
        Student-Nom   3-Cl-Nom   beer-Acc   drank
        'Three students drank beer'

   b.   **Haksayng-i** maykcwu-lul **sey myeng-i** masiessta
        student-Nom   beer-Acc   3-Cl-Nom   drank
        'Three students drank beer'

In Korean, unlike in Japanese, an FQ as well as an NP can be Case marked, as illustrated in (37a). What is interesting is that in the [NP-Case FQ-Case] constructions, the intervention of an object NP between a subject NP and its modifying FQ does not result in ungrammaticality as shown in (37b). Miyagawa's analysis, assuming the MCC and the nonscramblability of a subject, cannot account for the wellformedness of (37b). But our analysis readily rules in this example. For now, we leave the ungrammaticality of (37b) for further research.[15]

References

Abe, J. (1991) "The Nature of Anaphors and Distributy," ms. UConn
Ahn, S. -H. (1992) "Floated Quantifiers and Minimal Attachment," to appear in Chungmin Lee (ed.) *Korean Syntax and Semantics: 1991 LSA Linguistic Institute Workshop*, Seoul, Korea
Chae, -W. (1983) "A Study of Numerals and Numeral classifier Constructions in Korean," Language Research 19.
Choe, J. -W. (1987) "LF Movement and Pied-piping," in *Linguistic Inquiry* 18. 348-353
Chomsky, N. (1981) *Lectures on Government and Binding*, Dordrecht, Foris.
_____ (1986a) *Barriers*, LI monograph. The MIT Press.
_____ (1986b) *Knowledge of Language;Its Nature, Origin, and Use*, New York, Praeger.
_____ (1989) "Some Notes on Economy of Derivation and Representation," in I. Laka and A. Mahajan (eds.) *MIT Working Papers in Linguistics*, Vol. 10. 43-74
Fiengo, R. (1977) "On Trace Theory," Linguistic Inquiry 8.
Fiengo, R., C. -T. Huang, H. Lasnik, and T. Reinhart (1988) "The Syntax of Wh-in-situ," in *Proceedings of WCCFL* 7, 81-98.

---

[15] Ahn (1992) argues that the unacceptability of (35b) is due to the parsing difficulty. After considering the [NP-Case FQ-Case] constructions like (37), he deduces the difference between (35b) and (37b) by appealing to the Minimal Attachment Hypothesis (Frasier (1979)). We do not commit ourselves to this issue and leave it as an open question.

Frasier, L. (1979) *On Comprehending Sentences: Syntactic Parsing Strategies*, Ph. D. Diss., UConn

Fujita, N. (1991) "Negative Polarity Items and Floating Quantifiers in Japanese," ms.

Hoji, H. (1985) *Logical Form Constraint and Configurational Structures in Japanese*, Doctoral dissertation, Univ. of Washington.

Kawasaki, N. (1989) "Zibun-tati and Non-coreferential Anaphora," ms. UMass., Amherst. MA.

Lasnik, H. and M. Saito (1984) "On the Nature of Proper Government," in Linguistic Inquiry 15.

_____ (1992) *Move-α; Conditions on its Application and Output*, The MIT Press.

Mahajan, A. K. (1989) "On the A/A' Distinction: Scrambling and Weak Crossover in Hindi," ms. MIT

May, R. (1985) *Logical Form: Its Structure and Derivation*, The MIT Press.

Miyagawa, S. (1986) "Theme Subjects and Numeral Quantifiers," ms. Umass.

_____ (1989) *Structure and Case Marking in Japanese, Syntax and Semantics Vol 22*, Academic Press, NY.

Nishigauchi, T. (1986) *Quantification in Syntax*, Doctoral dissertation, UMass, Amherst.

Saito, M. (1985) *Some Asymmetries in Japanese and Their Theoretical Implications*, Ph. D. Diss., MIT.

_____ (1989) "Scrambling as Semantically Vacuous A'-Movement," in M. R. Baltin and A. S. Kroch (eds.) *Alternative Conceptions of Phrase Structure* The Univ. of Chicago Press. 182-200.

_____ (1991) "Long Distance Scrambling in Japanese," ms. UConn

_____ (1992) "The Additional-Wh Effects and the Adjunction Site Theory," ms. UConn

Sohn, K. (1992) "Syntactic Saving Effects, Scrambling and the ECP," ms. UConn

Tada, H. (1990) "Scrambling(s)," Handout distributed in the OSU Workshop on Japanese Syntax.

Takahashi, D. (1992) "Improper Movements and Chain Formation," ms. UConn, Storrs, CT.

Terada, M. (1990) *Incorporation and Argument Structure in Japanese*, Ph. D. Dissertation, Univ. of Massachusetts at Amherst.

Williams, E. (1980) "Predication," in Linguistic Inquiry 11. 203-208

The Boundedness of Scrambling

SHÛICHI YATABE
Stanford University

It has been claimed by Haig (1976), Kuno (1976, n. 11; 1980a; 1980b; 1988, n. 4), Harada (1977), Muraki (1979), Tonoike (1980), Saito (1985; 1989; 1992), and others that it is possible in Japanese to prepose phrases across clause boundaries. In this paper, I argue that all the examples that have been claimed to show the existence of long-distance preposing in Japanese should be reanalyzed as instances of something other than long-distance preposing and that the claim made by the above authors is therefore incorrect.

1 Pseudo-Raising

Let me start with the sentence shown in (1). A sentence like this has been analyzed by Saito (1985; 1992) and others as involving preposing of the object NP (*sono seisaku o* 'that policy') of the embedded clause to the sentence-initial position.

(1) [sono seisaku o]   [minna   ga]   [dareka   ga   itsuka
     [that policy   ACC] [everyone NOM] [someone NOM some day

     jisshi suru   daroo   to]   omotte   iru   (koto)
     implement-PRES it's likely COMP] think-GER be-PRES (NML)

     'everyone thinks that someone will implement that policy some day'

I claim that this type of sentence should be reanalyzed as an instance of what I would call pseudo-raising. More specifically, I suggest that in a sentence like this the main-clause predicate (*omotte* 'think') is functioning as a three-place predicate selecting a *ga*-marked NP, an *o*-

marked NP, and a clause that contains a zero pronoun coindexed with the *o*-marked NP.[1]

This view is supported by the following considerations.

First, as shown in (2), the sentence-initial phrase *sono seisaku* 'that policy' becomes a grammatical subject when the the verb *omotte* 'think' that heads the main clause is passivized.

(2) [sono seisaku ga] [minna   kara] [dareka ga   itsuka
     [that policy   NOM] [everyone from] [someone NOM some day

  jisshi suru   daroo   to]   omowarete   iru   (koto)
  implement-PRES it's likely COMP] think-PASS-GER be-PRES (NML)

  'it is believed by everyone that someone will implement that policy some day'

This observation shows that the phrase *sono seisaku o* 'that policy' in (1) is governed by the verb *omotte* 'think', and not by the verb *jisshi suru daroo* 'will implement'. It is not possible to regard sentence (2) as an instance of the so-called indirect (or adversity) passive construction, because (i) the grammatical subject must be animate in the indirect passive construction and (ii) the demoted logical subject cannot be marked by the postposition *kara* 'from' in that construction (Shibatani (1978)).[2]

Second,[3] the case of the sentence-initial NP in a sentence like (1) does not have to be the same as the case that the corresponding gap in the embedded clause receives, as shown in (3).

(3) [sono seisaku o] [minna   ga] [dareka ga   kitto
     [that policy   ACC] [everyone NOM] [someone NOM doubtlessly

  hantai suru   daroo   to]   omotte   iru   (koto)
  oppose-PRES it's likely   COMP] think-GER be-PRES (NML)

  'everyone thinks that someone will doubtlessly oppose that policy'

The embedded predicate *hantai suru* 'oppose' takes a dative object, not an accusative object, but the sentence-initial NP *sono seisaku o* 'that policy' is accusative. This observation favors the pseudo-raising analysis over the long-distance movement analysis.

Third,[4] the sentence-initial NP in a sentence like (1) can be accompanied by a long-winded marker *no koto o* rather than the simple accusative case marker *o*, as shown in (4).

---

[1] Hoji (1991) makes an analogous point.

[2] In the direct passive construction, a demoted logical subject can be marked by *kara* 'from' if it bears a source-like thematic role (Shibatani (op. cit.)).

[3] I owe this argument to Masayo Iida.

[4] I owe this argument to Makoto Kanazawa.

(4) [sono seisaku no koto o] [minna ga] [dareka ga
[that policy GEN matter ACC] [everyone NOM] [someone NOM

itsuka jisshi suru daroo to] omotte iru (koto)
some day implement-PRES it's likely COMP] think-GER be-PRES (NML)

'everyone thinks that someone will implement that policy some day'

This observation also favors the pseudo-raising analysis because the marker *no koto o* can be used only on the object NP of a verb like *omou* 'think',[5] and not on the object NP of a verb like *jisshi suru* 'implement' (cf. Kuno (1976)).

Fourth, the following binding fact, first noted by Yoshimura (1989; 1992), also indicates the basic correctness of the proposed account. Notice that in (5) the sentence-initial NP *nani o* 'who' is allowed to bind the zero pronoun contained in the matrix subject. ('pro' represents a zero pronoun, here and elsewhere.)

(5) [Nani o]$_i$ [pro$_i$ hitome mita hito ga]
[what ACC] [it a glance see-PAST person NOM]

[Mearii ga yonda to] omotta no?
[Mary NOM read-PAST COMP] think-PAST NML

'What$_i$ did a person who glanced at t$_i$ think that Mary had read t$_i$?'

The long-distance movement analysis (at least in its naive form) incorrectly predicts that this example should be unacceptable, because in such an analysis the sentence-initial NP *nani o* 'what' must be in an Ā-position (in Chomsky's (1981) sense) and should be incapable of binding the zero pronoun inside the matrix subject, just as the sentence-initial NP *who* in an English sentence like *Who does his mother think Mary likes?* is incapable of binding the pronoun *his* inside the matrix subject. Although technically it is not impossible to get around this problem while retaining the long-distance movement analysis (cf. Saito (1992)), the fact in question is left unexplained in such an analysis. The pseudo-raising analysis, on the other hand, correctly predicts that (5) should be acceptable; since in my account the sentence-initial NP *nani o* 'what' in (5) is an argument of the matrix predicate *omotta* 'thought' and is in an A-position, it is expected to be capable of binding the zero pronoun inside the following subject NP.

Fifth, there are languages in which verbs such as *think* and *say* clearly function as three-place predicates. (6) is a Dutch example.

---

[5] Some speakers do not allow inanimate NPs to be marked by the marker *no koto o*. For those speakers, the particular example given in the text is not acceptable.

(6) Dit is een boek waar$_i$ ik t$_i$ van denk dat Jan (er) naar verlangt.
     this is a   book which I   of think that Jan   to   longs

'This is a book about which I think that Jan longs for it.'
(from Huybregts and van Riemsdijk (1985))

In this example the verb *denk* 'think' is obviously a three-place predicate selecting a nominative NP, a PP, and a clause. (7) is a Makua example.

(7) Aráárima mwaán-ólé á-$\left\{\begin{array}{l} \text{hééríh-á} \\ \text{hómwééríh-á} \end{array}\right\}$ wiírá áhó-rúw-á   isímá.
     Ararima child-dem sa-t.oa.said-t   that sa.t-prepare-t porridge

'Ararima said (of) the child that (he) prepared porridge.'
(from Stucky (1983))

The fact that the main-clause predicate is accompanied by the object agreement marker, which is glossed as "oa" in this example, indicates that the NP referring to the child is an argument of that predicate.

    Thus, there seem to be good reasons to believe that a sentence like (1) is not a case of long-distance movement.

2 Argument Transfer

Let us consider the second type of putative instance of long-distance scrambling, exemplified in (8) and (9).

(8) [Tookyoo e] [kanojo ga] [shutchoo suru   koto o]
     [Tokyo   LOC] [she   NOM] [make_a_trip-PRES NML ACC]
     kangaete iru   (koto)
     think-GER be-PRES (NML)

'she is thinking of making a business trip to Tokyo'

(9) [Nihon kara] [karera ga] [buki o   tairyoo-yunyuu shiyoo
     [Japan from] [they   NOM] [weapon ACC import_massively-PRESUMP
     to]   mokuronde iru   (koto)
     COMP] scheme-GER be-PRES (NML)

'they are scheming to import a large amount of weapons from Japan'

Kuno (1980a), Saito (1985), and others have analyzed sentences like these as involving movement of the locative argument of the embedded clause to the sentence-initial position. Notice that these examples cannot be viewed as cases of pseudo-raising; the pseudo-raising analysis is applicable only when (i) the main-clause predicate is a verb expressing a propositional attitude and (ii) the seemingly dislocated expression that appears in the main clause is marked by the accusative case.

I claim that examples like (8) and (9) should be analyzed as cases of argument transfer (cf. Grimshaw and Mester (1988)) or, in my view equivalently, predicate raising (cf. Muraki (1978)). More specifically, I suggest that this type of example involves transfer of one or more argument slots of the embedded predicate to the main-clause predicate. For instance, in sentence (9), I suggest that the source argument slot of the embedded verb *tairyoo-yunyuu shiyoo* 'import massively' has been transferred to the predicate that heads the main clause. On this account, the structure of the example can be represented as in Figure 1, assuming the analysis of Japanese phrase structure suggested in Yatabe (1990).

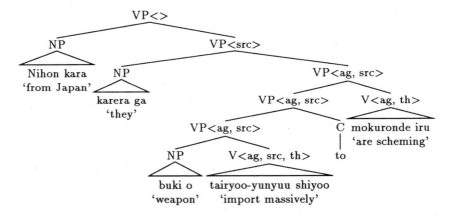

Figure 1: One possible structure of (9)

The verb *tairyoo-yunyuu shiyoo* 'import massively', which heads the embedded clause, has three argument slots, the agent slot, the source slot, and the theme slot. Only the theme slot is discharged within the embedded clause and the source slot is transferred to the predicate heading the main clause. On the other hand, the verb *mokuronde iru* 'are scheming', which heads the main clause, originally has an agent slot and a theme slot. The theme slot is discharged when the verb combines with the embedded clause; that is to say, the theme role is assigned to the embedded clause. At that point, the predicate inherits the source role that originally belonged to the embedded verb *tairyoo-yunyuu shiyoo* 'import massively'. As a result, the predicate heading the main clause now has two slots: the agent slot and the source slot, i.e., the agent slot that has belonged to it all along and the source slot that has been transferred to it from the embedded clause. This main-clause predicate discharges the agent slot and the source slot in that order, yielding the given sentence.

In the HPSG formalism (cf. Pollard and Sag (1987)), the proposed analysis can be realized by modifying the Subcategorization Principle so that argument slots are allowed to percolate up not only from heads to their mothers but also from controlled complements to their mothers. This analysis is in some sense equivalent to Muraki's (1978) analysis (see also Grimshaw and Mester (op. cit.)), as I mentioned above, and similar analyses have been suggested for German clause-union constructions by some authors including Bayer and Kornfilt (1991).

The proposed line of analysis is supported by the following considerations.

First, consider the sentences in (10) and (11),[6] which closely resemble (8) and (9) respectively.

(10)   [Tookyoo e]   [kanojo ga]   [shutchoo   o]   kangaete
      [Tokyo   LOC]   [she   NOM]   [making_a_trip ACC]   think-GER
      iru   (koto)
      be-PRES   (NML)

      'she is thinking of a business trip to Tokyo'

(11)   [Nihon kara]   [karera ga]   [buki   no   tairyoo-yunyuu   o]
      [Japan from]   [they   NOM]   [weapon GEN   massive importation   ACC]
      mokuronde iru   (koto)
      scheme-GER be-PRES   (NML)

      'they are scheming massive importation of weapons from Japan'

Sentences (10) and (11), unlike sentences (8) and (9) above, cannot reasonably be analyzed as instances of syntactic movement, since the sentence-initial phrases *Tookyoo e* 'to Tokyo' and *Nihon kara* 'from Japan', which are not (and cannot be) marked by the genitive case marker *no*, cannot have come from inside the NPs headed by *shutchoo* 'making a trip' and *tairyoo-yunyuu* 'massive importation' respectively; when a locative argument is inside an NP, it must be marked by *no*, as shown in (12).

(12)   ookina mondai to natta,   [[sono wakusei e   no/*∅]
      big   problem as become-PAST [[that planet   LOC GEN/∅]

---

[6] The possibility of constructing grammatical examples like these was first suggested by Ki-Sun Hong (personal communication, 1988). Yo Matsumoto discusses numerous examples of this type in Matsumoto (1992, chapter 3).

[nenryoo no]   yusoo]
[fuel   GEN] transportation]

'the transportation of fuel to that planet, which caused quite a stir'

Thus, the view that (8) and (9) involve long-distance preposing fails to cover examples like (10) and (11), while the argument transfer analysis, in which it is assumed that (8)–(11) involve transfer of the locative argument slot of the embedded predicate (*shutchoo* 'making a trip', *tairyoo-yunyuu* 'massive importation', etc.) to the predicate that heads the main clause, successfully accounts for (8)–(11) in a unified way.

Second, binding facts indicate that the sentence-initial expressions in sentences like (8) and (9) are in A-positions as predicted by the argument transfer analysis, and not in Ā-positions as predicted by simple versions of the long-distance movement analysis (Nemoto (1991)). Consider (13).

(13) [Dare ni]$_i$ [pro$_i$ ichido atta   dake no hito   ga]
      [who DAT] [him/her once meet-PAST only   person NOM]
      [hana-taba o   ageyoo   to]   kangaete iru   no?
      [bouquet   ACC give-PRESUMP COMP] think-GER be-PRES NML

'Who$_i$ is [a person who met t$_i$ only once] thinking of giving t$_i$ a bouquet?'

In this example the sentence-initial NP *dare ni* 'who' binds the zero pronoun inside the matrix subject NP. This indicates that the sentence-initial dative NP *dare ni* 'who' is in an A-position. Likewise, in (14), the sentence-initial accusative NP binds the reciprocal pronoun inside the subject NP of the matrix clause, indicating that the sentence-initial expression in this type of example is in an A-position.

(14) [Jon to   Bobu o]$_i$ [otagai$_i$ no chichioya ga]
      [John and Bob ACC] [each other GEN father   NOM]
      [rikai shiyoo   to]   kokoromita.
      [understand-PRESUMP COMP] attempt-PAST

'[John and Bob]$_i$, each other$_i$'s fathers tried to understand.'
(from Nemoto (1991))

Third, seemingly dislocated expressions in examples which I claim involve argument transfer are subject to the same linear precedence constraints that expressions that clearly have *not* been dislocated are subject to. The contrast between (15) and (16) provides one example of this phenomenon.

(15) [Taroo no koto o]   [hannin to]   [Hanako ga]
     [Taro GEN matter ACC] [culprit COMP] [Hanako NOM]
     [shinjikomu   tsumori de]   iru   (koto)
     [believe_firmly-PRES intention INST] be-PRES (NML)

     'Hanako intends to believe Taro to be the culprit'

(16) *[hannin to]   [Taroo no koto   o]   [Hanako ga]
     [culprit COMP] [Taro GEN matter ACC] [Hanako NOM]
     [shinjikomu   tsumori de]   iru   (koto)
     [believe_firmly-PRES intention INST] be-PRES (NML)

     'Hanako intends to believe Taro to be the culprit'

This contrast is presumably due to a linear precedence constraint that requires the accusative object of a verb like *shinjikomu* 'believe firmly' to precede the predicative complement of that verb (cf. Kuno (1976)). This situation is unexpected in the long-distance movement analysis; if the two sentence-initial constituents in an example like (16) had been preposed out of the embedded clause, then such a restriction on constituent order should apply to the *traces* of those constituents, not to the sentence-initial constituents themselves. Under the argument transfer analysis, on the other hand, the contrast in question poses no such puzzle, since on that account the relevant linear precedence constraint is correctly expected to apply to the sentence-initial constituents themselves, there being nothing else that the constraint can conceivably apply to.

It is not possible to account for the unacceptability of (16) in terms of the Proper Binding Condition, which states that a gap must be c-commanded by its filler (see Fiengo (1974)). Note that the accusative case marker *o* in (15) cannot be replaced by the nominative case marker *ga*, as shown in (17).

(17) *[[Taroo no koto   ga]   hannin to]   [Hanako ga]
     [[Taro GEN matter NOM] culprit COMP] [Hanako NOM]
     [shinjikomu   tsumori de]   iru   (koto)
     [believe_firmly-PRES intention INST] be-PRES (NML)

     'Hanako intends to believe Taro to be the culprit'

This observation suggests that the sentences in (15) and (16) do not have the hypothetical raising structures schematically shown in (18), which, if actual, could have made the analysis in terms of the Proper Binding Condition feasible.

(18) [Taroo no koto o]$_i$ [t$_i$ hannin to] ... (for (15))
     [t$_i$ hannin to] [Taroo no koto o]$_i$ ... (for (16))

The meaning of the noun *koto* 'matter', which appears in the accusative NP *Taroo no koto o* 'Taro's matter' in (15) and (16), also indicates that a verb like *shinjikomu* 'believe firmly' is a three-place predicate meaning 'believe a proposition X concerning (the matter of) Y' and not a true raising verb. Thus it seems to be something other than the Proper Binding Condition that is responsible for the contrast between (15) and (16).

The proposed analysis of sentences like (8) and (9) is based on the assumption that argument transfer, which Grimshaw and Mester (1988) view as a process that takes place in the lexicon, takes place in syntax. This assumption is motivated by two considerations.

First, Grimshaw and Mester's analysis of the argument transfer construction predicts that this construction can undergo further lexical processes such as passivization. This prediction is incorrect, as shown by (19).

(19) ?*Nooberu-shoo ga   Tanaka ni   juyo   o   sareta.
     Nobel prize   NOM Tanaka DAT awarding ACC do-PASS-PAST

'A Nobel prize was awarded to Tanaka.'

In Grimshaw and Mester's analysis, this example could be easily generated by first transferring the theme argument of the verbal noun *juyo* 'awarding' to the verb *s-* 'do' and then passivizing the verb. This sentence, however, is ungrammatical, in contrast to the sentence in (20), which involves a verb *juyo-s-* 'to award'.

(20) Nooberu-shoo ga   Tanaka ni   juyo sareta.
      Nobel prize   NOM Tanaka DAT award-PASS-PAST

'A Nobel prize was awarded to Tanaka.'

Arguably, the difference between (19) and (20) is that the sequence *juyo-s-* in (20) is constructed in the lexicon and hence can undergo passivization whereas the sequence *juyo o s-* in (19) is constructed in syntax and hence cannot undergo passivization, which is an operation that attaches the passive suffix to verb stems in the lexicon. (There is a possibility that the constituent structure of the string *juyo sareta* 'award-PASS-PAST' is [juyo [[s are] ta]], rather than [[[juyo s] are] ta]. If that is the case, the contrast between (19) and (20) does not provide a straightforward support for my view, though the unacceptability of (19) still poses a potential problem for Grimshaw and Mester's account.)

Second, when an argument slot σ has been transferred from a predicate α to another predicate β, the expression that fills the slot σ must precede α as well as β, as illustrated by the contrast between (8) and (21). This contrast is not explained in an account in which argument slots are allowed to be transferred from one predicate to another in the lexicon; in such an account, (8) and (21a, b) could both be generated by transferring the location argument slot of the verb *shutchoo suru* 'make a business trip' to the verb *kangaete (iru)* 'is thinking of' in the lexicon and letting the verb combine with its three arguments (one of which fills the location slot transferred from *shutchoo suru*) in syntax.

(21) a. *[kanojo ga]   [shutchoo suru   koto o]
            [she   NOM] [make_a_trip-PRES NML ACC]

            [Tookyoo e]   kangaete iru   (koto)
            [Tokyo   LOC] think-GER be-PRES (NML)

            'she is thinking of making a business trip to Tokyo'

      b. *[shutchoo suru   koto o]   [kanojo ga]
            [make_a_trip-PRES NML ACC] [she   NOM]

            [Tookyoo e]   kangaete iru   (koto)
            [Tokyo   LOC] think-GER be-PRES (NML)

            'she is thinking of making a business trip to Tokyo'

The proposed analysis correctly predicts that these sentences should be out because in neither case is there a constituent that can serve as a composite predicate that inherits the location argument slot of the verb *shutchoo suru* 'make a business trip'.

3 Extraposition

The sentence in (22) represents the third type of example that has been claimed to show the existence of long-distance preposing in Japanese (cf. Saito (1985)). The location argument of the verb *sawatta* 'touched' appears in the sentence-initial position, detached from the embedded clause headed by the verb.

(22) [sono hon ni] Ken ga   nazeka
      [that book DAT] Ken NOM somehow

      [Naomi ga   sawatta   to]   omotte   iru   (koto)
      [Naomi NOM touch-PAST COMP] think-GER be-PRES (NML)

      'Ken somehow thinks that Naomi touched the book'

This sentence cannot be analyzed as an instance of pseudo-raising because the scrambled expression (*sono hon ni* 'that book') is not an accusative NP, and it cannot be analyzed as an instance of argument transfer either because the embedded clause is not a controlled complement. Binding facts also indicate that an example like this is not a case of pseudo-raising or argument transfer; if it were an instance of pseudo-raising or argument transfer, then a sentence like (23) should be as acceptable as sentences like (5), (13), and (14) are.

(23) *[dono hon ni mo]ᵢ [sonoᵢ chosha ga]
 [which book DAT also] [its author NOM]

 [Naomi ga sawatta to] omotte iru (koto)
 [Naomi NOM touch-PAST COMP] think-GER be-PRES (NML)

 'every bookᵢ is such that itsᵢ author thinks that Naomi touched itᵢ.'

I submit that an example such as (22) should be seen as a case of extraposition, analogous to an English sentence like *John acted in a play last summer by that eccentric Polish writer, Witold Gombrowicz* (an example taken from Wittenburg (1987)), where the PP *by that eccentric Polish writer W. G.* is said to have been extraposed out of NP (and PP). Adopting Sag's (1987) and Rochemont and Culicover's (1990) view that extraposition does not induce any filler-gap dependency, I propose to assign the structure shown in Figure 2 to (22). The association between the verb *sawatta* 'touched' and its location argument *sono hon ni* 'that book' is assumed to be established by some variant of Sag's (op. cit.) Adjunct Constraint or Rochemont and Culicover's (op. cit.) Complement Principle.

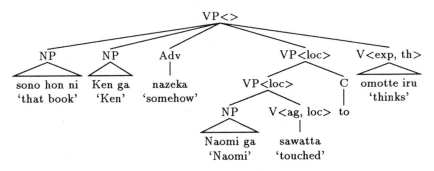

Figure 2: The structure of (22)

Examples like those in (24)–(27), whose resemblance to familiar English extraposition constructions is evident,[7] lend support to the idea that extraposition in Japanese shifts expressions to the left rather than to the right.

---

[7] It appears that, in Japanese, expressions can be extraposed out of an NP only when the NP is predicative.

(24) [Tanaka sensei no] tabun   kore ga [saigo no chosho ni]
     [Prof. Tanaka GEN] probably this NOM [last   book   DAT]

     naru   daroo.
     become-PRES it seems

     'This will probably become Prof. Tanaka's last book.'

(25) [Fudemame   datta   Taroo kara no]
     [fond of writing letters COP.PAST Taro   from GEN]

     kekkyoku sore ga [saigo no tegami to] natta.
     in the end that NOM [last   letter   as] become-PAST

     'In the end, that became the last letter from Taro, who was so fond
     of writing letters.'

(26) [Tanaka ga   koko ni   kita]   sore ga   jitsu wa
     [Tanaka NOM here DAT come-PAST] that NOM actually

     [hontoo no riyuu] na   no da.
     [real   reason] COP.PRES.ATTR NML COP.PRES

     'Actually that is the real reason why Tanaka came here.'

(27) [Sono mondai ni   tsuite   kakareta]   osoraku kore ga
     [that issue   DAT concern-GER write-PASS-PAST] probably this NOM

     [mottomo juuyoo   na   ronbun] desu.
     [most   important COP.PRES.ATTR paper] POL.COP.PRES

     'This is probably the most important paper that has ever been written
     concerning that issue.'

Notice that the proposed line of analysis correctly captures the fact that in (23) the quantifier expression *dono hon ni mo* 'to every book' is not allowed to bind the pronoun *sono* 'its', provided that extraposed phrases are assumed to be in Ā-positions. Thus my analysis offers a straightforward account for the contrast between examples like (23) and examples like (5), (13), and (14), which Saito (1992, n. 40) notes but leaves unexplained.

The proposed analysis of an example like (22) receives support from the following observations.

First, the existence of an example like (28) indicates that some instances of "long-distance scrambling" in Japanese are purely stylistic, that is, semantically vacuous, as claimed by Saito (1989; 1992), and thus quite different from standard cases of unbounded dependency such as English topicalization.

(28) ?[dono hon   o] Mearii ga [Jon ga
     [which book ACC] Mary NOM [John NOM

toshokan kara karidashita   ka] shiritagatte   iru   (koto)
library   from check_out-PAST Q] learn-want-GER be-PRES (NML)

'Mary wants to know which book John checked out from the library'
(from Saito (1989))

In the proposed analysis, this state of affairs is expected, as extraposition is known to be stylistic in the relevant sense (see J. R. Ross's argument discussed in Chomsky (1986, p. 41)). In an analysis like Saito's (op. cit.), which regards this sentence as a case of long-distance preposing, an additional assumption has to be made to explain why a sentence like *Who I wondered would go there* is not allowed as a variant of *I wondered who would go there* in English.

Second, seemingly dislocated expressions in an example like (22) are subject to the same linear precedence constraints that expressions that clearly have not been dislocated are subject to. For instance, consider the contrast between (29) and (30).

(29)(?)[Ken no   koto   o]   [hannin to]   Tanaka ga   [keisatsu ga
[Ken GEN matter ACC] [culprit COMP] Tanaka NOM [police   NOM

shinjikonde   iru   to]   omotte   iru   (koto)
believe_firmly-GER be-PRES COMP] think-GER be-PRES (NML)

'Tanaka thinks that the police firmly believe Ken to be the culprit'

(30) *[Hannin to]   [Ken no   koto   o]   Tanaka ga   [keisatsu ga
[culprit COMP] [Ken GEN matter ACC] Tanaka NOM [police   NOM

shinjikonde   iru   to]   omotte   iru   (koto)
believe_firmly-GER be-PRES COMP] think-GER be-PRES (NML)

'Tanaka thinks that the police firmly believe Ken to be the culprit'

The long-distance movement analysis fails to explain this contrast, because in such an analysis the relevant linear precedence constraint is expected to apply to the traces of the sentence-initial constituents, not to the sentence-initial constituents themselves, as I mentioned in connection with (15) and (16) as well.

Third, "long-distance scrambling" of the type being discussed in this section is *upward bounded* in Ross's (1967) sense, as noted by Nishigauchi (1986, pp. 9–10; 1990, pp. 7–8);[8] in a sentence like (22), no expression can be fronted over more than one clause boundary, as shown in (31)–(32). ((31) is slightly awkward due to multiple center-embedding.)

---

[8] Nishigauchi (op. cit.) simply states that scrambling in Japanese is upward bounded, without singling out the particular type of "long-distance scrambling" being discussed in the present section.

(31)(?)Taroo ga [keisatsu ga [Hanako ga daitooryoo ni atta
Taro NOM [police   NOM [Hanako NOM president DAT meet-PAST

to] shinjite iru to] omotte iru (koto)
COMP] believe-GER be-PRES COMP] think-GER be-PRES (NML)

'Taro thinks that the police believe that Hanako saw the president'

(32) *[daitooryoo ni] Taroo ga [keisatsu ga [Hanako ga atta
[president DAT] Taro NOM [police   NOM [Hanako NOM meet-PAST

to] shinjite iru to] omotte iru (koto)
COMP] believe-GER be-PRES COMP] think-GER be-PRES (NML)

'the president, Taro thinks that the police believe that Hanako saw'

The contrast between a sentence like (22) and a sentence like (32) is expected in the extraposition analysis, since extraposition is known to be upward bounded (Ross (1967)) unlike genuine cases of filler-gap dependency.

In order to rule out the string (not just the structure) shown in (32), it is necessary to rule out the following structure, in which three NPs, two VPs and a V are immediately dominated by the same VP node.

(33) [VP [NP daitooryoo ni] [NP Taroo ga] [NP keisatsu ga]
      [VP Hanako ga atta to] [VP shinjite iru to] [V omotte iru]]

A structure like this, which can be generated by first extraposing the lowest subject ('the police') and the most deeply embedded clause ('that Hanako met the president') out of the second most deeply embedded clause ('the police believe that Hanako met the president') and then extraposing the dative NP ('the president') out of the extraposed clause ('that Hanako met the president'), can be ruled out by setting up either (i) a constraint that prevents expressions from getting extraposed out of extraposed phrases or (ii) a constraint that prevents nominative subjects from getting extraposed. The choice between these two alternatives hinges on the grammaticality of an example like (35), which the first analysis but not the second analysis rules out.

(34) Taroo ga [[Hanako ga daitooryoo ni atta   to]
Taro NOM [[Hanako NOM president DAT meet-PAST COMP]

keisatsu ga shinjite iru to] omotte iru (koto)
police   NOM believe-GER be-PRES COMP] think-GER be-PRES (NML)

'Taro thinks that the police believe that Hanako saw the president'

(35) ??[daitooryoo ni] Taroo ga Hanako ga atta   to
[president DAT] Taro NOM Hanako NOM meet-PAST COMP

keisatsu ga   shinjite   iru   to   omotte   iru   (koto)
police   NOM believe-GER be-PRES COMP think-GER be-PRES (NML)

'the president, Taro thinks that the police believe that Hanako saw'

Since (35) seems to be significantly more acceptable than (32), the
second alternative should probably be preferred over the first; the low
acceptability of (35) can be attributed to processing difficulty.

In contrast to extraposition, pseudo-raising (cf. Saito (1985)) and
argument transfer (cf. Matsumoto (1992)) can give rise to seemingly
unbounded dependencies, as shown in (36) and (37).

(36) [sono hon   o]   Jon   ga   [[Mearii ga   katta   to]
      [that book ACC] John NOM [[Mary NOM buy-PAST COMP]

      Biru ga   itta   to]   omotte   iru   (koto)
      Bill NOM say-PAST COMP] think-GER be-PRES (NML)

      'that book, John thinks that Bill said that Mary bought'
      (from Saito (1985, subsection 3.3.2))

(37) [Nihon kara] karera ga   [[buki   o   tairyoo-yunyuu suru
      [Japan from] they   NOM [[weapon ACC import_massively-PRES

      koto o]   kokoromiyoo   to]   kangaete   iru   (koto)
      NML ACC] attempt-PRESUMP COMP] think-GER be-PRES (NML)

      'they are thinking of attempting to import a large amount of weapons
      from Japan'

In the analysis presented above, (36) is expected to be grammatical
because there is no reason why an anaphoric dependency between an
NP and a zero pronoun should be affected by the presence of an extra
clause boundary, and (37) is also correctly expected to be grammatical
because nothing prevents the source argument slot of *tairyoo-yunyuu
suru* 'import massively' from being transferred twice.

4 Conclusion

I have argued that scrambling in Japanese is strictly clause-internal and
that all the alleged instances of long-distance preposing in Japanese
should be reanalyzed as cases of pseudo-raising, argument transfer,
or extraposition. If this analysis is correct, then it becomes possible
to maintain that scrambling in a language like Japanese is essentially
the same phenomenon as scrambling in a language like German (pace
Fanselow (1990)).

Acknowledgments

I would like to thank Joan Bresnan, Kazuhiko Fukushima, Takao Gunji, Hajime Hoji, Hiroto Hoshi, Masayo Iida, Akira Ishikawa, Kiyoshi Ishikawa, Michio Isoda, Megumi Kameyama, Makoto Kanazawa, Tracy King, Yoshiko Masaki, Yo Matsumoto, Akira Nakamura, Tohru Noguchi, Bill Poser, Ivan Sag, Peter Sells, Yoshiko Sheard, and Noriko Yoshimura for invaluable help.

References

Bayer, J. and J. Kornfilt. 1991. 'Against Scrambling as Move-Alpha,' in T. Sherer, ed., *Proceedings of NELS 21*, GLSA, University of Massachusetts, Amherst, pp. 1–15.

Chomsky, N. 1981. *Lectures on Government and Binding: The Pisa Lectures*, Foris, Dordrecht.

Chomsky, N. 1986. *Barriers*, MIT Press, Cambridge, MA.

Fanselow, G. 1990. 'Scrambling as NP-Movement,' in G. Grewendorf and W. Sternefeld, eds., *Scrambling and Barriers*, John Benjamins, Amsterdam, pp. 113–140.

Fiengo, R. 1974. *Semantic Conditions on Surface Structure*, Ph.D. dissertation, MIT, Cambridge, MA.

Grimshaw, J. and A. Mester. 1988. 'Light Verbs and θ-Marking,' *Linguistic Inquiry*, 19, pp. 205–232.

Haig, J. H. 1976. 'Shadow Pronoun Deletion in Japanese,' *Linguistic Inquiry*, 7, pp. 363–371.

Harada, S.-I. 1977. 'Nihongo ni "Henkei" wa Hitsuyoo Da,' *Gengo*, vol. 6, no. 11, pp. 88–95 and no. 12, pp. 96–103.

Hoji, H. 1991. 'Raising-to-Object, ECM and the Major Object in Japanese,' handout for the talk given at the Japanese Syntax Workshop, University of Rochester, NY.

Huybregts, R. and H. van Riemsdijk. 1985. 'Parasitic Gaps and ATB,' in S. Berman, J.-W. Choe, and J. McDonough, eds., *Proceedings of NELS 15*, GLSA, University of Massachusetts, Amherst, pp. 168–187.

Kuno, S. 1976. 'Subject Raising,' in M. Shibatani, ed., *Japanese Generative Grammar (Syntax and Semantics 5)*, Academic Press, San Diego, pp. 17–49.

Kuno, S. 1980a. 'A Note on Tonoike's Intra-subjectivization Hypothesis,' in Otsu and Farmer (1980), pp. 149–156.

Kuno, S. 1980b. 'A Further Note on Tonoike's Intra-subjectivization Hypothesis,' in Otsu and Farmer (1980), pp. 171–184.

Kuno, S. 1988. 'Blended Quasi-Direct Discourse in Japanese,' in W. J. Poser, ed., *Papers from the Second International Workshop on Japanese Syntax*, CSLI, Stanford, pp. 75–102.

Matsumoto, Y. 1992. *On the Wordhood of Complex Predicates in Japanese*, Ph.D. dissertation, Stanford University, Stanford.

Muraki, M. 1978. 'The *shika nai* Construction and Predicate Raising,' in J. Hinds and I. Howard, eds., *Problems in Japanese Syntax and Semantics*, Kaitakusha, Tokyo, pp. 155–177.

Muraki, M. 1979. 'On the Rule Scrambling in Japanese,' in G. Bedell, E. Kobayashi, and M. Muraki, eds., *Explorations in Linguistics: Papers in Honor of Kazuko Inoue*, Kenkyuusha, Tokyo, pp. 369–377.

Nemoto, N. 1991. 'Scrambling and Conditions on A-Movement,' in D. Bates, ed., *The Proceedings of the Tenth West Coast Conference on Formal Linguistics*, Stanford Linguistics Association, Stanford, pp. 349–358.

Nishigauchi, T. 1986. *Quantification in Syntax*, Ph.D. dissertation, University of Massachusetts, Amherst.

Nishigauchi, T. 1990. *Quantification in the Theory of Grammar*, Kluwer, Dordrecht.

Otsu, Y. and A. Farmer, eds. 1980. *Theoretical Issues in Japanese Linguistics (MIT Working Papers in Linguistics 2)*, MIT, Cambridge, MA.

Pollard, C. and I. A. Sag. 1987. *Information-Based Syntax and Semantics, Vol. 1: Fundamentals*, CSLI, Stanford.

Rochemont, M. S. and P. W. Culicover. 1990. *English Focus Constructions and the Theory of Grammar*, Cambridge University Press, Cambridge.

Ross, J. R. 1967. *Constraints on Variables in Syntax*, Ph.D. dissertation, MIT, Cambridge, MA, reprinted in 1986 as *Infinite Syntax!*, ABLEX, Norwood.

Sag, I. A. 1987. 'Grammatical Hierarchy and Linear Precedence,' in G. J. Huck and A. E. Ojeda, eds., *Discontinuous Constituency (Syntax and Semantics 20)*, Academic Press, San Diego, pp. 303–340.

Saito, M. 1985. *Some Asymmetries in Japanese and Their Theoretical Implications*, Ph.D. dissertation, MIT, Cambridge, MA.

Saito, M. 1989. 'Scrambling as Semantically Vacuous A'-Movement,' in M. R. Baltin and A. S. Kroch, eds., *Alternative Conceptions of Phrase Structure*, University of Chicago Press, Chicago, pp. 182–200.

Saito, M. 1992. 'Long Distance Scrambling in Japanese,' *Journal of East Asian Linguistics*, 1, pp. 69–118.

Shibatani, M. 1978. *Nihongo no Bunseki: Seiseibunpoo no Hoohoo*, Taishuukan, Tokyo.

Stucky, S. 1983. 'Verb phrase constituency and linear order in Makua,' in G. Gazdar, E. Klein, and G. K. Pullum, eds., *Order, Concord and Constituency*, Foris, Dordrecht, pp. 75–94.

Tonoike, S. 1980. 'More on Intra-subjectivization,' in Otsu and Farmer (1980), pp. 157–170.

Wittenburg, K. 1987. 'Extraposition from NP as Anaphora,' in G. J. Huck and A. E. Ojeda, eds., *Discontinuous Constituency (Syntax and Semantics 20)*, Academic Press, San Diego, pp. 427–445.

Yatabe, S. 1990. 'Quantifier Floating in Japanese and the θ-Hierarchy,' in M. Ziolkowski, M. Noske, and K. Deaton, eds., *Papers from the 26th Regional Meeting of the Chicago Linguistic Society, Vol. 1: The Main Session*, CLS, Chicago, pp. 437–451.

Yoshimura, N. 1989. 'Parasitic Pronouns,' paper presented at the Southern California Japanese/Korean Linguistics Conference, University of California, Los Angeles.

Yoshimura, N. 1992. *Scrambling and Anaphora in Japanese*, Ph.D. dissertation, University of Southern California, Los Angeles.

Case, Agreement, and *Ga/No* Conversion

SHIGERU MIYAGAWA
Massachusetts Institute of Technology

0. Introduction[1]

In a simple clause in Japanese, the subject of the clause is commonly marked with the nominative case marker, as shown in (1).

(1) John-<u>ga</u>   piza-o   tabeta.
    John-<u>nom</u> pizza-acc ate
    'John ate pizza.'

In contrast, in a complex NP or a relative clause, the subject may optionally be marked with the genitive <u>no</u>, as shown in (2)a (cf. Harada 1971, 1976; Shibatani 1975). (2)b shows that the nominative case is also possible on the subject. This is what Harada called the <u>ga/no</u> Conversion in his 1971 article.

---

[1]Earlier versions of this paper were presented in a course on Japanese syntax at MIT in spring 1992 and at the Kansai Association of Theoretical Linguistics, July 1992, the Japanese/Korean Linguistics Conference at San Diego State University, August 1992, and a linguistics colloquium at the University of Connecticut, October 1992. I wish to thank those in attendance for many useful suggestions.

(2)a.   [$_{DP}$ [$_{IP}$ John-<u>no</u>   tabeta]   pizza]
      [$_{DP}$ [$_{IP}$ John-<u>gen</u>   ate]   pizza]
  'the pizza John ate'

  b.   [$_{DP}$ [$_{IP}$ John-<u>ga</u> tabeta] pizza]
              -<u>nom</u>

1. Previous Analysis

Harada (1971) does not entertain a structural difference between the genitive and the nominative subject, instead assuming that both are possible in the regular subject position. However, most other analyses suggest that the genitive subject resides in the higher DP, as illustrated in (3). These studies include Bedell 1972, Matsushita 1930, Miyagawa 1989, and Saito 1983.

(3)   [$_{DP}$ <u>John-no</u>   [$_{IP}$ ... tabeta]   piza]
    [$_{DP}$ <u>John-gen</u>   [$_{IP}$ ... ate]   pizza]

Saito (1983), for example, following a suggestion by Bedell (1972), proposes that the subject moves from the original IP position, leaving behind a trace, as illustrated in (4) (I have updated the structure).

(4)   [$_{DP}$ <u>John$_i$-no</u>   [$_{IP}$ t$_i$ tabeta]   piza]
    [$_{DP}$ <u>John$_i$-gen</u>   [$_{IP}$ t$_i$ ate]   pizza]

By identifying the subject NP with the higher DP, this family of analyses reduces the occurrence of the genitive case marker to the generalization that holds in Japanese that all XP's directly dominated by a projection of N or D must be marked with the genitive case marker. This point is illustrated with the simple nominal phrase in (5).

(5)   [$_{DP}$ Mary-<u>no</u>   nihon-de-<u>no</u>   suugaku-<u>no</u>   benkyoo]
    [$_{DP}$ Mary-<u>gen</u>   Japan-in-<u>gen</u>   math-<u>gen</u>   studying]
  'Mary's studying of math in Japan'

As we can see, both arguments and adjuncts in a nominal phrase must have the genitive particle.

However, this approach to the <u>ga/no</u> Conversion faces a serious empirical problem. As noted by Nakai (1980), a sentential adverb such as "yesterday" may occur to the left of the genitive subject.

(6) [DP [IP kinoo   Hanako-no   katta] hon]
    [DP [IP yesterday Hanako-gen   bought] book]
   'the book that Hanako bought yesterday'

Nakai correctly points out that such an adverb is associated with the IP, not the DP, so that in (6), the genitive subject Hanako-no must also be in the IP, and not directly dominated by the DP as most previous analyses would have it. Unlike in (6), a sentential adverb that is associated with the higher DP would have the genitive no.

(7) [DP kinoo-no   [IP Hanako-ga   itta]   paatii]
    [DP yesterday-gen [IP Hanako-nom   went]   party]
   'yesterday's party that Hanako went to'

2.   Analysis

I will propose that it is in fact possible to reconcile this sentential-adverb fact observed by Nakai with at least the spirit of the previous analyses. My analysis crucially depends on the notion that all morphological features including case features are checked at LF (cf. Chomsky 1992).

In Miyagawa (1991), I have proposed that case markers must be licensed by a functional category. As noted in (8)a, case markers such as the nominative ga and the accusative o must be licensed by verbal inflection.

(8)a. Infl: nominative ga, accusative o   (Miyagawa 1991)
   b. Det: genitive no

As shown in (8)b, I suggest that this extends to the genitive no, which is licensed by the functional head D, which heads DP. Thus, the previous analyses by Bedell, Saito, and others in which the genitive subject in ga/no Conversion occurs directly under the DP amounts to the requirement that the genitive case marker must be licensed by D. The question is, at what level does this licensing take place? If all morphological features are checked at LF as recently argued by Chomsky (1992), including Case features, then the Case-licensing requirement in (8) should hold at LF. I will give evidence that this is in fact correct. As shown in (9), this analysis predicts that when the subject has the genitive case, it moves at LF into Spec of DP, across the sentential adverb if such an adverb occurs.

(9)   The genitive subject moves at LF to have its case feature checked
        by D

    LF: [DP Hanako-no_i [IP kinoo   t_i   katta]   hon D]
        |_____<_____|
        [DP Hanako-gen_i [IP yesterday t_i   bought]   book D]
        'the book that Hanako bought yesterday'

3.   Evidence for LF Checking of Case Feature

        The type of evidence I will give involves a complex NP with a
head noun such as "reason" as exemplified in (10).

(10) [DP [IP Taroo-ga   itta]   riyuu]
      [DP [IP Taro-nom   went]   reason]
      'the reason why Taro went'

When the subject of this complex NP is marked with the nominative
ga, as in (11), the QP in the subject position, "John or Mary," always
has narrow scope over the head noun "reason."

(11) nominative subject
      [DP [IP (kinoo)   [John-ka Mary]-ga   kita]   riyuu]-o
      [DP [IP (yesterday) [John-or Mary]-nom came]   reason]-acc
      osiete.
      tell me
      'Tell me the reason why John or Mary came (yesterday).'
      reason > [John or Mary]; *[John or Mary] > reason

(11) only has an interpretation in which there is one reason for why
John or Mary came. This is not at all surprising since the nominative
subject would not ever be in a position that c-commands the head of the
complex NP.[2] In sharp contrast to this, in (12) below, in which the
subject QP is marked with the genitive case, the QP may take wide
scope over the head noun "reason."

---

[2]Other complex NPs that behave like the "reason" complex
NP include those headed by hi 'day' and mama 'while'. See Yamashita
(1992) for a detailed analysis of complex NP's with a variety of heads.

(12) genitive subject

[$_{DP}$ [$_{IP}$ (kinoo)   [John-ka Mary]-<u>no</u> kita]   riyuu]-o
[$_{DP}$ [$_{IP}$ (yesterday) [John-or Mary]-<u>gen</u> came]   reason]-acc
osiete.
tell me
'Tell me the reason why John or Mary came (yesterday).'
reason > [John or Mary]; [John or Mary] > reason

This sentence has an interpretation in which there are two reasons, one each for John coming and Mary coming. Crucially, this wide-scope reading of the genitive subject QP is possible even with the sentential adverb "yesterday" occurring in front of the subject. Based on this contrast between the two sentences, it would be reasonable to assume that in (12), the genitive subject moves at LF to a position that c-commands the head noun "reason," as shown in (13).

(13) **LF**

[$_{DP}$ [John-ka Mary]-<u>no</u>$_i$ [$_{IP}$ kinoo t_i kita] riyuu D]
[$_{DP}$ [John-or Mary]-<u>gen</u>$_i$ [$_{IP}$ yesterday t_i came] reason D]

This constitutes evidence for LF movement of the genitive subject to the Spec of DP. This movement can only be motivated by case checking. It cannot, for example, be an instance of QR because QR would only raise the subject QP to the IP-adjoined position. This position would not c-command the head noun of the complex NP. We therefore have evidence for (14):

(14) Morphological features such as the Case feature are checked at LF (cf. Chomsky 1992)

Following are other examples that illustrate the same point. In the last pair, the complex NP is headed by "day" instead of "reason." This "day" complex NP has the same property of not allowing the subject QP to take scope over the head "day" if the QP is nominatively marked.

(15)a. nominative subject

    [$_{DP}$ [$_{IP}$ sensyuu   [subete-no gakusei]-<u>ga</u>   kita]   riyuu]-o

    [$_{DP}$ [$_{IP}$ last week   [every-gen student]-<u>nom</u>   came]   reason]-acc

    osiete.

    tell me

 'Tell me the reason why every student came last week.'

 reason > [every student]; *[every student] > reason

   b. genitive subject

    [$_{DP}$ [$_{IP}$ sensyuu   [subete-no gakusei]-<u>no</u>   kita]   riyuu]-o

    [$_{DP}$ [$_{IP}$ last week   [every-gen student]-<u>gen</u>   came]   reason]-acc

    osiete.

    tell me

 'Tell me the reason why every student came last week.'

 reason > [every student]; [every student] > reason

(16)a. nominative subject

    [$_{DP}$ [$_{IP}$ kinoo   [John-to Mary]-<u>ga</u>   kita]   riyuu]-o

    [$_{DP}$ [$_{IP}$ yesterday   [John-and Mary]-<u>nom</u>   came]   reason]-acc

    osiete.

    tell (me)

 'Tell me the reason why John and Mary came yesterday.'

 reason > [John and Mary]; *[John and Mary] > reason

   b. genitive subject

    [$_{DP}$ [$_{IP}$ kinoo   [John-to Mary]-<u>no</u>   kita] riyuu]-o

    [$_{DP}$ [$_{IP}$ yesterday   [John-and Mary]-<u>gen</u>   came] reason]-acc

    osiete.

    tell me

 'Tell me the reason why John and Mary came yesterday.'

 reason > [John and Mary]; [John and Mary] > reason

(17)a. nominative subject

    [$_{DP}$ [$_{IP}$ raigetu   daremo-<u>ga</u>   kuru]   hi]-o   osiete.

    [$_{DP}$ [$_{IP}$ next month   everyone-<u>nom</u> come]   day]-acc   tell me

 'Tell me the day when everyone will come next month.'

 day > everyone; *everyone > day

b. genitive subject

[DP [IP raigetu   daremo-<u>no</u>   kuru]   hi]-o   osiete.

[DP [IP next month   everyone-<u>gen</u>   come]   day]-acc   tell me

'Tell me the day when everyone will come next month.'

day > everyone; (?)everyone > day

4. Scope of Subject QP and Head Noun "reason"

I will now turn to an issue regarding complex NP's headed by the head noun "reason," which I used above to argue for LF movement of the genitive subject. In particular, I will look to see why the nominative subject QP cannot take scope over the head noun "reason." This is again illustrated in (18).

(18)   [DP [IP subete-no   gakusei]-<u>ga</u>   itta]   <u>riyuu</u>]-o   osiete.

     [DP [IP every   student]-<u>nom</u>   went] <u>reason</u>]-acc   tell me

  'Tell me the reason why every student went.'

  reason > every student; *every student > reason

In contrast to this, when we consider a relative clause such as (19) in which the gap in the relative clause corresponds to an argument position, the QP subject may take scope over the head noun "book."

(19)   [DP [CP OP$_i$ [IP [subete-no   gakusei]-ga   t$_i$ katta]]   hon$_i$]-o

     [DP [CP OP$_i$ [IP [every   student]-nom t$_i$ bought]] book$_i$]-acc

     misete.

     show me

  'Show me the book that every student bought.'

  book > every student; every student > book

It is reasonable to assume operator movement in this structure, and as shown, the nominative subject QP may take wide scope over the head of the relative clause, presumably through the operator chain and the coindexation of the head of the chain to the head noun "book." We would have the solution to the absence of wide-scope reading for the subject QP in "reason" complex NP if it can be shown that no operator movement occurs in this construction. Murasugi (1991) gives evidence that this is in fact the case. The "reason" complex NP differs from a normal "argument" relative clause in not allowing long-distance construal of the head.

(20) [DP[CP OP$_i$ [IP Hanako-ga   [CP John-ga   t$_i$ katta   to]

    [DP[CP OP$_i$ [IP Hanako-nom   [CP John-nom   t$_i$ bought comp]

    omotta] hon$_i$]

    thought] book$_i$]

  'the book that Hanako thought that John bought'

(21) *[DP [CP [IP Hanako-ga   [CP John-ga   naita to]   omotta]

    [DP [CP [IP Hanako-nom [CP John-nom cried comp] thought]

    riyuu]

    reason]

  'the reason why Hanako thought that John cried'

The long-distance construal of the head "book" in (20) is accounted for by operator movement that associates the head noun with the trace in the lower clause. The failure of long-distance construal in the "reason" complex NP suggests that no operator movement takes place.

5. A Locality Condition on A-chain

I now return to the main concern of this paper, ga/no Conversion. Up to now, we have only looked at instances of subject ga/no Conversion. However, it is possible in stative constructions for the object as well as the subject to be associated with the genitive case. As shown in (22), in a stative construction the object as well as the subject may be marked with the nominative ga.

(22) John-ga   aisukuriimu-ga suki da.

    John-nom ice cream-nom   like   cop

    'John likes ice cream.'

As shown in (23), this construction in combination with ga/no Conversion gives rise to four possible case arrays.

(23)a.　John-<u>ga</u>　aisukuriimu-<u>ga</u>　　suki　na　koto (nom-nom)
　　　　John-<u>nom</u>　ice cream-<u>nom</u>　　　like　cop　fact
　　　　'the fact that John likes ice cream'

　　　b.　John-<u>no</u>　aisukuriimu-<u>ga</u>　suki　na　koto　(gen-nom)
　　　　　John-<u>gen</u>　ice cream-<u>nom</u>　like　cop　fact

　　　c.　John-<u>no</u>　aisukuriimu-<u>no</u>　suki　na　koto　(gen-gen)
　　　　　John-<u>gen</u>　ice cream-<u>gen</u>　like　cop　fact

　　　d.　John-<u>ga</u>　aisukuriimu-<u>no</u>　suki　na　koto　(nom-gen)
　　　　　John-<u>nom</u>　ice cream-<u>gen</u>　like　cop　fact

Let us now look at scope interaction in the stative construction. We already know that the genitive subject may take scope over the head noun "reason" in complex NP. This is again illustrated in (24) this time with a stative structure.

(24) [$_{DP}$ [John-ka Mary]-<u>no</u>　tenisu-ga　　dekiru　riyuu]-o
　　　[$_{DP}$ [John-or Mary]-<u>gen</u>　tennis-nom　can　　　reason]-acc
　　　osiete.
　　　tell me
　　'Tell me the reason why John or Mary can play tennis'
　　reason > John or Mary; John or Mary > reason

What about a QP in the object position? The possible combinations are given in (25).

(25)a. (nom-nom)
　　　John-<u>ga</u>　　[subete-no　daitooryoo　koohosya]-<u>ga</u>　sukina
　　　John-<u>nom</u>　[every　　　presidential　candidate]-<u>nom</u>　like
　　　riyuu-o　　osiete
　　　reason-acc tell me
　　　'Tell me the reason(s) why John likes every pesidential candidate'
　　　reason > [every pres. candidate]; *[every pres. cand.] > reason

　　b. (gen-nom)
　　　John-<u>no</u>　　[subete-no daitooryo　koohosya]-<u>ga</u>　sukina riyuu
　　　John-<u>gen</u>　[every　　　presidential candidate]-<u>nom</u> like　　reason
　　　'the reason why John likes every pesidential candidate'
　　　reason > [every pres. candidate]; *[every pres. cand.] > reason

c. (gen-gen)

John-<u>no</u> [subete-no daitooryoo koohosya]-<u>no</u> sukina riyuu
John-<u>gen</u> [every presidential candidate]-<u>gen</u> like reason
'the reason why John likes every pesidential candidate'
reason > [every pres. candidate];
<u>?[every pres. cand.] > reason</u>

d. (nom-gen)

John-<u>ga</u> [subete-no daitooryoo koohosya]-<u>no</u> sukina riyuu
John-<u>nom</u> [every presidential candidate]-<u>gen</u> like reason
'the reason why John likes every pesidential candidate'
reason > [every pres. candidate];
<u>*[every pres. cand.] > reason</u>

In (a) and (b), the object QP cannot take scope over the head noun
"reason." This is expected because the object is marked with the
nominative case, not the genitive. In (c), in which the object as well as
the subject is marked with the genitive case, the object QP may take
scope over the head noun. Presumably, at LF both the genitive subject
and the genitive object raise to the higher DP. Now look at (d). The
object is marked with the genitive case, yet, as indicated by the
underlined impossible scope interpretation, this genitive object cannot
take scope over the head noun "reason." Clearly the culprit here is the
nominative case on the subject, since in (c) above, the genitive object
may take scope over the head noun as long as the subject is also
genitive. Why can't the genitive object raise by A-movement to the
higher DP at LF if the subject is nominative?

I wish to suggest a locality condition on A-chains to account for
why the genitive object cannot raise across the nominative subject by A-
movement. As shown in (26), if the genitive object raises over the
nominative subject, this results in a structure in which the trace of the
genitive object is locally c-commanded by the nominative subject.

(26) [$_{DP}$ object-<u>no</u>$_i$ [$_{IP}$ subject-<u>ga</u> t$_i$ .....

Based on this observation, I suggest the locality condition on A-chains
given in (27).

(27) Locality Condition on A-chains

> The trace of an A-chain cannot be locally c-commanded by a
> member of another A-chain checked by a different-type functional
> category.

(28) Two Different Types of Functional Categories
Infl: checks nominative, accusative
Det: checks genitive

According to this condition, the problem with (26) is that while the genitive object is checked by Det, its trace is locally c-commanded by the subject with nominative case, which is checked by Infl.[3] This violates the locality condition because the nominative case, which is checked by Infl, locally c-commands the trace of the genitive object, which is checked by the Determiner.[4]

---

[3]The Locality Condition on A-chains may be viewed at least in part as an extension of Relativized Minimality (Rizzi 1990). A problem with Relativized Minimality is that it makes the wrong prediction for clause-internal scrambling. It is well-known that the chain formed by clause-internal scrambling of the object over the subject has A properties (cf. Mahajan 1990, Miyagawa 1991, Saito 1992, Tada 1990, Webelhuth 1989, among others). However, Relativized Minimality would predict that this instance of scrambling should be A'-movement, since it "crosses" an A-position. The Locality Condition proposed above gets us out of this dilemma, since "crossing" A-chains are allowed as long as both chains are checked by the same-type functional head (e.g., verbal inflection).

[4]A problem that arises here is, how is the genitive case on the object licensed in (25)d? One possibility is that Det licenses the genitive case by Government Transparency (cf. Baker 1988). Terada (1990) has suggested that the verb in the relative clause incorporates into the head noun to license the genitive case (see also Kamio 1983 and Matsunaga 1983 for a similar analysis).

(i) $[_{DP} [_{IP} \ldots t_v] \text{ V-N D}]$
$|\_>\_|$

By having the verb incorporate into the head noun, and, presumably, this entire structure incorporating into D, D can govern the original governing domain of the verb by Baker's Government Transparency Corollary, as Terada (1990) suggests. Thus, if the verb incorporates into the head noun, there is no need for the genitive phrase to move into the Spec of DP. See Miyagawa (1993) for an alternative analysis. There are speakers who do not get the wide-scope reading noted in, e.g., (12) with the sentential adverb; these speakers apparently favor this

We can find independent evidence for this locality condition on A-chains in the original study on ga/no Conversion by Harada (1971). He makes an interesting observation that it is not possible to scramble, say, the object across the genitive subject, as shown in (29).

(29) *hon-o$_i$ John-no   t$_i$ katta   mise

   book-acc$_i$ John-nom t$_i$ bought   store

   'the store where John bought a book'

Under the previous analyses such as Bedell's or Saito's, this receives a straightforward explanation. In their analysis, the genitive subject John-no is in Spec of DP, as illustrated in (30), hence it would be impossible to scramble the object hon-o in front of it. (29) is fine if the subject is marked with the nominative instead of the genitive marker.

(30)   hon-o$_i$ [$_{DP}$ John-no$_j$ [$_{IP}$ t$_j$ t$_i$ katta] mise]

   *|_____<_____|

However, under the analysis I am pursuing this explanation is unavailable because the genitive subject may be in the original Spec of IP at S-structure. Therefore, as shown in (31), the scrambling we see here may simply be IP-adjunction, which should result in a grammatical structure.

(31)   [$_{DP}$ [$_{IP}$ hon-o$_i$ John-no   t$_i$ katta] mise]

   |___<_____|

This structure is effectively excluded by the Locality Condition on A-chains I proposed above. The accusative object crosses the genitive subject, hence the trace of the accusative object is locally c-commanded by the genitive subject, in violation of the locality condition. Our analysis has the advantage of providing the same solution to this scrambling problem and to the prohibition against LF A-movement of genitive object we saw above for (25)d.[5] There is yet another advantage

_____(25)

alternative way of licensing genitive case in this context. Many speakers who get the reading find it somewhat weak, suggesting that the alternative licensing method is preferred in general in this context.

[5]In footnote 3 above, I suggested that the Locality Condition on A-chain may in part be an extension of Relativized Minimality. If this is correct, the fact that it is impossible to scramble an accusative object across the genitive subject, as we have seen, leads to a view of

that the present analysis has. The previous analyses exclude all instances of scrambling across the genitive subject. However, there are instances in which scrambling seems possible. For example, as shown in (32), scrambling of the goal NP of a ditransitive verb across the genitive subject appears grammatical, although there is some degradation in acceptability.

(32) ?[[minna-ni$_i$ John-no t$_i$ ageta] hon]-wa kore da.
    [[everyone-to$_i$ John-gen t$_i$ gave] book-top this cop
  'This is the book that John gave everyone'

This can be accounted for if we suppose that only the nominative and the accusative case markings are checked directly by the relevant functional heads, possibly Agr-s and Agr-o, and the goal NP with <u>ni</u> is not uniquely identified with a functional head. It is therefore able to escape the constraint imposed by the locality condition on A-chains in (32).

6. Conclusion

In this paper I gave evidence for LF movement for the purpose of Case checking using the so-called *ga/no* Conversion phenomenon in Japanese. The Locality Condition on A-chains, which was suggested to account for those instances in which this LF A-movement for Case checking is apparently blocked, also has the advantage of overcoming the difficulty posed by scrambling for Relativized Minimality.

---

clause-internal scrambling that is different from the generally accepted view. Mahajan (1989) argues that the clause-internal scrambling is A or A' (see also Saito 1992, for example). However, according to the data we see, clause-internal scrambling is (at least) always A-movement. Because the genitive subject resides in an A-position, the scrambling cannot sustain the A-property, thus it is out. See Miyagawa (1993) for an expansion of this analysis.

References

Baker, Mark. 1988. Incorporation: a theory of grammatical function changing. University of Chicago Press.

Bedell, George. 1972. On no. Studies in East Asian syntax. UCLA Papers in Syntax, no. 3.

Chomsky, Noam. 1989. Some notes on economy of derivation and representation. MIT working papers in linguistics, Vol. 10.

Chomsky, Noam. 1992. Minimalist program for linguistic theory. MIT working papers in linguistics occasional papers 1.

Harada, Shin-Ichi. 1971. Ga-no conversion and idiolectal variations in Japanese. Gengo kenkyuu 60.

Harada, Shin-Ichi. 1976. Ga-no conversion revisited -- a reply to Shibatani. Gengo kenkyu 70.

Kamio, Akio. 1983. Meishiku no koozoo. Nihongo no kihon koozoo, ed. by Kazuko Inoue. Sanseido.

Kuno, Susumu. 1973. The structure of the Japanese language. MIT Press.

Mahajan, Anoop. 1990. The A/A-bar distinction and movement theory. Doctoral dissertation, MIT.

Matsunaga, Setsuko. 1983. Hisotrical development of case marking in Japanese. M.A. thesis, Ohio State University.

Matsushita, D. 1930. Hyoojun Nihon koogohoo. Benseisha (reprinted in 1977).

Miyagawa, Shigeru. 1989. Structure and Case Marking in Japanese, Syntax and Semantics 22. Academic Press.

Miyagawa, Shigeru. 1991. Scrambling and Case realization, ms.

Miyagawa, Shigeru. 1993. LF Case-checking, ms.

Murasugi, Keiko. 1991. Noun phrases in Japanese and English: a study in syntax, learnability, and acquisition. Doctoral dissertation, University of Connecticut.

Nakai, Satoru. 1980. A reconsideration of ga-no conversion in Japanese. Papers in linguistics 13.

Rizzi, Luiggi. 1990 Relativized minimality. MIT Press.

Saito, Mamoru. 1983. Case and government in Japanese. Proceedings of WCCFL.

Saito, Mamoru. 1985. Some asymmetries in Japanese and their theoretical implications. Doctoral dissertation, MIT.

Saito, Mamoru. 1992. Long-distance scrambling in Japanese. Journal of East Asian Linguistics 1.

Shibatani, Masayoshi. 1975. Perceptual strategies and the phenomena of particle conversion in Japanese. Papers from the Parasession on Functionalism. Chicago Linguistics Circle.

Tada, Hiroaki. 1990. Scramblings. Ms., MIT.

Takezawa, Koichi. 1987. A configurational approach to case marking in Japanese. Doctoral dissertation, University of Washington, Seattle.

Terada, Michiko. 1990. Incorporation and argument structure in Japanese. Doctoral dissertation, University of Massachusetts.

Webelhuth, Gert. 1989. Syntactic saturation phenomena and the modern Germanic languages. Doctoral dissertation, University of Massachusetts, Amherst.

Yamashita, Hiroko. 1992. Relative clause formation in Japanese. Ms., Ohio State University.

Analyzing the Verbal Noun:
Internal and External Constraints

CHRISTOPHER MANNING
Stanford University

Japanese verbal nouns such as *sakugen* 'reduction' and *saikuringu* 'cycling' appear initially noun-like, in morphology and distribution. They normally take adjectives and nominal case marked arguments (that is, preceding arguments and modifiers are case marked with the genitive *-no* or an oblique particle followed by *-no*, such as *-e-no* 'to-GEN'), as in (1a).[1] In such a sentence, verbal case marked arguments (by which I mean use of particles like *-ga* and *-o* to mark subject, object and oblique grammatical roles) is impossible, as shown in (1b).

(1) a. [Nihon-**no** bōeki-kuroji-**no** ōhaba-na SAKUGEN-ga]
    Japan-GEN trade-surplus-GEN drastic reduction-NOM
    nozomarete-iru
    desire.PASS-PROG.PRES
    'Japan is required to drastically reduce its trade surplus.'

[0]My thanks to the many people who have helped me with this paper. First and foremost should be mentioned Peter Sells and Masayo Iida upon whose work this paper builds. I have also received advice and comments (relating to data or linguistic analyses, though generally the latter) from Lynn Cherny, Hye-won Choi, Mary Dalrymple, Yookyung Kim, Yoshiko Matsumoto, Shigeru Miyagawa, Bill Poser, Yoshiko Sheard and Shûichi Yatabe. My email address is manning@csli.stanford.edu.

[1]Verbal nouns are written in small capitals in all the examples. I will largely restrict myself to discussing non-native verbal nouns (of Chinese and Western origin). See Tsujimura (forthcoming) for a discussion of native deverbal nouns.

b. *[Nihon-**ga** bōeki-kuroji-**o** ōhaba-ni SAKUGEN-**ga**]
nozomarete-iru

Verbal nouns are θ-assigners with their own argument structure and thus similar to English complex event nominals, such as *arrival*, even though verbal nouns are in general not synchronically derived from verbs. However, verbal nouns are also verblike: when acting as the main predicate of a sentence in conjunction with the pro-verb *suru* 'do', as in (2), their arguments can or must take verbal case marking:

(2) Jon-wa   murabito-ni ōkami-ga kuru-to
John-TOP villager-DAT wolf-NOM come.PRES-COMP
KEIKOKU-o   shita
warning-ACC do.PAST
'John warned the villagers that the wolf was coming.'

It is often suggested that *suru* licenses the verbal case marking of these arguments, perhaps as the result of argument transfer of θ-roles from the verbal noun to *suru* (Grimshaw and Mester 1988). However, Sells (1988) demonstrated that this cannot be the explanation in all cases. In a sentence such as (3), *suru* could not be assigning the first noun phrase Case because that would violate the 'Double-*o* constraint' (specifically, the part of the 'Double-*o* constraint' that prevents two nominals from bearing the same abstract Case, see Poser (1989) for discussion). Rather, accusative Case must be being assigned directly by the verbal noun, even though the NP has scrambled from the verbal noun's projection as shown:[2]

(3) [Kaiketsu-no hōkō   -wa /?-o]$_i$ sono hōkokusho-ga
solution-GEN direction TOP/ACC   that report-NOM
Mari-ni [$_{NP}$ t$_i$ SHISA-o]   shite-iru
Mary-to   suggestion-ACC do-PROG.PRES
'This report suggests to Mary the direction of the solution.'

Iida (1987) presented a considerable amount of additional evidence that verbal nouns can assign verbal case by showing that it happens in at least three other contexts: when verbal nouns genitively modify certain temporal nouns such as *sai* or *ori* 'occasion' (4a); with certain 'temporal affixes' such as -*chū* 'in the middle of' or -*go* 'after' (4b); and in controlled purpose clauses (4c):[3]

---

[2]While scrambling out of NPs is generally impossible, it is possible when the constituents are verbal case marked (Sells 1991). Thus, scrambling is also possible with the verbal case marked constructions which I consider below, but this 'long distance scrambling' is not further discussed in this paper.

[3]A verbal noun can also appear with preceding verbal case marked arguments

(4) a. [Sōridaijin-**ga**   Amerikataishi-**to**
         Prime minister-NOM American.Ambassador-with
         KAIDAN-no] ori-ni   Tarō-wa   tsūyaku-o
         meeting-GEN occasion-at Tarō-TOP translation-ACC
         tsutometa
         perform-PAST
         'When the Prime Minister met the American ambassador,
         Tarō acted as translator.'

      b. [Jikken-**ga**   buji-ni SHŪRYŌ-**go**] wareware-wa
         experiment-NOM safely finish-after we-TOP
         minna-de shukuhai-o ageta
         together   toast-ACC   raise-PAST
         'We raised a toast after the experiment was safely
         completed.'

      c. Kikuko-ga   Amerika-ni [Eigo-**o**   BENKYŌ-**ni**-wa]
         Kikuko-NOM America-to English-ACC study-PURP-FOC
         kyonen   itta-ga
         last year went-but
         'Kikuko went to America last year to study English (, but)'

In this paper, I wish to analyze the behavior of the verbal noun in these
contexts that Iida discussed, and examine how the existence of words
of apparent mixed categorial status impacts on possible theories of UG.
Similar data occur also in Korean (and are discussed in Saiki and Cho
1987 and Y.-S. Lee 1991), but I will concentrate on Japanese.

1   The Data

In each of the three contexts just described, a verbal noun can be
preceded by either nominal or verbal case marking:[4]

(5) a. [Kanai-**ga**   Amerika-**o**   HŌMON-no ori-ni-wa],
         my.wife-NOM America-ACC visit-GEN occasion-on-TOP
         iroiro   osewa-ni   narimashita
         various hospitality-ADV.PART become.POLITE.PAST

---

in some other special contexts, such as newspaper headlines (Kageyama 1977:120),
as in (i), but it cannot normally license verbal case marking by itself (recall (1b)).

   (i) Nihon-josei Himaraya ni TOZAN!
        'Japanese women climb the Himalayas!'

   [4] This paper tacitly assumes the argument structure of a verbal noun is the same
in its nominal and verbal usages, but I have recently become aware of Hasegawa
1991 which argues convincingly that this is not always so. I have yet to fully
incorporate her observations (which deal mainly with *suru* constructions), but feel
that categorial underspecification will remain a useful part of a complete analysis.

'Thank you for your generous hospitality when my wife visited America.'

b. [Kanai-no   Amerika-no   HŌMON-no ori-ni-wa], ...
   my.wife-GEN America-GEN visit-GEN   occasion-on-TOP

(6) a. [Jon-ga   ainugo-o   KENKYŪ-chū-ni]   dareka
       John-NOM Ainu.language-ACC research-during-at someone
       kite   shimatta
       come end.up.PAST
       'Someone (unfortunately) came in the middle of John's
       research into Ainu.'

   b. [Jon-no   ainugo-no   KENKYŪ-chū-ni]   ...
      John-GEN Ainu.language-GEN research-during-at

(7) a. Kenzō-ga   [shinsaku-o   HAPPYŌ-ni]   Tōkyō-ni itta
       Kenzō-NOM   new.line-ACC introduce-PURP Tokyo-to went
       'Kenzō went to Tokyo to introduce his new (product) line.'

   b. Kenzō-ga   [shinsaku-no   HAPPYŌ-ni]   Tōkyō-ni itta
      Kenzō-NOM   new.line-GEN introduce-PURP Tokyo-to went

Additionally, as observed by Sells (1988), one gets mixed case marking
(some arguments have verbal case marking while others have nominal
case marking), as in (8a–b). This is only possible when the verbal case
marked arguments are higher on the θ-hierarchy than the nominal case
marked ones, and they appear higher up in the S-structure tree (i.e.,
to the left) (8c). These data prevent an analysis in which a word like
kenkyū-chū is simply specified disjunctively as either a verb or a noun.

(8) a. Tarō-**ga**   Tōkyō-e piza-**no**   YUSŌ-chū-ni,   ...
       Tarō-NOM Tokyo-to pizza-GEN sending-during-at
       'While Tarō was sending the pizza to Tokyo, ...'

   b. Tarō-**ga**   Nihon-**no** RYOKŌ-no ori-ni,   ...
      Tarō-NOM Japan-GEN travel-GEN occasion-at
      'When Tarō was traveling in Japan, ...'

   c. *Tarō-**no** Nihon-o   RYOKŌ-no ori-ni,   ...
      Tarō-GEN Japan-ACC travel-GEN occasion-at

I will omit examples showing the scrambling possibilities (see Sells
(1991) and especially Lee (1991)[5]), but the proposal I will present also

---

[5]But note that scrambling of nominal case marked arguments is not possible
in Japanese, even when the sentence contains additional arguments or adjuncts –
such sentences can only be interpreted with appropriate pauses as sentence repairs.
Their acceptability in Korean varies greatly between speakers, as noted by Lee.

handles cases with clause internal scrambling.

Even when a temporal suffix is attached to a verbal noun, the phrase has the same external distribution as any other noun phrase, regardless of whether the case marking of its arguments is verbal, nominal or mixed. For example, such a phrase can appear as subject or object (marked with -*ga* or -*o*) as in (9a), in a topic or contrastive position (marked with -*wa* or -*mo*), before the copula as in (9b), modifying another noun genitively (marked with -*no*), or as a time adverbial. This distribution corresponds closely to the distribution of an adverbial NP headed by a 'temporal' noun such as *toki* 'when'.[6]

(9) a. Tarō-wa sono henji-o   suru jiki toshite [Hawaii-ni
       Tarō-TOP that answer-ACC do   time as   Hawaii-in
       RYOKŌ-chū-o] eranda
       travel-mid-ACC chose
       'Tarō chose the period of traveling in Hawaii as the time to
       make his response.'

    b. Kaisha-ga   [shukusha-o   KENCHIKU-chū] **da**
       company-NOM dormitory-ACC construct-mid   is
       'The company is in the midst of building dormitories.'

2   On the proper treatment of 'mixed-category' items

There are many other cases of 'mixed-category' items like verbal nouns, such as the nominalized verbs in Quechuan languages (described in Lefebvre and Muysken 1988), and the English gerund, as in (10).

(10) John's joining the Ku Klux Klan was foolish.

While there are also important differences between these constructions, they have a common thread: their external distribution is NP-like, but internally there are arguments which one would expect to appear only in a projection headed by a verb or some Infl-like functional category.

A recently popular explanation of mixed category items is the use of functional projections. Functional projections allow a 'clean' way for the apparent nature of a phrase to change as one moves up the tree, while maintaining endocentricity. Thus Abney's (1987) analysis of gerunds as VP complements to D simultaneously explained the internal verbal character of the phrase and its external nominal character (once a noun phrase is reanalyzed as a DP).

---

[6] And the differences in distribution between *toki* phrases and other noun phrases are being regarded as purely semantic, following from the fact that the head noun is a time rather than a thing.

Despite their widespread adoption in recent work, there are problems in using functional categories in the analysis of Japanese and Korean. Sells (1992) raises such general concerns as the arbitrariness and undermotivation that results when functional heads are null or head-movements are string vacuous, and various problems with selection, locality and functional category ordering. A particular problem, which makes a DP-style treatment of the verbal noun suspect, is the following. While the Japanese verbal noun and the English gerund both allow mixed case marking (compare (8a) and (10)), the ordering is the opposite: in English the verbal case marking must appear internal to the nominal case marking, whereas with Japanese verbal nouns, verbal case marking must appear external to nominal case marking. This means that while an Abney-style approach works well in English, it is unmotivated in Japanese. Such an analysis does not explain why the external distribution of the verbal noun phrase is nominal.

3 Previous Analyses

3.1 Miyagawa (1991)

Miyagawa (1991) proposed the structures shown in (12) for cases in which a verbal noun plus -*chū* has verbal and nominal case marking:

(11) a. Mari-ga eigo-o kenkyū-chū

    b. Mari-no eigo-no kenkyū-chū

    c. Mari-ga eigo-no kenkyū-chū
       'while Mary is doing research on English'

    d. *Mari-no eigo-o kenkyū-chū

(12) a.

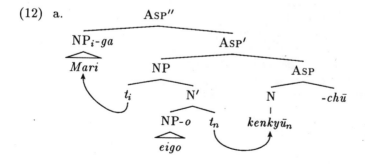

b.

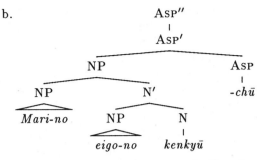

In other situations (such as example (1a)), where only nominal case marking is possible, Miyagawa proposed that we have simply an NP. The ability to assign verbal Case occurs 'only if the nominal clause itself is a part of a larger clause headed by an aspectual element' (p. 6). But, as observed in Sells (1991), this analysis predicts that a clause 'headed' by a verbal noun is sometimes an NP and sometimes an AspP, and this would only be justified if these two phrases had different syntactic distributions, which they don't. Further, AspP is usually regarded as a projection that appears above VP, not NP (Rivero 1990, Mitchell 1991).

The internal structure of this proposal is also undermotivated and problematic. The analysis of subject case marking involves the subject NP moving to [Spec, AspP], but (as Lee 1991 observes) there does not seem to be any independent evidence indicating that movement has occurred here. Conversely, object case marking involves the head verbal noun incorporating into Asp^0. Miyagawa's proposal for the mixed case marking asymmetries (why (11c) is okay, but (11d) is bad) relies crucially on the stipulation that licensing of genitive case is not transmitted under government (so that if *kenkyū* incorporates into *-chū* to license accusative case on *eigo*, it no longer licenses genitive case on *Mari*). But this stipulation is unwarranted: in languages which have noun incorporation, a genitive case marked possessor can be left 'stranded' when incorporation occurs (see Baker 1988:96–105). Also, on Miyagawa's analysis, one should be able to get an adjective or demonstrative modifying the verbal noun or its trace (cf. Baker 1988:93–96 for the incorporation case), but a sentence like (13) is impossible:

(13) *Jon-ga   Mari-no   ronbun-o   [$_{NP}$kibishii t_i] HIHAN$_i$-go-ni
      Jon-NOM Mary-GEN thesis-ACC   severe   criticism-after-at

3.2   Lee (1991)

Y.-S. Lee (1991) argued for base generation of the arguments of a verbal noun phrase – a position I endorse. Her analysis thus lacks the technical problems of phrase internal structure just discussed, but the problem of the verbal noun phrase's external distribution remains the same. The equivalent of Miyagawa's AspP in Lee's analysis is an XP[+V]. Late in the paper, she suggests that this XP[+V] is in fact a PP (while conceding that this is inconsistent with the featural decomposition of Chomsky (1970)).

This means analyzing suffixes like -*chū* as prepositions, and recall that Miyagawa (1991) regarded them as members of the functional category Asp. Neither of these proposals seems very appealing. In traditional Japanese grammar, items like -*chū* are classified simply as nouns. While *chū* does have a few specialized independent uses such as *chū o toru* 'to take the middle course', in the use we are concerned with here, -*chū* cannot stand alone, even if suitably modified (**benkyō-no chū* 'while studying'). Thus, this -*chū* is a bound morpheme (and behaves much like the many other Sino-Japanese morphemes that are bound nominal suffixes). But it still seems entirely reasonable to regard suffixes like -*chū* as of category N. Their behavior is special only in so far as they are bound forms with a temporal aspectual meaning. There is no evidence for suffixes like -*chū* behaving like postpositions and such a proposal does not explain why the external distribution of an XP[+V] is the same as that of a regular noun phrase.

3.3   Shibatani and Kageyama (1988)

In an earlier paper, Shibatani and Kageyama (1988) solved the problem of external distribution by proposing an NP-over-S phrase structure:

(14)

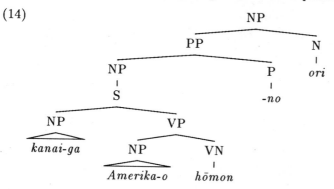

This is an obvious (if not very theoretically attractive) response to the internal verbal case marking and external nominal character of such examples. One could try to 'fix' a functional categories analysis along the same lines by proposing another null-headed functional category, so that what I am calling a 'verbal noun phrase' really looks like (15):

(15)

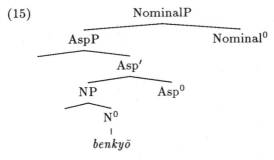

But unconstrained use of functional categories in this manner allows anything to be changed into anything else, so the resultant grammatical theory becomes largely devoid of content. Moreover, even this proposal seems unable to explain the purpose clause data I will present below.

4 Proposed Analysis

If the behavior of the verbal noun is accounted for purely categorially (as in Miyagawa and Lee's proposals), then, in cases of verbal or mixed case marking, there will always be a contradiction. Phrase internally, the upper reaches of the clause appear verbal while the external distribution is that of any other noun phrase. Thus some theoretical innovation is required. Sells (1991) chose to maintain that the verbal noun is categorially an N, but this forced him to the view that taking verbal case marked arguments and being modified by adverbs are not properties of being a verb, but of something else (having dependents, something that one might claim to be a semantic notion, but that leaves unresolved how Japanese event nouns differ from English event nouns). I find this direction unappealing and would like to maintain such basic intuitions as the fact that adverbs modify verbs. So, I will suggest moving to a more sophisticated notion of categoriality. The account has three ingredients: morphological licensing, along the lines suggested by Iida (1987), the use of categorial underspecification, and the division of the concept of category into two parts, categorial information and combinatoric information, as proposed by Cho and Sells (1991).

4.1 Morphological licensing

While a verbal noun can license verbal Case on arguments in some contexts, it cannot do so generally (recall (1b)). Thus words and suffixes like *sai* or *-chū* play a crucial role in allowing verbal nouns to assign verbal case. Iida (1987) suggested that these forms have an aspectual feature [+ASP] which they transfer to the verbal noun, and which licenses it to assign verbal case. Let us generalize this proposal, and suggest that all words in Japanese can only assign verbal case if they are aspectually licensed – a similar intuition appears in Miyagawa (1991). For verbs and adjectives, inflectional endings provide aspectual licensing (except for the *ren'yōkei* which can thus only appear when it inherits aspectual licensing from another verb to its right or the purpose marker -*ni*). For verbal nouns, the aspectual endings on *suru* can license the verbal noun to assign verbal case, but verbal nouns can also be aspectually licensed by forms like -*chū* and *sai*, or the purpose marker -*ni*: these forms provide the feature [+ASP] which percolates to the verbal noun by the usual mechanisms of morphological feature percolation and Spec-Head agreement.[7]

4.2 Categorial underspecification

Next I propose that the verbal noun is an underspecified category that is compatible with behaving as either a verb or a noun. The idea that the verbal noun has both a nominal and a verbal character is not new (for example, Inoue (1976) suggested that a verbal noun could be inserted under either an N or a V node (in the latter case suffixed by *suru*)). The mixed case marking constructions show the insufficiency of a simple disjunction and so I will introduce a concept of categorial underspecification, based on using a partially ordered hierarchy of sorts.

One way to implement a hierarchy of sorts is via a featural decomposition of categories. In Chomsky's (1970) system, the sort [+V] is sort-compatible with both verbs and adjectives (which are [+V, −N] and [+V, +N] respectively). I cannot use this featural decomposition, because, within it, there is no feature that is shared by verbs and nouns, but I could adopt another one. For example, Jackendoff (1977:31) suggested 'there are many rules which generalize across supercategories N and V' and proposed a feature decomposition in which verbs and nouns share the features [+Subj, +Comp]. This featural decomposition has recently been supported by Grimshaw (forthcoming), who advocated an idea of categorial neutralization similar to the one I am exploring.

However, it is not necessary for there to be a featural decomposition of categories. It is sufficient to give a hierarchy that shows sort compatibility. Let me thus merely suggest that the sort of verbal nouns, which I will call VN, is sort compatible with being a verb or a noun. So, part of the categorial sort hierarchy for Japanese looks like (16):

---

[7] For exceptional cases like newspaper headlines, let me just suggest that aspectual licensing is being provided by the discourse context.

(16)

The idea is that when some word or affix SELECTS for a certain category, any category that is sort-compatible with the desired category can fill the slot. A word is sort-compatible if its category is less than or equal to the category being selected for in the above partially ordered set. Thus, in cases of selection, a verbal noun can appear anywhere that a verb can and anywhere that a noun can, retaining its own sort in the phrase structure tree. And, rather than requiring categorial identity between a phrase and its head, the head need merely be sort-compatible. However, it is also possible for another word to SPECIFY the sort of a sister. In this case, the sort of the sister becomes the sort which is specified. Below, I will denote SELECTION with just a category name, and SPECIFICATION with a category name followed by an exclamation mark, for example, by V vs. V!.

4.2.1 Evidence from purpose clauses

The suggestion that verbal nouns can, ceteris paribus, appear wherever a verb is selected is non-standard, but ultimately an attraction of my proposal. Normally the result of doing so is ruled out independently by the aspectual licensing requirement, since verbal words require aspectual licensing, and verbal nouns (like regular nouns) are morphologically defective and cannot host normal verbal inflections. However, where aspectual licensing is being provided by another element, such as the purpose marker -*ni*, a verbal noun can appear in a slot where otherwise only verbs appear.

Two lines of argument show that the purpose marker -*ni* only attaches to verbs and not to the segmentally identical deverbal noun derived from verbs. First, note that one gets purpose clauses with verbs which lack a corresponding deverbal noun, such as, *taberu* 'eat':

(17) Kinō-wa   isogashikute hirugohan-o **tabe-ni-mo**   ikanakatta
     Yesterday busy   lunch-ACC   eat-PURP-even go.NEGPAST
     'I was so busy yesterday I never even went to have lunch.'

Secondly, for some verbs the accent on the *ren'yōkei* differs from that on the deverbal noun (Kawakami 1973, Poser 1984). For example, if the verb is simplex and accented, normally the *ren'yōkei* has its accent on the penultimate mora while the deverbal noun has its accent on the final mora as in (18):

(18) a. Jon-wa   umi-de **oyógi**, Mari-wa   kawa-de oyoida
      John-FOC sea-at swim   Mary-FOC river-at swim.PAST
      'John swam in the ocean and Mary swam in the river.'

   b. Jon-wa   **oyogí**-ga   umai
      John-TOP swimming-NOM skillful
      'John is good at swimming.'

The purpose morpheme -*ni* is accentually inert when it attaches to an accented word, so we can see in (19) that it attaches to a verb (the *ren'yōkei*) and not to the deverbal noun:

(19) a. umi-e **oyógi**-ni   iku   b. *umi-e **oyogí**-ni iku
      sea-to swim-PURP go.PRES
      'I go to the beach to swim.'

Consider then (20), which shows that a verbal noun can appear before the purposive -*ni* with or without *shi*, the *ren'yōkei* of *suru* 'do':

(20) a. Jon-wa   sūgaku-o KENKYŪ-ni   Furansu-e itta
      John-TOP math-ACC research-PURP France-to go.PAST
      'John went to France to do mathematical research.'

   b. Jon-wa sūgaku-o KENKYŪ-shi-ni Furansu-e itta

Under any proposal where the verbal noun is just a noun categorially, this behavior is inexplicable. The data can only be described via some gross disjunction such as Tsujimura's (forthcoming) '*ni* can take either a noun or the *renyōkei* form of a verb, except when a native word is involved, in which case only the *renyōkei* form of a verb is allowed.'

However, under my account, these facts fall out simply: the purpose marker -*ni* selects a verb to attach to, and since VN is sort-compatible with V, it is predicted that a verbal noun can appear before -*ni*. Of course, the verbal noun does not appear everywhere the *ren'yōkei* is licensed. This is captured by Cho and Sells's (1991) distinction between categorial and combinatoric information. While the purpose marker -*ni* attaches morphologically, selecting for category V, in other places where the *ren'yōkei* appears, its distribution is governed by the syntax, which is partly determined by combinatoric information, and the combinatoric information of the *ren'yōkei* differs from that of the verbal noun.

4.3   Categorial information vs. Combinatoric information

Cho and Sells (1991) propose that the features which are normally presumed to reflect a word's category are divided into two types of

information: CATEGORIAL INFORMATION and COMBINATORIC INFOR-
MATION. The aim is to capture the sense in which the inflectional
morphology is left-headed (so that *hanasu*, *hanashitari* and *hanashite*
are all verbs) while still capturing the fact that inflectional endings
affect how words combine in the syntax. See Sells (1992) for a more
extensive justification of this scheme.

For categorial information Sells uses traditional labels such as N,
V and A, while for combinatoric information, words are given a type:
N-SIS or V-SIS for things that appear as arguments of a nominal or
verbal head, and SENTENCE for items that stand alone or engage in
sentential conjunction (that is, the *ren'yōkei*).[8] Categorial information
is everything that is selected for by another head. Combinatoric information adds to the very general information given by a one bar level X'
structure (of the sort proposed by Fukui 1986) to correctly determine
the distribution of categories. Combinatoric information is consistently
inherited from the righthand sister, and serves to constrain only syntactic combination (so word-internal combinatoric information serves
no function). Thus, while both *Tōkyō-e-no* and *Tōkyō-e* are nouns,
the former appears inside an NP because it is [TYPE: N-SIS] while the
latter appears inside a VP because it is [TYPE: V-SIS!]:

(21) a.

$$N_{\text{N-SIS}}$$

$$N_{\text{V-SIS!}} \qquad Af_{\text{N-SIS}}$$

$$N \qquad Af_{\text{V-SIS!}} \qquad -no$$

$$T\bar{o}ky\bar{o} \qquad -e$$

b.

$$N_{\text{V-SIS!}}$$

$$N \qquad Af_{\text{V-SIS!}}$$

$$T\bar{o}ky\bar{o} \qquad -e$$

4.3.1 Clauses with -*chū* or *sai*

Together these ideas combine to give a satisfactory analysis of clauses
with forms like -*chū* or *sai*. The verbal noun, an underspecified VN,
can appear as the head of either a V' or an N'. The combinatoric
information of a phrase ending in -*no* is [TYPE: N-SIS] and it can
therefore modify an N or a VN (without changing its categorial status).
However, an adjective or demonstratives like *sono* will specify that they
are the sister of a noun, and so they potentially further determine the
sort of the head, and this information will then percolate upwards.
Similarly, a verbal case marked daughter or various other adjuncts such
as adverbs will specify their head sister by being [TYPE: V-SIS!]. Saying
that -*no* only selects (rather than specifying) its sister captures the
asymmetry between nominal case marking and verbal case marking in

---

[8] Sells referred to these forms as ¬TYPE.

mixed case marking constructions. In this way, the model explains the basic facts about nominal, verbal and mixed case marking, as shown in (24).

(22) a. $[benkyō]_{VN_{V\text{-}SIS}}$ b. $[sono]_{Det_{N\text{-}SIS!}}$

c. $[kibishii]_{A_{N\text{-}SIS!}}$ d. $[kibishiku]_{Adv_{V\text{-}SIS!}}$

e. $[-no]_{Af_{N\text{-}SIS}}$ Case marker suffixed to N

f. $[-ga]_{Af_{V\text{-}SIS!}}$ Case marker suffixed to N

g. $[-ni]_{Af_{V\text{-}SIS!}}$ Purpose marker suffixed to V

(23) a. Jon-ga ronbun-o kibishiku HIHAN-chū, ...
John-NOM thesis-ACC severely criticism-during
'During John's severe criticism of the thesis, ...'

b. Jon-ga Ainugo-no KENKYŪ-no sai, ...
John-NOM Ainu.language-GEN research-GEN occasion
'While John was doing research into Ainu, ...'

(24) a.

b.

c.

d.

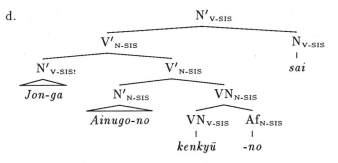

With verbal case marked arguments as in (24a), the clausal projection is specified as verbal, but the combinatoric information is always just inherited from the righthand daughter, so in this and the following examples, the clause remains [TYPE: V-SIS], that is, it has the same external distribution as any other noun phrase. (24b) shows that one cannot have elements that specify a verbal and nominal sister in the same clause, as the result is contradictory. However, a phrase like *ronbon-no* only selects for an N sister, and VN is sort-compatible with N, so the sort of mixed case marking shown in (24c) is correctly predicted to be possible. This prediction cannot be captured by simply suggesting that the verbal noun is disjunctively specified as either a verb or a noun. Also, this analysis does not require *-chū* to be a separate head in order to explain mixed case marking. This is highly desirable, given that mixed case marking also occurs with independent nouns like *sai* (for which such an analysis is less plausible). Here such cases receive an identical analysis, as indicated in (24d).[9]

4.3.2 Purpose clauses revisited

These same ideas also yield a satisfying account of the case marking possibilities in purpose clauses. The analysis is indicated in (26):

(25) a. Ainugo-no benkyō-ni   b. *Ainugo-no benkyō shi-ni

---

[9]Finally, to correctly predict the possibilities for clause-internal scrambling, an additional constraint is needed. The constraint is that if at least one of any pair of arguments of a VN is nominally case marked, then the linearly first argument must be superior to the second on the thematic hierarchy. Restated formally:

(i) If at least one of (any) two arguments p and q of a verb is nominal case marked, then:

$$p >_\theta q \iff p \succ q$$

where $>_\theta$ means 'is higher on the θ-hierarchy' and $\succ$ can be read as 'c-commands' or 'linearly precedes' (i.e., either reading is adequate). This sort of thematic precedence condition is similar in sort to the one that appears in Grimshaw and Mester (1988).

b. Ainugo-o benkyō-ni   d.   Ainugo-o benkyō shi-ni
   'in order to study Ainu'

(26) a.

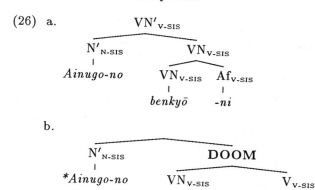

b.

Note especially (26a) which provides crucial evidence for the categorial underspecification analysis presented here. *Ainugo-no* selects for a nominal sister while *-ni* selects a verb as its morphological host. Nevertheless, (26a) is grammatical, as is correctly predicted by a categorial underspecification account. This result could not be obtained if the verbal noun were just specified disjunctively. Conversely, when the *ren'yōkei* of *suru*, *shi*, appears, verbal case marked arguments are still possible, but nominal case marking is now impossible, and this is again correctly predicted, as indicated in (26b).

5   Conclusion

The data requires an analysis that explains nominal, verbal and mixed case marking within a verbal noun phrase while still capturing the fact that a verbal noun phrase has the same distribution as any other noun phrase. I have argued that functional categories do not give a good solution to this problem; rather the only available solution trivializes the problem. I then presented my own three-part solution. Two of the parts have been suggested independently, so the new idea I wish to emphasize is how the use of categorial underspecification can provide a good solution to problems of mixed categorial status.

References

Abney, S. P. 1987. *The English Noun Phrase in its Sentential Aspect.* PhD thesis, MIT.

Baker, M. C. 1988. *Incorporation: A Theory of Grammatical Function Changing.* Chicago, IL: University of Chicago Press.

Cho, Y. Y., and P. Sells. 1991. A lexical account of phrasal suffixes in Korean. MS, Stanford University.

Chomsky, N. 1970. Remarks on nominalization. In R. Jacobs and P. Rosenbaum (Eds.), *Readings in English Transformational Grammar*, 184–221. Waltham, MA: Ginn.

Fukui, N. 1986. *A Theory of Category Projection and Its Applications.* PhD thesis, MIT.

Grimshaw, J. forthcoming. Extended projection. MS, Brandeis University.

Grimshaw, J., and A. Mester. 1988. Light verbs and θ-marking. *Linguistic Inquiry* 19:205–232.

Hasegawa, N. 1991. On head movement and Japanese: the case of verbal nouns. In *Proceedings of Sophia Linguistics Society 6*, 8–32.

Iida, M. 1987. Case assignment by nominals in Japanese. In M. Iida, S. Wechsler, and D. Zec (Eds.), *Working Papers in Grammatical Theory and Discourse Structure: Interactions of Morphology, Syntax, and Discourse*, 93–138. Stanford, CA: CSLI.

Inoue, K. 1976. *Henkei-Bunpoo to Nihongo.* Tokyo: Taishukan.

Jackendoff, R. 1977. *X-Bar Syntax: A Study of Phrase Structure.* Cambridge, MA: MIT Press.

Kageyama, T. 1977. Incorporation and Sino-Japanese verbs. *Papers in Japanese Linguistics* 5:117–155.

Kawakami, S. 1973. Dooshi kara no tensei meishi no akusento. *Imaizumi Hakase Koki Kinen Kokugogaku Ronsoo* 55–70.

Lee, Y.-S. 1991. Case alternation and word order variation in nominal clauses. MS, University of Pennsylvania. Revised version of Japanese/Korean Linguistics Conference paper.

Lefebvre, C., and P. Muysken. 1988. *Mixed categories: nominalizations in Quechua*. Dordrecht: Kluwer Academic.

Mitchell, E. 1991. Evidence from Finnish for Pollock's theory of IP. *Linguistic Inquiry* 22:373–379.

Miyagawa, S. 1991. Case realization and scrambling. MS, Ohio State University. Second revision; presently being revised.

Poser, W. J. 1984. *The Phonetics and Phonology of Tone and Intonation in Japanese*. PhD thesis, MIT.

Poser, W. J. 1989. What is the 'Double-*o* constraint' a constraint on? MS, Stanford University.

Rivero, M.-L. 1990. The location of nonactive voice in Albanian and Modern Greek. *Linguistic Inquiry* 21:135–146.

Saiki, M., and Y. Y. Cho. 1987. Verbal nouns in Korean and Japanese. In S. Kuno et al. (Ed.), *Harvard Studies in Korean Linguistics 2*, 434–442.

Sells, P. 1988. More on light verbs and θ-marking. MS, Stanford University.

Sells, P. 1991. Properties of verbal nouns and category status in Japanese. MS, Stanford University.

Sells, P. 1992. Korean and Japanese morphology from a lexical perspective. MS, Stanford University.

Shibatani, M., and T. Kageyama. 1988. Word formation in a modular theory of grammar. *Language* 64:451–484.

Tsujimura, N. forthcoming. Licensing nominal clauses: The case of deverbal nominals in Japanese. To appear in *Natural Language and Linguistic Theory*.

A Semantic Parameter: The Progressive in Japanese and English

WILLIAM MCCLURE
Cornell University

1.0 Introduction

The PROGRESSIVE (or rather, the *te-iru* construction) in Japanese consists of the verbal gerund (the *te*-form of the verb) combined with some form of the verb *iru* 'be in a location (animate)'. Applied to ACTIVITY verbs as in (1), the result corresponds straightforwardly to the English progressive.

(1) Activity
     W-ga hasite-iru
     W-NOM run-be
     'W is running'

As students of the Japanese language are continually learning, however, the progressive of an ACHIEVEMENT verb such as kuru 'come' is not progressive at all. In (2), the *te-iru* form of an achievement is semantically equivalent to the English perfective.

(2) Achievement
     W-ga kite-iru
     W-NOM come-be
     'W has come/is here' (*W is coming)

---

*I am indebted to Takao Gunji, Takeo Kurafuji, Michinao Matsui, and Norio Naka of the Faculty of Language and Culture at Osaka University for their help in formulating my ideas about the Japanese progressive. At Cornell, John Whitman and Takashi Nakajima keep my Japanese syntax straight while Gennaro Chierchia keeps my semantics honest. Remaining errors and oddities are of course my fault alone.

There is in fact no way in Japanese to form the progressive of an achievement, and imminence of a discrete event can be expressed only by using expressions such as *about to* or *looks like* with imperfect verb forms. This is the basis of the puzzle. Why does one aspectual class in Japanese allow a progressive interpretation while another class does not?

Clearly, no existing account of the progressive in English explains the distribution of the progressive in Japanese or its relationship to the *te-iru* construction. Typical accounts of the English progressive (Dowty 1979, Parsons 1990, Landman 1992) rely on some kind of event-part or stage. The progressive intuitively means that an event is underway or that some of its stages have occurred, but it never has a perfective meaning. It is of course possible to hypothesize that there are two homophonous morphemes at work here, one progressive and one not (there is in fact evidence for this theory in Korean and some Japanese dialects[1]), but the two-morpheme hypothesis does not explain the distribution of meanings. Why should just activities be progressive and achievements not? And why is the *te-iru* form of an achievement equivalent to the perfective and not some other aspect?

---

[1] Compare the following sentences from Korean.

(1) Activity
   a. Perfective
      *ttwi-**a** iss-ta
      run-**INFINITIVE** be-INDICATIVE
      'has run'

   b. Progressive
      ttwi-**ko** iss-ta
      run-**ing** be-INDICATIVE
      'is running'

(2) Achievement
   a. Perfective
      o-**a** iss-ta
      come-**INFINTIVE** be-INDICATIVE
      'has come/is here'

   b. Progressive
      *o-**ko** iss-ta
      come-ing **INDICATIVE**-be
      'is coming'

Perfective and progressive meanings are represented by two different morphemes, *a* and *ko* respectively. Paralleling Japanese, only the activity predicate has a progressive interpretation.

The theory I propose explains these apparently arbitrary facts within Japanese while reducing the difference between English and Japanese to a single parametric switch. My proposal is essentially a refinement of event based analyses of the progressive, although it exploits a compositional event-based definition of Dowty's (1979) aspectual operators. The modifications I propose allow for a simple explanation for the behavior of Japanese achievement, and that such verbs receive a perfective interpretation rather than a progressive interpretation is shown not to be an accident.

2.0 Japanese aspectual phenomena

In traditional discussions of Japanese aspect such as that of Kindaichi (1976), verbs in Japanese behave much the same as their English counterparts. The aspectual classes of Vendler (1967) and Dowty (1979) are found in Japanese with similar sets of verbs falling into each class. Which tests are used to determine the aspectual categories and how these test work, however, are rather different in the two traditions. Dowty's distribution is based on a collection of tests for aspect and volitionality. While no test classifies perfectly, the progressive test as outlined in (3) is easily the most robust. Kindaichi, on the other hand, relies solely on the use and meaning of the **te-iru** construction. The Japanese classification is given in (4).

(3) English aspectual types (Dowty 1979 and many others)
   a. Stative
      progressive is not possible
      (*know, love, stink*, etc.)

   b. Achievement
      progressive does not entail perfective
      is dying → *has not yet died*
      (*arrive, sink, open, recognize*, etc.)

   c. Activity
      progressive entails perfective
      is running → *has already run (some distance)*
      (*swim, walk, run, push*, etc.)

   d. Accomplishment
      both achievement and activity patterns are possible
      (*read a book, build a house*, etc.)

(4) Japanese aspectual types (Kindaichi 1976)
   a. Stative (I)
      te-iru is not possible
      (*iru* 'be', *aru* 'have', etc.)

   b. Achievement
      te-iru is perfective
      sinde-iru 'is dead' → *sinda* 'has died' NOT 'is dying'
      (*tuku* 'arrive', *aku* 'open', etc.)

   c. Activity
      te-iru is progressive
      hasite-iru 'is running' *hasita* 'has run (some distance)'
      (*oyogu* 'swim', *aruku* 'walk', etc.)

   d. Stative (IV)
      te-iru is mandatory
      (*sobiete-iru* 'towers over', *nite-iru* 'resembles', etc.)

While, there are clear parallels between English and Japanese, there are several obvious differences between the classifications in (3) and (4). First, while achievements and activities both allow the *te-iru* construction, the interpretation of *te-iru* is completely different. Achievements are perfective while activities are progressive. The point of this discussion is to account for this difference. Second, Kindaichi does not posit a separate class of ACCOMPLISHMENTS, preferring instead to classify such complex predicates as achievements. Third, although Kindaichi distinguishes two kinds of STATIVES, I argue below that class IV statives are in fact all achievements. Further, although it is not apparent in (4), it should also be noted that there are in fact very few Japanese stative verbs anyway. Perhaps only three verbs prohibit the *te-iru* construction. Verbs such as *ai-suru* 'love', *wakaru* 'understand', and *niru* 'resemble' which are stative in English are in fact activities (*ai-suru*) and achievements (*wakaru*, *niru*) in Japanese. The revised understanding of aspectual class which I argue for makes possible an aspectual characterization parallel to that of English. The *te-iru* construction is progressive for activities, perfective for achievements, and impossible with statives. Accomplishments have both the activity and achievement interpretation. This characterization of Japanese aspectual classes makes it possible to define the Japanese progressive in a manner similar to that already laid out for English. The apparently bizarre behavior of the Japanese progressive will no longer be an accident.

2.1 Accomplishments
Kindaichi does not posit a class of accomplishment verbs for Japanese because he prefers to classify such verbs as achievements. As argued by Jacobsen (1992), however, this is counterintuitive because it ignores the

activity-like characteristics of such verbs. As in English, predicates such as *mado o akeru* 'open a window' or *hon o yomu* 'read a book' can have either an achievement or an activity interpretation. As stated already, the achievement interpretation of such predicates is perfective and not progressive.

(5) Japanese accomplishment
(W-ga) keeki-o tukutte-iru
W-NOM cake-ACC make-is
'(W) is making a cake'
-or-
'(W) has made a cake'

Clearly, accomplishments as a class of predicates exist in Japanese as well as English, and, parallel to English, they can be defined as the set of predicates which exhibit both achievement and activity behavior.

2.2 Statives

In this discussion I first look at the two stative classes which Kindaichi defines. One class prohibits *te-iru* while the stative IV class requires *te-iru*. I argue that independent aspectual tests in Japanese indicate that the members of the stative IV class are actually all achievements. A true stative class can therefore be identified by verbs which do not allow the *te-iru* construction. It turns out, however, that there are at most three verbs which do not allow the *te-iru* construction: *iru* 'be (animate)', *aru* 'be (inanimate), have' and *iru* 'need'. This brings up a second question. Since there are so few statives in Japanese, many English statives such as *love* and *stink* and *understand* apparently do not have stative counterparts in Japanese. What is the aspect of such predicates in Japanese?

Turning to Kindaichi's two stative classes, one set of verbs is incompatible with the *te-iru* construction while the other class apparently requires it. As verbs of either class are generally equivalent to some kind of English stative, it is tempting to collapse the two classes and ignore their grammatical differences. As noted by Jacobsen and a number of other scholars, however, many apparently stative verbs in Japanese are actually achievements which refer ambiguously to the state resulting from a change or to the change itself. According to Koizumi, et. al. (1989), *sinu* 'die', *wakaru* 'understand' and *magaru* 'bend' are three such verbs. Thus, *sinu* can mean that I have just died, in its change interpretation, or it can mean that I am already dead, in its resulting state interpretation. Similarly for *wakaru* and *magaru*. Significantly, *niru* 'resemble' and other class IV statives also display this same kind of ambiguity. Intuitively, the verb is stative, but aspectual tests taken from Moriyama (1988) which rely on compounding with *hazimeru* 'begin', *tuzukeru* 'continue', and *owaru* 'finish' and adverbial tests adapted from Dowty (1979) indicate that *niru* is clearly an achievement like *sinu* 'die'. The relevant tests are summarized in (6) for *sinu* and (7) for *niru*. For the sake of comparison, I give an example of an activity in (7).

(6) Classification of *sinu* (achievement)
 a sinihazimeru 'begin to die'
 b. *sinituzukeru 'continue to die'
 c. *siniowaru 'finish dying'
 d. sanzikan kakkate sinu 'take three hours to die'
 e. *sanzikan sinu 'die for three hours'
 f. allows *te-iru* with perfect interpretation
  (resulting state)

(7) Classification of *niru* (achievement)
 a. nirihazimeru 'begin to resemble'
 b. *nirituzukeru 'continue to resemble'
 c. *niriowaru 'finish resembling'
 d. sanzikan kakkate niru 'take three hours to resemble'
 e. *sanzikan niru 'resemble for three hours'
 f. allows *te-iru* with perfect interpretation
  (resulting state)

(8) Classification of *hasiru* (activity)
 a hasirihazimeru 'begin to run'
 b. hasirituzukeru 'continue to run'
 c. hasiriowaru 'finish running'
 d. *sanzikan kakkate hasiru 'take three hours to run'
 e. sanzikan hasiru 'run for three hours'
 f. allows *te-iru* with progressive interpretation
  (ongoing process)

Niru 'resemble', like *sinu* 'die', can be compounded with *hazimeru* 'begin to' but not with *tuzukeru* 'continue to' or *owaru* 'finish'. It is also acceptable with expressions such as *sanzi-kan kakkate* meaning 'to take three hours to'. Note that *hasiru* 'run' is acceptable with all compounding and takes the time adverbial *sanzikan* meaning 'for three hours'. *Niru* should therefore be thought of not as a state but as an achievement meaning 'come to resemble'. *Sobieru* means 'come to tower over'. *Wakaru* means 'come to know', and *magaru* means 'bend'. Like other Japanese achievements, these verbs refer ambiguously to the change or to the state resulting from the change, although in the case of *niru* or *sobieru*, and unlike *aku* or *sinu*, for example, almost all the emphasis is on the resulting state. The other feature that all of these verbs have in common is that they allow the *te-iru* construction with a perfective interpretation. *Nite-iru* therefore properly means 'has come to resemble'. The change has taken place, and the state resulting from the change now holds. These same facts are true of all verbs classified by Kindaichi as class IV statives. As such, class IV statives are not a separate aspectual class. While it is true that intuitively they look stative, grammatical tests clearly indicate that class IV statives are all achievements.

I therefore propose that only verbs which never allow the *te-iru* construction are true statives. To my knowledge, there are only three such verbs in Japanese: *iru* 'be (animate)', *aru* 'have, be (inanimate)', and *iru* 'need'. In (9), we see that these stative verbs pattern very differently from achievements or activities.

(9) Classification of *aru* (stative)
   a   *arihazimeru 'begin to have'
   b. arituzukeru 'continue to have'
   c. *ariowaru 'finish having'
   d. *sanzikan kakkate aru 'take three hours to have'
   e. sanzikan atta 'have for three hours'
   f. does not allow *te-iru*

If this aspectual classification is accurate, however, how can we account for the variety of statives in English which apparently do not exist in Japanese? I have already argued that predicates such as *understand* ('wakaru') and *be bent* ('magaru') are both achievements in Japanese. Applying the aspectual tests outlined above would show that verbs like *ai-suru* 'love' or *nikumu* 'hate' which assign accusative case to their direct objects are actually activities in Japanese. Jacobsen (1992: 31) also confirms this analysis. The lesson from all this is that translation into English is not a very good way to determine aspectual class. Any individual concept can be expressed in any language, but membership in a particular aspectual class is truly a syntactic phenomena. Regardless of what our intuitions tell us about the duration or agentivity of a particular predicate, the grammar of a particular language may indicate otherwise.

2.3 Restatement of aspectual classes
Summing this discussion, Japanese has four aspectual classes of verbs, most easily distinguished by the behavior of the *te-iru* construction. Again, the behavior of the *te-iru* form parallels that of the English progressive (which is to say, progressive with activities and impossible with statives) except for the achievement class where it is perfective rather than progressive. The Japanese classes are thus similar to those of English, although the membership of each class differs cross-linguistically. Achievements and accomplishments are characterized by their inherent conclusions, while statives and activities are characterized by their open-endedness. Kindaichi's class IV statives have been subsumed into the achievement class. Examples from each class are listed in (10).

(10) Japanese aspectual types (revised)

    a.   Stative
        te-iru is not possible
        (*iru* 'be', *aru* 'have', etc.)

    b.   Achievement
        te-iru is perfective
        sinde-iru 'is dead' → *sinda* 'has died' NOT 'is dying'
        (*tuku* 'arrive', *aku* 'open', *niru* 'resemble', etc.)

    c.   Activity
        te-iru is progressive
        hasite-iru 'is running' → *hasita* 'has run (some distance)'
        (*oyogu* 'swim', *aruku* 'walk', etc.)

    d.   Accomplishment
        both achievement and activity patterns are possible
        (*mado o akeru* 'open window', *hon o yomu* 'read a book', etc.)

3.0 Dowty's aspectual semantics

Dowty's aspectual semantics derives the four verb classes in (3) and (10) from underlying stative forms by means of the aspectual operators BECOME and DO in combination with the connective CAUSE. Semantically, Dowty's operators are defined as outlined in (11).

(11) Dowty's aspectual operators (1979)

$$\text{BECOME } (\alpha) = 1 \text{ iff} \neg \alpha \text{ then } \alpha$$
$$\text{CAUSE } (\alpha, \beta) = 1 \text{ iff} \neg \alpha \rightarrow \neg \beta$$
               (Lewis-style conditional)
$$\text{DO } (x, \alpha (x)) \rightarrow \text{volitional } (x)$$
               (material implication)

A state α BECOMEs when it comes into existence. Although Dowty's definition is given in terms of interval semantics, its intuitive meaning is obvious, and BECOME is in some sense a pair of states, before and after the moment of change. CAUSE is somewhat more abstract, but at its most basic level, one event CAUSEs another when the absence of the first entails the absence of the second. The full semantics for CAUSE as given by Dowty actually involves counterfactuals, and I do not address the nature of causation in this paper. Finally, in Dowty's theory, DO turns out to represent mainly the volitionality of the subject. It means that the subject is a sentient being, theoretically in control of the course of events. Consequently, DO does not have an interval semantic or model theoretic definition. Unlike BECOME, it is not clear that DO can be thought of as a situation or as a set of situations, and as such it is left to play a minor role in Dowty's theory.

In Dowty's aspectual calculus, every verb is therefore characterized by an underlying state and one or more of the aspectual operators. An achievement such as *die* is represented as in (12a). 'Dead' is a state. 'BECOME dead' means 'to die'. Examples of the other three classes are listed in (12b-d).

(12) Dowty's aspectual calculus
    a.   Achievement
        W dies = BECOME (^dead (W))

    b.   Stative
        W stinks = stink (W)

    c.   Activity
        W runs = DO (W, ^run (W))

    d.   Accomplishment
        W builds a house
        = ∃P CAUSE (^P(W), ^BECOME(^built (house)))

States are basic so no operators are incorporated into their representation. All of the knowledge contained in a state is available by looking at the world at a single point of time. A state is therefore represented by a possible situation. Activities, however, entail a DOing, by somebody, of something like running or swimming. Accomplishments are the most complex because they entail a DOing by somebody which results in the BECOMEing of something else. An accomplishment such as 'W builds a house' entails both that W builds and that this activity necessarily results in the creation of a house. The theoretical representation of (12d) entails both these parts, while the CAUSE connective formally defines the relationship between W's activity and the creation of a house. It says that without the activity this particular outcome would not be realized.

The various operators in Dowty's representations are then used to explain a host of aspectually related phenomena in syntax including the distribution of adverbials and the behavior of the progressive. In the semantics I propose, I hope to incorporate many of these results wholesale. My semantics differs from Dowty's in that I use situation-based definitions for Dowty's operators, and I give a situation-based definition for DO. I propose that a DOing is in fact a kind of change characterized by a particular aspectual structure. In particular, I argue that DO is composed of a collection of BECOMEings.

4.0 Situation-based aspectual semantics

Along the lines of Higginbotham (1985) and Parsons (1990), in my semantics I assume that verbs are predicates of eventualities with arguments fed in locally under government by means of theta-roles. This means that all verbs have the general event structure outlined in (13), while (14) is the specific representation for 'W is in Ithaca'. The stative predicate *in Ithaca* is predicated of the eventuality s for stative and *W* is assigned the relevant theta-role. In this representation, s stands for a possible situation. 'W is in Ithaca' is the set of all possible situations s such that s is a being in Ithaca situation and W is marked by the particular theta-role of the situation.

(13) General eventuality structure (Parsons)
    $Verb = V(e)$
    $NP + Verb = V(e) \ \& \ \theta(NP, e)$

(14) 'W is in Ithaca'
    $= \{s \mid in\ Ithaca\ (s) \ \& \ \theta(s, W)\} = \lambda s\ (in\ Ithaca\ (s) \ \& \ \theta(W, s))$

In Parsons' event semantics, there is a basic split between states and events, but all kinds of eventualities are represented by a general event argument. In my semantics, I define each eventuality type. STATES, EVENTS, and PROCESSES each have specific internal structures. Further, the eventuality types I propose are all compositionally defined to reflect the intuitions of Dowty's aspectual operators. Like Dowty, I assume that single situations are the simplest and therefore the most basic. As situations have no internal structure they may be as short as a moment in time or they may occupy an open interval. They do not, however, entail any change which can represent an endpoint. Returning then to the definitions in (11), recall that a BECOMEing can be intuitively represented as a pair of states, the state before and the state after a point of change. The change is in fact defined by the two situations, and BECOME can always be thought of as a pair of situations. Further, a BECOMEing is in some sense defined by a closed interval, the point of change equaling the point of closure.

The DO operator is then a set of these BECOMEings. Dowty has basically equated the DO operator with volitionality, but I believe that processes can in fact be represented by particular sets of changes. Intuitively, the activity *run* is a continuous process composed of discrete cycles represented by stepping from one place to another. These steps are a set of achievements which are chained to define the process. The cycles represented by stepping, however, are simply the most obvious manifestation of the particular predicate *run*. Discrete cycles as such are not an inherent feature of process predicates. Moving is an activity not composed of any obvious cycles, entailing rather a chain of instantaneous changes of location from one point to the next. While each of these changes may or may not constitute a cycle of some kind, it is clear that the change of location entailed by *move* is not of any fixed length and may of course become infinitesimally small. One may move distances that are always half of the previous movement without ever reaching a particular destination.

Returning then to running, if we look into the steps of running, we can see that running too is in some sense composed of infinitesimally small changes. While the characteristic cycles of running (i.e. the steps) are clearly of a relatively standard length, the physical changes which compose running are equally clearly not of any fixed length. Instead of dividing running up into achievements representing a full step, one may just as easily divide the process up into changes which represent half steps or quarter steps or eighth steps. For any partition of the activity, one may always identify a partition with twice as many steps. In this sense, running, like moving, is composed of changes which may be instantaneous in length and therefore infinite in number, and we may consequently argue that any process is composed of a dense set of situations where any two ordered situations represent an achievement.

Let us say then that in general any process can be represented by a dense collection of states where any two ordered states represent an achievement. Processes can therefore be conceptualized as longer intervals composed of the well-defined closed intervals of the particular achievements. In addition, the DO operator requires that this collection of states be connected in the proper fashion. A set of random changes produced by random people is not a DOing because the many small events are not necessarily connected in space and time. Moreover, these changes are not centered on a particular protagonist. A collection of changes cannot form a DOing unless it is spatio-temporally connected and all of the changes are made by a single individual who is in some sense responsible for the changes. This individual is typically identified as the agent, and its theta-role is assigned by the DO operator in my system. A process with these basic conditions may then have or not have a well-defined final member. Processes which do not have such a member are realized as activities, while processes which do have a final member are accomplishments. In terms of interval semantics, an activity is therefore a dense open interval itself composed of an unspecified number of closed intervals. An accomplishment is a dense closed interval composed of an unspecified number of smaller closed intervals.

The aspectual structures and logical types outlined in the preceding discussion are summarized in (15) and (16).

(15)   Aspectual structures
       states = s, a situation
       achievements = $<s_1\ s_2>$
       activities = $\{<s_1\ s_2> <s_2\ s_3> <s_3\ s_4>...<s_n\ s_{n+1}>\}$
              where n is, in general, infinite
       accomplishments = $\{<s_1\ s_2> <s_2\ s_3> <s_3\ s_4>...<s_n\ s_{n+1}>\}$
              where n is finite

(16)   Logical types
       BECOME: sets of states $\rightarrow$ sets of pairs of states
       DO: sets of becomings $\rightarrow$ sets of sets of becomings
                              with same protagonist

Given that states are basic, achievements are represented by pairs of states, and activities are represented by open-ended sets of pairs of states. Accomplishments are closed sets of pairs of states. Both activities and accomplishments are characterized by the process associated with a DO operator, although only accomplishments have a well-defined final state. Processes are therefore composed of events which are themselves composed of states. Thus, while my representations of particular predicates do not differ from those of Parsons, the semantic interpretations of these representations reflect the compositional hierarchy defined in (12). The semantic interpretation of a simple state involves no aspectual operators, while an achievement requires the BECOME operator which itself entails two states. The DO operator subcategorizes for both a protagonist and a set of BECOMEings, themselves composed of states. The process defined by the DO operator may then be open-ended or finite depending on the status of its final state.

       Further, each of the representations in (15) can be assigned to a particular interval in time by the TEMPORAL TRACE function τ. This function is give in (17) which is read 'the temporal trace of an eventuality is i, an interval in time'. The temporal trace of an eventuality is important because it tells us when all or part of an eventuality is true. It tells us when a particular state holds or when a particular activity is going on.

(17)   Temporal trace function
       $\tau (s) = i$, a moment or interval in time

The temporal trace of a state may be as brief as a moment or as long as an unbounded interval. All that matters is that only the single state pertain throughout the interval. Achievements then require that the temporal trace of the initial state strictly precede the temporal trace of the final state. The moment of change then defines the boundary of a closed interval. Activities are unbounded collection of these closed intervals while accomplishments are a bounded collection of closed intervals.

       Formal semantic definitions for each eventuality type are given in (18). The predicate *stink* in (18a) selects arguments and an appropriate basic state.

Stink is defined as the set of all situations where someone or something stinks. 'W stinks' is the subset of stinking situations where W is also present and W is in fact stinking. W plays a particular role in the situation and is marked by the theta-role selected by the predicate. The achievement in (18b) also selects a basic state and arguments, but in addition, an achievement predicate must also specify a condition on change. Two states, one which precedes the other, are paired to realize the achievement. The condition on change which specifies the relationship between these two states is realized through application of the BECOME operator. Finally, an activity has the semantic structure given in (18c). Activities are characterized by the unbounded repetition of a BECOMEing, in this case, moving from one location to the next. In addition, activities must specify how these changes are linked and who links them. This condition on chaining and the identity of the causal agent are both specified by the DO operator. In (18c), the condition on change is 'by moving arms and legs quickly' while the agent is identified as the individual *W*. A typical activity is therefore a dense linear order bounded by an open interval where any two consecutive situations define a change, and all changes are caused by a single individual. Accomplishments have similar structure with a well-defined final change.

(18) Aspectual structures

    a.   Stative

        'W stinks' $= \lambda s$ [stink(s) & $\theta(s, W)$] (s)

    b.   Achievements

        'W falls' = BECOME (λs [fallen (s) & $\theta(s, W)$])(e)

        $= \{ \ e \mid \exists \ s_1 \ s_2, s_1 \neq s_2, e = <s_1 \ s_2> \ \&$

            λs [fallen (s, W)] (s_2) &

            λs [standing (s, W)] (s_1) &

            $\tau(s_1) < \tau(s_2)\}$

    c.   Activity

        'W runs' = DO (BECOME (λs [in (s, W)]))

        & Cause (W, α) & by moving arms and legs (α)]

        where $\alpha = \{in_1, in_2, in_3...in_n\}$

        & $\forall in_n, in_{n+1} \in \alpha$, BECOME $<in_n \ in_{n+1}> = 1$

        & $\neg \exists n_n$ s.t. $n_n \in \alpha \ n_{n+1} \notin \alpha$

Based on the structures outlined in (18), two further sub-structures must be defined before the semantics for the progressive can be specified. First, a SEGMENT of an eventuality is defined in (19).

(19) Segment σ of an eventuality
    a.   Stative s
        $\sigma = \{s\}$, the entire eventuality α

    b.   Achievement $<s_1\ s_2>$
        $\sigma = \{s_1, s_2, <s_1\ s_2>\}$

    c.   Activity $\{s_1\ s_2\ s_3\ s_4...s_n\}$
        $\sigma =$ any ordered subset $\{s_1...s_x\}$ where $1 \leq x \leq n$

    d.   Accomplishment $\{s_1\ s_2\ s_3\ s_4...s_n\}$
        $\sigma =$ any ordered subset $\{s_1...s_x\}$ where $1 \leq x \leq n$

Accordingly, a FINAL SEGMENT of an eventuality is defined as follows.

(20) Final segment σ of an eventuality α
    σ is final segment of α iff
    σ is a segment of α &
    $\exists s_n, s_n \in \sigma \in \alpha$ & $s_{n+1} \notin \alpha$

A final segment is one which contains a state that does not have a next state in the eventuality. Note that by this definition, the single situation of a stative predicate is both a segment and a final segment. Furthermore, activities never have final segments because they do not have final states by definition.

    A particular segment σ of an eventuality α is then realized if the temporal trace function of the segment precedes whatever is taken to be the moment of evaluation. This moment of evaluation is conceptually similar to Reichenbach's (1947) point of reference. If we are looking at the real world, a particular segment of an eventuality is actualized if its temporal trace function precedes the present moment. A segment is realized if it is a part of the real history of the world at this point in time. A particular eventuality is completely realized if all of its situations have been realized. Thus:

(21) Realization
    Real (σ) iff $\tau(\sigma) \leq i$ (moment of evaluation)

Keep in mind that the moment of evaluation is not to be equated with the actual present. Rather, the absolute location of the evaluation in time is determined by tense and it will result in past, present, and future progressive. Only when the moment of evaluation actually is the real present does the present progressive result. If actualization is relative to moment in the past, the past progressive will result. Similarly for the future.

5.0 The progressive

Intuitively, then, the English progressive is used when an eventuality is incomplete, regardless of when in time it is incomplete. In my terms, an eventuality is in progress if some but not all of its situations have been realized relative to some point of reference. (22) gives my truth conditions for the progressive in English.

(22) The Progressive (English)

PROG (Predicate P) = 1 iff
$\exists$ σ a segment , $\exists$ α an eventuality s.t.
P(α) & σ $\in$ α &
$\neg$Final (σ, α) & Real (σ) &
$\forall$ σ'[Final (σ', e) $\rightarrow$ $\neg$Real (σ', w)]]

The progressive is true for a particular verb (realized as the set of states α) if (i) there exists a non-final segment of the eventuality which has been realized in the relevant world and time, and (ii) all final segments of the eventuality have not been realized. The English progressive is true when the eventuality has begun but is not yet complete.

Turning now to Japanese, the intuition for achievements seems to be that the *te-iru* construction indicates some kind of completion while activities behave like their English counterparts. While an account of these facts may seem difficult from the traditional English perspective, given the semantic structures I have developed for each aspectual class, truth conditions for the Japanese *te-iru* construction are nearly identical to the truth conditions for the English progressive. (23) gives my truth conditions for the Japanese.

(23) The Progressive (Japanese)

PROG (Predicate P) = 1 iff
$\exists$ σ a segment , $\exists$ α an eventuality s.t.
P(α) & σ $\in$ α &
$\neg$Final (σ, α) & Real (σ) &
$\forall$ σ'[Final (σ', e) $\rightarrow$ Real (σ', w)]]

The progressive is true for a particular verb (represented by the set of situations α) if (i) there exists a non-final segment of the eventuality which has been realized in the relevant world and time, and (ii) all final segments of the eventuality have also been realized. The only difference between (22) and (23) is the status of the final segments. This is the parameter. In English, final segments cannot be realized. In Japanese, all final segments must be realized.

These definitions then interact with the aspectual structures in a very straightforward fashion to derive the necessary distributions. Because activities never have final segments in any language by definition, the universal at the end of the conjunct in (22) and (23) is always true and activities allow the progressive as soon as a segment which is in some pragmatic sense long enough has been actualized. Statives never allow the progressive because the single situation of a stative is itself a final segment. There is no such thing as a non-final part of a stative so the first existential is never satisfied. Achievements, however, are pairs of states, and the only possible non-final segment is simply the initial situation. In English and Japanese, this initial state must be actualized to satisfy the first existential. A final segment is any segment which is not followed by more states. For an achievement, any segment which contains the second situation will be final. This means that for the English progressive only the initial state will be realized but for the Japanese *te-iru* the entire eventuality will be realized. That the *te-iru* form of an achievement is equivalent to the perfective is therefore not an accident. *Te-iru* is possible only when all the situations in the eventuality are actualized. The perfective is intuitively true under the same conditions. Accomplishments work in a parallel fashion, allowing either the activity or the appropriate achievement reading.

6.0 Conclusion

We see therefore that the straightforward situation-based analysis for verbal eventualities defined in (18) and the parameterized definition of the progressive given in (22) and (23) systematically account for the observed differences between Japanese and English, as well as for the facts within Japanese. The general aspectual semantics I have given is also derived from existing theories and as such accounts for the behavior typically associated with each aspectual class. The details of the semantics I have outlined here is explained in detail in McClure (in prep). And while the theory I have developed in this paper may not be the only way to account for the aspectual differences between Japanese and English, any theory of the progressive will have to incorporate some version of these proposals if Japanese and English are to be treated in a unified manner.

References

Dowty, D. (1979). Word Meaning and Montague Grammar. Reidel, Dordrecht.

Higginbotham, J. (1985). 'On Semantics'. Linguistic Inquiry 16.547-593.

Jacobsen, W.M. (1992). The Transitive Structure of Events in Japanese. Kurosio, Tokyo.

Kindaichi, Haruhiko. (1976). Nihongo Doosi no Asupekuto (Aspect in Japanese Verbs). Mugi Syoboo, Tokyo.

Koizumi, T, et. al. (1989). Nihongo Kihon Doosi Yoohoo Ziten (A Dictionary of Basic Japanese Verbs). Taisyuukan Syoten, Tokyo.

Landman, F. (1992). 'The Progressive'. Natural Language Semantics 1.1-32.

McClure, W. (to appear). "Unaccusativity and 'Inner' Aspect". Proceedings of WCCFL XI, Kurel. M. et. al. (eds). CSLI, Stanford.

McClure, W. (in preparation). Syntactic Projections of the Semantics of Aspect. Cornell University dissertation.

Moriyama, T. (1988). Nihongo Doosi Zyutugobun no Kenkyuu (Investigations of Japanese Verbal Predicates). Meiji Syoin, Tokyo.

Parsons, T. (1990). Events in the Semantics of English. MIT Press, Cambridge, MA.

Reichenbach, H. (1947). Elements of Symbolic Logic. Free Press, New York.

Vendler, Z. (1967). Linguistics in Philosophy. Cornell University Press, Ithaca.

Do *aru* and *iru* Exist as Verbs of Existence in Japanese?

SUSAN STRAUSS

University of California at Los Angeles

1   Introduction[1]

This paper presents an alternative analysis of the two verbs of existence in Japanese, <u>aru</u> and <u>iru,</u> from a Form-Content perspective.   The Form-Content approach differs from the more traditional approaches, in that its primary goal is to discover a single and invariant meaning for the linguistic form in question, instead of describing and listing the various properties and phenomena of the form under investigation, which generally results in an enumeration of multiple descriptions and multiple meanings for the same linguistic form. The Form-Content approach 'proceeds from the theoretical position that the structure of language is fundamentally determined by its function as an instrument of human communication.' (Reid 1991:6). By proposing a single and invariant meaning for each of

---

[1]   I am grateful to Noriko Akatsuka and Robert Kirsner for their encouragement and support from the first version of this paper through its current stage. I would also like to thank Patricia Clancy, Yoko Collier-Sanuki, Motoko Ezaki, Hiroko Furuyama, Shoichi Iwasaki, Akio Kamio, Mihoko Miki, Kuniko Tada, and Eri Yoshida for their thoughtful comments and feedback. Any misconception, misrepresentation or error that may be in the text of the paper or in the theory underlying the words is my own.

these two verbs 'of existence' in place of the traditionally held diverse notions of existence, location, possession, ownership, belonging, group membership, etc., certain inconsistencies and puzzles pervading the current literature may begin to become somewhat clearer.

The results of the study will show that these verbs are actually inextricable elements of a larger system of Japanese grammar. This alternative approach will also encompass into its analysis the occurrence of the prenominal modifier aru 'a certain', 'a particular', which has until now been considered by grammarians and native speakers alike as a simple instance of coincidental homonymy with its 'existential' verb counterpart. Furthermore, I am hoping to expand the analysis into a future study to include these verbs as they co-occur with other verbs in compound forms in an attempt to account for additional puzzles in meaning relating to tense, aspect, and transitivity which remain the subject of interest of many of even the most current and up to date linguists.[2]

2 The Traditional View

According to virtually all known reference grammars and textbooks on the Japanese language (Alfonso 1966, Jorden 1987, Makino and Tsutsui 1986, Martin 1975, McGloin 1989, Mizutani and Mizutani 1977, Ono 1973, etc.) the choice between the two existential verbs is fundamentally governed by the animacy or inanimacy of the subjects with which they occur. Aru[3] is regarded as the existence verb for inanimate subjects and iru, for animates. Consider the following examples taken from Mizutani and Mizutani (1977:21):

---

[2]   Iru, as do the other three verbs treated in this paper, combines with the -te form of main verbs to express a rich combination of spatio-temporal and aspectual messages. The -te iru combination, depending upon the type of main verb with which it occurs, signals what appear to be mutually contradictory aspectual messages including perfective, stative as well as progressive (Jacobsen 1992).

[3]   a) The verb aru will appear in the various examples in this paper in the following additional forms:

arimasu	non past
arimashita	past
o ari desu	non past (deferential)

b) The verb iru will appear in the following additional forms:

imasu	non past
imashita	past

(1) Asoko   ni   kissaten   ga   <u>arimasu</u> ne.   (aru)
Over there LOC coffee shop SUBJ exist PRT
'There's a coffee shop over there.'

(2) Asoko   ni   otoko no hito   ga   <u>imasu</u> ne.   (iru)
Over there LOC man SUBJ exist PRT
'There's a man over there.'

The literature generally and consistently accounts for the meanings of the verbs as 'to be', 'to exist', 'to be in a place', etc., with the choice of <u>aru</u> vs <u>iru</u> determined by whether or not its subject is animate. However, there are cases where the feature of simple subject animacy/inanimacy is not sufficient to account for verb choice, since <u>aru</u> is often used with animate subjects and <u>iru</u> with inanimate subjects. It is in explaining this type of phenomenon that the restrictions and qualifications governing verb choice in the literature are less and less consistent with each other. There is actually little uniformity in description from reference to reference; some references cover only certain exceptional restrictions while other references cover only other restrictions.

In *A Reference Grammar of Japanese* (1975), Martin's (ibid.,193-8) introductory paragraph for the section on these verbs opens with the statement that the linguistic devices used to encode notions such as existence, location, and possession overlap in many languages, as they do in Japanese, 'because in a three-dimensional world, if something exists it must have a location; and in a personalized world OWNERSHIP (emphasis Martin's) can be imputed (to supernatural beings if to no one else) for whatever exists.' Hence, the following examples of possession extracted from Martin (ibid.) indicate perfect acceptability of <u>aru</u> with animate subjects representing the 'thing being possessed':

(3) Dare ni/ga   kodomo   ga   <u>arimasu</u>   ka
Who DAT/SUBJ child(ren) SUBJ exist Q PRT
'Who has a child/children?' (informal)

(4) Donata ni/ga   kodomo   ga   o <u>ari</u> desu   ka
Who DAT/SUBJ child(ren) SUBJ exist (pol) Q PRT
'Who has a child/children?' (deferential)

In *Japanese Language Patterns* (1966), Alfonso (ibid.,104-11) indicates that family members are regarded as 'belonging' to a particular person. By extension, noun subjects such as 'friends' or 'guests' also fall into the category of family membership since they are 'considered by

Japanese as such', thereby attributing to the acceptability of aru, as in (5), excerpted from Alfonso (ibid.):

(5) Uchi ni   wa   okyakusan ga   arimasu.
    House LOC TOP guest(s)   SUBJ exist
    'There is/are guests at home.'

Alfonso also mentions that iru may be used with vehicles of transportation, but includes in his description the somewhat tight restriction that the motion be 'on the point of taking place'. He illustrates such use through the following made up scenario: 'a person leaves the station thinking that his bus has probably already gone, but he finds it still there and about to leave...', thus calling for the use of iru by Alfonso's (ibid.) hypothetical speaker as reproduced below in (6):

(6) Mada basu ga   imashita
    Still bus   SUBJ exist--past
    'The bus was still there.'

Still other references impose restrictions on only one of the verbs, such that aru is used with family members who are alive now, when stating a universal fact, when telling an old story or a historical fact (Ono 1973:47), or with someone who maintains a very close relationship with the possessor, such as a family member, a relative or a friend; with events such as parties and concerts; and, to express the notion of possession not expressible with the compound verb motte iru (Makino & Tsutsui 1986:73-6). These two sources mention no special properties of iru outside the basic animacy requirement. Jorden (1987) limits her discussion of these verbs to the core notion of animacy/inanimacy.

One additional use of aru, occurring prenominally and meaning 'a particular', 'a certain', 'one', as in aru hito 'a particular man', aru hi 'one day', aru teido made 'to a certain degree', is not mentioned whatsoever by any researcher as being related in any way to its 'existential' verbal counterpart.

3   An Alternative Approach

As has been noted above, the aru vs iru problem is one of fundamental importance within the grammar of Japanese. At the same time, it seems to be a subject for which there is only minimal overlap among descriptive and prescriptive accounts by linguists in terms of the qualifications, restrictions, and exceptions to the basic animate/inanimate distinction.

The current analysis is proposing that instead of signalling many diverse concepts such as those of existence, location, ownership, possession, family membership, motion about to happen, etc., these verbs are actually inextricably linked to a larger system of Japanese grammar. Additionally, the semantic scope of this larger system does not even relate specifically, explicitly, nor directly to the notion of existence at all. Rather, the system being proposed here centers around the potential movement of an entity through both space as well as time, whether that entity is animate or inanimate, whether it is concrete or abstract.

This alternative system, then, instead of being one of 'existence', is actually one of motion, and is comprised of four basic verbs: the two verbs traditionally classified as verbs of 'existence', <u>aru</u> and <u>iru</u>, together with the two deictic verbs <u>kuru</u> 'come' and <u>iku</u> 'go'. The schema for this system is illustrated below in example (7):

(7) meanings of all four verb signals[4]:

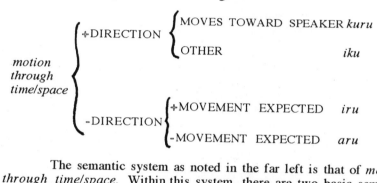

The semantic system as noted in the far left is that of *motion through time/space*. Within this system, there are two basic semantic distinctions affecting such motion, i.e., +DIRECTION and -DIRECTION, with the verbs <u>kuru</u> and <u>iku</u>, generally coinciding with English 'come' and 'go' respectively, comprising the +DIRECTION category and the verbs <u>iru</u> and <u>aru</u>, the -DIRECTION category.

Additional evidence for combining the four verbs into the same semantic system is the striking fact that in *keigo*, the Japanese honorific system, the verbs <u>kuru</u>, <u>iku</u> and <u>iru</u> can all be expressed with one form, <u>irassharu</u>, as illustrated in (8), (9), and (10) below:

(8) Katosan wa koko ni kimashita. <u>(kuru)</u>   'Mr. K. came here'
     Tada sensei wa koko ni <u>irasshaimashita</u>.   'Prof. T. came here'

---

[4]   This schema is based on the Columbia School representation of the interrelationship between semantic system, substance and value. See Garcia (1975), Kirsner (1979), Reid (1991), and others.

(9) Katosan wa gakkoo e ikimashita (iku)   'Mr. K went to school'
     Tada sensei wa gakkoo e <u>irasshaimashita</u>.   'Prof. T. went to school'

(10) Katosan wa koko ni imasu. (iru)   'Mr. K. is here'
     Tada sensei wa koko ni <u>irasshaimasu</u>.   'Prof. T. is here'

Furthermore, although not mentioned by any reference grammar or textbook reviewed to date, the verb <u>aru</u> can also be expressed using <u>irassharu</u>, as in the honorific variation of the question 'How many children do you have?', as illustrated in (11):

(11) kodomo wa nannin arimasu ka? (aru)   non-honorific form
     okosama wa nannin <u>irasshaimasu</u> ka?   honorific form

The phenomenon as noted in examples (8) - (11) is a clear indication that all four verbs comprising this system are indeed related as a verbal representation of the interrelationship between the concepts of directionality and expectation of movement in Japanese.

In contrast with Martin's rationale that 'if something exists it must have a location...', the system being proposed here is based more strongly on the motion (or lack of it) through time and space. If something or someone is regarded from the point of view of its motion, then its existence must be presupposed. According to this system, <u>aru</u> and <u>iru</u> are not verbs of state or disposition as represented by the traditional literature. Rather, they are verbs of activity, just like their +DIRECTION counterparts, <u>kuru</u> and <u>iku</u>. Example (12) indicates the imperative forms of all four verbs.

(12)
a. koko ni   kinasai.   (kuru)
    here LOC come
    'come here'

b. asoko   ni   ikinasai   (iku)
    there   LOC go
    'go there'

c. koko ni /asoko ni   inasai   (iru)
    here LOC/ there LOC stay
    'stay here/there'

d. *arinasai   (aru)

With <u>aru</u> signalling -DIRECTION, -EXPECTATION OF MOVEMENT, it is not at all surprising that it resists the imperative, since its semantic message excludes the expectation of any spatio-temporal displacement with respect to its subject.

Also, the active quality of <u>aru</u> becomes clear in sentences such as (13), where it takes on a meaning such as 'to happen', 'to take place':

(13)   Ano hoteru   de osoroshii satsujin jiken ga arimashita
          That hotel   LOC terrible murder case SUBJ exist--pst
          'A terrible murder took place at that hotel.'

Here, it is the interrelationship between the verb itself and the particle <u>de</u>[5] which creates the truly active sense of the verb <u>aru</u>. Notice the contrast between the particle <u>de</u> in (13) with the particle <u>ni</u> in (1), (2), (5), (12a-c).

The schema in (7) represents a model of native speaker behavior (albeit at a potentially subconscious level) with respect to the four tightly related linguistic forms under consideration. It is precisely due to this connectedness and strong interrelationship between the four verbs themselves and their respective semantic signals that the choice of one major distributional category (+DIRECTION or -DIRECTION) over the other and the choice of one particular verb over the other, are of prime importance. These verbs represent competing meanings within a single semantic domain. The choice of one necessarily excludes the choice of any competing forms. According to Kirsner (1979:33), 'the more two meanings have "something to do with each other", the more intense will be their competition and the more the choice of one in order to communicate a given message will be understood to constitute a rejection of the other'. What is represented in (7), then, is nothing more than a schematic manifestation of particular oppositions of exclusion that ultimately constitute what motivates native speakers to make particular choices within the domain of *motion through time/space.*

The two verbs traditionally considered as verbs of direction or deictic verbs, i.e., <u>kuru</u> 'come' and <u>iku</u> 'go' both signal the meaning +DIRECTION in opposition with their <u>iru</u> and <u>aru</u> counterparts of -DIRECTION. Each sub-category member also maintains its own oppositions with its counter-member. For example, <u>kuru</u>, maintaining the traditional meaning signal of 'toward speaker' refers to movement through time and/or space in the one and only direction of toward speaker. This verb

---

[5] The particle <u>de</u> as it appears in the structure [place + <u>de</u> + activity verb] typically indicates the location of a particular action. The contrast between these locative particles is based primarily on differences in type and scope of activity. This contrast of particles and their interrelationship with the verbs with which they occur could potentially be the subject of an entirely independent study and will not be dealt with in greater detail at this point.

is but one example of the single most definite human reference point from which all other motion through space and time can be described, namely the speaker. Iku, on the other hand, captures every other direction, again, in time and/or space, which is not toward the speaker. Many traditional grammarians define iku in an inverse linear manner as kuru, or 'away from speaker', however, while kuru is by its very definition linear and therefore highly specific, iku is not necessarily linear at all with regard to the speaker. For example, if Mr. Tanaka went with Mr. Smith to Shinjuku Station, the directional vector, to Shinjuku Station, has nothing whatsoever to do with the speaker's location at the time of the utterance. It simply states that they did not go to where the speaker was. Instead of 'away from speaker', then, iku signals any direction but toward the speaker, which explains why OTHER is the category label in the system, in direct semantic opposition to its TOWARD SPEAKER counterpart.

The two verbs iru and aru signalling -DIRECTION or no particular dislocation in space and/or time also oppose each other, but not based upon whether the subject is animate or inanimate, a family member still alive now, a guest or friend considered to be a family member, a historical fact, or motion about to take place. Rather, the opposition between the two verbs is based upon whether the speaker expects some self-actualized displacement of the entity through space and/or time. Since no one would expect a subject such as a book, a tree, or a desk to displace itself on its own, the verb aru would invariably be used when referring to its existence. However, when we consider the choice of aru vs iru for referents which would be less easily categorizable according to traditionalists, such as an elevator being stopped at the second floor of some building, or the notion of having children (in the sense of being a parent), the distinction between aru and iru becomes much clearer when we look at verbs from the point of view of expectation of movement, as the examples in sentences (14) and (15)[6] show:

(14) erebeetaa wa   rooka no   tsukiatari ni   aru / *iru
     elevator TOP hall GEN   end   LOC exist
     'The elevator is at the end of the hall.'

(15) erebeetaa wa   nikai   ni   iru   / *aru
     elevator TOP 2nd flr LOC exist
     'The elevator is on the second floor.'

The occurrence of the verb iru in (14) would be crashingly ungrammatical, precisely because of the concept of expectation of movement. In (15), the converse is true, with the substitution of aru yielding an ungrammatical

---

6   I am grateful to Sandy Thompson for these examples.

utterance, unless somehow the elevator were either broken or the building had been specially designed for the elevator service to begin at the second floor rather than at ground level.

Examples (16) and (17) illustrate the use of aru and iru with family members:

(16) kodomo   ga   aru
      child/children SUBJ   exist
      'I have a child/children.'

(17) kodomo   ga   iru
      child/children SUBJ   exist
      I have a child/children
                or
      'There is a child/are children.'

To some Japanese, aru, as in (16) is more acceptable than iru, in spite of the inherent animacy of the referent. Aru, in a declarative statement such as this clearly signals the unambiguous message 'I have children.' On the other hand, while kodomo ga iru is still perfectly acceptable to express the identical notion as its aru counterpart, this iru-signalled message could also ambiguously express some temporary physical location of the child or children in question in addition to the 'existential' reading.

Therefore, the aru signal is highly specific in terms of both space and time. It is the most specific of the four verbs in that it helps define the entity by the very notion that the signal combination of -DIRECTION and -EXPECTATION OF MOVEMENT locks it into a definite point where space and time intersect. The entity and the location, whether that location is a place, a person, or an abstract notion, are very closely related to each other, to the degree that the entity, the space it occupies and the zero expectation of movement from that space are one. From this standpoint, the example sentences in (18), (19), and (20) are all messages of one and the same signal, -DIRECTION and -EXPECTATION OF MOVEMENT, rather than individual occurrences of various messages such as existence, historical fact, possession, etc.

(18) ano yama   no ue ni   wa   furui otera ga   aru.
      that mountain's top LOC TOP old   temple SUBJ exist
      'There's an old temple on top of that mountain'

(19) Kamakura jidai ni Minamoto no   Yoritomo
      Kamakura era LOC Minamoto GEN   Yoritomo

to	iu	hito	ga	<u>arimashita</u>.[7]
QUOT	say	person	SUBJ	exist--past

'There was a person named Minamoto no Yoritomo
in the Kamakura era.'

(20) Musuko wa netsu ga <u>aru</u>.
son   TOP fever SUBJ exist
'My son has a fever'

Evidence from Classical Japanese also seems to corroborate the analysis being proposed here.[8] Classical Japanese uses ar=u for the traditional notion of 'existence', with no constraint regarding the animacy or inanimacy of the subject. However, in the *Hamamatsu chunagon monogatari* (ca. 1068 AD) and the *Sarashina nikki* (ca. 1079), the verb form wi=ru appears when it refers to a person just before setting off to go somewhere. Further, there may be evidence of this form being used in the *Sarashina nikki* to refer to inanimate subjects in motion, as in personal possessions, during a move across the river. These passages, and others, will be examined in greater detail in a future study.

As mentioned above, the present framework also seems to account for one more occurrence of <u>aru</u> which is considered by the very vast majority of Japanese speakers as merely coincidentally homophonous with the <u>aru</u> 'of existence', namely that of the prenominal modifier as in <u>aru hi</u> 'one day' or <u>aru onna</u> 'a certain woman'. By considering the highly specific meaning of <u>aru,</u> which is achieved by locking the entity to its time and place, it is clear that the signal for prenominal <u>aru</u> is one and the same as the signal for the <u>aru</u> of 'existence'.

Prenominal <u>aru</u> is used frequently as a determiner in a construction similar to a relative clause in Japanese, with the verb preceding the noun being modified. In a language such as Japanese which does not have an article system, the use of the prenominal <u>aru</u> construction parallels, in a way, a modified indefinite article system for first mention nouns. <u>Aru</u> as a first mention noun modifier functions somewhere between an indefinite and definite article. <u>Aru onna no hito</u> 'a certain woman' expresses a greater degree of differentiation than would simply 'a woman' and a lesser degree of differentiation than 'the woman. Further, it is not as quantity specific as <u>hitorino onna no hito</u> 'one [human classifier] woman'. <u>Iru</u>, being similar from the point of view of -DIRECTION, but lacking a zero expectation of movement, is therefore, not specific enough to lock the entity into its

---

[7]   Ono (1973:47)

[8]   I am deeply indebted to Alexander Vovin for his personal observations which are expressed in this paragraph.

time/place coordinate nor to convey the notion of differentiation or specificity. The +EXPECTATION OF MOVEMENT message signalled by iru precludes a locking of the entity into a fixed spatio-temporal location. Note the differences in meaning conveyed by the two signals of aru vs iru respectively in (21) a) and (21) b):

(21) a) aru[9]   onna   no   hito
       exist woman GEN person
       'a certain woman'
    (in a particular place, at a particular time, i.e.
    -DIRECTION, -EXPECTATION OF MOVEMENT)

    b) *iru   onna   no   hito
       exist woman GEN   person
       *'a woman'
    (in a particular place, with dislocation expected, i.e.
    -DIRECTION, +EXPECTATION OF MOVEMENT)

With the aru message serving to lock an entity into a single particular spatio-temporal coordinate, thereby resulting in an extreme definiteness in time/space, it is predicted that its use as a prenominal modifier would favor singular referents. A pilot study of this pronominal modifier in written discourse was conducted involving a 2,000 word corpus, 'Guides (Excerpts)' by Terada Torahiko from the textbook *Intensive Course in Japanese, Intermediate*. The results show a total of 10 tokens of aru + noun (or aru + modified noun), all of which are in fact singular[10]. The ten tokens are as follows: aru kankyoo 'a particular interest, aru hitori 'one of the people in particular', aru heya 'a certain room', aru mado 'a particular

---

[9]   While modern Japanese uses different Chinese characters for prenominal aru and 'existential' aru, the Koojien dictionary (1991) indicates that the character used for 'existence' also means 'a particular' or 'a certain' when it precedes a noun. Also, some native speakers of Chinese have indicated through personal communication that either of the two characters, when it precedes the character for 'woman' conveys the meaning of 'a certain woman'.

[10]   These findings are consistent with Contini Morava's (1975) study of Swahili locatives, particularly with respect to the PA-existential. '*Pa*, referring to a space which is geometrically homogeneous, i.e., spatially undifferentiated, should avoid co-occurring with plural nouns, because a plurality of entities contradicts a homogeneous interpretation. That is to say, a plurality of entities, being made up of several individuals leads one to expect heterogeneity of location: each individual will tend to define its own *pa*-space.' In the case of Japanese, the aru signal locks the particular entity into time/space by virtue of its meaning of zero direction, zero expectation of movement, thereby designating a single point, which is most easily occupiable by a single or a singular entity.

window', aru miyako no daigaku 'a university in a certain capital city', aru
kibutsu ka e ka 'a certain vessel or picture', aru imi de wa 'in a certain
sense', aru fushigi na maryoku 'a certain strange magical power', aru mono
'a certain entity'.

4 The Data

The majority of the data used for the present paper is based on
questionnaire surveys conducted among native speakers. Respondents for
the first data set range in age from 20 to 54 and have varying educational
backgrounds. The questionnaire for this set consists of twenty sentence
pairs (or triplets), resulting in a total of 44 sentences. Twenty-three
subjects were asked to rank the sentences on a scale of 1 to 5 based on the
general acceptability of the utterance using aru and an almost identical
counterpart sentence using iru. A score of 1 represents the level of least
acceptability, 3 represents an awkward or unnatural sentence, and 4 and 5
both represent acceptable utterances, with 5 being the highest level of
acceptability. The ranking scale with a sample sentence pair taken from the
actual questionnaire sheet has been reproduced in (22):

(22)

LEAST ACCEPTABLE	1
Not Acceptable	2
Awkward/Unnatural	3
Acceptable	4
VERY ACCEPTABLE	5

Madonna ni wa otoko ga aru _____
Madonna ni wa otoko ga iru _____
'Madonna has a lover'

In Questionnaire A, eleven of the twenty sentences have animate
subjects, eight have inanimate subjects, and one uses the word kamisama
'God' as subject. Table 1 indicates the responses given based on the number
of response tokens and corresponding percentages of interviewees who accept
aru, who reject aru, who accept iru, and who reject iru. For the purpose of
this study, scores of 3, indicating an awkward or unnatural sentence were not
counted[11], which explains why a particular utterance may show less than a
total of 23 response tokens or less than 100% for the combined responses of

---

11   In these instances, the majority of respondents recommended that an
alternative verbal expression would render the utterance grammatical. These
proposed alternative verbal expressions coupled with the present framework will
serve as additional data for future study.

acceptance/rejection for a particular verb form cooccurring with a particular subject.

Table 1
Questionnaire A Results Summary

n = 23	aru		iru	
Animate subjects	ACCEPT	REJECT	ACCEPT	REJECT
grandmother	8 (35%)	11 (48%)	20 (87%)	1 (4%)
older sister	10 (43%)	8 (35%)	22 (96%)	0
children	11 (48%)	10 (43%)	22 (96%)	0
King (Egypt)	1 (4%)	18 (78%)	23 (100%)	0
cat	1 (4%)	21 (91%)	23 (100%)	0
customers in shop				
a) always	7 (30%)	11 (48%)	20 (87%)	1 (4%)
b) now	2 (9%)	17 (74%)	23 (100%)	0
students				
a) at school	0	22 (96%)	23 (100%)	0
b) in front of something	0	23 (100%)	23 (100%)	0
lover	4 (17%)	15 (65%)	21 (91%)	1 (4%)
unemployed people	2 (9%)	15 (65%)	23 (100%)	0
Inanimate subjects				
book	23 (100%)	0	0	23 (100%)
chess king	20 (87%)	3 (13%)	5 (22%)	14 (61%)
ship--open sea	10 (43%)	6 (26%)	15 (65%)	4 (17%)
boat--in port	15 (65%)	1 (4%)	10 (43%)	8 (35%)
subway	22 (96%)	1 (4%)	1 (4%)	21 (91%)
bus				
a) garage	14 (61%)	5 (22%)	7 (30%)	15 (65%)
b) bus stop	7 (30%)	12 (52%)	17 (74%)	4 (17%)
taxi	7 (30%)	13 (57%)	19 (83%)	3 (13%)
God as **subject**	5 (22%)	12 (52%)	23 (100%)	0

Notice that in spite of the number of clear cut animate vs inanimate subjects, only 2 of the 44 total utterances show a 100% preference of one form with a 100% rejection of another, i.e., the utterance, 'the book is on the table', unanimously attracted an aru response, while unanimously rejecting iru; and 'the students are in front of the blackboard' unanimously accepts iru, while totally rejecting aru. Also, it is clear that for the animate category, iru is overwhelmingly preferred for all referents. However, note the progression of acceptability according to type of family membership: 11 of the 23 interviewees (48%) accept aru for 'children', 10

(43%) for 'older sister', and 8 (35%), in the Japanese version of 'do you have a grandmother?'[12].

7 respondents accept <u>aru</u> for the sentence 'there are always a lot of customers in that shop'. However, by altering this particular survey question slightly from the customers always being in a shop to 'there are a lot of customers now', acceptability dropped to 2 respondents or 9%. Thus, once the location to entity link begins to weaken, so do the response acceptabilities for <u>aru</u>, such that the conceptions of people having a cat or a lover, for example, or a State having a lot of unemployed people, are considered transitory and temporary, rather than a seemingly inalienable part of the subject in question, as implied by the <u>iru</u> or +MOVEMENT EXPECTED preference for the verb.

This difference becomes even more salient with inanimate subjects where varying degrees of expectation of subject dislocation come into play. <u>Iru</u> is shown to be perfectly acceptable with 'ship', 'boat', 'bus', and 'taxi'. In fact, in the Japanese equivalent to the statement 'there is a taxi in front of the house', <u>iru</u> is preferred by 19 of the 23 respondents or (83%). Bear in mind that this particular utterance contains no other contextual information to lead the respondent to believe one way or another that the motion may or may not be 'on the point of taking place', as Alfonso (ibid.) seems to specifically require as a constraint for <u>iru</u> usage with vehicles.

Notice the almost perfect mirror image of acceptability judgments for the ship being in the open sea in contrast with the boat being in port. In the case of the former, 43% accept <u>aru</u> and 65% also accept <u>iru</u>. In the case of the latter, 65% accept <u>aru</u> and 43% also accept <u>iru</u>. The widest differential occurs among the rejection of <u>aru</u>, with 26% rejecting it for a ship being in the open sea, and only 4% rejecting it for the boat being in port.

Almost all of the inanimate subjects in Questionnaire A which show a relatively high acceptance ratio for <u>iru</u> involve some type of vehicle of transportation. One or two respondents seemed to feel that the decisive factor for accepting <u>iru</u> is that the vehicles in question might be populated by animates, thus causing the <u>iru</u> reading. In an attempt to rule out this potential influence, Questionnaire B was designed and circulated among an additional 31 respondents. The rating scale is identical to that of Questionnaire A. The new survey contains only six sentence pairs of inanimate subjects only, including <u>taifuu</u> 'typhoon', <u>UFO</u> 'UFO' (unidentified flying object), and <u>robotto</u> 'robot', plus three other contextually related subjects involving different types of boats at sea: <u>chimbotsusen</u> 'a

---

[12]   One interesting observation in this regard is that some of the older interviewees seemed to actually prefer <u>aru</u> to <u>iru</u> when referring to family members, even lovers, while the majority of the younger interviewees seemed to prefer <u>iru</u>.

shipwreck', <u>junshisen</u> 'a patrol boat', and the generic <u>booto</u> 'boat'. The results of this Questionnaire are shown in Table 2. Scores of 3, considering the utterance awkward or unnatural, are not included in the table, as with Questionnaire A.

Table 2
Questionnaire B Results Summary[13]

n = 31	**aru**		**iru**	
Inanimate subjects	ACCEPT	REJECT	ACCEPT	REJECT
boat at sea	19 (61%)	4 (13%)	21 (68%)	8 (26%)
shipwreck at sea	27 (87%)	1 (3%)	4 (13%)	19 (61%)
patrol boat at sea	18 (58%)	7 (23%)	26 (84%)	4 (13%)
R-2 D-2	28 (90%)	0	26 (84%)	2 (6%)
typhoon	9 (29%)	14 (45%)	23 (74%)	4 (13%)
UFO	22 (71%)	3 (10%)	26 (84%)	2 (6%)

The responses for the various 'boat' subjects clearly indicate the notion of expectation of movement. Note the progression of acceptability from an almost identical percentage of acceptance of <u>aru</u> (61%) and <u>iru</u> (68%) with the generic 'boat', a strong preference for <u>aru</u> (84%) with an equally strong rejection of <u>iru</u> (13%) for 'shipwreck', and a greater preference of <u>iru</u> (84%) over <u>aru</u> (58%) with 'patrol boat', although the percentage of <u>aru</u> as being acceptable is still relatively high.

Further, the 'robot' subject generated responses such that <u>aru</u> is perfectly acceptable if the robot is a toy, perhaps sitting on a shelf, and <u>iru</u> is fine for a robot that moves.

Finally, respondents seemed to prefer <u>iru</u> (74%) overwhelmingly to <u>aru</u> (29%) for the 'typhoon' as subject, which points clearly to the concept of motion with virtually no possibility that the existence of an animate entity would be the influential factor for the choice of one over the other.

One final example of the interplay between <u>iru</u> and <u>aru</u> and their interrelated notions of expectation of motion comes from actual discourse, taken from Clancy's (1978) language acquisition data, in which a mother, in talking about a hypothetical world to her two year old son, switches from <u>iru</u> in one line to <u>aru</u> in a closely following line, when referring to <u>bubu</u>, which is baby talk for 'car(s)':

---

[13]   The order of inanimate subjects as noted in Table 2 does not represent the order in which the subjects actually appeared in the questionnaire. The actual order was designed per the following, in order to avoid the 'boat' subjects occurring in any way sequentially: 'boat at sea', 'R-2 D-2', 'shipwreck at sea', 'typhoon', 'UFO', 'patrol boat at sea'.

(23) Line 1043: abunai? abunakunai? bubu takusan <u>itara</u>? (<u>iru</u>)
      Line 1047: futachu mo mitchu mo <u>attara</u> bubu butsukaranai
                  ka naa?   (<u>aru</u>)

Loosely translated as:
Line 1043: is it dangerous or not <u>if there are</u> a lot of cars?
Line 1047: won't the cars bump into each other <u>if there are</u>
            a lot? [literally: 'as many as 2 or 3']

The hypothetical world created here involves one of cars being drawn on a piece of paper. The son asks his mother to continue drawing more cars, and the response to this request is reproduced in lines 1043 and 1047 above. This is a prime example illustrating that the motivating force behind native speaker verb choice is clearly not driven by the strict animate/inanimate distinction regarding the referent.

5 Conclusion

In sum, it has been my endeavor to show that the animacy/inanimacy distinction which characterizes virtually all traditional accounts of the 'existence' verbs in Japanese is a highly imprecise convention for describing a phenomenon that is in actuality a far more complex cognitive and perceptual process. By considering these two 'existential' verbs rather as verbs of 'motion' together with other traditionally recognized motion verbs, it becomes clearer just how much and to what degree the concept of motion through time/space plays a role in the grammar of Japanese.

References

Alfonso, Anthony. 1966.   Japanese Language Patterns, A Structural Approach, volumes 1 and 2. Tokyo. Sophia University L.L., Center of Applied Linguistics.

Contini Morava, Ellen.   Statistical demonstration of a meaning: the Swahili locatives in existential assertions. Studies in African Linguistics. 7(2): 137-56.

Garcia, Erica. 1975. The Role of Theory in Linguistic Analysis: The Spanish Pronoun System. Amsterdam. North-Holland Publishing Company.

Intensive Course in Japanese. Intermediate. Main Text. 1980. Tokyo. Language Services Co., Ltd.

Jacobsen, W.M. 1992. The Transitive Structure of Events in Japanese. Tokyo. Kurosio Publishers.

Jorden, Eleanor Harz & Noda, Mari. 1988. Japanese: The Spoken Language. Part 1. New Haven. Yale University Press.

Kirsner, Robert. 1979. The Problem of the Presentative Sentences in Modern Dutch. Amsterdam. North-Holland Publishing Company.

Makino, Seichi & Tsutsui, Michio. 1986. A Dictionary of Basic Japanese Grammar. Tokyo. The Japan Times.

Martin, Samuel. 1975. A Reference Grammar of Japanese. New Haven. Yale University Press.

Mizutani, Nobuko & Mizutani, Osamu. 1977. An Introduction to Modern Japanese. Tokyo. The Japan Times.

McGloin, Naomi Hanaoka. 1989. A Students' Guide to Japanese Grammar. Tokyo. Taishukan Publishing Company.

Ono, Hideichi. 1973. Japanese Grammar. Tokyo. The Hokuseido Press.

Reid, Wallis. 1991. Verb & Noun Number in English. New York. Longman, Inc.

Case-Marking in Korean Post-Verbal Negation

YOOKYUNG KIM
Stanford University

Introduction

In this paper, I will discuss the case alternation in post-verbal negation constructions in Korean. Korean has two ways of negating a sentence: one is to modify the verb with the negation adverb *an*, and the other is to embed the main verb under the negation verb *anh-ta*,[1] as illustrated in (1).

(1) a. John-i   phyenci-lul an   sse-ss-ta.
        John-NOM letter-ACC   NEG write-PAST
        'John didn't write a letter.'

     b. John-i   phyenci-lul ssu-ci   anh-ass-ta.
        John-NOM letter-ACC   write-COMP NEG-PAST
        'John didn't write a letter.'

---

[1] This form may be considered as a contraction form of *ani ha-ta* 'neg do'.

My paper concerns the second type of negation in (1)b which is called "post-verbal" or "long form" negation, contrasted with the first one in (1)a. Regarding case-marking, this construction shows a peculiar property such that the content verb may be case-marked.

(2) a. John-i   phyenci-lul ssu-ci-**lul/*ka**   anh-ass-ta.
         John-NOM letter-ACC write-COMP-ACC/*NOM NEG-PAST
         'John didn't write a letter.'

     b. pang-i   kkaykkusha-ci-**lul/ka**   anh-ass-ta.
         room-NOM be clean-COMP-ACC/NOM NEG-PAST
         'The room was not clean.'

There must be some restriction on the case-marking. Accusative marking is allowed in either case, but nominative marking is allowed in only one sentence in (2). It seems that if the content verb is non-stative, only the accusative case is possible, while if the verb is stative, both accusative and nominative are possible. However, I will show in the following section that the semantic feature "stativity" does not make accurate predictions, and another apparent factor "agentivity" also is not enough to account for the case alternations. It will turn out that Grimshaw's analysis (1990) of the argument structure which involves both thematic structure and aspectual structure effectively accounts for the problems in question.

1. Stativity vs. Agentivity

1.1. Stativity

As indicated in the literature on Korean linguistics (Sells 1992, Young-joo Kim 1990 among others), so-called Korean adjectives are not distinguished from verbs in that they do not appear with copula when used as predicates, and are directly inflected for tense, aspect, and modality. More importantly, it is hard to find any categorial distinction between them in a morphotactic sense. Instead, we must depend on a semantic feature called "stativity", if we need to distinguish them at all. All adjectives and a few verbs such as *iss* 'exist', *sokha* 'belong' are [+stative]. The [+stative] feature applies to something that is not a process but a state or quality. Progressive formation constitutes a good test for the stativity of a verb in Korean. Only non-stative verbs can occur with the progressive form.

(3) a. John-i   phyenci-lul ssu-ko   iss-ta. [−stative]
         John-NOM letter-ACC   write-COMP be
         'John is writing a letter.'

    b. *pang-i   kkaykkus-ha-ko iss-ta. [+stative]
        room-NOM be clean-COMP   be
        'The room is cleaning.'

It seems that there is a correlation between stativity and the possibility of nominatve case marking after content verbs: only stative verbs (which don't allow the progressive form as in (3)b) may have nominatve case marking under negation. But this apparent generalization cannot hold as we have non-stative verbs which allow nominative marking.

(4) a. elum-i   nok-ko   iss-ta. [−stative]
         ice-NOM   melt-COMP be
         'The ice is meltiing.'

    b. elum-i   nok-ci-**ka**   anh-nun-ta.
        ice-NOM   melt-COMP-NOM NEG-PRES
        'The ice doesn't melt.'

Therefore, we see that a verbal classification relying on the progressive formation is not a necessary condition for deciding nominative case marking in the negation construction.[2]

1.2. Agentivity

Another semantic classification of verbs regards agentivity. Imperative formation is a test for agentivity.[3]

(5) a. phenci-lul sse-la. [+agentive][−stative]
         letter-ACC write-IMP
         'Write a letter.'

    b. *kkaykkusha-yela. [−agentive][+stative]
        be clean-IMP
        'Be clean.'

    c. *nok-ala. [−agentive][−stative]
        melt-IMP
        'Melt.'

---

[2] Since Accusative case is possible regardless of the class of content verbs, I will concern myself to Nominative marking for the time being.

[3] Cooccurrence with adverbs like *deliberately*, verbs like *stop, start* is another test for agentivity.

Since a stative verb. in (5)b and an unaccusative verb in (5)c make a natural class as "non-agentive" and both allow nominative marking under negation, we may make a second hypothesis: the verb has Nominative case under negation iff the verb is non-agentive.

However, consider the following example.

(6) a. cengcikha-yela. [+agentive][+stative]
         be honest-IMP
         'Be honest.'

     b. John-i   cengcikha-ci-**ka**   anh-ta.
         John-NOM   be honest-COMP-NOM   NEG
         'John is not honest.'

This example is quite puzzling according to our second hypothesis, as the verb has nominative marking in spite of its agentivity. Now, we have a dilemma. We cannot make any statement for a positive condition of Nom marking in terms of either stativity or agentivity. If we consider only these semantic features, we can make only a weak statement that the verbs which are agentive as well as nonstative can NOT take nominative marking under negation. But this is not desirable, since it does not tell us why this should be so. Considering the general assumption that case-marking on dependents is a property of the head, it would be a quite unusual case if some kinds of dependent reject some certain case marking. Instead, if we could find a common property of the three cases which do allow nominative marking, we would be one step closer to finding an underlying reason for the case alternations.

1.3. Grimshaw's Argument Structure (1990)

I propose that we look for an answer in the argument structure of the verbs. Among various approaches to argument structure, I adopt an analysis of Grimshaw (1990) and assume that the argument structure has two dimensions of representation, thematic prominence and aspectual prominence. In this theory, the notion of external argument is defined differently from the study in which William (1981a) first introduced this notion.[4] Grimshaw attempts to derive the notion of external argument from the level of lexical semantic representation rather than syntactic configuration. The external argument is defined as the most prominent argument in the

---

[4] According to Williams (1981), the argument structure of a lexical item is an unordered list of θ-role labels, and one of the arguments is distinguished as an external argument, of which the maximal projection of the predicate is predicated.

argument structure, which is the most prominent along two dimensions: thematic and aspectual representations.

The argument structure is a structured representation of prominence relations among arguments. The prominence relations are jointly determined by the thematic properties of the predicate (via the thematic hierarchy) and by the aspectual properties of the predicate. The following scheme gives the proto-argument-structure for the thematic dimension:

(7)   (Agent(Experiencer(Goal/Source/Location(Theme))))

In this scheme, a more embedded role represents a less prominent role.[5]

On the other hand, each verb has associated with it an event structure, which when combined with elements in the clause, provides an event strucutre for the entire sentence. The event structure, which represents the aspectual analysis of the clause, breaks down into aspectual subparts: activity and state.

(8)

An accomplishment like *x constructs y* is analyzed as an activity in which x engages in construction ("activity") plus a resulting state in which existence is predicated of *y*. In this case, *x* (Agent) is more prominent than *y* (Patient) in the thematic analysis, since a Patient role is far more embedded than an Agent role in the Thematic Hierarchy given in (7), and prominent also in the aspectual analysis, since an argument which participates in the first sub-event is more prominent than an argument which participates in the second sub-event.

An unergative verb such as *work* may be analyzed as having only the "activity" part, which is the first sub-event of accomplishment verbs. Since the only argument of an unergative verb is engaged in the first sub-event of the event structure, it will count as maximally prominent. Accordingly, an unergative verb has an external argument in this theory.

Contrasted with this case, an unaccusative verb can be assumed to have "state/change of state" as its event structure. Since this corresponds to the second sub-part of an accomplishment, the argument which may

---

[5] Bresnan & Kanerva 1989 assume a different order of prominence among thematic roles: Agent<Experience<Goal<...<Theme<Location

be the most prominent argument in terms of thematic dimension[6] cannot count as maximally prominent. It follows that unaccusative verbs lack an external argument.

1.4. "No External Argument" Condition

Grimshaw's (1990) two dimensional account of argument structure can shed light on our case alternation problem. By incorporating the aspectual property into the argument structure of a verb, we can distinguish verbs which allow nominative case under negation from verbs which do not. While the classification in terms of stativity in the previous section depends on the progressive formation, we may now consider the lexical conceptual structure of a verb, that is, whether the argument is involved in an activity or state/change of state. The four types of verbs in terms of $\pm$ stative and $\pm$ agentive can be reanalyzed as follows, and distinguished into two groups: those which have an external argument and those which do not.

(9) a. ilk 'read' [− stative, + agentive] $(x(y))$

   b. kkaykkusha 'be clean' [+ stative, − agentive] $((x))$

   c. nok 'melt' [− stative, − agentive] $((x))$

   d. cengcikha 'be honest' [+ stative, + agentive] $((x))$

When we consider the aspectual part of these verbs, all cases except 'read' in (9)a are associated with "state or change of state", which is the second sub-part of an accomplishment; thus these lack external arguments. Double parenthesis embedding represents this property. Interestingly, these three verb classes are just those which allow Nominative case under negation. The verb 'melt' which was a problematic case for the "stative" hypothesis does not cause any problem in this classification, since the argument of 'melt' is surely involved in a "change of state" rather than an "activity". Neither does the agentive adjective 'be honest' cause a problem. Since externality is not determined simply by the thematic label, even though the argument of 'be honest' may be identified with the "Agent" role of other verbs, the aspectual part prevents it from being an external argument. Recall that Agent is always the maximally prominent argument (external argument) only because it is a "Cause" argument which is always most prominent in the aspectual dimension. However, it is impossible to assume a "Cause" argument in the case of 'be honest'.

---

[6] Since prominence is determined in a relative sense, a Theme role may actually be the most prominent, if there is no other more prominent role.

To conclude this section, given the analysis of Grimshaw (1990), the following generalization regarding case alternations in post-verbal negation constructions can be made:

> *The verb can be Nominative marked iff it lacks an external argument, whereas any verb can be marked Accusative case regardless of its argument structure.*

2. Suppression of External Argument

In this section, I will consider lexical rules which are generally assumed to involve suppression of the external argument such as Passivization (Bresnan 1982, Levin & Rappapport 1986 etc.). The conclusion which we drew in the last section will be tested for derived lexical items by such suppression rules.

2.1. Passivization

The Korean lexical passive is formed with an suffix (*i/hi/li/ki*), as follows.

(10) a. John-i   kencho-lul thulek-ey   sil-ess-ta
John-NOM   hay-ACC   truck-LOC   load-PAST
'John loaded hay in the truck.'

b. kencho-ka (John-eyuihaye) thulek-ey   sil-I-ess-ta.
hay-NOM   John-by   truck-LOC   load-PASS-PAST
'The hay was loaded in the truck by John.'

Concerning the argument structure of passive verbs, we find them to follow the universal pattern of passivization: suppression of the external argument (Agent role). Since the Agent role is suppressed, it cannot be counted as the most prominent role, and the next prominent argument becomes the subject. We may wonder why the next prominent argument cannot be an external argument. Considering the aspect of passive sentences, we may find an answer. Passive verbs have a complex event structure when the adjunct *by*-phrase is explicitly expressed as in (11). The first sub-part "activity" is identified by Agentive role expressed by *by*-phrase, and the subject (Theme) of a passive sentence serves to identify the resulting state. Thus, this argument cannot be the external argument.

The following is the argument structure of passive verb form.

(11)   sil-I-ta 'be loaded' (x-ϕ (y))
                             Agent   Theme

If this assumption is right, we may expect the passive verbs to allow nominative case under negation even if the active counterpart does not. This prediction is borne out in these examples:

(12) a. John-i   kencho-lul thulek-ey sil-ci(-**lul/*ka**)   anh-assta
      John-NOM hay-ACC   truck-LOC load(-ACC/*NOM) NEG-PAST
      'John didn't load hay in the truck.'

   b. kencho-ka thulek-ey sil-I-ci(-**lul/ka**)   anh-ass-ta.
      hay-NOM   truck-LOC load-PASS(-ACC/NOM) NEG-PAST
      'The hay was not loaded in the truck.'

2.2. Resultative Intransitivization

Korean has an auxiliary verb -e *iss-ta* which is called the intransitivizing resultative construction.[7]

(13) a. John-i   pwul-ul   khi-n-ta.
      John-NOM light-ACC turn on-PRES
      'John turns the light on.'

   b. pwul-i   khy-e   iss-ta.
      light-NOM turn on-COMP be
      'The light is on.'

As we see in the English translation, the complex predicate *V-e iss* expresses the resulting state caused by the activity denoted by the content verb. Thus, contrasted with the sentence in (13)a which clearly represents an "activity", the sentence in (13)b cannot be associated with an "activity" event, but represents a "state". Therefore, this complex predicate can be assumed to involve the suppression of the external argument. Presumably, the process may not be simply a suppression[8] but a total deletion of the external argument, since it is impossible to have the Agent argument expressed, even optionally in this construction. Whatever formalization we might make, it is clear that this complex predicate lacks an external argument. The following contrast confirms this position.

---

[7] See Matsumoto (1990) for a Japanese construction of the same type.

[8] Recall that Grimshaw (1990) argues for the dual status of *by*-phrase in the passive sentence: an adjunct, at the same time, an argument. This is attributed to the fact that the argument structure of the passive form keeps the Agent role, even though demoted.

(14) a. John-i   pwul-ul   khi-ci(-**lul/*ka**)   anh-nun-ta.
       John-NOM   light-ACC   turn on(-ACC/*-NOM)   NEG-PRES
       'John doesn't turn the light on.'

     b.   pwul-i   khy-e   iss-ci(-**lul/ka**)   anh-ta.
       light-NOM   turn on-COMP   be(-ACC/-NOM)   NEG
       'The light is not on.'

Before leaving this subject, it is good to consider the other complex predicate which also represents "resulting state" as its sub-part of event structure.

(15)   emeni-ka   kwaca-lul   kwu-e   noh-ass-ta.
       mother-NOM   cookie-ACC   bake-COMP   put-PAST
       'Mother has baked cookies (for future use).'

It is true that the complex predicate *kwu-e noh* expresses that the 'cookies' (Theme) now exist ("state"), but in addition, this represents an "activity" of cooking by 'mother' (Agent). Thus, this complex predicate has a complex event structure and the Agent which is involved in the first sub-part is maximally prominent in both the thematic and aspectual dimension: hence it would count as an external argument. Then, we predict that this predicate cannot be marked Nom under negation.

(16)   emeni-ka   kwaca-lul   kwu-e noh-ci(-**lul/*ka**) anh-assta.
       mother-NOM   cookie-ACC   bake   put(-ACC/*NOM   NEG-PAST
       'Mother has not baked cookies (for future use).'

In this section, we have considered two kinds of constructions which involve suppression of an external argument: passivization and resultative intransitivization. As expected, the verbs which don't allow nominative case will allow it after each lexical rule or process affecting the argument structure. Since derived passive verbs and certain complex predicates lack an external argument, it follows from the generalization that they can be nominative marked under negation.

3. Adding an External Argument

One further piece of evidence comes from causativization, a lexical rule which adds an external argument to the argument structure of the base verb.

3.1. Causativization

Let's consider a pair of an underived verb and a causativized verb.

(17) a.   elum-i   nok-ci-**ka**   anh-ass-ta.
        ice-NOM melt-COMP-NOM NEG-PAST
        'The ice din't melt.'

    b.   John-i   elum-ul   nok-i-ci(***-ka**)   anh-ass-ta.
        John-NOM ice-acc   melt-CAUS-COMP-NOM NEG-PAST
        'John didn't melt the ice.'

As generally assumed in the literature (Alsina to appear, Bratt 1991), the lexical causative gets a new Causer role by the lexical rule. This added role is surely an external role, since it is maximally prominent thematically and aspectually. Thus, the contrast given in (17) naturally follows from each lexical form of content verb. In (17)a, the verb 'melt' is a so-called unaccusative verb which denotes a "change of state"; hence it is predicted that this verb can be nominative marked. In (17)b, on the contrary, the causativized verb is no longer an unaccusative verb but denotes an "activity" and a lexical rule guarantees this to have an external argument; hence, this derived verb may not have nominative case under negation.

3.2. Inchoatives

It is worthwhile to look at the class of inchoative verbs.

(18) a.   tanphwung iph-i pwulk-ci-**ka**   anh-ta.
        maple leaf-NOM   red-COMP-NOM   NEG
        'Maple leaves are not red.'

    b.   tanphwung iph-i pwulk-e-ci-ci-**ka**   anh-ass-ta.
        maple leaf-NOM   red-COMP-incho-COMP-NOM   NEG-PAST
        'Maple leaves didn't redden.'

What I am trying to show is that Inchoativization does not involve any externalization of a role. Even though a sentence which has an inchoative verb has a different aspectual meaning from that with a pure stative verb, the change of meaning is expressed inside the second sub-part of the schematic event structure. In other words, by adding an inchoative morpheme *-e ci* to a verbal stem, we express "change of state" rather than "activity". Therefore, we may assume that inchoativization cannot affect the argument structure of the stem. Inchoativization is a case which shows that every change of meaning does not necessarily cause a change in argument structure. Since the case marking on content verb under negation is determined by the argument structure of the verb itself, no change of case marking is expected in this case, as in (18).

    To sum up, the generalization made in section 1 is confirmed in section 2 and 3, where we considered lexical rules which affect the argument structure of the base verb. Causativization shows that the new external argument surely blocks the Nom case marking which was possible before applying the rule.

4. An Account of Case Marking

4.1. Argument Structure of Complex Predicates

Following Sells (1991), I claim that the auxiliary verb may participate as a head (a part of the head) in a sentence by the mechanism of "argument structure sharing" with the content verb. Unlike VP or S complement verbs such as *seltukha* 'persuade' and *malha* 'tell' which have independent argument structures, the auxiliary verbs have associated with them partially or totally underspecified argument structures. While a sentence which has a VP or S complement verb shows biclausal properties,[9] the sentence which has an auxiliary verb shows monoclausal properties, as if there is just one predicate. The argument sharing and event structure sharing between the content verb and the auxiliary verb makes them constitute a complex predicate. The following is the argument structure of the complex predicate which contains the negation verb.

(19)   kkaykkusha-ci anh-ta

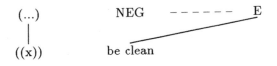

The dots inside the parentheses indicate that all arguments would be inherited from the argument structure of the content verb. One specification of E(vent) linked between two verbs indicates that there is one event involved in this complex predicate.

Note that the negation verb which combines with a verb not having an external argument eventually comes to lack an external argument, since its argument structure is just the same as that of the content verb. Then we have a quite striking fact. The negation verb which lacks an external argument "assigns" accusative case to the content verb. This does not

---

[9] The higher verb or the embedded verb may be modified separately, and may take a separate time adverbial, and different tense.

follow Burzio's generalization which states that "any verbs which fail to assign an external theta role, also fail to assign Accusative case (Burzio 1986)." Before explicating an analysis of accusative marking on the content verb, we need to consider the other case where the content verb does have an external argument.

(20)   ssu-ci anh-ta

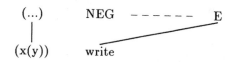

As the negation verb takes the whole argument structure of the content verb in its argument structure, it may have an external argument in this case.[10] Recall that nominative case cannot be attached to the content verb in this case.

4.2. Nominative Marking

Before accounting for case marking in the post-verbal negation construction, let's consider general properties of case marking in Korean. Korean has two kinds of psych verb constructions which show aspectual differences.

(21) a. John-i   kohyang-ul   kuliwe-ha-n-ta.
         John-NOM   hometown-ACC   miss-do-PRES-DECL
         'John is longing for his hometown.'

    b. John-i   kohyang-i   kulip-ta.
        John-NOM   hometown-NOM   miss-DECL
        'John misses his hometown.'

The verb in (21)a, considered as an action verb in Korean,[11] may have the progressive form and imperative form. But this is not true for the verb in (21)b. This verb denotes a state. As we may predict, Nominative case is

---

[10] It is not easy to imagine what kind of activity is involved in "not writing", but let me assume it as a kind of activity, unlike "not being clean" which is a state.

[11] As Koreans regard *believe* as a (psychological) action, not simply a psychological state, the same is true for this verb.

possible only after the second type of psych verb under negation. Thus, we may assume that this verb lacks an external argument.[12] Note that even though this second type of psych verb has two complements, neither of those complements have Accusative case in (21)b. As a matter of fact, there is no instance in which the verb without an external argument assigns Accusative case to its complements. We may generalize that only verbs which lack an external argument assign Nominative Case to their non-subject complement in Korean.[13]

From this generalization, we can account for the nominative marking under negation. As explicated in the previous section, the negation auxiliary verb shares its argument structure with the content verb. Thus, if the content verb lacks an external argument, it follows that the negation verb as well lacks an external argument. Since the content verb itself is a complement of the negation verb, it is predicted to be Nominative marked in this case. On the contrary, if the content verb has an external argument, the negation verb also has an external argument, hence there is only accusative marking on the content verb which is its non-subject complement.

(22)   John-i   kohyang-i$_{non-subj}$ kulip-ci-**ka**$_{non-subj}$ anh-ta.
        John-NOM hometown-NOM   miss-COMP-NOM   NEG-DECL
        'John doesn't miss his hometown.'

By assuming that the property of the complement (content verb) inherits to the head (negation verb) by argument structure sharing, we could account for the case marking in the post-verbal negation construction in the same manner as for the general case.

There is another interesting account of nominative marking by Heycock & Lee (1989). According to them, Korean and Japanese nominative marking depends on predication. According to them, a nominative marked nominal is a syntactic subject, but need not be an argument of the verb. This analysis works well for the multiple nominative constructions.

(23)   John-i$_{subj2}$ [son-i$_{subj1}$ khu-ta$_{pred1}$]$_{pred2}$.
        John-NOM   hand-NOM big
        'John has big hands. / John is generous.'

---

[12] Passivization is also impossible with this verb.

[13] Many previous studies including Kim (1990) and Hong (1991) have assume the nominative case as default, and tried to find a condition for accusative markings. But, for our concern, the case marking seems to be going on the other way around, since the accusative case is allowed anytime, while the nominative is restricted. While it relies on naive intuition, it seems that nominative marking on non-subject complements is a marked case and should not be treated as default.

If we adopt this analysis, we should regard the CI-marked content verb as a syntactic subject. While in cases of multiple nominative constructions, the predicate extends by incorporating an inner nominative marked complement, in our case, the syntactic subject should be assumed to extend by incorporating inner predicate.

(24) [elum-i$_{subj1}$ nok$_{pred1}$-ci-ka]$_{subj2}$ anh-ass-ta$_{pred2}$.
       ice-NOM   melt-COMP-NOM   NEG-PAST-DECL
       'The ice didn't melt.'

In order to pursue this account, we should find evidence that the CI-marked content verb is a nominalized form, since a verb cannot be the subject. There is no case when the complements of the content verb can be marked by genitive case in the post-verbal negation construction, so it is not clear whether nominalization is involved here or not. Moreover, it would be difficult to account for the fact that nominative case is not possible when the content verb has an external argument. Does nominalization depend on the class of verbs?

4.3. Accusative Marking

The Accusative marking on the content verb under negation can be explained as follows. According to Grimshaw & Mester's (1988) account of the light verb construction in Japanese, the light verb *suru* lacks a thematic argument structure but has the accusative case to assign to the verbal noun. Their account applies to the Korean counterpart *ha-ta*.

(25) John-i   yenge-lul   kongpwu-**lul** ha-n-ta.
       John-NOM English-ACC study-ACC   do-PRES-DECL
       'John studies English.'

What is interesting is that the same verb *ha-ta* is involved in both light verb construction and post-verbal negation construction. Thus, we may adopt Grimshaw & Mester's account for our problem: the negation verb has an Accusative case to assign to its sister, while it lacks an independent argument structure. This accusative case which is not associated with the predicate-argument relation functions as a kind of emphatic marker.[14] In this sense, this accusative case may be regarded as similar to delimiters such as *man* 'only', *to* 'also' which attach not only nominals but also other categories including verbs and adverbs.

---

[14] See Ahn (1990), for a discussion of the emphatic accusative case after verbal nouns in light verb constructions in Korean.

(26) a. pang-i   kkaykkusha-ci-**to**   anh-ta.
         room-NOM   be clean-COMP-also   NEG-DECL
         'The room (is not wide and) is not even clean.'

   b.   pang-i   kkaykkusha-ci-**lul**   anh-ta.
         room-NOM   be clean-COMP-ACC   NEG-DECL
         'The room is not CLEAN.'

However, unlike the other delimiters, the emphatic accusative marker is allowed only before the light verb or negation verb. Thus, it is not unreasonable the accusative case marking is the property of the verb, specifically *ha* 'do', even though its function is the same as the other delimiters.

4.4. Semantic Properties

From a semantic point of view, there is an interesting point in a negated sentence which has an emphatic accusative case. Generally, it is assumed that post verbal negation sentence has two scope readings, unlike preverbal negation sentence.

(27) a. ta   an   yeppu-ta.
         every one NEG be pretty
         'Every one is not pretty. (every(not...))'

   b.   ta   yeppu-ci   anh-ta.
         every one be pretty-COMP NEG
         'Every one is not pretty. (every(not...)) / (not(every...))'

As we see in this pair of examples, the pre-verbal negation marker negates only the verb, and it cannot scope over the subject, whereas the post-verbal negation may scope over the whole sentence. In this repect, the negation verb may be a propositional operator. However, if the Accusative case occurs on the content verb, the sentence is unambiguous.

(28)   ta   yeppu-ci-lul   anh-ta.
         every one be pretty-COMP-ACC NEG-DECL
         'Every one is not pretty. (every(not...))'

Although the sentence in (28) involves a post-verbal negation, it has a different reading from (27)b.[15] This contrast may be due to the fact that the accusative case gives an emphasis on the verb, and makes the negation have a scope only over the verb. In other words, the negation verb is not a propositional operator in that case.

---

[15] As for the sentence which has Nom case on the content verb, there seems to be no preferred reading but it is just ambiguous as usual.

5. Conclusion

I have discussed case alternations in post-verbal negation constructions in Korean. According to the argument structure of the content verb, or even more specifically, given the existence of an external argument, Nominative marking is possible on the content verb. The internal structure of the argument structure of a verb is determined by both thematic and aspectual representations. The verbs which denote a "state" or "change of state" are distinguished from verbs which denote an "activity". This aspectual difference is encoded in the lexical form of each verb by specifying only the latter kinds of verbs to have an external argument in their argument structures. We can make a generalization that verbs without external arguments may be nominative marked under negation. This generalization is confirmed by applying a few lexical rules which are assumed to affect the argument structure of the base verb. Even though the base verb allows the nominative marking, the causativized form cannot, and the base verb which may not be nominative marked can be marked after passivization.

I have claimed that Accusative marking which is possible regardless of the verb class should be considered in the same line of accusative marking on verbal nouns in the light verb constructions. In both cases, the case assignee is not a thematic argument of the verb, and the accusative case functions as a kind of emphatic marker. The Nominative marking is accounted for in that the negation verb inherits the case marking property along with the argument structure of the content verb. Since only verbs without an external argument assign nominative case to their non-subject complement, it is predicted that the nominative case is not allowed in every case. In other words, the case-marking property, which is related to the argument structure of the content verb, is eventually responsible for the nominative marking on itself by means of an "argument structure sharing" process.*

References

Alsina, Alex. to appear. On the Argument Structure of Causatives. *Linguistic Inquiry.*

Ahn, Hee-Don. 1989. On Light Verb Construction in Korean and Japanese. In Hajime Hoji (ed.) *Proceedings of the first Southern California Conference on Japanese/Korean Linguistics.* CSLI, Stanford Linguistics Association, 221–237.

---

* I would like to thank Peter Sells for his valuable discussions and comments.

Bratt, Elizabeth Owen. 1991. Korean Periphrastic and Lexical Causatives. Ms. Stanford University.

Bresnan, Joan. 1982. The Passive in Lexical Theory. In J. Bresnan, ed., *The Mental Representation of Grammatical Relations.*

Bresnan, Joan and J. Kanerva. 1989. Locative Inversion in Chichewa: A Case Study of Factorization in Grammar. *Linguistic Inquiry* 20, 1-50

Burzio, L. 1986. *Italian Syntax,* D. Riedel, Dordrecht.

Cho, Jae Ohk. 1988. Suffixed Verb Forms and Compound Verb Constructions. In Eung-Jin Baek (ed.), *Papers from the Sixth International Conference on Korean Linguistics,* International Circle of Korean Linguistics, 77-106.

Grimshaw, Jane. 1990. *Argument Structure.* Linguistic Inquiry Monograph. The MIT Press.

Grimshaw, Jane and A. Mester. 1988. Light-Verbs and θ-Marking. *Linguistic Inquiry* 19, 205-232.

Hong, Ki-Sun. 1991. *Argument Selection and Case Marking in Korean.* Doctoral Dissertation, Stanford University.

Heycock, Caroline & Young-suk Lee. 1989. Subjects and Predication in Korean and Japanese. In Hajime Hoji (ed.) *Proceedings of the First Southern California Conference on Japanese Korean Linguistics.* CSLI, Stanford Linguistics Association.

Kim, Young-joo. 1990. *The Syntax and Semantics of Korean Case: The Interaction between Lexical and Semantic Levels of Representation.* Doctoral Dissertation, Harvard University.

Levin, B. and M. Rappaport. 1986. The Formation of Adjectival Passives. *Linguistic Inquiry* 17, 623-662

Matsumoto, Yo. 1989. Constraints on the 'Intransitivizing' Resultative *-te aru* Construction in Japanese. In Hajime Hoji (ed.) *Proceedings of the First Southern California Conference on Japanese Korean Linguistics.* CSLI, Stanford Linguistics Association.

Rosen, Sara. 1990. *Argument Structure and Complex Predicates.* Doctoral Dissertation, Brandeis University.

Sells, Peter. 1991. Complex Verbs and Argument Structures in Korean. *Proceedings of the Fourth Harvard Workshop on Korean Linguistics.*

Sells, Peter. 1992. Korean and Japanese Lexical Morphology. Ms. Stanford University.

Williams, Edwin. 1981. Argument Structure and Morphology. *Linguistic Review* 1, 81-114.

From Zero to Overt Nominalizer NO: A Syntactic Change in Japanese

KAORU HORIE

University of Southern California

0. Introduction[1]

One of the clearest syntactic differences distinguishing

---

[1]. This is a revised version of the paper presented at USC and at the ABC Japanese/Korean Functional Linguistics Meeting (May 92). My thanks go to Bernard Comrie, Jack Hawkins, Shoichi Iwasaki, Sung-Ock Sohn, and Roger Woodard. I am also grateful to Dwight Atkinson, Maria Polinsky, Satoshi Uehara, and Alexander Vovin, for their helpful comments. Needless to say, I am solely responsible for any possible errors.

The following abbreviations are used in glosses: Acc = Accusative marker; Adn = Adnominal form; Emp = Particles expressing emphasis; Gen = Genitive marker; Ger = Gerundive form of predicates; Imp = Imperative mood marker; Mood = Sentence-final mood marker; Neg = Negative; Nom = Nominative marker; Noml = Nominalizer; Past = Past tense marker; Perf = Perfect aspect marker; Pol = Auxiliary verb expressing politeness toward the addressee; Pre = Present tense marker; Quot = Quotation marker; Res = Auxiliary verb expressing respect toward the person expressed by the grammatical subject; Top = Topic marker.

Classical Japanese (CJ)[2] from Modern Japanese (MJ) is the
latter's replacement of bare ADNOMINAL PREDICATE
FORMS by OVERT NOMINALIZERS in nominalized clauses,
as shown below:
(1) [Te tatake-ba yamabiko-no *kotauru*]   ito urusasi.
    hand clap-as echo-Gen   answer=Adn very annoying
        (Genji monogatari, 11th century; Kondo 1988: 22)
(1') [Te-o tataku-to kodama-ga kotaeru *no/?koto/*ⁿⱺ*]-wa
    Acc clap-when echo-Nom answer   Top

    taihen huyukai-da.
    very annoying-be
     'It is very annoying that there is an echo when (he) claps
     (his) hands'
     In CJ, as seen in (1), bare adnominal predicate forms
(traditionally referred to as 'rentai-kei' in Japanese grammar)
nominalize clauses which don't have overt syntactic heads. In
MJ, on the other hand, adnominal forms, which have merged
with sentence-final forms ('syuusi-kei'), no longer nominalizes
clauses on their own. Hence overt nominalizers are used in
order to nominalize such clauses as seen in (1'). Of the
nominalizers used in MJ, *no* is worthy of particular attention.
No in fact occurs in many of the syntactic environments where
bare adnominal predicate forms once occurred in CJ. (cf.
Yoshikawa 1950, Haraguchi 1978, 1980) Complement clauses
and adjunct clauses, which are illustrated in the following
sentences for both CJ and MJ, are representative of such
environments:

complement clauses
(2) (CJ) [kaguyahime-no yamome   *naru*] -o
            Gen unmarried one be=Adn-Acc
      nageka-si-kere-ba,...
      lament-Res-Past-because
      'because (she) was lamenting that Kaguyahime was
      unmarried (Taketori monogatari, early Heian period;
      Akiba 1978: 64)

---

[2]. By Classical Japanese, I mean the language used from the
9th to the 13th centuries A.D.

(3) (MJ) [Taroo-ga siken-ni sippai si-ta *no*]-o
　　　　　　Nom　exam-in　fail-Past　Noml-Acc

　　sitte　　　　　odoroi-ta.
　　know = Ger　　be surprised-Past
　　'I was surprised to learn that Taroo had failed in the
　　exam'

<u>adjunct clauses</u>
(4) (CJ) [...to tigira-se-tamahi-*si*]-ni, kanawa-zari-keru
　　　　　　Quot pledge-Res-Res Past = Adn　come true-Neg-Past

　　inoti.
　　fate
　　'A life which, although he made a pledge, has not gone
　　according to his wishes' (Genji mogogatari, approx. 11th
　　century; Ikeda 1975: 211)

(5) (MJ) [Taroo-ga yamero-to　　it-ta　　*no*] ni...
　　　　　　stop = Imp-Quot　say-Past
　　'Though Taroo said "Stop it!"...'

　　　　Examples (2) through (5) indicate both an important
similarity and an important difference between CJ and MJ.
　　　　As for the similarity, MJ continues to employ particles
such as *o* or *ni* to mark argument (complement) or adjunct
clauses.
　　　　As for the difference, CJ employed bare adnominal
predicate forms to nominalize entire complement and adjunct
clauses, as in *naru* and *si* of (2) and (4). In MJ, in contrast, the
overt nominalizer *no* is used to nominalize these clauses, as in
(3) and (5).
　　　　In this paper, I will address the following questions:

　　　　(i) Is the replacement of bare adnominal predicate
forms by *no* historically complete? If not, how can we
characterize the contexts which are resistant to the change?

(ii) Can we observe any difference between complement and adjunct clauses regarding the way this syntactic change has taken place?

In order to answer these questions, I will first look at the roles played by particles in encoding complement clauses and adjunct clauses in CJ and MJ.

1. Particles marking complement and adjunct clauses in CJ and MJ

In this section, I will compare the manner in which particles mark complement and adjunct clauses in CJ and MJ in order to see whether any difference can be observed between these two environments regarding the syntactic change in question.

1.1. Particles marking complement clauses in CJ and MJ

Japanese has a number of monosyllabic particles which encode grammatical relations, semantic roles and pragmatic functions. The three major grammatical relations, i.e. subject, direct object, and indirect object, are encoded by the particles *ga*, *o*, and *ni* respectively, as shown below:

(6) Taroo-*ga* ki-ta. (subject)
        come-Past
  'Taroo came'
(7) Taroo-ga hon-*o* kat-ta. (direct object)
        book   buy-Past
  'Taroo bought a book'
(8) Taroo-ga Hanako-*ni* hon-o yat-ta. (indirect object)
                  give-Past
  'Taroo gave a book to Hanako'

Significantly, the particles *ga*, *o* and *ni* mark the nominal clauses which occur as arguments of predicates, i.e. complement clauses. As mentioned in the above section, CJ and MJ present a striking contrast in the way complement clauses are nominalized.

In CJ, the three particles *ga*, *o* and *ni* marked complement clauses nominalized by adnominal predicate forms, as shown below:

(9) [Nati no taki-wa kumano-ni ari   to   *kiku*]-*ga* aware-nari.
    Gen waterfall-Top in exist Quot hear = Adn impressive-be
    'It is impressive to hear that Nati waterfall exists in
    Kumano' (Makura no soshi, approx. 10th century;
    Yamazaki 1965: 405)

(10) [Wakaki nyooboo   nado-no *yomu*]-*o*   kiku-ni...
    young female servant   Gen read = Adn   listen-when
      'When (the prince Kaoru) hears female servants read...'
      (Genji monogatari; Mitani 1965: 85)

(11) ... wasure   tamau-o   [*uresiki*]-*ni*
    forget Res = Adn-Acc   happy = Adn -as
    omoinase-do...
    consider-though
      'Though (the woman) considered (it) a happy thing that
      (he) forgot about (it)' (Genji monogatari; Kitayama
      1951: 59)

In MJ, the particles *ga*, *o* and *ni* continue to mark complement clauses. However, since bare adnominal predicate forms can no longer nominalize complement clauses, the overt nominalizer *no* is commonly used, as shown below:

(12) [Taroo-ga sono mise-kara okane-o nusun-da *∅/no*]-*ga*
    Nom that shop-from money-Acc steal-Past
    hanmeisi-ta.
    turn out-Past
      'It turned out that Taroo had stolen money from the
      shop'

(13) Taroo-wa [Mariko-ga mise-kara detekuru *∅/no*]-*o* mi-ta.
        Top   Nom shop-from come out   Acc see-Past
    'Taroo saw Mary come out of the shop'

(14) Taroo-wa [Mariko-ga totuzen naki-dasi-ta *∅/no*]-*ni*
                suddenly cry-start-Past
    odoroi-ta.
    be surprised-Past
      'Taroo was surprised that Mariko had suddenly started
      to cry'

As seen in (12)-(14), it is normally unacceptable to use bare adnominal form predicates to encode complement clauses before *ga*, *o* and *ni* in MJ. However, there remain semi-lexicalized idioms in MJ which allow bare adnominal predicate forms before *ga*, *o* and *ni*:

(15) [Yatte   *miru*] -*ga* ii.
　　　do=Ger see=Adn   good
　　　'(lit.) It is good to try and do (it)'
　　　'(meaning) Why not do it?'
(16) [Mitome-*zaru*]-*o*   e-nai.
　　　admit-Neg=Adn   obtain-Neg
　　　'(lit.) (I) do not obtain not admitting (it)'
　　　'(meaning) (I) cannot but admit (it)'
(17) Taroo-wa [*hasansuru*]-*ni*   ita-tta.
　　　　　　go bankrupt=Adn reach-Past
　　　'(lit.) Taroo reached going bankrupt'
　　　'(meaning) Taroo ended up going bankrupt'

It is interesting to note that this type of bare adnominal clause is not evenly distributed across the contexts of *ga*, *o* and *ni*. The following figures, which are based on Martin (1988: 890-896) as well as my own counts, demonstrate the uneven distribution of this type of adnominal clause:

(A) Number of existing idioms taking bare adnominal clauses before *ga*, *o* and *ni* in MJ
　　ga: 6
　　o: 2
　　ni: 36

What these figure suggest is that the particle *ni* is more likely to allow bare adnominal clauses like those found in CJ than the other two particles. We will consider the significance of this finding in section 2.

1.2. Particles marking adjunct clauses

The particles *ga*, *o*, and *ni* were also employed to mark another type of clause, i.e. adjunct clauses, in CJ. The following examples illustrate the use of *ga*, *o*, and *ni* as adjunct-markers:

(18) [Mukasi-yori ooku-no sirabyoosi   ari-*si*]-*ga*,
    old times from many-Gen   exist-Past = Adn   though

kakaru mai-wa   imada mi-zu.
such dance-Top   yet see-Neg

> 'Though there had been a lot of Sirabyoosi dances from
> old times, I have never seen such a (wonderful) dance'
> (Heike monogatari, 13th century; Konishi 1969: 107)

(19) [Kokorobosoku oboe-*haberu*]-*o*,   ima namu nagusami
    uneasy   feel-Pol = Adn-though   now Emp calm down

haberi-nuru.
Pol-Perf
> 'Though I have been feeling uneasy, now I'm feeling at
> home' (Genji monogatari; Konishi 1969: 562)

(20) [Ayasigarite yorite   *miru*]-*ni*,   tutu-no
    wonder = Ger approach = Ger see = Adn-when, tube-Gen

naka hikari-tari.
inside glitter-Perf
> 'Wondering what it was, they approached and looked
> inside; the inside of the tube was glittering' (Taketori
> Monogatari; Konishi 1969: 398)

(21) [Kogane-wa kono kuni-ni   naki   mono to
    gold-Top   this country-in not exist   thing Quot

omoe-*ru*] -*ni*,   odanokoori...ni ari.
think-Perf = Adn though   in-exist

> 'Though it was thought that in this land there was no
> gold, (it is found) in Odanokoori' (Shoku Nihongi, 9th
> century; Sansom 1928: 277)

Note that, structurally speaking, the adjunct clauses in
(18)-(21) are identical to the complement clauses in (9)-(11).
That is, both types of clauses are nominalized by adnominal
predicates forms.

As we saw in (12)-(14), the complement-clause marking
function of particles was transferred from CJ to MJ through the

help of overt nominalizer *no*. The adjunct-clause marking function of particles, on the other hand, does not appear to have transferred from CJ to MJ in a straightforward manner. Rather, of the three particles *ga*, *o*, and *ni*, only *ni* appears to have successfully maintained its adjunct-clause marking function in MJ through the medium of *no*:

(22) [Mariko-wa kita] *no ni*, Taroo-wa ko-na-katta.
       Top came   come-Neg-Past
    'Though Mariko came, Taroo didn't'

It is of interest to note that the semantic domains covered by *ni* in CJ have become specialized to encode primarily antithesis (cf.(20), (21) and (22) above). In fact, the combination of an overt nominalizer *no* and a particle *ni* is lexicalized in MJ and the *no ni* functions as one conjunction with the meaning 'although'.

In contrast, neither particles *ga* nor *o* are employed in MJ in a similar way.[3]

(23) *[Mariko-wa ki-ta] *no ga*, Taroo-wa ko-na-katta.
       Top come-Past
    'Although Mariko came, Taroo didn't'

(24) *[Mariko-wa ki-ta] *no o*, Taroo-wa ko-na-katta.
    'Although Mariko came, Taroo didn't'

As noted by Martin (1988) and Cu (1988), there are, however, some instances where the combinations *no ga* and *no o* appear to have taken on an antithetical function:

---

[3]. In MJ,however, the particle *ga* can introduce the following type of coordinate structure, indicating the weak antithetical contrast between two events:
[Taroo-wa ki-(masi)-ta]-*ga* , Hanako-wa ki-masen-desita.
Top come-Pol-Past   Pol = Neg-Past
   'Taroo came, but Hanako didn't'
However, the bracketed clause in this example is not structurally equivalent to the nominalized clause introduced by *ga* in CJ. In fact, it is more plausible to consider the bracketed clause as not involving nominalization. For one thing, the addressee politeness marker -*mas*, which is normally disallowed in adnominal clauses, is perfectly acceptable in this clause.

(25) [Kin no tamago-o umu hazu da-tta   *no*] *ga*, tadano
     gold Gen egg-Acc lay is supposed to-Past   ordinary

    tamago-ni natte   sima-tta.
        to become = Ger   end up-Past

      'Though (the chicken) was supposed to lay golden eggs,
      ordinary eggs turned up' (Cu 1988: 98)

(26) [Okaasan-ga "sekigunha-e   itte mo   ii ga,
     mother-Nom Red Army group-to go = Ger even good but

    uti-ni ite okure" to iu *no*] *o*, mata uti-o   de-tyatta.
    home-at stay give Quot say   again home leave-ended up

      'Though his mother said, "You may join the Red Army
      Group but please live at home", yet he left home
      again'(Martin 1988: 854)

     These examples suggest that the combinations *no ga*
and *no o* may be undergoing lexicalization as has *no ni*.
However, it is not certain at this stage whether such
lexicalization will in fact take place.[4]

---

[4]. The lexicalization of nominalizers and particles is not a
phenomenon peculiar to Japanese. For instance, Korean also
lexicalizes the combination of nominalizers with certain case
particles (Sung-Ock Sohn and Nam-Kil Kim, personal
communication), e.g. *ki + ey*, *(u)m + (u)lo* (i.e. *ki* and
(u)m are nominalizers; and *ey* ('at/in') is a particle which
partially overlaps in meaning with the Japanese particle *ni*; and
(u)lo ('by/with') is a particle which partially overlaps in
meaning with the Japanese particle *de*), as shown below:

Nemwu pissa   { *ki ey* }   an sa-sse-yo.
too   expensive { *m lo* }   Neg buy-Past-Mood

'Because (it) was too expensive, (I) didn't buy (it)'
In fact, both of these combinations, *ki ey* and *(u)m lo*, are
lexicalized and listed in dictionaries as single conjunctions with
the meaning 'because,' just like the Japanese *no de* (cf.
Tsukamoto and Kitajima 1985: 399, 937).

The fact that such combinations as *no ga* and *no o* are not highly lexicalized in MJ is remarkable, especially in light of such expressions as *no de*:[5]

(27) [Mariko-ga ki-ta] *no de*, Taroo-wa ko-na-katta.
'Because Mariko came, Taroo didn't'

De is a particle encoding instrument, means and cause. In contrast to *ga* and *o*, *de* did not take a nominalized clause until fairly recently (i.e. probably not before 17th or 18th centuries, cf. Nihon Kokugo Daijiten 1975, vol. 14: 140). An example of the conjunctive use of *de* is illustrated below:

(28) [Hiatari   no ii]   *de*,   ookina fuki-ga   hae.
     sunniness Gen good   large butterbur-Nom grow
     'A large butterbur has grown as (the place where it has grown) is sunny' (Haihuu Yanagidaru, 18th Century; Haraguchi 1978: 32)

At this stage, suffice it to note that the particle *ni* is allowed to retain its function of marking adjunct clauses through the medium of a nominalizer *no* (i.e. *no ni*), while *ga* and *o* appear to have lost this function (e.g. ?*no ga*, ?*no o*). I will consider the significance of this finding in section 2.

1.3. Summary

To sum up the points made thus far, we have seen how the particles *ga*, *o* and *ni* in CJ transferred their functions of marking complement and adjunct clauses into MJ. The function of marking complement clauses was transferred from CJ to MJ through the medium of an overt nominalizer *no*. The particle *ni*

---

[5]. In traditional Japanese grammar, there are at least two theories regarding the origin of *no de*. One theory argues that it derives from the CJ particle *de* (encoding cause or means) directly taking the adnominal clause, as illustrated in (28) (cf. Nagano 1978). The other theory has it that *no de* derives from the expression *no da* ('it is that') (cf. Cho 1988). The present paper finds the former theory to be more plausible in view of the parallel development of *no ni* from the CJ *ni* directly taking the adnominal clauses.

appears to be more resistant to this functional transfer than *ga* and *o*. This is clearly shown by the existing semi-lexicalized idioms allowing bare adnominal clauses before *ni*, which outnumber the idioms allowing bare adnominal clauses before *ga* and *o* (cf. 1.1).

The function of marking adjunct clauses has been successfully preserved (though semantically narrowed) only in the case of the particle *ni*. This was again made possible through the medium of nominalizer *no*, and the combination *no ni* is lexicalized as one conjunction in MJ. *Ga* and *o*, on the other hand, have apparently lost the function of marking adjunct clauses in a parallel way (cf. 1.2).

The above-mentioned syntactic change can be illustrated as follows:

(B) Functional transfer of particles from CJ to MJ

1. <u>marking complement clauses</u>

CJ	adnominal forms + *ga*	adnominal forms + *o*	adnominal forms + *ni*
MJ	*no* + *ga*	*no* + *o*	*no* + *ni*

adnominal forms less   <   adnominal forms more
likely to be retained   likely to be retained

2. <u>marking adjunct clauses</u>

CJ	adnominal forms + *ga*	adnominal forms + *o*	adnominal forms + *ni*
MJ	?*no ga*	?*no o*	*no ni*

less likely to lexicalize   <   more likely to lexicalize
as one conjunction   as one conjunction

2. Syntactic positions resistant to syntactic change

In the previous section, we observed how the functions of marking complement and adjunct clauses were transferred from CJ to MJ with regard to three particles *ga*, *o* and *ni*. We also observed that there are syntactic environments in MJ in which the transfer of these functions is incomplete (cf. Fig. B). If we compare those syntactic environments in each of the two functional domains, we are led to the following observations:

(I) *Ni* is more resistant than *ga* and *o* to the process of transferring the complement-clause marking function by means of an overt nominalizer *no*.

(II) *Ga* and *o* are more resistant than *ni* to the process of transferring the adjunct-clause marking function by means of an overt nominalizer *no*.

The opposite orientations of these two groups of particles can be illustrated as follows:[6]

(C) Accessibility of particles to functional transfer from CJ to MJ

Complement-clause marking function (transferred through *no*)

more accessible <--------------------> less accessible

$$ga, o \quad > \quad ni \quad > \quad de$$

Adjunct-clause marking function (transferred through *no*)

more accessible <--------------------> less accessible

$$de \quad > \quad ni \quad > \quad ga, o$$

This table makes it possible to understand why some syntactic positions (encoded by particular particles) are more/less accessible to a particular functional transfer mediated by the nominalizer *no*.

Ga and *o* are more or less grammaticalized as subject and direct object marker respectively in MJ. These two particles

---

6. The instrument-coding particle *de*, which we briefly mentioned in (28), is also taken up again in the following table.

are more accessible to the complement-clause marking function than the adjunct-clause marking function. Hence the syntactic positions marked by *ga* and *o* are more receptive to the spread of *no* when these particles encode complement clauses, while resistant to the introduction of no when they encode adjunct clauses.

Like *ga* and *o*, particle *ni* can encode what is referred to in Relational Grammar as TERMS (i.e. subject, direct object and indirect object, cf. Perlmutter and Postal 1983). *Ni* can thus partake in the argument structure of predicates and mark complement clauses. Therefore, the syntactic position marked by *ni* is subject to the spread of *no* when the particle encodes complement clauses. In this respect, *ni* is different from other postpositions such as *de*, which do not mark obligatory arguments and which have not been affected by syntactic change in argument positions. This characteristic of *ni* is illustrated by the following syntactic test:

(29) Co-occurrence with genitive marker *no*

{ **ga-no* , **o-no* , **ni-no* } { *de-no* }

According to this test, *ni* patterns more with the 'grammaticalized' particles like *ga* and *o* than the 'postposition' *de*.

However, *ni* shares certain grammatical functions with other postpositions like *de*, specifically the function of adjunct (clause) marker. Therefore, the syntactic position marked by *ni* is also subject to the spread of *no* when the particle encodes adjunct clauses. Hence the lexicalization of *no ni* took place. This characteristic of *ni* is highlighted by the following syntactic test:

(30) Co-occurrence with topic marker wa

{ **ga-wa* , **o-wa* } { *ni-wa* , *de-wa* }

According to this test, *ni* patterns more with the 'postposition' *de* than the 'grammaticalized' particles *ga* and *o*.

This ambivalent aspect of the particle *ni* has been pointed out by Shibatani (1978) in relation to the application of QUANTIFIER FLOAT. According to Shibatani, while *ga*-marked NPs and *o*-marked NPs freely allow quantifies to float, *ni*-marked NPs split between those which do and those which don't, as shown below:

(31) a. Boku-wa onna no hito-*ni* san yo nin   kite mora-tta.
           women   three four person come receive-Past
    'I received the favor of three or four women coming to me'

  b. *? Kado-o maga-tta tokoro de, boku-wa sira-nai hito-*ni*
     corner turn-Past moment at   know-Neg person-to

    ni sannin   butuka-tta.
    two three person bump into-Past

    'The moment I turned the corner, I bumped into a couple
    of strangers'
  c. *Boku-wa kodomo-*ni* sannin   hon-o   ya-tta.
    I-Top kids-to   three person book-Acc give-Past
  'I gave books to three children' (Shibatani 1978: 352-3)

Though behaviorally ambivalent, *ni* is more accessible to the adjunct-clause marking function than the complement-clause marking function. This point is brought out by the *ni* being more resistant to the introduction of *no* when it encodes complement clauses than when it encodes adjunct clauses.

3. Conclusion and prospectus

In this paper, we observed how the bare adnominal form of predicates in CJ was replaced by the overt nominalizer *no* in MJ. It was further observed that the syntactic positions marked by particles *ga*, *o* and *ni* were more receptive/resistant to the syntactic change, depending on whether these particles encoded complement clauses or adjunct clauses. The degree of receptiveness/resistance to syntactic change highlights the inherent accessibility of these three particles with regard to two distinct functions, i.e. complement-clause marking and adjunct-clause marking. It was shown that *ga* and *o* are more accessible to the complement-marking function, while *ni* is more accessible to the adjunct-marking function.

Before concluding this paper, it should be pointed out that the type of accessibility scale mentioned above has been observed in other linguistic phenomena in Japanese. For instance, Shibatani (1978) proposed the following hierarchy of particles in terms of their accessibility to a variety of syntactic operations (e.g. quantifier float):

(D) Hierarchy of particles (Shibatani 1978: 369)
   $ga > o > ni, (e) >$ other postpositions

Compare this hierarchy to the accessibility scale proposed in the present case, as repeated below:

(C) Accessibility of particles to functional transfer from CJ to MJ

Complement-clause marking function (transferred through no)

more accessible <---------------------> less accessible

ga, o > ni > de

Adjunct-clause marking function (transferred through no)

more accessible <---------------------> less accessible

de > ni > ga, o

Although the accessibility scale (C) does not completely coincide with Shibatani's hierarchy (D), we can still observe that the same relative ordering of particles holds in both cases, i.e., ni is situated between the 'grammaticalized' particles ga and o on the one hand, and postpositions like de on the other.

Furthermore, it is interesting to note that the language-specific accessibility hierarchy and scale (Figures C,D) are reminiscent of the NP ACCESSIBILITY HIERARCHY proposed by Keenan and Comrie (1977), which is shown below:

(E) NP accessibility hierarchy
   Subject > Direct Object > Indirect Object > Oblique >
   Genitive > Object of Comparison (Keenan and Comrie
   1977: 66)

It should be noted here that Keenan and Comrie's NP accessibility hierarchy refers to grammatical relations, while the accessibility hierarchy and scale proposed by Shibatani and here refer to specific case particles. Needless to say, case particles do not necessarily exhibit one-to-one correspondences with specific grammatical relations. Nevertheless, what strikes me as extremely significant is the recurrence of accessibility hierarchy scales underlying a variety of linguistic phenomena, both synchronic and diachronic, and also across languages.

At this stage, it is not entirely clear what kind of human cognition and/or perceptual strategies are represented in these recurrent patterns on accessibility scales. However, it is hoped that the continued development of COGNITIVE LINGUISTICS will shed some real light on this problem in the future.

References

Akiba, Katsue. 1978. A historical study of old Japanese syntax. Unpublished doctoral dissertation. UCLA.

Cho, Sanbun. 1988. *Kara* to *node*. [*Kara* and *node*] Nihongogaku 7. 63-77.

Cu, Le Van. 1988. *No* ni yoru umekomi kozo no hyogen to kino. [Expression and function of structures embedded by *no*] Tokyo: Kuroshio Shuppan.

Haraguchi, Hiroshi. 1971. *No de* no teichaku. [How *no de* came to be used] Bulletin of Shizuoka Joshi Daigaku 4. 31-43.

____. 1978. Rentaikei juntaiho no jittai. [Actual use of bare nominalized forms] Festschrift for Prof. Kasuga Kazuo, 431-50. Tokyo: Oufusha.

____. 1980. Juntai joshi *no* no teichaku. [How the nominalizer *no* came to be used] Kokugogaku 123. 47-57.

Horie, Kaoru. 1991. Event nominalizations in Japanese and Korean: a cognitive perspective. Harvard Studies in Korean Linguistics 4. 503-12.

Ikeda, Tadashi. 1975. Classical Japanese grammar illustrated with texts. Tokyo: Toho Gakkai.

Iwasaki, Shoichi. to appear. Functional transfer in the history of Japanese language. Japanese and Korean Linguistics 2. Stanford: CSLI

Keenan, Edward. and Bernard, Comrie. 1977. Noun phrase accessibility hierarchy and universal grammar. Linguistic Inquiry 8. 63-99.

Kitayama, Keita. 1951. Genji monogatari no goho. [Word usage in the tales of Genji] Tokyo: Iwanami Shoten.

Kondo, Yasuhiro. 1981. Chukogo no juntai kozo ni tsuite. [On
    the nominalized structure of Heian Japanese]
    Kokugo to Kokubungaku 58. 18-31.

Konishi, Jin'ichi. 1969. Kihon kogo jiten. [Basic dictionary of
    classical Japanese] (Revised edition) Tokyo: Taishukan.

Martin, Samuel. 1988. A reference grammar of Japanese.
    Tokyo: Tuttle.

Mitani, Eiichi. 1965. Sogo genji monogatari yokai.
    [Comprehensive exposition of the tales of Genji] Tokyo:
    Saneisha.

Nagano, Masaru. 1979. *Kara* to *node* wa doo chigau ka. [How
    do *kara* and *node* differ?] Nihon no gengogaku
    [Linguistics in Japan] 4. 467-88. Tokyo: Taishukan.
    Nihon kokugo daijiten [Encyclopedia of the Japanese
    language] vol.14. 1975. Tokyo: Shogakkan.

Ono, Susumu et al. (ed.) 1990. Iwanami kogo jiten. [Iwanami
    classical Japanese dictionary] Tokyo: Iwanami Shoten.

Perlmutter, David M. and Postal, Paul M. 1983. The relational
    succession law. In Perlmutter, David M. (ed.) Studies in
    relational grammar 1. 30-80. Chicago: The University of
    Chicago Press.

Sansom, G.B. 1928. An historical grammar of Japanese. Oxford:
    Clarendon Press.

Shibatani, Masayoshi. 1978. Nihongo no bunseki. [Analysis of
    Japanese] Tokyo: Taishukan.

Tsukamoto, Osamu. and Shizue, Kitajima. 1985. Chosengo
    daijiten. [Encyclopedia of the Korean language] vol.1.
    Tokyo: Kadokawa Shoten.

Yamazaki, Yoshiyuki. 1965. Nihongo no bunpo kino ni
    kansurukenkyu.[Study of the grammatical functions in
    Japanese] Tokyo: Kazama Shobo.

Yoshikawa, Yasuo. 1950. Keishiki meishi *no* no seiritsu.
    [Development of a formal noun *no*] Nihon bungaku
    kyositsu, 29-38. Tokyo: Someisha.

Part III

Phonology

Rhythmic Lengthening and Shortening in Korean

HEE-BOK JUNG

University of Washington

1. Introduction

In metrical theory, stress is viewed as a rhythmic distribution of metrical structure (Liberman and Prince 1977).   The representation of stress is encoded suprasegmentally in the metrical structure. Early research in metrical theory has been devoted to providing the basis for a more accurate representation of metrical structure, setting parameters on metrical structure to create a more constrained theory. In a recent work, Hayes (1991) attempts to develop a new parametric metrical theory on bounded feet.   In his theory, foot construction is grounded in a parametric law of rhythmic structure 'Iambic/Trochaic Law' (see section 3). Under this law, he proposes two fundamental parameters: the restriction on foot inventory and the ban on degenerate feet.   In the first parameter (the restriction on foot inventory) he reduces the bounded foot inventory to three canonical foot types, iambs, moraic trochees, and syllabic trochees.[1] Iambs should have the canonical foot type in (1)a and moraic trochees and syllabic trochees should have the canonical foot types in (1)b and c respectively:[2]

---

*I am grateful to Ellen Kaisse and Sharon Hargus for much useful discussion of this material. Errors of form or interpretation are my own.
[1]   The term 'canonical foot' may be understood as a well-formed foot.
[2]   Iambs and moraic trochees are quantity-sensitive, while syllabic trochees are quantity-insensitive.

(1)   Canonical foot types
   a.   Iambs: (.   x)   (x)
                        ∨ -   or   -
   b.   Moraic trochees: (x   .)   (x)
                        - ∨   or   -
   c.   Syllabic trochees: (x   .)
                        σ σ
  (where /∨/ = light σ and /-/ = heavy σ.)

The second parameter (the ban on degenerate feet) is an attempt to parameterize the minimum size of metrical feet. Hayes defines degenerate feet as logically the smallest possible feet. He introduces three types of degenerate feet: single light syllables in iambs and moraic trochees and single syllables in syllabic trochees.

(2)   Degenerate feet (p. 75)
   a.   Iamb   b.   Moraic trochee   c.   Syllabic trochee
    (x)   (x)   (x)
     ∨   ∨   σ

He proposes that languages ban degenerate feet on a parametric basis as stated below:[3]

(3)   Degenerate foot parameter (p. 76)
   a.   Strong prohibition: absolutely disallowed
   b.   Weak prohibition: allowed only in strong position: i.e. when
                              dominated by a higher grid marker

The languages adopting the strong prohibition do not construct degenerate feet at all, while those adopting the weak prohibition permit degenerate feet early in the derivation, but they are repaired by metrical rules (rhythmic lengthening or shortening) or reparsing of foot boundaries.

   The question addressed in this paper is what is the role of these parameters (the restriction on foot inventory and the ban on degenerate feet) in determining stress patterns in Korean. I first consider a formal analysis of the stress pattern of Korean spoken in Seoul, focusing on the stress pattern in the domain of the word.[4] From a metrical analysis of

---

[3]   There is a third value of the degenerate foot parameter proposed in Hayes (1991), which refers to a non-prohibition on degenerate feet. In languages with this non-prohibition, degenerate feet may be freely constructed.
[4]   The Seoul dialect in Korean has been described as a stress language informally in S. N. Lee (1960), H. B. Lee (1974) and (1989), and H. Y. Lee (1990). I benefited

Korean, I conclude that Korean has both lengthening and shortening rules that can be understood in terms of the realization of the canonical iamb. I also show that minimal word phenomena can only explain a subset of the lengthening phenomena. Finally, I conclude that Korean is an iambic stress language and respects the weak prohibition on degenerate feet.

2. Stress pattern

Korean establishes a binary distinction involving the weight of a syllable, dividing syllables into heavy and light syllables. If we consider the stress rules on the rime projection, the distinction can be characterized as one of branching (heavy) versus non-branching (light) rimes:

(4)a.　　light (/ ∨ /)　　　　　b.　　heavy (/ - /)

$$
\begin{array}{ccc}
\sigma & \sigma & \sigma \\
| & /\backslash & /\backslash \\
\mu & \mu\,\mu & \mu\,\mu \\
/\,| & /|\ | & /|\ | \\
C\ V & C\ V\ V \quad \text{or} \quad & C\ V\ C
\end{array}
$$

　　　Take a look at the following examples which are all multisyllbic words. (Some examples of monosyllabic words will be presented in section 4.1.1.) Stress falls on the initial syllable if it is heavy as illustrated in (5)a and the second syllable if the initial syllable is light as shown in (5)b.[5]

(5)a.　/ - ∨ /　　　t.ɛ:sa　　　　　'matter of great concern'
　　　　　　　　　　s.i:kye　　　　'visibility'
　　　　　　　　　　p.oksu　　　　'revenge'
　　　　/ - - /　　　t.ɛ :so:　　　　'great and small sizes'
　　　　　　　　　　s.i:caŋ　　　　'market'
　　　　　　　　　　s.ipsa:　　　　'fourteen'
　　　　　　　　　　n.aks∂n　　　　'defeat in an election'
　　　　/ - - - /　　p.akmulkwan　'museum'
　　　　　　　　　　ky.o:hwe:taŋ　'church'
　　　　/ - - ∨ /　　p.o:to:pu　　　'press section'
　　　　　　　　　　s.a:kunca　　　'four gentlemanly plants'
　　　　　　　　　　n.ankoŋsa　　　'difficult construction work'
　　　　/ - ∨ ∨ /　ky.o:toso　　　'prison'

---

much from reading H. B. Lee (1989) which describes a regular interaction of syllable quantity with stress in Korean.
[5]　Note that because of typographical limitations stressed syllables are represented by a lowered dot: e.g. [.a] represents stressed [a].

	c.amcari	'dragon fly'
/ - ∨ - /	.i:sacaŋ	'chief director'
	m.uncipaŋ	'threshold'
/ - ∨ ∨ ∨ /	y.okc'ik∂ri	'abusive language'
	.aktakuri	'brawl'
/ - - ∨ ∨ /	s.a:my∂nchoka	'be surrounded by foes on all sides'
/ - - - ∨ /	p.ansinpulsu	'hemiplegia'

b.	/ ∨ ∨ /	pup.u	'husband and wife'
		muc.i	'lack of knowledge'
		im.a	'forehead'
	/ ∨ - /	tos.i:	'city'
		pum.o:	'father and mother'
		par.am	'wind'
		suc.ip	'collection'
	/ ∨ ∨ ∨ /	toc.aki	'pottery and porcelain'
		c∂k.ori	'(traditional) upper garment'
		poc.aki	'wrapper'
	/ ∨ ∨ - /	muc.ehan	'limitless'
	/ ∨ - ∨ /	cat.oŋcha	'automobile'
		toy.e:ka	'pottery artist'
	/ ∨ - - /	suc.iks∂n	'perpendicular line'
		cih.a:sil	'basement'
	/ ∨ ∨ ∨ ∨ /	muc.imakci	'rudeness'
		ac.um∂ni	'aunt'

The generalization is thus that Korean stress rules refer to a distinction between heavy and light syllables as illustrated in (4) above. A foot construction rule forms iambs from left to right and a word layer rule places a grid mark in the left-most position.[6]

(6) Korean stress
   a. Syllable weight: / - / = CVV or CVC,   / ∨ / = CV

---

6   Historically Korean has been losing the vowel length contrast. Due to this change, some variational stress patterns are found in the Seoul dialect today, which are different from the stress pattern analysed in this paper. I will briefly consider one example here. Among young people we can find a dialect in which the vowel length is no longer distinctive. Only CVC syllables count as heavy syllables in this dialect. The loss of the quantity opposition in vowels produces changes in stress rules.

b.　Foot construction:　Form iambs from left to right
c.　Word layer:　　　　 End Rule left[7]

Given these rules (6), we can now derive the stress pattern as demonstrated below:

(7)a.　(x 　　)
　　　　(x)
　　　　 -　 ∨
　　　　 t ɛː s a
　　　　'matter of great concern'

b.　(x 　　　　)　　　Word layer
　　 (x) (.　 x)　　Foot construction
　　　 -　∨　 -
　　　 iː　s a c a ŋ
　　　'chief director'

c.　(　 x 　)
　　 (.　 x)
　　　∨　 -
　　　p a r a m
　　　'wind'

d.　(x 　　　　)　　　Word layer
　　 (x) (x)　　　 Foot construction
　　　 -　 -　 ∨
　　 n a n k o ŋ s a
　　 'difficult construction work'

e.　(　 x)
　　 (.　 x)
　　　∨　∨
　　 p u p u
　　 'husband and wife'

f.　(　 x 　)　　　　 Word layer
　　 (.　 x)　　　　 Foot construction
　　　∨　∨　∨
　　 t o c a k i
　　 'pottery'

One interesting point here is that when a word begins with two light syllables, an even iamb (/ ∨ ∨ /) is constructed as presented in (7)e and f. Considering the canonical foot type of iambs in (1)a (namely, / ∨ - / or / - /), it would seem that this even iamb here constitutes a contradiction. However in the next sections I will show that lengthening rules adjust this situation.

3.　Iambic/Trochaic Law

Let us briefly consider the 'Iambic/Trochaic Law' which is a central concept in Hayes (1991). In traditional metrical analysis, the foot template of iambs is considered as a single heavy syllabic foot or a disyllabic foot in which the right member is strong and the left member must be a light syllable. Under such an analysis, the following three types of the foot template are found:

---

[7]　In Hayes (1991) the term 'End Rule (left/right)' is used to describe a metrical rule with the following effects: 1) create a new metrical constituent on top of the existing structure and 2) place a grid mark forming the head of this constituent in the (leftmost/rightmost) available position (p. 50).

(8)a .　(x)　　　b.　　(. x)　　　c.　　(. x)

　　　　-　　　　　　　∨ ∨　　　　　　　∨ -

Hayes proposes a slightly different formulation of the iambic foot template. He doesn't allow the even foot (/ ∨ ∨ /) like (8)b for the iambic foot template. As we have already seen in (1)a above, he claims that the canonical foot types of iamb only include (/ - /) and (/ ∨ - /). His claim is based on perceptual results of the prefered groupings of durational and intensity contrast as illustrated in (9)a and b respectively.

(9)a.　Durational contrast: ... [– —] [– —] [– —] [– —] [– —] ...
　　b.　Intensity contrast:　...　[x x] [x x] [x x] [x x] [x x] [x x] ...

The durational contrast reveals the pattern of iambic groupings, while the intensity contrast shows the structure of trochaic groupings. Based on such perceptual results, Hayes proposes the law of well-formed rhythmic structure, 'Iambic/Trochaic Law' as follows:

(10)　Iambic Law:　elements contrasting in duration naturally form
　　　　　　　　　　　groupings with final prominence.
　　　Trochaic Law: elements contrasting in intensity naturally form
　　　　　　　　　　　groupings with initial prominence.

Given the Iambic/Trochaic Law (especially the Iambic Law), we can see here that the even iamb (/ ∨ ∨ /) is not a well-formed rhythmic structure in that it does not construct a durational contrast, hence it can not be the canonical foot type of the iamb.

4.　Segmental rules

In this section we will consider some segmental rules (rhythmic lengthening and shortening) which can be construed as phonological processes creating canonical iambic feet and respecting the ban on degenerate feet.

4.1.　Rhythmic lengthening

4.1.1.　Light monosyllabic words

Korean contains monosyllabic words which may be light (CV) or heavy (CVV and CVC). In metrical structure the light monosyllabic words would produce degenerate feet like (11)a below, whereas the heavy monosyllabic ones will produce canonical feet like (11)b.

(11)a. (x)   b. (x)

         ∨   -

Some examples of lexically light monosyllabic words are given in (12)a and I also show some examples of lexically long monosyllabic words as presented in (12)b.

(12)a. /CV/   b. /CVV/

/so/	'cow'	/so:/	'lawsuit; small'
/tɛ/	'(bamboo) culm'	/tɛ:/	'generation; large'
/pi/	'rain'	/pi:/	'ratio'
/pɛ/	'ship'	/pɛ:/	'double'
/i/	'tooth'	/i:/	'two'

cf. /so-kacuk/ [sog.a:cuk]   /so:-kacok/ [s.o:gacok]
      'cow-leather'   'small-familly'
      /tɛ-namu/ [tɛn.a:mu]   /tɛ:-tɛ:-ro/ [t.ɛ:dɛro]
      'bamboo-tree'   'from generation to generation'
      /pi-ka/   [pig.a:]   /pi:-ka/   [p.i:ga]
      'rain-subjetive'   'ratio-subjective'

Since these light monosyllabic words in (12)a consist of only a degenerate foot, we can see here that Korean is not a type of language adopting the strong prohibition on degenerate feet like (3) which disallows degenerate feet absolutely. Korean does not allow degenerate feet freely, either, since no light monosyllables are found in surface forms. In Korean they are all lengthened phonetically as illustrated in (13).

(13)   so   [so:]
        tɛ   [tɛ:]
        pi   [pi:]
        pɛ   [pɛ:]
        i   [i:]

Here we can see that a process of vowel lengthening makes it possible for unstressable words to be stressed. Korean can thus be analysed as invoking the weak prohibition on degenerate feet like (3)b which allows degenerate feet in a metrically strong position. The syllables in the light monosyllabic words may be construed as being dominated by a higher grid mark since they all bear a main stress. Degenerate feet can be created early in the derivation, but they are repaired by a rhythmic lengthening rule (apparently vowel lengthening here) creating the canonical iamb in (1)a and respecting the weak prohibition on degenerate feet in (3)b. The rhythmic lengthening rule may be stated as follows:

(14)   Rhythmic lengthening

$$
\begin{array}{c}
(\ x\ ) \\
\sigma \\
|\ \backslash \\
\phi \rightarrow \mu\ /\ \ \mu\ \text{--}
\end{array}
$$

This rule is illustrated in the following derivation.

(15)

$$
\begin{array}{ccccc}
 & & (\ x\ ) & & (\ x\ ) \\
\sigma & & \sigma & & \sigma \\
| & & | & & /\backslash \\
\mu & & \mu & & \mu\ \mu \\
/\,| & & /\,| & & \backslash\ / \\
s\ o & \rightarrow & s\ o & \rightarrow & s\ o\text{:} \quad \text{'cow'}
\end{array}
$$

Foot construction   Rhythmic lengthening

The application of the rhythmic lengthening rule phonetically neutralizes the underlying length difference between light monosyllabic words and lexically long monosyllabic words as contrasted below.

(16)a. /CV/   b. /CVV/

/so/	[so:]	/so:/	[so:]
/tɛ/	[tɛ:]	/tɛ:/	[tɛ:]
/pi/	[pi:]	/pi:/	[pi:]
/pɛ/	[pɛ:]	/pɛ:/	[pɛ:]
/i/	[i:]	/i:/	[i:]

McCarthy and Prince (1986) argue that there is a minimum placed on the size of a word ('minimal word' phenomena). Languages have a tendency not to allow words of a single degenerate foot.[8] Korean appears not to allow such words in a light monosyllable, but only in surface forms. In Korean, as we have seen above, the light monosyllabic words are allowed in underlying representations, but they are converted to heavy ones by a lengthening rule, hence no light monosyllabic words can be found in phonetic realizations. We can see here that the requirement of the

---

[8]   There are languages in which every word must contain at least two moras (e.g. Fijian, Hawaian, Palestinian Arabic, etc.). Content words in these languages cannot consist of a single light syllable. There are also languages which require at least two syllables for every content word (e.g. Pintupi, Mohawk, Anguthimri, etc.).

word minimum, in Korean, can be understood in terms of the realization of the canonical iamb. However, this requirement can only explain a subset of the lengthening phenomena.

4.1.2. Multisyllabic words

Korean shows another rhythmic lengthening rule. In multisyllabic words, as we have seen in (5)b, stress falls on the second syllable when the initial syllable is light. The second syllable which is stressed can be either heavy or light. If the second syllable is heavy, the application of the metrical rule in (6) will produce canonical iambs like (1)a, but if the second syllable is light, then it would create an ill-formed rhythmic structure (namely, an even iamb ($\vee \vee$)) which violates the Iambic Law. In Korean , however, we can observe that the short vowel in the metrically strong position is pronounced longer than that in the metrically weak position, as in the following examples:[9]

(17)   pup.u   [pub.u:]   'husband and wife'
        muc.i   [muj.i:]   'lack of knowledge'
        toc.aki   [toj.a:gi]   'pottery and porcelain'
        muc.ehan [muj.e:han] 'limitless'

The short syllable in a metrically strong position is, thus, lengthened to create a well-formed foot template (namely, a canonical iamb). This second rule of rhythmic lengthening can be represented as follows:

(18)   Rhythmic lengthening

$$(\ . \quad x \ )$$
$$\sigma \quad \sigma$$
$$| \quad | \ \backslash$$
$$\phi \ \rightarrow \ \mu \ / \ \mu \ \mu \ \text{--}$$

This rule is illustrated in the following derivations:

(19)a.

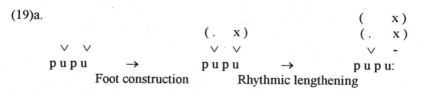

               Foot construction   Rhythmic lengthening

---

[9]   It should be noted that these lengthened vowels are underlyingly short. Evidence can be drawn from words in which such vowels are not in the second position. As we will see in the following examples, they are all short and unstressed when they are word-initial, e.g. puin [pu.in] 'wife', cisik [cis.ik] 'knowledge', caki [cak.i:] 'porcelain', and cehan [ceh.an] 'limit'.

b.

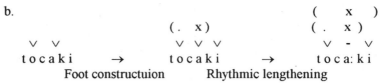

| Foot constructuion | Rhythmic lengthening |

The application of the rhythmic lengthening rule, thus, creates canonical iambic feet, changing (/ ∨ ∨ /) to (/ ∨ - /). Now we might recapitulate the rhythmic lengthening rules both in (14) and (18) under a single and unified representation as demonstrated below.

(20) Rhythmic lengthening

$$
\begin{array}{c}
((\,.\,)\ \ x) \\
(\sigma)\ \ \sigma \\
|\quad\ |\ \backslash \\
\phi\ \rightarrow\ \mu\ /\ (\mu)\ \mu\ \text{--}
\end{array}
$$

4.2. Rhythmic shortening

Korean also contains a phonological process of rhythmic shortening. In multisyllabic words stress falls on the first syllable when it is heavy, no matter what type of weight the rest of the syllables may have. The rest may be either heavy or light. Consider the following examples.

(21) s.o:tosi: [s.o:dosi]   'small (urban) town'
       s.i:min   [s.i:min]   'townspeople'
       s.o:si:min   [s.o:simin]   'lower middle class townspeople'

Focusing on the surface form of /si:/ in each example, we can see that it turns out short (namely, [si]) whenever it is located in a metrically weak position (namely, /si:/ in /so:tosi:/ and /so:si:min/). This process of rhythmic shortening contributes to creating culminativity in the sense that each word has a single prominent syllable. The rule of rhythmic shortening changes metrically weak long vowels (VV) to short ones (V) in the word layer.

(22) Rhythmic shortening

| (x   ) | (x   ) | Word Layer |
| (x) ((.) x) | (x) ((.) x) | Foot Construction |

Consider now the derivational processes. In the example /so:tosi:/ in (21), the word-initial heavy /so:/ and the word-final heavy /si:/ form canonical iambs separately at the foot construction level. The word layer rule will create a new constituent including both /so:/ and /si:/ and the end rule left will place a higher grid mark on the initial syllable /so:/. At this stage now the word-final /si:/ is metrically weak, hence it is visible to the rule (22) and is changed to a short [si].

(23)
```
( x ) ( .    x )
  σ    σ    σ
  Λ    |    Λ
  μμ   μ    μμ
  V    |    V
  so:  to   si:        Foot construction


( x              )
( x ) ( .    x )
  σ    σ    σ
  Λ    |    Λ
  μμ   μ    μμ
  V    |    V
  so:  to   si:        Word Layer


( x              )
( x ) ( .    x )
  σ    σ    σ
  Λ    |    |
  μμ   μ    μ
  V    |    |
  so:  to   si         Vowel shortening
```

Now consider the example /so:si:min/ in (21). The application of the foot construction rule will produce three metrically strong feet, since they are all heavy. In the word layer, however, only the initial syllable will be stressed according to the end rule left. The second syllable which is a long vowel gets metrically weak, hence finally it undergoes shortening.

(24)
```
( x )  ( x )  ( x )
  σ      σ      σ
  Λ      Λ      Λ
  μμ     μμ     μμ
  V      V      ||
  so:    si:    min        Foot construction
```

```
( x                )
( x ) ( x ) ( x )
  σ     σ     σ
  Λ     Λ     Λ
 μμ    μμ    μμ
  V     V    ||
 so:   si:   min          Word layer


( x                )
( x ) ( x )( x )
  σ     σ    σ
  Λ     |    Λ
 μμ     μ   μμ
  V     |   ||
 so:    si  min           Rhythmic shortening
```

Here are more examples found in Korean which illustrate the same rhythmic shortening rule in (22).

(25)	ye:po:ka	[y.e:boga]	'forecaster'
	tɛ:so:py∂n	[t.ɛ:soby∂n]	'urine and faeces'
	tɛ:kwa:k∂	[t.ɛ:gwag∂]	'past perfect tense'
	sa:mu:sil	[s.a:musil]	'office'
	sinbi:kam	[s.imbigam]	'mysticism'
	c∂ŋpo:pu	[c.∂ŋbobu]	'information bureau'

The application of the rhythmic shortening rule (22) makes it possible for each word to preserve not only the well-formed foot structure but also culminativity.

5.   Conclusion

In metrical theory, current research is contributing to the formalization of a tightly constrained universal foot inventory. Hayes (1991) proposed two fundamental parametric principles of the metrical theory: the restriction on foot inventory and the ban on degenerate feet. In this paper I have tried to show that these parameters are crucial to an account of the stress pattern of Korean. Korean has both lengthening and shortening rules that can be best understood in terms of the realization of the canonical iamb and these rules contribute to creating culminitivity. Korean respects the weak prohibition on degenerate feet and the minimal word phenomena can only explain a subset of the lengthening phenomena.

References

Everett, D. L. 1988. On Metrical Constituent Structure in Pirahã. Natural Language and Linguistic Theory 6. 207-246.

Hayes, B. 1981. A Metrical Theory of Stress Rules. Indiana University Linguistics Club.

Hayes, B. 1984. The Phonology of Rhythm in English. Linguistic Inquiry 15. 33-74.

Hayes, B. 1991. Metrical Stress Theory: Principles and Case Studies. Ms., UCLA.

Kim, C. K.1980. Tonal Systems in Kyongsangdo Dialect (in Korean). Seoul: Kwahaksa.

Kiparsky, P. 1979. Metrical Structure Assignment is Cyclic. Linguistic Inquiry 10. 421-441.

Ladd, D. R. 1986. Intonational Phrasing: the Case for Recursive Prosodic Structure. Phonology Yearbook 3. 311-340.

Lee, H. B. 1974. The Rhythm and Intonation in Seoul Speech (in Korean). Language Research 10-2. Seoul.

Lee, H. B. 1989. Korean Grammar. Oxford University Press.

Lee, H. Y. 1990. The Structure of Koean Prosody. Ph.D. Dissertation. University College London.

Lee, S. N. 1960. A Study of Accent in Modern Seoul Speech (in Korean). Kugohak Nongo. Seoul:Tongyang Chulphansa.

Liberman, M. and A. Prince. 1977. On Stress and Linguistic Rhythm. Linguistic Inquiry 8. 249-336.

McCarthy, J. and A. Prince. 1986. Prosodic Morphology. MIT Press, Cambridge.

Moon, H. K. 1974. A Descriptive Study of Korean Tone (in Korean). Seoul: Sejong Chulphan Kongsa.

Nespor, M. and I. Vogel. 1986. Prosodic Phonology. Fortis, Dordrecht.

Prince, A. 1983. Relaing to the Grid. Linguistic Inquiry 14. 19-100.

Notes on Some Japanese-Korean Phonetic Correspondences

ALEXANDER VOVIN

The University of Michigan

The goal of this paper is to provide some critical comments on several Japanese-Korean phonetic correspondences proposed in John Whitman's dissertation (1985). Whitman's work is of outstanding scholarly quality and it provides a solid basis for the further investigation of the genetic relationship between Japanese and Korean. Some of Whitman's proposals, such as his theory of the loss of *-r- and *-m- in Proto-Japanese (PJ) are extremely important, since they uncover a significant number of new etymologies. However, some correspondences established by Whitman are doubtful and require reconsideration. Samuel E. Martin believes that Whitman's etymologies demonstrating Proto-Japanese-Korean (PJK) *g and *z are unconvincing (1991: 273). I will add to this list also Whitman's PJK *š, *y and his hypothesis on the origin of Middle Korean (MK) aspirates.

I base my criticism on four major points: 1) a new phoneme proposed for a proto-language should not be in complementary distribution with another phoneme; 2) Japanese-Korean comparative linguistics has to acknowledge old achievements and recent developments in Altaic comparative studies; 3) the best way to disprove an etymology is to offer a better etymology; 4) while

338

there is a superb PJ reconstruction (Martin 1987), the lack of Proto-Korean (PK) reconstruction as a whole seriously hampers Japanese-Korean comparative studies. Thus, straightforward comparison of Old Japanese (OJ) or even PJ with MK may lead to wrong results.

Whitman's PJK*g > OJ k-, MK n- is based on four etymologies:

1) PJK *gar > MK nal H 'day', OJ -ka (counter), key 'day'. There is a better traditional etymology for the Middle Korean word, proposed by G. Ramstedt: Mongolian nara(n) 'sun' (1949: 159). PJ *ka-Ci 'day' ?1.3a (Martin 1987, 430) may be compared in its turn to MK hoi H 'sun' < PK *x[a/o]Ci, both yielding Proto-Altaic (PA) *k^h[a/o] 'day', 'sun'.

2) PJK *gat > MK nas- L 'is better than', OJ kat- 'is better than'. It seems that the meaning of the Japanese verbal is cited from the Iwanami kogo jiten (Ohno 1974: 304), based on poem 3450 in the Manyôshû (ca 758 AD):
Wokusa=wo=to Wogusa=zuke=wo=to sipo=pune narabe=te mi=reba Wogusa kat=imeri
Wokusa=man=and Wogusa=suke=man=and tide=boat put side by side look=if Wogusa win/surpass=seems
If to compare sea boats of the man from Wokusa (place name) and of suke (title) from Wogusa, it seems that Wogusa['s boat] beats/surpasses [that of Wokusa].

The form katimeri here allows the interpretation 'it seems that it is better', but it is obvious that this meaning is secondary and is derived from 'to beat', 'to surpass', 'to win'. Thus, the cited meaning of the Japanese form is doubtful, even leaving aside the phonetic difficulty: the correspondence OJ t : MK s < ñ (Vovin, forthcoming).

3) PJK *go(+-i) > MK noy H 'smoke', 'vapor'; OJ key 'smoke'. Again, there is another etymology for the Korean word which is far more satisfactory from the phonetic point of view: Proto-Manchu-Tungus (PMT) *nu[b/w]- 'soot', 'to smoke (something)' (Ramstedt 1949: 158). Martin reconstructs PJ *keyburi 3.1 ?< *k^a/oCinpu-r[a-C]i (1987: 448), and Starostin proposes PJ *kaiN=puri (1991: 277). Neither is satisfactory, since OJ key is obviously attested in the meaning 'smoke', e.g. in the compound po-key 'smoke of the fire'. Thus, following Whitman, I suggest PJ *kaCi 2.1 'smoke'. The comparison with Proto-Mongolian *kei 'wind', 'air' (Starostin 1991: 277) is dubious, since there is no evidence for an intervocalic consonant loss in Mongolian. I propose a comparison with OT (Old Turkic) qalïq 'air', 'aerial space', 'sky' (note that OJ key may also be used in reference to fog) < PA *k[^h]al̦i 'air', 'smoke'.

4) PJK *gimü > MK nim R, OJ kyimu-/kyimyi id. To the best of my knowledge, there is no kimu- in OJ. The citation is probably based on Middle Japanese (MJ) kimuti 'you', attested in the Kagerô nikki (ca. 950 AD) (Ohno 1974: 372). In light of MJ namudi 'you' (cf. OJ na 'you'), it is not possible to analyze kimuti as kimu-ti. In any case, a better etymology for the Japanese word probably is MK -kum in nim-kum 'king'. Keeping in mind the primary sacred function of sovereigns in Japan and Korea, cf. also Proto-Turkic (PT) *kjam 'shaman' (Old Turkic qam, Tuvinian xam 'shaman',

Chuvash *jum-ša* 'sorcerer'). It may be that PJ **kamu-* 2.3 'god' and Ancient Korean **kam* 'goddess' (attested in the *Zhou shu*) are also related.

I will also demonstrate that PJK **š* is in complementary distribution with PJK **s*. Whitman provides nine etymologies to illustrate PJK **š* > MK *h-*, OJ *s-* (1985, 235-236) as opposed to PJK **s* > MK *s-*, OJ *s-*. This new protophoneme has quite a peculiar distribution: it occurs only in initial position.

1) The comparison of MK *ho* L, *hon* L, *honolh* LL 'one' with OJ (more exactly MJ, since the word in question is attested only from Heian period) *su* L 'plain', 'simple', 'unadorned' needs to be rejected. The Japanese word is an obvious loanword from Middle Chinese *swo* 'plain', 'simple', 'unadorned'.

2) MK *hwowak* LH 'mortar' is compared with OJ *usu* LH 'mortar' with a note that the first vowel in Japanese form is prothetic. The basis for such a conclusion remains unclear. Therefore, the etymology ought to be rejected until the prothetic nature of the first vowel in OJ *usu* is proved.

3) The comparison of MK *heli* LH 'waist' with OJ *sǫ-/se* '(anatomical) back' overlooks traditional comparison with OJ *kǫsi* 'waist' which is a better semantical and phonetical fit than OJ *sǫ-/se* . PA **kʰäl₂i* 'waist'.

4) MK *hye* H < *hyel* 'tongue' and OJ *sita* LL 'tongue' might stand a chance if there were no better etymologies: PMT **xileŋu* 'tongue' (Ramstedt 1948, 61) and PM **kele-*. PA **kʰile* 'tongue'. Given this, we can conclude that the Japanese word is not related.

5) The comparison of MK *hun=ho* LL 'is plentiful' with OJ *sǫdar=* < *sǫn=tar=* 'is plentiful' and *sǫnapey=* 'completely supplies', 'makes an offering to the gods' also seems dubious. *Sǫn=* in OJ *sǫdar=* may be anything, since *tar=* alone means 'is plentiful', 'is enough'. Besides, there is no proof that *sǫn=* in *sǫnapey=* is related to the *sǫn=* in *sǫdar=*. That makes comparison of MK *hun=ho=* with OJ *sǫnapey=* dubious semantically.

Now we come across three etymologies where MK *h-* really corresponds to *s-* in Japanese and/or other Altaic languages. But in all these cases MK *h-* is followed by MK *-o-* which corresponds to [i] or an iodized vowel in other languages:

6) MK *ho=* 'does', OJ *su-* 'does'. The underlying stem of the OJ verbal is really *si=* as can be seen on the basis of the mizenkei (imperfective 'base') *se-* : *semu* < **si=am=u* 'will do', *senu* < **si=an=u* 'does not do (participle)'. Thus, *si+u* > *su*. MK *ho=* contains the reduced vowel /o/ which probably goes back to **i*. PA **si=* 'does'. This sugestion is supported by the two following etymologies.

7) MK *hoi=* H 'white', OJ *sirwo=* LL, *sira=* LL 'white'. Cf. also well-known etymologies from the other Altaic languages: PT **siɔrï* 'white', 'yellow' (Chuvash *šurǝ* 'white', OT *sarï* 'yellow'), PM **sira* 'yellow'. The combined evidence from Japanese, Turkic and Mongolian demonstrates that

the PA vowel in the first syllable was either *i* or iodized. PA *si[V]r₁a* 'white'.

8) MK *holk* L 'earth', 'soil', 'clay' as Whitman notes himself has parallels in Tungusic and Mongolian languages which all have the vowel /i/ in the first syllable: PMT *sir[a/u]* 'sand', PM *siruga* 'dust', 'soil', 'earth'. OJ *su* 'sand' cited by Whitman probably also belongs here, being a result of contraction: *siru* > *siu* > *su*. PA *siru=k* 'earth', 'sand'.

Thus, I come to the conclusion that *s*- and *h*- in Middle Korean as reflexes of PA *s* are in complementary distribution, with *ho*- being a special reflex of PA *si*-. As such, there is no need to propose a new protophoneme *š.

9) The only one etymology where MK *h*- corresponding to OJ *s*- is not followed by MK /o/ < PA *i* is the comparison of MK *hanolh* 'sky' with OJ *swora* 'sky' < PJ *saCura* < *sanura*. However, one etymology is obviously not enough for the establishment of a new protophoneme. Therefore, I prefer to dismiss the case of PJK *š.

Only two etymologies support the reconstruction of PJK *z:

1) The comparison of MK *sil* R 'thread' < PK *sirV* and OJ *ito* L H 'thread' is unconvincing in light of PMT *sire* 'thread' and PM *sir=* 'thread' (SSTM II 1977: 98).

2) The comparison of MK *sel* R 'new year', 'year of age' < PK *selV* and OJ *-zo* 'year' (?— A.V.) in *kozo* 'last year' is also dubious from the phonetic and semantic points of view. OJ /z/, as Whitman notes himself, undoubted goes back to *-ns-*. In addition, the semantic derivation 'last year' < *'this year' seems to be completely unrealistic. I suggest a comparison with PMT *see* 'year of age' < *se[r]e*.

There are five etymologies supporting the reconstruction of PJK *y-*. However, two of them have better parallels for the Japanese counterparts in Tungusic, and two have troubled semantics:

1) Even if the comparison of MK *yet*- L < *yot*- L in *yetulp* 'eight' with OJ *ya=* H 'eight' were true, it would be strange that Japanese and Korean share only one numeral 'eight'. Whitman overlooks comparisons of Japanese and Tungusic system numerals proposed by Murayama Shichirô. Murayama demonstrated that numerals 4, 7-9 in Japanese and Tungusic are cognates (1962, 166). With additions concerning 'five' and 'ten' (Miller 1972: 221), 'six' (Starostin 1991) and 'three' (Vovin, forthcoming) we have the following system of numerals, common for Proto-Japanese and Proto-Manchu-Tungus:

	Proto-Japanese	Proto-Manchu-Tungus	Proto-Altaic
'three'	*mi= < *ñi=	*[ñ]ila=	*ñïl₁ï=
'four'	*do=	*du=	*dV=
'five'	*itu=	*tu=	*[i]tV=
'six'	*mu= < *ñu=	*ñuŋu=	*ñuŋu=
'seven'	*nana=	*nada=	*na[n]da=
'eight'	*da=	*jab=	*jab=

| 'nine' | *kǫkǫnǫ | *xegɐn | *kʰekVn |
| 'ten' | *tǫbo | *ǰuwa= | *čuba= |

From this point of view, the comparison of PJ *da= 'eight' with PMT
*ǰab= "eight" is better than with MK. Moreover, I suppose that it is possible
to analyze MK yetulp 'eight' as a compound of the opposite count: ye < yelh
'ten' +tulp < tuWul 'two'.

2) The comparison of MK yewuy= LH 'gets thin', 'gets emaciated' with
OJ yase= 'gets thin', 'gets emaciated' faces a serious phonological problem
with a correspondence MK [-Ø-] : OJ [-s-]. It is true that MK yewuy= should
result from PK *yeCuy=, but there is no evidence that this $C = *s$. I suggest
that it is better to compare OJ yase= < PJ *dasa=Ci= with PMT *lalV= 'gets
thin', 'gets emaciated', 'starves', which will together yield PA *Lal₂a=[1] 'gets
thin', 'gets emaciated'.

3) The comparison of MK yelp= 'thin', 'weak' (?) with OJ ywowa= 'weak'
< PJ *daCuba < *daruba is very attractive phonetically, but at the same time
it is quite doubtful from the semantic point of view, since MK yelp= does
not really have the meaning 'weak' (it seems to me that Whitman here brings
in the English idiomatic translation of the word in question, like yelpun cha
'weak tea', lit. 'thin tea').

4) The same applies to the comparison of MK yel= R 'ties it' with OJ
yǫr= 'braids it', 'twines it': there is a phonetic resemblance, but the semantics
is dubious.

5) Thus, we are left with the well-known comparison of MK yeleh LH
'many' and OJ yǫrǫdu 'ten thousand', 'many'. MK yelh 'ten', also here cited
by Whitman should be rejected from the start, since it is hardly better semantically than a well-known comparison of Turkic on 'ten' with MK on
'hundred'. Besides certain doubts whether or not the Japanese word had the

---

[1] I reconstruct PA *l- on the basis of correspondences PJ *n- : PK *n- : PMT *l- :
PM *l-/*n- : PT *j- and PA *L- (phonetically, probably [tˡ] or [dˡ]) on the basis
of correspondences PJ *d- : PK *n- : PMT *l- : PM *l-/*n- : PT *j-. Examples:
PA *l-:
PA *lamV "wave", "sea" > PMT *lamu "sea", "wave"; PJ *nami "wave".
PA *luk= "to take off" > PMT *luk= "to take off", PJ *nuk= (OJ nuk=, MJ nug=)
"to take off".
PA *lobä "swamp", "marsh" > PMT *lewe "swamp", "marsh", PJ *numa
"swamp", "marsh", PK *nu[p/b]V=k (MK nuph) "swamp", "marsh", PM
*lob[V]=ku (WM lobxu) "swamp", "marsh".
PA *L-:
PA *Lel₂u "armour" > PMT *lelu "breast plate", "armpit armour"; PJ *dǫrǫ=pi
"armour".
PA *Lukʰi "quiver", "arrow" > PMT *lukii "arrow", PJ *duki "quiver".

original meaning 'many',[2] it is obvious that one etymology is not sufficient for the establishment of a protophoneme. Other solutions, like the possibility of borrowing, may also be taken into consideration.

Whitman's theory on the origins of aspiration in Korean, explaining it as a result of initial vowel loss, is based on four Japanese-Korean etymologies involving MK *ph-* and six etymologies with MK *th-*. Recently, S. Robert Ramsey proposed an alternative hypothesis concerning MK aspirates. Ramsey suggested that MK /ph/, /th/ and /kh/ go back to PK clusters of *Ck or *CH type, that is *pk/*pH, *tk/*tH, *kk/*kH. These clusters resulted in turn from the loss of a minimal vowel between the consonants (Ramsey 1991: 231). Ramsey's theory is more plausible because: 1) It parallels exactly the origin of Korean fortis consonants, also resulting from consonant clusters; 2) the evidence not only from Japanese, but also from other Altaic languages provides a considerable amount of etymologies supporting Ramsey's and not Whitman's point of view; 3) Whitman does not provide any etymologies involving MK /kh/ and /ch/.

1) It is better to compare MK *tho=* H 'burns' not with OJ *atu=* 'is hot' as proposed by Whitman but with OJ *yak=* < PJ **dak=* 'burns', PMT **deg=je=* 'burns' and PT **jak=* 'burns'. MK *tho=* < PK **tVKV=* < PA **dak=* 'burns'.

2) In the same way, MK *thi=* H 'hits it' < PK **tVki=* is related not to OJ *ut=* 'hits it', but to OJ *tuk=* 'strikes it', 'stabs it'; PMT **tooki=* 'hits it', 'strikes it'; PM **toksi=* 'strikes it', 'knocks'; and PT **tokï=* 'hits it', 'strikes it' < PA **t^hok^h[i]=* 'hits it', 'strikes it'.

3) The comparison of MK *thwoski* HL 'hare', 'rabbit' with OJ *usagi* LHH 'hare', 'rabbit' with proposed analysis of *thwoski* as prefix *th-* or *thwo* (Sino-Korean 'rabbit') + *woski* seems to be a little bit too imaginative. MK *thwoski* < PK **tVkwoski* is either related to PMT **tuksa* 'hare' or represents an early loanword from Tungusic (several Tungusic languages have the derived form *tuksa=ki*; the word itself may thus be derived from PMT **tuksa=* 'to run' (SSTM II 1977, 208)).

---

[2] It seems to me that in OJ texts of the eighth century *yorodu* always means "ten thousand". This belief of mine comes from the fact that the samples of oldest Japanese poetry are rather precise in their descriptions and lack the flavor of undecisiveness and vagueness of the later Heian poetry. Besides that, there are two other Japanese stems with the meaning "many": *mane=* and *opo=*, used exactly according to their meaning. At least, I do not know any single OJ context where *yorodu* cannot be translated as "ten thousand". The situation changes in the early Heian, when *yorodu* appears for the first time with a definite meaning "many". It is interesting to note that Old Russian had a numeral *t∞ima* "ten thousand" (an obvious loanword from Middle Persian *tumaan* "ten thousand" via Turkic *tümän* "ten thousand"), which later began to mean "uncountable multitude" and now, in Modern Russian after contamination with pure Slavic *temnota* "darkness", means "darkness". I suspect that OJ *yorodu* underwent a similar process.

4) Whitman follows Ohno 1974 and compares K *thek* 'chin', 'lower jaw' with MJ (Whitman cites as OJ, but the word is not attested phonetically before tenth century (Ohno 1974: 225), (JDB 1967: 151)) *otogaFi* LHH? 'chin', 'lower jaw'. The Japanese word is obviously a compound and, thus, its original semantics is problematic. Martin suggests PJ **otǫ=n=kap[a=C]i* 'lower joining' (1987, 513). Strangely enough, Whitman does not cite MK *thok* H 'chin', 'lower jaw' ([1]Yu 1964/1987: 710). A glance at the different forms of this word attested in Modern Korean dialects: *thak, thɛgari, thɛk, thək, thek,*

thoksugari, thøk, thʋk (Choy 1987, 416-20) will naturally lead to the conclusion that a kind of diphthong should be reconstructed here for a PK form. I propose to reconstruct PK **tVk=Vik/*tVk=iVk* 'chin', 'lower jaw'. Then PMT **ǰeag/*ǰiag* < **diag* 'chin', 'lower jaw' is a better candidate for a cognate. PA **diak* 'chin', 'lower jaw'.

5) Whitman rejects the traditional comparison of MK *thwop* H 'fingernail' with OJ *tumey/tuma=* HH 'fingernail' (Martin 1966: 228) on the basis that 'the K /p/ : J /m/ correspondence is irregular' (Whitman 1985: 219). However, MK /-W-/ < PK **-b-* undergoes neutralization in the word-final position, and there is no way to tell whether we had PK **thwop[V]* or **thwob[V]*. PK **-b-* reflects PA **-b-* and PJ **-m-* is an alternative reflex for PA **-b-*. Examples:

PA **djube* 'two' > PK **twubwu=rh* 'two' (MK *tulh* R, Kyelim [1]yusa *tubur*, Hyangka **[tu]bur*), PMT **ǰuwe* 'two', PM **ǰĭw=ri* 'two' (fem.), PJ **tuma* 'spouse' < ***'pair';

PA **c[h]Vba=* 'cold' > PK **chib=* (MK *chiW=* H) 'cold', PJ **tuma=Ci=ta=* (MJ *tume=ta=*) 'cold to the touch', 'cold'.[3]

PA **subV* 'water', 'liquid' > PK **swubwur* 'rice wine', PT **sub* 'water' (cf. Slavic *vod=a* 'water' and *vod=ka* 'vodka', both from IE **Hwedh* 'water');

PA **guba* 'beatiful' > PK **kwobV=* 'to be beautiful', PM **gu[w]a* 'beatiful';

PA **t[h]ibV=* 'to be[come]' > PK **toboy=* 'to become', PMT **tiw[a]* 'to be', 'to live';

?PA **bem* 'tiger' > MK *pem* 'tiger', *tay=Wem* 'big tiger' (attested in the *Yongpi ethyenka* 87, 1446 AD), Nanai *beme* 'tiger'.[4]

PA **daba* 'mountain', 'mountain pass' > PJ **dama* 'mountain', PMT **dawa=* 'mountain', 'mountain pass', PM **daba=* 'mountain pass'.

---

[3]There is a crazy *kokugogaku* etymology of the word (Ohno 1974, 870): *tumey* "fingernail" and *ita=* "is painful". First of all, fingernails are the least sensitive part of the hand, second, *tumeta=* is not limited to the meaning "cold to the touch".

[4]This word is not presented in any Nanai dictionary and was recorded by one of my colleagues in St. Petersburg.

Thus, the correspondence K /p/ : J /m/ might be quite regular. As for initial aspiration, it is necessary to note that there are some cases when it comes from the end of a word, like K *kho* 'nose' < MK *kwoh*. I suggest PK *twob[V]h* < *twobVk* 'fingernail'. The comparison of the Korean word with PJ *oyubi* 'finger' proposed by Whitman is quite doubtful semantically.

6) The comparison of MK *tho=* H 'is susceptible to it', 'is a target for it' with OJ[5] *atar=* 'is touched by', 'comes into contact with', 'corresponds to' is very weak from the semantic point of view.

Below I present four more MK etymologies with initial *th-*, supporting Ramsey's cluster theory:

7) MK *theh* H 'foundation', 'base' < PK *tVke=k*. Cf. PMT *teke* 'root', 'base' and PJ *tǫkǫ* 'floor'.

8) MK *theli* LH, *thel* L 'hair', 'fur' < PK *tVker*. Cf. PMT *tiki=/*tike=* 'skin with hair', 'hair', 'fur'.

9) MK *thul=* 'turns it', 'winds it', 'twists it' < PK *tVkur=*. Cf. PMT *tokor=* 'turns around', 'winds', 'twists'; PM *tokir* 'twisted', 'bent'. PA *t^{h}okVr=* 'twists', 'winds'.

10) MK *thi=* H 'puts into' < PK *tVki=*. Cf. PMT *ciki= < *tiki=* 'puts into', PM *ciki= < *tiki=* 'puts into'. PA *t^{h}ik^{h}i=* 'puts into'.

Now let us look at Whitman's etymologies with initial *ph-*:

1) The comparison of MK *phol* H, *pholi* HH 'fly' with OJ *amu* 2.5, J *abu* < PJ *am[p]u* 2.5 'horsefly' should be rejected since Whitman himself notices that a correspondence J /m/ : K /p/ is irregular (1985: 219). I suppose that OJ *papey* 'fly' < PJ *papaCi* might be a reduplication *pa=pa=Ci*. In that case it is comparable with the Korean word, yielding PA *p^a/or$_{1,2}$/*p^a/ol$_1$/*p^a/od* 'fly'. The Korean aspiration may be secondary in this case (see above).

2) It is doubtful that MK *phul* H 'grass' is a nominalization of MK *phulu=, pholo=, phala=, phele=* 'blue/green'(Whitman 1985: 213). The lack of any derivational suffix in *phul* makes me suggest the opposite development: MK *phulu=* etc. is derived from *phul* 'grass'. A comparison of MK *phul* with OJ *awi* 'indigo' is doubtful: *awi* has green leaves (as any plant), but reddish flowers, and the color of indigo used as a dye is not that of grass. I do not know any Altaic cognates for MK *phul* < PK *pVkul*. There is a possibility that the word is a loanword from the Easternmost Indoeuropean: Tocharian *pikul* 'grass'. Moreover, *awo=* in Japanese, mostly is used in the meaning 'blue', while 'green' is predominantly described as *midǫri*, attested already in OJ (Igarashi 1969, 135).

3) Whitman's #47 MK *phu=* H 'opens', 'spreads', 'comes out' and #48 MK *pheti=* HH 'spreads out', 'gets broad' compared with OJ *opiy=* 'sprouts', 'grows' and OJ *opo=* 'is big' are obviously based on the same root. Therefore, I count them as one etymology, not two. Whitman claims that OJ *opiy=* goes back to PJ *opu=Ci=* (Whitman's *opU=*), but the basis for such a con-

---

[5]Really MJ, since the word is attested phonetically only in the tenth century.

clusion is not clear to me. There is also a possibility that OJ *opiy=* goes back to PJ **opǫ=Ci*, which seems to be preferable in light of OJ *opo=* 'big'. Thus, both Japanese words in question are also based on the same root. The semantic side of the comparison is far from ideal, and I prefer the comparison of PJ **ǫpǫ=* 'big' with PMT **amba* 'big'. The latter is faced with a phonetic problem of a sonorant loss in Japanese, which is not expected, but semantically it is considerably better.

4) The comparison of MK *pho=* H 'digs it' with OJ *uwe=* 'plants it' is also weak semantically. I prefer to compare MK *pho=* 'digs it' < PK **pVku=* with PM **[h]uku=* 'digs it', yielding PA **p^huku=* 'digs it'.

I am unable to provide additional Altaic etymologies supporting the consonant cluster origin of MK *ph-*, but this is not strange, since we have considerably fewer native words with *ph-* than with *th-*. The same is true of MK *kh-*. However, there are some Altaic etymologies for MK *ch-*:

1) MK *cho=* H 'is full' < PK **cVho=*. Cf. PMT **cak* 'full'. PA **c^hak[h]* 'full'.

2) MK *cho=* H 'cold to touch' < PK **cVho=*. Cf. PMT **jǔke* 'ice'. PA **jǔk[h]V* 'ice-cold'.

3) MK *cho=* H 'kicks' < PK **cVho=*. Cf. PMT **jǔg=* 'beats', 'pushes'. PA **jǔk/g[V]=* 'kicks', 'beats'.

The last issue I would like to discuss here is Whitman's proposal for reconstruction of PJK vocalism. Whitman establishes the following correspondences and proposes the reconstructions:

OJ	MK	PJK
a	a	*a
i	i	*i
u	wo	*u
a/-o	e	*e
-u-/a	o	*o
u	wu	*ü
o	u	*ö

The proposed system may be criticized from different points of view. As Martin noticed, there is at least one correspondence not reflected in the chart above: OJ /ǫ/ : MK /e/: MK *cek* L 'time', OJ *tǫki* LL 'time'; MK *ep=* L 'bears', OJ *op=* L 'bears' (1991: 274). I can add at least one other: OJ /a/ : MK /u/.

1) OJ *kari* 2.4 'wild goose', MK *kuryeki* LLH 'wild goose', OT *kaz* 'goose', PTM **gaarV* 'swan' < PA **gaar₂V* '[wild] goose'.

2) OJ *ta* 1.3a 'rice-field' < pre-PJ **tara*, MK *turuh* LH 'field', PT **tala* 'field', 'steppe', PM **tala* 'field', 'steppe' < PA **t^halɉa* 'field', 'steppe'.

3) OJ *tati* plural marker, MK *tulh* plural marker < PA **t^har₂i* plural marker.

What protophonemes are we supposed to reconstruct for these two correspondences? I believe none, since not every correspondence reflects a protophoneme.

We know perfectly well now that PJ vocalism included four vowels: *a, *i, *u, *ϱ. But so far we know nothing about PK vocalism. To equate MK vocalism with a PK one is a very dangerous enterprise. For example, according to the above chart, MK o < PK *o and MK u < PK *$\ddot{o}$. But such a claim does not make any sense, because these vowels have very limited distribution in Middle Korean[6] and are obviously a result of vowel reductions. Therefore, the 'correspondences' of these vowels with Proto-Japanese vowels will yield fictitious 'protophonemes'. Even the comparison of Proto-Japanese vowels with the remaining five basic Middle Korean vowels: a, i, wu, e, wo may still be inadequate before the reconstruction of Proto-Korean vocalism is properly done.

I believe that it is a wrong tendency in Korean or Tungusic studies to try to reconstruct the vocalism of proto-language *a là* Turkic or Mongolian with seven or eight vowels with vowel harmony. As already indicated, this 'system' turns out to be fictitious for PMT (Starostin 1991: 22-3). I largely suspect that the same can be true for Proto-Korean, since we have only five basic vowels in Middle Korean, vowel harmony in Middle Korean only partially reminds us of vowel harmony in Turkic, and, finally, there are too many exceptions to the vowel harmony rules.

Finally, I would like to mention briefly the hypothesis on the affinity of Japanese and Korean. The greatest merit and contribution in recent Japanese-Korean comparative studies certainly must be attributed to S. Martin, for he not only provided many important Japanese-Korean etymologies and advertized the very idea that Japanese and Korean are related — in an academic world less than friendly to comparative studies in the sixties and seventies, but also prepared several new scholars working in this field. However, the work on Japanese-Korean genetic relationship in North America was carried on with little or almost no connection to Altaic studies, with the exception of work done by R. A. Miller (1967, 1972, 1980, 1991), who works mostly on Japanese and classical Altaic triad (Turkic, Mongolian, and Tungusic), but does not use as much data from earlier stages of Korean as S. Martin. Recently, S. Starostin, on the basis of the glottochronological calculations, also came to the conclusion that Japanese and Korean are more closely related to each other than to any other Altaic language (1991). I support the general idea that Japanese and Korean are related. Morever, I believe that both are members of the Altaic language family. However, the more I work on external connections of Japanese and Korean, the more I disbelieve the hypothesis that they constitute any kind of unity opposed to other members of Altaic. As it seems to me now, this hypothesis is based primarily on numerous lex-

---

[6]MK o never occurs in the word initial position. MK u occurs in this position only twice in native vocabulary.

ical correspondences, and more or less ignores grammar elements. Two excellent recent surveys of common grammar elements by S. Martin reveal a surprisingly low quantity of these elements (1990, 1991). It is always difficult to try to organize language groups within a linguistic family to unities of intermediate level, just as, for example the best documented unity within Indo-European, Balto-Slavic, faces some insurmountable difficulties. However, if we give it a try within Altaic, I suspect that the closest 'relative' of Japanese will be not Korean but Tungusic.[7] Evidence for a common numerical system of Japanese and Tungusic was given above. Here I will add to it the possible cognates from other Altaic languages, including Korean.

	PJ	PMT	PK	PM	PT	PA
'one'	*pito=	—	—	—	*bir$_1$	*pir$_1$V
'two'	—	*ǰuwe	*twubwu-r	*ǰiw=ri	—	*djube
'three'	*mi=<*ñi	*[ñ]ïla=	*se=<*ñe[8]	—	—	*ñïl$_1$ï=
'four'	*do=	*du=	*de=[9]	*dö=	*dö=	*tV=
'five'	*itu=	*tu=	*ta=	*ta=	—	*[i]t^{h}V=
'six'	*mu=<*ñu	*ñuŋu=	—	—	—	*ñuŋu=
'seven'	*nana=	*nada=	—	—	*jedi	*na[n]da=
'eight'	*da=	*ǰab=	—	—	—	*ǰab=
'nine'	*kokono	*xegun	—	—	—	*k^{h}ekVn
'ten'	*tobo	*ǰuwa=	—	—	—	*čuba=
'hundred'	*mwomwo	*ñama	—	—	—	*ñVmV

One can easily see that Proto-Korean shares fewer common numerals with either Japanese or Tungusic than the latter two share between themselves. The same situation may be observed for personal pronouns:

	PJ	PMT	PK	PM	PT	PA
'I'	*ban[u]	*bi/*bin=	*na	*bi/*na=	*ben	*bV=n
'thou'	*so=[10]	*si/*sin=	*ne	*ti/*ca=	*sen	*sV=n

---

[7] This idea does not belong to me; it was proposed before by Murayama Shichirô (Murayama 1962, 1988).

[8] (Vovin, forthcoming).

[9] Reconstructed on the basis of the North Hamkyeng $d^{TM}i$ "four" (King & Vovin, 1989).

[10] OJ *na* "you" is attested in Ryukyu only as a honorific pronoun. On the other hand, OJ *si/so=* which has limited attestation in even in Nara period, has good reflexes in Ryukyu. That is why I suggest that OJ *na* may be an early loanword from Ancient Korean *ne "you", while OJ si probably represents a PJ pronoun. Anyway, even if we would reconstruct PJ *na "you" as well, still we would have the genetically related pronoun for Japanese and Korean only for the second person, and this situation provides evidence against Japanese-Korean unity rather than supports it.

Here Proto-Japanese, Proto-Manchu-Tungus and PT all share the same personal pronouns, but PK has quite a different set. PK *na* 'I' may be compared to PM *na=* 'I', a stem of oblique cases, but there are no other obvious cognates. Similar evidence may also be cited from the verbal systems; I will present the evidence in another publication.

PJ and PK also share just one phonological innovation: a merging of PA *l̦* and *r̦* into [r], and it seems to me that they have no common archaic features whatsoever. On the other hand, Tungusic and Japanese also share some innovations, e.g., PA *-c-* is reflected in both languages as *-s-*, but what is more important, they have many common important archaic features, like retention of second syllable vowels and restriction to combinations of certain vowels within a word (Starostin 1991: 23), which further developed into vowel harmony in Turkic, Mongolian, and MK.

In conclusion, I would like to repeat that Whitman's work represents a significant step forward in Japanese and Korean comparative studies. However, like any other work in the field, it is not free of shortcomings. I tried here to survey these shortcomings, one being his very limited usage of the other Altaic languages. Japanese and Korean are not isolated in East Asia; typologically and genetically they are linked to a larger linguistic stock, and further work on their origins will be considerably more fruitful if we do not limit ourselves to Japanese and Korean only.

Abbreviations

H	High pitch
IE	Indo-European
L	Low pitch
MJ	Middle Japanese
MK	Middle Korean
OJ	Old Japanese
OT	Old Turkic
PA	Proto-Altaic
PJ	Proto-Japanese
PJK	Proto-Japanese-Korean
PK	Proto-Korean
PM	Proto-Mongolian
PMT	Proto-Manchu-Tungus
PT	ProtoTurkic
R	Rising pitch
WM	Written Mongolian

References

Choy, Hakkun 1987. Hankwuk pangen sacen. Seoul: Hyenmunsa. .
Igarashi, Jin'ichi 1969. Jôdai kanazukai jiten. Tôkyô: Shôgakkan.
King, J. Ross P.,and Vovin, Alexander 1989. Unpublished field materials on Soviet Korean.

JDB 1967. Jidai betsu kokugo dai jiten. Jôdai hen. Tôkyô: Sanseidô.

[1]Yu, Changton 1964/1987. *[1]Yico e sacen*. Seoul: Yensey tayhakkyo.

Martin, Samuel E. 1966. Lexical Evidence Relating Japanese to Korean. Language 42/2.185-251

Martin, Samuel E. 1987. The Japanese Language Through Time. New Haven and London: Yale University Press.

Martin, Samuel E. 1990. Morphological Clues to the Relationships of Japanese and Korean. Linguistic Change and Reconstruction Methodology, 483-509. Berlin and New York: Walter de Gruyter.

Martin, Samuel E. 1991. Recent Research on the Relationships of Japanese and Korean. Sprung from Some Common Source, 269-292. Stanford: Stanford University Press.

Miller, Roy A. 1967. The Japanese Language. Chicago: Chicago University Press.

Miller, Roy A. 1972. Japanese and the Other Altaic Languages. Chicago: Chicago University Press.

Miller, Roy A. 1980. Origins of the Japanese Language. Seattle: University of Washington Press.

Miller, Roy A. 1991. How many Verner's Laws Does an Altaicist Need? Studies in the Historical Phonology of Asian Languages, Studies Current Issues in Linguistic Theory, #77, 176-204. Amsterdam and Philadelphia: John Benjamins Publishing Company.

Murayama, Shichirô. 1962. Nihongo no tsungûsu go teki kôsei yoso. Minzokugaku kenkyû 26/3.157-169.

Murayama, Shichirô. 1988. Nihongo no kigen to gogen. Tôkyô:

Ohno, Susumu, et al. 1974. Kogo jiten. Tôkyô: Iwanami.

Ramsey, S. Robert. 1991. Proto-Korean and the Origin of Korean Accent. Studies in the Historical Phonology of Asian Languages, Studies Current Issues in Linguistic Theory, #77, 215-238. Amsterdam and Philadelphia: John Benjamins Publishing Company.

Ramstedt, Gustav, J. 1949. Studies in Korean Etymology. Memoires de la Société Finno-Ougrienne, XCV. Helsinki: Suomalais Ugrilainen Seura.

Starostin, Sergei A. 1991. Altaiskaia problema i proiskhozhdenie iaponskogo iazyka. Moskva, Nauka.

SSTM I-II 1975, 1977. Sravnitel'nyi slovar' tunguso-man'chzhurskikh iazykov. Leningrad, Nauka.

Vovin, Alexander. forthcoming. 'On the Phonetic Value of the Middle Korean Grapheme Δ 'triangle". To appear in Bulletin of the School of Oriental and African Studies (BSOAS).

Whitman, John B. 1985. The Phonological Basis for the Comparison of Japanese and Korean. Doctoral. dissertation, Harvard University.

Index